# American Education

ELEVENTH EDITION

## Joel Spring
New School University

Boston   Burr Ridge, IL   Dubuque, IA   Madison, WI   New York
San Francisco   St. Louis   Bangkok   Bogotá   Caracas   Kuala Lumpur
Lisbon   London   Madrid   Mexico City   Milan   Montreal   New Delhi
Santiago   Seoul   Singapore   Sydney   Taipei   Toronto

# McGraw-Hill Higher Education

*A Division of The **McGraw-Hill** Companies*

AMERICAN EDUCATION

Published by McGraw-Hill, a business unit of the McGraw-Hill Companies, Inc., 1221 Avenue of the Americas, New York, NY, 10020. Copyright © 2004, 2002, 2000, 1998, 1996, 1994, 1991, 1989, 1985, 1982, 1978 by The McGraw-Hill Companies, Inc. All rights reserved. No part of this publication may be reproduced or distributed in any form or by any means, or stored in a database or retrieval system, without the prior written consent of The McGraw-Hill Companies, Inc., including, but not limited to, in any network or other electronic storage or transmission, or broadcast for distance learning.

Some ancillaries, including electronic and print components, may not be available to customers outside the United States.

This book is printed on acid-free paper.

1 2 3 4 5 6 7 8 9 0 FGR/FGR 0 9 8 7 6 5 4 3

ISBN 0-07-255884-9

Publisher: *Jane Karpacz*
Sponsoring editor: *Jane Karpacz*
Developmental editor: *Terri Wise*
Senior marketing manager: *Pam S. Cooper*
Media producer: *Lance Gerhart*
Project manager: *Diane M. Folliard*
Production supervisor: *Carol A. Bielski*
Freelance design coordinator: *Gino Cieslik*
Lead supplement producer: *Marc Mattson*
Art editor: *Robin Mouat*
Cover design: *Gino Cieslik*
Interior design: *Gino Cieslik*
Typeface: *10/12 Palatino*
Compositor: *ElectraGraphics, Inc.*
Printer: *Quebecor World Fairfield Inc.*

**Library of Congress Cataloging-in-Publication Data**

Spring, Joel H.
    American education / Joel Spring.— 11th ed.
      p. cm.
    Includes bibliographical references and index.
    ISBN 0-07-255884-9 (softcover : alk. paper)
      1. Education—Social aspects—United States. 2. Education—Political aspects—United States. 3. Educational equalization—United States. 4. Education and state—United States.
    I. Title.
    LC191.4 .S684 2004
    370'.973—dc21                                                                2002043111

www.mhhe.com

# About the Author

JOEL SPRING is on the faculty of the New School University. He received his PhD in educational policy studies from the University of Wisconsin. His major research interests are history of education, multicultural education, Native American culture, the politics of education, global education, and human rights education. He is the author of many books, the most recent of which are *Education and the Rise of the Global Economy*; *The Universal Right to Education: Justification, Definition, and Guidelines*; *Globalization and Educational Rights*; and *Educating the Consumer Citizen: A History of the Marriage of Schools, Advertising, and Media*.

# Contents

## 3   Equality of Educational Opportunity: Race, Gender, and Special Needs

## 4   Student Diversity

Part II
POWER AND CONTROL IN AMERICAN EDUCATION

# Preface

The No Child Left Behind Act of 2001 is the most important educational event since the publication of the previous edition of *American Education.* In this eleventh edition, the No Child Left Behind Act is discussed throughout the book. For instance, in Chapter 1, I discuss the implications of the "Character Education" section of the legislation. In Chapter 5, I examine the impact of the legislation on transforming bilingual education into English acquisition education. I discuss the impact of the No Child Left Behind Act on charter schools and school choice in Chapter 6. In Chapter 7, I discuss the legislation's requirement of high-stakes testing and academic standards and analyze the reading, school violence, and drug-prevention sections of the legislation. In Chapter 9, I examine the censorship problems created by the legislation's requirements for high-stakes testing and academic standards. And in the book's last chapter, Chapter 10, I discuss the sections in the No Child Left Behind Act designed to ensure school prayer and the right of Boy Scouts, despite their discrimination against gay youth, to use school facilities.

The major structural change in this eleventh edition is the combining of two previous chapters, "The Profession of Teaching" and "Teachers Unions and Teacher Politics," into a single chapter titled "The Profession of Teaching." In addition, I moved the chapter "The Profession of Teaching" from "Part I: School and Society" to a more logical place as Chapter 8 in "Part II: Power and Control in American Education."

The other significant structural change is the addition of time lines to Chapters 1, 3, and 4. Chapter 1, "The Purposes of Public Schooling," integrates a critical examination of the goals of education with a historical summary of American education. Chapter 3 highlights the history of the struggle for equal educational opportunity and Chapter 4 provides a historical overview of the experiences of Asian Americans, Native Americans, and Mexican Americans in U.S. schools. The addition of time lines to these chapters allows the reader to better grasp key events that helped to define American education from the nineteenth century to the present.

Besides the discussion of the No Child Left Behind Act and structural changes, each chapter has been revised and updated. Below is a list of chapter revisions.

## Chapter 1

- Discussion of character education section of the No Child Left Behind Act.
- Expanded discussion of the schools' attempts to stabilize family life, marriages, and the American diet.
- Discussion of the controversy surrounding the Pledge of Allegiance.

## Chapter 2

- New chapter title, "Education and Equality of Opportunity."
- Addition of the high-stakes testing model of equality of opportunity.
- Updated tables.
- New section on real estate values and the quality of schools titled "Education, Social Class, and Real Estate Brokers."
- New section titled "Shopping for a Public School."

## Chapter 3

- Addition of a time line of the struggle for equal educational opportunity.
- New section discussing Census Bureau definitions of race titled "What Race Am I?: Racial and Cultural Self-Identification."
- Updated and expanded material on the education of students with disabilities, including new sections titled "Students with Disabilities," "Public Law 94–142: Education for All Handicapped Children Act (Individuals with Disabilities Education Act)," "Writing an IEP," "Which Children Have Disabilities?" "Integrating Children with Disabilities into the Regular Classroom," "An Inclusion Success Story," "The Inclusion Debate," and "President George W. Bush's Commission on Excellence in Special Education."

## Chapter 4

- Addition of time lines for Mexican American Students, Asian American Students, and Native American Students.

## Chapter 5

- Discussion of the English Language Acquisition Act of 2001, which is a section in the No Child Left Behind Act.

## Chapter 6

- Expanded and updated section on site-based management.
- Discussion of the No Child Left Behind Act regarding school choice and charter schools.

- New section titled "Teacher Cooperative: A Charter School Model."
- A discussion of the American Federation of Teachers report: "Do Charter Schools Measure Up?"
- New section titled "Edison Schools Inc.: A Tale of an Education Company in Search of Profit."
- New section titled "The Edison Design."

## Chapter 7

- Discussion of the No Child Left Behind Act regarding high-stakes testing, academic standards, reading, school violence, and drugs.
- Discussion of the U.S. Department of Education and U.S. Justice Department report "Indicators of School Crime and Safety: 2000."
- Historical review of proportion of revenues from state, federal, and local sources going to education.

## Chapter 8

- New section titled "Disparities in Teacher Salaries and Equality of Educational Opportunity."
- Addition of new tables comparing teacher salaries with other professions.
- Addition of new tables showing disparity in teacher salaries between high-income and low-income school districts.
- New section entitled "American Board for Certification of Teacher Excellence: Alternative Routes to Teaching."

## Chapter 9

- Discussion of the censorship of literary selections on the New York State Regent's examination.
- New section titled "Web Scrub: A New Form of Censorship?"
- Discussion of the academic standards requirements of the No Child Left Behind Act.
- Expanded discussion of the debate about evolution and creationist theories in academic standards for science.
- Discussion of the latest controversies involving censorship of textbooks by the Texas State School Board.
- Discussion of the impact of The Child Online Protection Act of 1999 on e-learning.

## Chapter 10

- Discussion of the school-prayer section of the No Child Left Behind Act.
- A discussion of *Zelman v. Simmons-Harris* in which the U.S. Supreme Court upheld Ohio's Pilot Project Scholarship Program which allows the use of vouchers to attend religious schools.

- A discussion of the U.S. Supreme Court ruling in *Board of Education of Independent School District No. 92 of Pottawatomie County et al. v. Earls et al.*, which allows schools to administer drug tests to students participating in competitive extracurricular activities.
- New section titled "Gays, Boy Scouts, and the No Child Left Behind Act of 2001" dealing with the access of Boy Scout organizations to public school buildings.

I would like to thank the following professors for their feedback during the development of the eleventh edition:

Jim Allan, *Loras College*
Bill Bassett, *Mount St. Mary College*
Beverly Cross, *University of Wisconsin—Milwaukee*
Russell Dennis, *Bucknell University*
Jo Victoria Goodman, *The University of Pittsburgh*
Robert P. Green, Jr., *Clemson University*
Steve Grineski, *Minnesota State University—Moorhead*
Michael T. Hayes, *Washington State University*
Kerry Holmes, *University of Mississippi*
Lawrence Klein, *Central Connecticut State University*
Guy Larkins, *The University of Georgia*
Joyce Woelfle Lehman, *The State University of New York—Geneseo*
K. Fritz Leifeste, *Angelo State University*
Charles Litz, *Kansas State University*
Donna Martin, *Northern Illinois University*
Richard McEwing, *Youngstown State University*
Diane B. Napier, *University of Georgia*
Steve Oates, *Northern Michigan University*
Ken Paulli, *Siena College*
Monte Piliawsky, *Wayne State University*
Richard J. Reynolds, *Eastern Connecticut State University*
William Riggs, *University of Minnesota—Morris*
Larry Rosenberg, *Millersville University of Pennsylvania*
Paul Singer, *California State University—Northridge*

# PART ONE

# School and Society

## CHAPTER 1

# The Purposes
# of Public Schooling

Why do we have public schools? Does this sound like a simple question? Consider the 2002 federal law, No Child Left Behind. This law is the backbone of President George W. Bush's educational agenda. The "Partnerships in Character Education" section of the law provides for the integration of character education into classroom instruction. After passage of the legislation, President Bush defined his goals for public education to a White House Conference on Character and Community:

> The thing I appreciate is that you understand education should prepare children for jobs, and it also should prepare our children for life. I join you in wanting our children to not only be rich in skills, but rich in ideals. Teaching character and citizenship to our children is a high calling. It's a really high calling. And I'm grateful for your work. (June 19, 2002)

On the surface, the goal of preparing students for jobs does not seem highly controversial. This has been a goal for education since the nineteenth century. Most Americans would probably support this as an important educational goal. However, as I discuss later in this chapter, there are important issues about how to prepare students for the job market. Should schools prepare students to be lifelong learners for a world where they might have to change careers several times during their life span? Should students be prepared to enter specific sectors of the job market, such as service industries, manufacturing, or information industries? Or, should students be educated for specific jobs?

Similar to job preparation, most people, including teachers, would not object to character and citizenship education. However, there is a problem in defining good character and good citizenship. For instance, the No Child Left Behind law refers to "integrating *secular* character education into curricula and teaching methods of schools [my emphasis]." The use of *secular* in the legislation is to make a distinction from character education based on religious values. As examples of the elements of secular character education, the legislation provides the following:

a. Caring
b. Civic virtue and citizenship
c. Justice and fairness
d. Respect
e. Responsibility
f. Trustworthiness
g. Giving

While public schools can't teach religion, some religiously oriented people would object to "secular character education." Christian fundamentalist groups refer to this form of character education as secular humanism. The simplest definition of secular humanism is that it comprises a set of ethical standards that place primary emphasis on a person's ability to interpret and guide his or her own moral actions. This is against the Christian fundamentalist viewpoint, which holds that the sources of ethical and moral values should be the Bible and God. Secular humanism relies on the authority of human beings, while Christian fundamentalism relies on the authority of the Scriptures. From this perspective, ideas like caring, respect, responsibility, and giving should only be taught in a religious context.

The controversy surrounding the goals of character education are illustrated by a 1986 legal suit brought by a group of parents against the Hawkins County School District in Tennessee for requiring students, on a threat of suspension, to read from the Holt, Rinehart and Winston basic reading series.

**"I'm here to emphasize values. Remember . . . work hard, aim high and always use your parents' connections."**

*Source:* Bruce Beattie/Copley News Service

*Source:* Adrian Raeside/Victoria Times Colonist

Specifically, the parents objected to selections in the readers from *The Wizard of Oz, Rumpelstiltskin,* and *Macbeth.* The parents claimed that the textbook series contained explicit statements on secular humanism and taught values contrary to the religious beliefs of their children. In the words of presiding U.S. District Judge Thomas Gray Hull, "The plaintiffs believe that, after reading the entire Holt series, a child might adopt the views of a feminist, a humanist, a pacifist, an anti-Christian, a vegetarian, or an advocate of a 'one-world government'."

Does the concept of "respect" included in the character education section of No Child Left Behind include teaching respect for households headed by gay and lesbian couples? In 1992 New York City adopted the "Children of the Rainbow" curriculum, which required elementary schools to teach tolerance toward gays and lesbians. Among the books recommended for use in classrooms were *Daddy's Roommate* and *Heather Has Two Mommies.* Both books show pictures of gay couples, including a drawing of two men in bed. Standing on top of a truck outside the school chancellor's office, Mary Cummins, the president of the local Queens district board of education, led a demonstration against the curriculum. "It is bizarre," she said, "to teach six-year-olds this [referring to the gay and lesbian content of the curriculum]. Why single out [homosexuals] for respect? Tomorrow it will be skinheads." Catholic, Pentecostal, and Baptist churches along with Orthodox synagogues protested that homosexuality is a sin and that schools should not teach respect for gay and lesbian lifestyles. Neil

Lodato, a construction worker, shouted outside his daughter's school, "They should stick to teaching these babies that $1 + 1 = 2$, instead of what daddy and his boyfriend are doing in the bedroom."

Should schools teach "respect" for other cultures? In *The De-Valuing of America: The Fight for Our Culture and Our Children*, William Bennett, former U.S. Secretary of Education, expresses his objections to teaching respect for other cultures. Bennett argues that U.S. cultural traditions have produced the best society on earth. Why teach respect for inferior cultures? Bennett maintains that U.S. schools should focus on transmitting the European roots of American culture.

So what does "respect" mean if it doesn't include appreciation of other lifestyles and cultures? Does it mean respect for one's own person with regard to sexual activities? The Sex Respect program began in 1983 with a curriculum guide designed to motivate teens to practice chastity. The program's current goal is "to enable each individual to progressively develop responsible behavior, positive self-esteem, and respect for others as he/she makes decisions involving the use of his/her sexual freedom." Sex Respect defines sexual freedom as the freedom to say no. Today, the program is being used in all 50 states and 23 foreign countries. The program's growth was made possible by Title V of the welfare-reform act of 1996 in which Congress authorized federal funds to be provided to the states in the form of block grants to promote chastity until marriage. Title V requires states to fund education that:

a. Has as its exclusive purpose, teaching the social, psychological, and health gains to be realized by abstaining from sexual activity;
b. Teaches abstinence from sexual activity outside marriage as the expected standard for all school-age children;
c. Teaches that abstinence from sexual activity is the only certain way to avoid out-of-wedlock pregnancy, sexually transmitted diseases, and other associated health problems;
d. Teaches that a mutually faithful monogamous relationship in the context of marriage is the expected standard of human sexual activity.

Both the federally funded Sex Respect program and the goals of Title V raise important questions about the meaning of respect and the goals of public schools. Should schools be involved in sex education or should this area of instruction be left to parents, the community, or religious groups? Should government legislation define a "faithful monogamous relationship in the context of marriage . . . [as] the expected standard of human sexual activity" for all people? Should public schools focus on birth control methods as opposed to abstinence from sexual activity?

While the above are important questions there is still the real public problem of AIDS and the transmission of sexual diseases. Do these public problems require schools to teach particular moral values such as sexual abstinence before marriage? Or, should these public problems be addressed by teaching about methods of protection against sexually transmitted diseases?

# THE PUBLIC BENEFITS OF SCHOOLS

Public schools exist to serve public goals. The public goals of schooling are determined by elected representatives in local, state, and federal governments. U.S. public schools were established to reduce political and social unrest by teaching future citizens a common set of political values and patriotism; to reduce social tensions by promising equality of opportunity; to decrease crime by teaching morality; and to eradicate poverty by stimulating economic growth. Twentieth- and twenty-first-century concerns with urbanization, industrialization, racial and cultural harmony, juvenile crime, nutritional health, epidemic diseases, and globalization add to these early goals.

Taken as a whole, these public goals place a heavy burden on schools, particularly on administrators and teachers, and arouse a great deal of controversy. Think of the burden placed on the public school teacher. Can teachers actually integrate character education into their teaching as recommended by the 2002 legislation No Child Left Behind? Can teachers of reading, writing, arithmetic, English, history, science, and other school subjects actually impart knowledge and values that will reduce crime, promote racial and economic harmony, increase employment opportunities, stabilize the political system, and prepare for globalization?

In addition, there is the potential conflict between personal and public goals. Of course, personal and public goals can be the same. Parents might want the schools to prepare their children for employment while, at the same time, elected officials are stressing employment skills as important for economic growth. Teachers might also agree that schools should prepare students for work. On the other hand, what about parents who believe schools should concentrate on academic skills and the transmission of culture and not worry about the job market? What about parents who believe the political and economic values taught to students are too liberal or too conservative? Or parents who object to teaching evolutionary theory in required science courses? What about teachers who object to the values they are asked to stress in the classroom?

The conflict between personal and public goals for schools is an ongoing problem. It is important for all citizens, including teachers, students, school administrators, and elected officials to understand the deep-rooted controversies surrounding the functioning of public schools. In evaluating the various public goals for education, you should consider the broader question of public benefits versus parental or personal educational goals.

- Do you think there are public benefits that should override the objections of parents and other citizens regarding the teaching of particular subjects, attitudes, or values?
- Should elected representatives determine the subject matter, attitudes, and values taught in public schools?
- What should teachers do if they are asked to teach values that are in conflict with their own personal values?

## ARE SCHOOLS ALWAYS A PUBLIC GOOD?

Most people assume that public schooling is necessary for the advancement of society. However, public schools have been used to advance political and economic ideologies that did not improve the condition of human beings. For instance, in the 1930s Nazis enlisted schools in a general campaign to educate citizens to believe in the racial superiority of the German people, to support fascism, and to be willing to die at the command of Hitler. Racial biology and fascist political doctrines were taught in the classroom; patriotic parades and singing took place in the schoolyard. A similar pattern occurred in South African schools in attempts to maintain a racially divided society. Many totalitarian countries, particularly former communist countries, used their schools to instill allegiance to dictatorial control.

Consequently, the reader should be aware that "education" does not always benefit the individual or society. Public and personal benefits depend on the content of instruction. To think critically about education means to think critically about the content of instruction and the potential effect of that content on society. For instance, history can be taught in schools for the purpose of political indoctrination or to raise critical questions about the human condition. In the following sections, my goal is to enhance your critical awareness of the issues surrounding the goals of public education.

## HISTORY AND THE GOALS OF SCHOOLING

Since the nineteenth century, the goals of public schools have increased as society encounters new problems. Most of the original goals of schooling still guide the work of educators. For instance, in the 1830s advocates of public schools claimed schools were necessary to educate future citizens, reduce crime, and provide equality of opportunity. These three educational goals remain present in the twenty-first century. However, since the 1830s the schools have been called on to deal with a variety of other issues ranging from stabilizing marriages and families to globalization. The multiplicity of things schools are now asked to do is a result of this historical process. Consequently, a critical analysis of educational goals will also provide a brief history of public schools.

In the 1820s and 1830s, Horace Mann, the often-called father of American education, and other educational supporters, campaigned for a school system for white children that would teach a common set of moral and political values, and improve economic opportunities. Native Americans and enslaved Africans were excluded from this initial school system. Since the time of Horace Mann to the present, educational institutions have adjusted their goals to deal with problems resulting from the end of slavery, the granting of citizenship to Native Americans, urbanization, industrialization, a lengthy Cold War with the former Soviet Union, and globalization.

For the purpose of analysis, I have divided my discussion into "The Political Goals of Schooling," "The Social Goals of Schooling," and "The Economic Goals of Schooling." Each of the following sections will trace the history of these goals to the present. In each section, I will list critical questions about the role of schooling in society. I have also created two time lines. Figure 1–1 indicates the approximate decades when public schools adopted particular educational goals to meet changing social and economic conditions. Missing from this time line are the changes in the teaching profession. The teaching profession time line is presented in Chapter 2. Figure 1–2 provides a time line of events mentioned in my discussion.

## THE POLITICAL GOALS OF SCHOOLING

Public schools in the U.S. were originally charged to educate qualified leadership for a republican government. After the American Revolution, many worried about the selection of political leaders. In his first message to Congress in 1790, President George Washington proposed a national university for training political leaders and creating a national culture. He wanted attendance by students from all areas of the country. Washington's proposal was criticized as elitist. Requiring a college education, some protested, would result in politicians being primarily recruited from the rich and national university graduates considering themselves superior to the general public. In this case, a hereditary aristocracy would be replaced by an aristocracy of the educated. If none but the rich had access to higher education, then the rich could use higher education as a means of perpetuating and supporting their social status.

To avoid the problem of elitism, Thomas Jefferson suggested using education to promote a meritocracy. A *meritocracy* is an educational system that gives an equal chance to all to develop their abilities and to advance in the social hierarchy. Advancement within the educational system and society is based on the merit or achievements of the individual. For instance, consider the following situation: students A and B are given an equal chance to attend school; student A is very

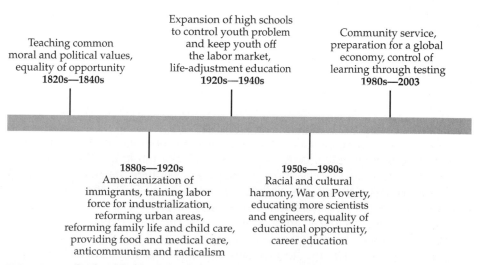

FIGURE 1–1. Goals of Public Schools in the U.S., 1820–2003

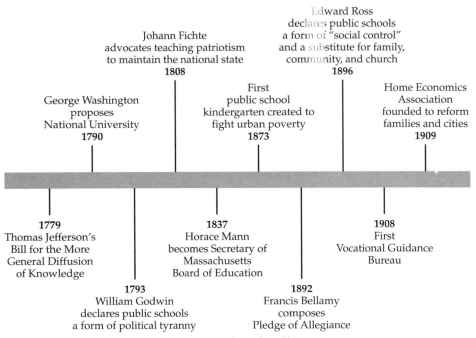

FIGURE 1–2.  Time Line of Events Discussed in This Chapter

successful but student B fails. Within the framework of an educational meritocracy, their success or failure in school determines their later position in society.

Since Jefferson was concerned with finding the best politicians, A's educational success would mean the possibility of assuming political leadership. On the other hand, B's educational failure would mean being disqualified from political leadership. But both had been given an equal chance to succeed. In this case, the school becomes the key institution for training and sorting citizens.

In the 1779 Bill for the More General Diffusion of Knowledge, Jefferson proposed three years of free education for all nonslave children. The most talented of these children were to be selected and educated at public expense at regional grammar schools. From this select group, the most talented were to be chosen for further education. Thomas Jefferson wrote in *Notes on the State of Virginia,* "By this means twenty of the best geniuses will be raked from the rubbish annually, and be instructed, at the public expense."

The details of Jefferson's plan are not as important as the idea, which has become ingrained in American social thought, that schooling is the best means of identifying democratic leadership. This idea assumes that the educational system is fair in its judgments. Fairness of selection assumes that judgment is based solely on talent demonstrated in school and not on other social factors such as race, religion, dress, and social class. Meritocracy fails if schools favor individuals from certain racial, religious, and economic groups.

What happens when meritocracy fails, but citizens continue to believe that it is still operating fairly? For instance, schools might claim to be operating accord-

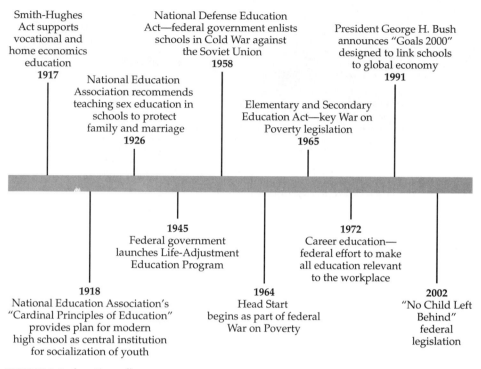

FIGURE 1–2. (continued)

ing to merit while favoring privileged economic and racial groups. This situation might result in perpetuating these favored groups. If students are taught to believe that schools select fairly, then they might believe in the superiority of the social groups favored by the school. In other words, all students might be taught to accept the social hierarchy perpetuated by the educational system. Acceptance might obscure inequalities in society. For instance, if the educational system favored those with wealth, then all members of society might come to accept differences in wealth as differences in talent as determined by educational institutions.

Besides educating political leadership, schools are also to educate future citizens. However, opinions are divided on how this should be accomplished. For instance, Thomas Jefferson and Horace Mann differed on the best method of citizenship education. Jefferson proposed a very limited education for the general citizenry. The three years of free education were to consist of instruction in reading, writing, and arithmetic, with reading instruction using Greek, Roman, English, and American history. Jefferson did not believe that people needed to be educated to be good citizens. He believed in the guiding power of natural reason to lead the citizen to correct political decisions. Citizens were to receive their political education from reading newspapers published under laws protecting freedom of the press. Citizens would choose between competing political ideas found in newspapers. Consequently, the important function of schools in preparing citizens was to teach reading.

"—AND IF AMERICA'S CHILDREN DON'T WORK HARD AND APPLY THEM-
SELVES IN SCHOOL, WHERE WILL THEY END UP?"

*Source:* © Tribune Media Services, Inc. All rights reserved. Reprinted with permission.

Interestingly, while Jefferson wanted political opinions to be formed in a free marketplace of ideas, he advocated censorship of political texts at the University of Virginia. These contradictory positions reflect an inherent problem in the use of schools to teach political ideas. There is always the temptation to limit political instruction to what one believes are correct political ideas.

In contrast to Jefferson, Horace Mann wanted schools to instill a common political creed in all students. Mann felt that without commonly held political beliefs society was doomed to political strife and chaos. Mann developed these ideas and his reputation as America's greatest educational leader while serving as secretary of the Massachusetts Board of Education from 1837 to 1848. Originally a lawyer, Mann became an educational leader because he believed schooling was the key to improving society.

Horace Mann feared that growing crime rates, social-class conflict, and the extension of suffrage would lead to violence and mob rule. Commonly held political values, Mann believed, would curtail political violence and revolution, and maintain political order. For Mann, the important idea was that all children in society attend the same type of school. This was what was meant by "common." It was a school common to all children. Within the common school, children of all religions and social classes were to share in a common education. Basic social disagreements were to vanish as rich and poor children, and children whose parents were supporters of different political parties, mingled in the schoolroom.

Within the walls of the common schoolhouse were to be taught the basic principles of a republican form of government. Mann assumed there was general agreement about the nature of these general political values, and they could be taught without objection from outside political groups. In fact, he argued against teaching politically controversial topics because of their potential for destroying the public school. The combination of common schooling and the teaching of a common political philosophy would establish, Mann hoped, shared political beliefs that would ensure the survival of the U.S. government. Political liberty would be possible, according to Mann's philosophy, because it would be restrained and controlled by the ideas implanted in students by the public school.

Is there a common set of political values in the United States? Since the nineteenth century, debates over the content of instruction have rocked the schoolhouse. Throughout the twentieth century, conservative political groups such as the Christian Coalition, American Legion, and the Daughters of the American Revolution pressured local public schools to not teach left-wing ideas. On the other hand, liberal organizations, and particularly labor unions and the People for the American Way, have pressured schools to teach their particular political doctrines.

There is also strong dissent to public schools teaching any political doctrines. Some argue that the teaching of political doctrines is a method of maintaining the political power of those in control of government. In the late eighteenth century, English political theorist William Godwin warned against national systems of education because they could become a means by which those controlling government could control the minds of future citizens. Writing in 1793, Godwin stated, "Their views as institutors of a system of education will not fail to be analogous to their views in their political capacity: the data upon which their instructions are founded."

Another problem is that American schools never achieved Mann's dream of children from all walks of life sharing the same classroom. All races, religions, and social classes do not mingle within a single common school. Racial segregation continues to exist even after massive efforts at desegregation in the 1960s and 1970s. A variety of religious groups, the largest being Catholic, maintain separate parochial schools. Children in wealthy suburbs attend private schools or public schools that are quite different from those in poorer school districts. Consequently, Horace Mann's goal of mixing students from differing social backgrounds to reduce social and political tensions was never achieved.

Mann's political and social objectives focused on the concept of socialization. Simply defined, *socialization* refers to what students learn from interacting with other students, following school rules, and participating in school social events. Socialization can be contrasted with *academic learning*, which refers to classroom instruction, textbooks, and other forms of formal learning. Some might argue that socialization is the most important learning that takes place in school, because students learn to get along with others.

For many educational leaders, socialization is a powerful means of political control. Learning to obey the rules of the school is socialization for obedience to the rules of government. Advocating the use of schools as political control, Johann Fichte, a Prussian leader in the early nineteenth century, asserted that schools should prepare students for conformity to government laws by teaching obedience to school rules and developing a sense of loyalty to the school. He argued that students will transfer their obedience to school rules to submission to government laws. According to Fichte, loyalty and service to the school and fellow students prepares citizens for service to the country. The school, according to Fichte, is a miniature community where children learn to adjust their individuality to the requirements of the community. The real work of the school, Fichte said, is shaping this social adjustment. A well-ordered government requires citizens to go beyond mere obedience to written constitutions and laws. Fichte believed children must see the government as something greater than the individual and must learn to sacrifice for the good of the social whole.

To achieve his goals, Fichte recommended teaching patriotic songs, national history, and literature to increase a sense of dedication and patriotism to the government. This combination of socialization and patriotic teachings, he argued, would produce a citizen more willing and able to participate in the army and, consequently, would reduce the cost of national defense.

In the United States, patriotic exercises and the fostering of school spirit were emphasized after the arrival of large numbers of immigrants from southern and eastern Europe in the 1890s. In 1892, Francis Bellamy wrote the Pledge of Allegiance and introduced it in the same year to educators attending the annual meeting of the National Education Association. A socialist, Bellamy wanted to include the word "equality" in the Pledge but this idea was rejected because state superintendents of education opposed equality for women and African Americans. The original Pledge of Allegiance was: "I pledge allegiance to my Flag and to the Republic for which it stands, one nation, indivisible, with liberty and justice for all." Bellamy's Pledge of Allegiance became popular classroom practice as educators worried about the loyalty of immigrant children.

In the 1920s, the American Legion and the Daughters of the American Revolution thought that the Pledge's phrase "I pledge allegiance to my Flag" would be construed by immigrants to mean that they could remain loyal to their former nations. Consequently, "my flag" became "the flag of the United States." It was during this period that schools initiated Americanization programs. Americanization involved teaching immigrant children the laws, language, and customs of the United States. Naturally, this included teaching patriotic songs and stories. With the coming of World War I, the Pledge of Allegiance, the singing of patriotic songs, participation in student government, and other patriotic exercises became a part of the American school. In addition, the development of extracurricular activities led to an emphasis on school spirit. The formation of football and basketball teams, with their accompanying trappings of cheerleaders and pep rallies, was to build school spirit and, consequently, prepare students for service to the nation.

Teaching patriotism creates problems for a society with a variety of religious, ethnic, and political groups. Some religious groups object to pledging allegiance to the flag because it involves worship of a graven image. In *West Virginia State Board of Education v. Barnette* (1943), the U.S. Supreme Court ruled that expulsion from school of children of Jehovah's Witnesses for not saluting the flag was a violation of their constitutional right to freedom of religion. Some teachers view patriotic exercises as contrary to the principles of a free society. In Chapter 10, which deals with legal issues, there is a lengthy discussion of the court cases related to academic freedom and loyalty oaths as well as the conflict between patriotic requirements and students' rights.

In the 1950s, the Pledge of Allegiance underwent another transformation when some members of the U.S. Congress and religious leaders campaigned to stress the role of religion in government. In 1954, it was recommended that the phrase "under God" be added to the Pledge. The new Pledge referred to "one nation, under God." Congressional legislation supporting the change declared that the goal was to "acknowledge the dependence of our people and our Government upon . . . the Creator . . . [and] deny the atheistic and materialistic concept of communism." For similar reasons, Congress in 1955 added the words "In God We Trust" to all paper money.

Reflecting the continuing controversy over the Pledge, a U.S. Court of Appeals ruled in 2002 that the phrase "one nation, under God" violated the U.S. Constitution's ban on government-supported religion. The suit was filed by Michael Newdow, the father of a second-grade student attending California's Elk Grove Unified School District. Newdow argued his daughter's First Amendment rights were violated because she was forced to "watch and listen as her state-employed teacher in her state-run school leads her classmates in a ritual proclaiming that there is a God, and ours is 'one nation under God'."

In reaction to the Court's decision, which was being appealed, Anna Quindlen wrote in the July 15, 2002, edition of *Newsweek*, "His [Bellamy's] granddaughter said he would have hated the addition of the words 'under God' to a statement he envisioned uniting a country divided by race, class and, of course, religion." Another dimension of the story was that Bellamy was a socialist during a period of greater political toleration than today. In contrast to the 1890s, today it would be difficult to find a professional educational organization that would allow an outspoken socialist to write its patriotic pledge.

In recent years, community service has also become an important consideration in citizenship training. For instance, in the fall of 1998, Chicago became the nation's largest school system to require students to perform community service to receive a high school diploma. Beginning with the sophomore class, students are required to spend forty hours at community service work and are required to submit proof of that work in the form of an essay, video, or oral report. "We want students to learn the importance of community," said Bruce Marchiafava, speaking for the nation's third-largest school system behind New York and Los Angeles. "They need to know that community is about giving, not just getting."

The immediate problem for Chicago officials was defining and identifying community service. This problem was compounded by the headache of finding enough community service activities for all the students. "If you let students work for an antihandgun group," Marchiafava said, "do you also let them work for the NRA [the National Rifle Association, which opposes strong gun control laws]?" Are political activities community service? Does volunteer work at for-profit schools and hospitals increase profits for these institutions by decreasing labor costs? Also, who decides what is community service? What happens if the person making this decision identifies work with religious organizations as community service? Would this be a violation of the Constitution's prohibition of government aiding religion? What about objections by some people to religious groups such as the Native American Church, which uses peyote, a hallucinogenic drug, in its ceremonies? Will students be able to volunteer to work for organizations advocating the legalization of marijuana?

None of the issues surrounding the political goals of education are easily resolved. Can they even be achieved? For instance, consider the following questions:

- Should there be a consensus of political values in the United States and should public schools develop that consensus?
- Should the public schools develop emotional or patriotic attachments to symbols of the State through the use of songs, literature, and history?
- Should the purpose of teaching history be the development of patriotic feelings?
- Does the teaching of patriotism in schools throughout the world increase the potential for international conflict?
- Who or what government agency should determine the political values taught in public schools?
- Have the public schools created a consensus of political values?

## THE SOCIAL GOALS OF SCHOOLING

Improving society through public schooling became an article of American faith. Horace Mann believed the school was the key to social improvement. He argued that past societies failed to stop crime by government and laws. To stop crime, Mann reasoned, schools must instill moral values in students. Later, this approach to controlling crime was referred to as putting a police person in every child's heart. Mann even suggested that America might see the day when the training in the schoolhouse would significantly reduce the number of police required by society.

The problem for Horace Mann and later educational leaders was determining which moral values to teach in schools. His approach was to teach moral values common to most Protestant denominations. A variety of religious groups disagreed with his ideas. The Catholic Church was the largest single religious group to reject Mann's plan and establish its own system of schools. The argument of Catholic Church leaders was that all education by its very goal of shaping behavior was religious and that it was impossible for a public institution to claim that it could satisfy the needs of all religious groups. Even if the public school eliminated all religious and moral teaching, this alternative could not be accepted because education would then become irreligious.

Despite the conflicts over what morality should be taught by public schools, Mann's dream of education as the key to social improvement remains alive. For many Americans, the school is the symbol and hope for achieving the good society. This hope is best illustrated by a story told to kindergartners in the early twentieth century about two children who bring a beautiful flower from their school class to their dirty and dark tenement apartment. The mother takes the flower and puts it in a glass of water near a dirty window. She decides the flower needs more light to expose its beauty. The mother proceeds to wash the window, which allows more light into the apartment and illuminates the dirty floors, walls, and furniture. The added light sends the mother scurrying around to clean up the now-exposed dirt. In the meantime the father, who is unemployed because of a drinking problem, returns to the apartment and is amazed to find his grim dwelling transformed into a clean and tidy house. The transformation of the apartment results in the father wanting to spend more time at home, and less time at the local bar. The father's drinking problem is solved, he is able to find work, and the family lives happily ever after. This story characterizes the hope that the social influence of the school will penetrate the homes and neighborhoods of America.

This story also illustrates the importance attached to the school as a central social institution by sociologist Edward Ross. Writing in the 1890s, Ross referred to education as a key mechanism for social control. He divided social control into external and internal forms. Traditionally, he argued, internal forms of control centered on the family, the church, and the community. The family and church inculcated moral values and social responsibility in the child, which ensured social stability and cohesion. In modern society, Ross declared, the family and church were being replaced by the school as the most important institution for instilling internal values. Ross saw reliance on education for control becoming characteristic of American society. "The ebb of religion is only half a fact," Ross wrote. "The other half is the high tide of education. While the priest is leaving the civil service, the schoolmaster is coming in. As the state shakes itself loose from the church, it reaches out for the school."

While Edward Ross was declaring schools a means for social control, the home economics profession, currently called Family and Consumer Sciences, was calling upon schools to play a major role in improving the quality of American families, changing the lifestyles of women, bettering urban conditions, and reforming the American diet. Schools responded by adding home economics courses for girls and school cafeterias. Founded in 1909, the American Home Economics Association spearheaded the creation of educational goals linked to home and urban improvement projects.

Home economics courses were designed to train women to be scientific housekeepers who would be freed from kitchen drudgery through a reliance on packaged and processed foods. Home economics courses taught cooking, household budgeting, sewing, and scientific methods of cleaning. The result was to be more free time for housewives to pursue further education and work to improve municipal conditions. The family model was that of woman as consumer of household products and educator, and husband as wage earner. By teaching women household budgeting, worker discontent over wages was to be reduced by families learning to live within their means. By teaching housewives to keep a clean and cheerful house, alcoholism was to be reduced because the husband would want to hurry home from work rather than stop at a tavern. Also, by teaching women how to cook healthy meals, husbands would have more vigor for work. And, of course, freed to receive more education, the housewives were to improve the political and cultural level of the American home.

In *Perfection Salad: Women and Cooking at the Turn of the Century,* Laura Shapiro credits home economists with the development of a distinctive American cuisine. She argues that during the latter part of the nineteenth century home economists "made American cooking American, transforming a nation of honest appetites into an obedient market for instant mashed potatoes." Jell-O and Wonder Bread, a factory-baked white bread, became symbols of American cuisine. These home economists paved the way for America's greatest contributions to global cuisine, the fast-food franchise.

Home economists helped to make school and hospital cafeteria food healthy, inexpensive, and bland. Through the school cafeteria, home economists hoped to persuade immigrant children to abandon the diet of their parents for the new American cuisine. A founder of the home economics movement, Ellen Richards projected a liberating role for prepared food in a 1900 article titled, "Housekeeping in the Twentieth Century." In her dream home where the purchase of cheap, mass-produced furniture allowed more money for "intellectual pleasures," the pantry was filled with a large stock of prepared foods—mainly canned foods and bakery products. A pneumatic tube connected to the pantry speeded canned and packaged food to the kitchen where the wife simply heated up the meal. In addition, the meal would be accompanied by store-bought bread. Besides being unsanitary, home economists believed that homemade bread and other bakery goods required an inordinate amount of preparation time and therefore housewives should rely on factory-produced bread products. Ellen Richards dismissed the issue of taste with the comment, "I grant that each family has a weakness for the flavor produced by its own kitchen bacteria, but that is a prejudice due to lack of education." People would stop worrying about taste, she argued, when they fully realized the benefits of the superior cleanliness and consistency of factory kitchens and bakeries.

Concern about the American diet continued into the twenty-first century when in 2002 the U.S. Congress began considering the Obesity Prevention and Treatment Act that would initiate a campaign to improve the eating habits in the nation, where more than 60 percent of adults are overweight. Public schools also jumped on the campaign to control student diets. Referring to the nationwide income of $750 million earned by schools from companies that sell snack or processed food in schools, Steve O'Donoghue, a teacher at Fremont High School in California, commented, "Should schools be co-conspirators in promoting unhealthy diets? Even if we can't change a single kid's behavior, the message we send by having all these deals with junk food peddlers is that this stuff is OK." To control student diets, Fremont High School has banned junk and snack foods. However, the Center for Consumer Freedom objects to the restrictions as a denial of student freedom of choice. Who should control students' eating habits?

In addition to the family, community, health, and diets, schools were called on to exercise social control over youth. Traditionally, the high school focused on teaching academic subjects. Broader goals were established for high schools in the National Education Association's 1918 report, *The Cardinal Principles of Secondary Education.* This report set the stage for the high school to become the major public institution for the socialization of youth through school dances, athletics, student government, clubs, and other extracurricular activities. Attended by only a small portion of the population prior to the 1920s, the high school became a mass institution by the 1930s.

High school extracurricular activities aimed to control adolescent sexuality and prepare youth for future family roles. In 1926, the NEA's Committee on Character Education recommended sex education courses as a means of combating the decline of the family and regulating sexual impulses for the good of society. The recommendation defined the purpose of human life as: "The creation of one's own home and family, involving first the choice and winning of, or being won by, one's mate." Sex education was to prepare youth to fulfill this purpose. Similar to today's emphasis on sexual abstinence before marriage, these early sex education courses taught that sexual control was necessary for "proper home functioning, which includes the comfort and happiness of all, maximum development of the mates, proper child production, and effective personal and social education of children." Students were warned that sexual intercourse outside marriage should be avoided because of its potential threat to the stability of the family.

Ironically, the high school heightened the possibility of early sexual activity by bringing large numbers of youth together within one institution. High school activities created a shared experience for youth. In *From Front Porch to Back Seat: Courtship in Twentieth-Century America,* Beth Bailey argued that the high school standardized youth culture in the United States. A common youth culture was spread by radio and magazines. The result of this close contact was the development of ritualized dating. High school marriage texts and manuals built sexual boundaries around dating. According to Bailey, early high school sex education books dealt with the issue of petting, which meant anything from hand-holding to sexual acts short of actual penetration. All the books warned against promiscuous petting. High school girls were cautioned that heavy petting would lead to a decline of their dating value in the marketplace. Women were given the task of ensuring that petting did not go too far. They were warned that boys tended to sit around and talk about their sexual exploits. The worst thing that could happen to a girl was to become an object of locker room discussions. Girls were told to achieve a balance between being known as an "icicle" or a "hot number."

By the 1930s, the senior prom was the pinnacle of the high school dating experience. In *Prom Night: Youth, Schools, and Popular Culture,* Amy Best argues that as a growing number of youth attended high school, "School clubs, school dances, and student government increasingly became a significant part of the kids' lives." Proms became widespread in the 1930s as the high school became a mass institution. They were considered a poor or middle-class version of the debutante ball which instructed youth in proper dating and mating rituals. Amy Best contends, "Proms were historically tied to a schooling project used to govern the uncontrollable youth. By enlisting you to participate in middle-class rituals like the prom, schools were able to advance a program that reigned in student's emerging and increasingly public sexualities."

By the 1940s, high schools had created a national youth culture given the name "teenagers." After World War II spending patterns changed as symbolized by the publication *Seventeen* magazine with its slogan "Teena means business." The word "teenager," according to Kelly Schrum, was invented by advertisers. At first advertisers experimented with "teenster" and "Petiteen," then "teenager" was popularized during the 1940s to mean a group defined by high school attendance. Defined as a major consumer market, it was believed that teenagers needed to be trained in the arts of consumption. Reflecting this trend, high school home economics courses were replaced by Family and Consumer Science courses.

Today, the sexual education of teenagers remains a controversial issue. Many people turn to the schools in efforts to exert control over adolescent sexual behavior. In recent years, the most heated value conflicts centered on AIDS education. These debates pitted those who believe in a strong moral code to control sexual behavior against those who believe in the right of free sexual activity between consenting adults. Those who believe in a strong moral code tend to support AIDS education programs that advocate sexual abstinence outside marriage and take a strong line against homosexual activities. Those at the other end of the value spectrum emphasize educational programs that teach safe sexual procedures and advocate the dispensing of condoms in public schools.

Despite the fact that the historical record indicates that moral instruction has not reduced crime, controlled teenage sexuality, or ended substance abuse, society still turns to public schools as the cure for many social problems. Certainly, the school can teach subjects that will improve society without engaging in moral instruction that will light the fires of religious controversy. For instance, early home economists advocated teaching about sanitation and diseases as a means of promoting public health. High school courses can teach about the results of alcoholism and substance abuse without entering the realm of morality; for example, is cigarette smoking "evil" or just bad for your health? Social studies, history, and economics courses can study social conditions that might contribute to crime and violence. However, even in this seemingly neutral approach to social issues there is always lurking in the background the potential for conflict over moral values.

By the time of the 2002 passage of the "Partnerships in Character Education" section of No Child Left Behind, with its list of ideal character traits, there had already been a long and complex history of attempts by schools to mold students' characters. The legislation's call for a "secular character education" that would include traits such as caring, respect, responsibility, and trustworthiness is offensive to those who believe that character education requires religious instruction. Also, what do these terms mean? Does "caring" mean that the individual should support a strong welfare government that guarantees all citizens health care, shelter, and adequate nutrition? Or does "caring" mean eliminating welfare programs so that the poor are forced to work and learn to be economically independent?

Attempts to use public schools to solve social problems will continue to raise problems about what values should dominate character education and how to reconcile secular and religious values. Consider the following questions:

- What are legitimate areas of social concern for public schools? Should public schools attempt to solve social problems, such as the AIDS epidemic or other epidemics, the destructive use of drugs and alcohol, teenage pregnancy, poverty, and child abuse?
- What government agency, organization, or group of individuals should decide the moral values to be taught in public schools?
- Should instruction related to social and moral issues be mandatory for all students?
- Should teachers be required to teach only the moral and social values given in the school district's curriculum?

## THE ECONOMIC GOALS OF SCHOOLING

In justifying the necessity of a public school system, Horace Mann proposed two major economic objectives. One was what we now call "human capital." Simply stated, *human capital theory* contends that investment in education will improve the quality of workers and, consequently, increase the wealth of the community. The second was the idea of "equality of opportunity." By going to school, everyone was to be given an equal opportunity to compete for jobs and wealth.

Horace Mann used human capital theory to justify community support of schools. For instance, why should an adult with no children be forced to pay for the schooling of other people's children? Mann's answer was that public schooling increased the wealth of the community and, therefore, even people without children economically benefitted from schools. Mann also believed that schooling would eliminate poverty by raising the wealth of the community and by preparing everyone to be economically successful.

Human capital arguments played a major role in the legislative outcomes of the War on Poverty programs of the 1960s. This legislation continues to affect public schools. The economic model of the War on Poverty in Figure 1–3 exemplifies current and past ideas about schooling and poverty. Notice that poor-quality education is one element in a series of social factors that tends to reinforce other social conditions. As you move around the inner part of the diagram, an inadequate education is linked to low-income jobs, low-quality housing, poor diet, poor medical care, health problems, and high rates of absenteeism

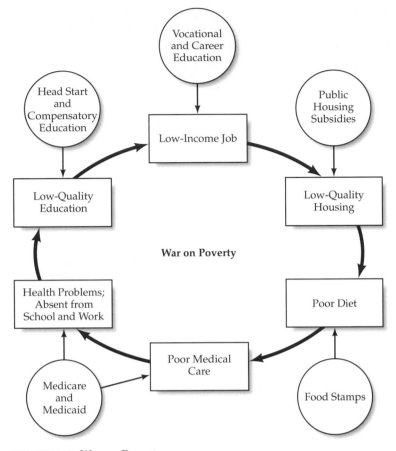

FIGURE 1–3. War on Poverty

from school and work. This model suggests eliminating poverty by improving any of the interrelated points. For instance, the improvement of health conditions will mean fewer days lost from school and employment, which will mean more income. Higher wages will mean improved housing, medical care, diet, and education. These improved conditions will mean better jobs for those of the next generation. Antipoverty programs include Head Start, compensatory education, vocation and career education, public housing, housing subsidies, food stamps, and medical care.

Today, Head Start programs are premised on the idea that some children from low-income families begin school at a disadvantage in comparison to children from middle- and high-income families. Head Start programs provide early childhood education to give poor children a head start on schooling that allows them to compete on equal terms with other children. Job-training programs are designed to end teenage and adult unemployment. Compensatory education in fields such as reading are designed to ensure the success of low-income students.

Besides the issue of poverty, human capital arguments have directly influenced the organization of schools. In the twentieth and twenty-first centuries, the dominant model for linking schools to the labor market is the "sorting machine." The image of the sorting machine is that of pouring students—called *human capital* or *human resources*—into schools where they are separated by abilities and interests. Emerging from the other end of the machine, school graduates enter jobs that match their educational programs. In this model, the school counselor or other school official uses a variety of standardized tests to place the student into an ability group in an elementary school classroom and later in high school into a course of study. Ideally, a student's education will lead directly to college or a vocation. In this model, there should be a correlation among students' education, abilities, and interests and their occupations. With schools as sorting machines, proponents argue, the economy will prosper and workers will be happy because of the close tie between the schools and the labor market.

In the twenty-first century, American workers are competing in a global economy. As U.S. companies seek cheaper labor in foreign countries, American workers are forced to take reductions in benefits and wages to compete with foreign workers. The only hope, it is argued, is to train workers for jobs that pay higher wages in the global labor market.

Preparation for the global economy shifts the focus from service to a national economy to a global economy by preparing workers for international corporations and for competition in a world labor market. This is important to understand because the premise is not reducing inequalities in salaries between jobs but educating all workers into higher-paying jobs.

The architect of educational policies for the global economy, former Labor Secretary Robert Reich, writes in *The Work of Nations*, "Herein lies the new logic of economic capitalism: The skills of a nation's workforce and the quality of its infrastructure are what makes it unique, and uniquely attractive, in the world economy." Reich draws a direct relationship between the type of education provided by schools and the placement of the worker in the labor market. He believes that many workers will be trapped in low-paying jobs unless their employment skills are improved. Reich argues, "There should not be a barrier between education and work. We're talking about a new economy in which lifelong learning is a necessity for every single member of the American workforce."

Reich's education and economic goals are based on human capital concepts. In schools, human capital is students, and the development of human capital simply means preparing students to be efficient workers, who, it is hoped, can find employment in their area of training. Economic growth pays for the investment in education. In the framework of human capital illustrated in Figure 1–4, an important consideration is the return on investment.

- Does investment in education produce worthwhile economic returns?
- Should governments invest in schools if there are few economic rewards?

Horace Mann's other economic goal was equality of opportunity. The idea of equality of opportunity resolves the conflict between promises of equality

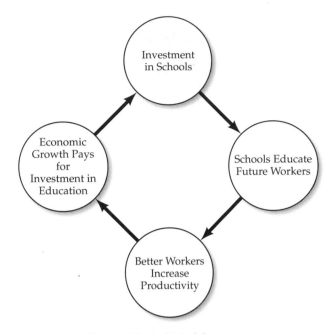

FIGURE 1–4.  Human Capital Model

and the existence of a society strongly divided by economic inequalities. Equality of opportunity does not mean equal income, living conditions, or status, but rather equality to compete for wealth. Horace Mann envisioned schools providing children of the rich and poor an equal education so that when they graduated they would be on equal terms to compete for jobs. He believed that the idea of equality of opportunity would reduce social tensions between the rich and poor by instilling the belief in people that everyone had an equal chance to succeed. It didn't matter whether equality of opportunity actually existed because social tensions would be reduced simply by people *believing* that the school provided everyone with an equal chance for success.

Equality of opportunity plays an important role in human capital theory. The War on Poverty and the No Child Left Behind legislation are premised on the idea that improved schooling will provide an equal opportunity for poor children in the labor market. It also assumes that equality of opportunity will improve the efficiency of the labor market by letting talented children from poor families achieve occupations commensurate with their abilities. Allowing talented children to achieve despite family conditions will, theoretically, contribute to economic growth.

*Educational inflation,* however, might fly in the face of equality of opportunity and human capital arguments. Increasing the number of high school and college graduates might result in decreasing the economic value of education. It is a simple story of supply and demand. With educational inflation, the educational requirements of jobs increase while the actual skills required for the jobs do not change. This results in the declining economic value of high school and college diplomas. Educational inflation first appeared in the early 1970s when the labor market was flooded with college graduates, and scholars with doctorates were driving taxicabs and cooking in restaurants. In this situation, the occupational structure did not expand to meet the increased educational training of the labor force. The response of educational institutions was to reorganize for more specific career training and call for more limited educational aspirations. The important lesson was that the nature of the labor market was more important in determining employment than was the amount of education available to the population. Educational inflation can hinder the ability of increased schooling to end poverty. There must be an increase in the number of jobs actually requiring higher levels of education for increased schooling to effectively raise levels of income. Education alone cannot solve the problems of poverty.

In addition to human capital improvement and provision of equality of opportunity, schools are believed to benefit the economy by socializing students for work. The school is the first formal public organization encountered by the child and provides the preparation and training needed to deal with other complex social organizations. The school's attendance requirements, tardiness rules, instruction in completing tasks and following directions, and obedience to authority are preparation for the workplace.

Arguments for the school's role in socializing for the workplace can be found throughout U.S. history. In the nineteenth century, schools emphasized marching, drills, and orderliness as preparation for the modern factory. Lining up for class as well as marching in and out of the cloakroom and to the blackboard were justified as training for factory assembly lines. Today, some students are prepared for job interviews and filling out employment forms. However, there is the question of whether the school is simply educating workers who are obedient, conforming, and passive, and who are, consequently, unwilling to join or form unions to actively struggle for workers' rights.

In recent years, there has been discussion of the school's role in promoting a learning society and lifelong learning so that workers can adapt to constantly changing needs in the labor force. A learning society and lifelong learning are considered essential parts of global educational systems. Both concepts assume a world of constant technological change, which will require workers to continually update their skills. This assumption means that schools will be required to teach students how to learn so that they can continue learning throughout their lives. These two concepts are defined as follows:

- In a learning society, educational credentials determine income and status. Also, all members in a learning society are engaged in learning to adapt to constant changes in technology and work requirements.
- Lifelong learning refers to workers engaging in continual training to meet the changing technological requirements of the workplace.

In the context of education for the global economy, the larger questions include the following:

- Should the primary goal of education be human capital development?
- Should the worth of educational institutions be measured by internal and external efficiency?
- Will the learning society and lifelong learning to prepare for technological change increase human happiness?

## HUMAN CAPITAL AND THE ROLE OF BUSINESS IN AMERICAN EDUCATION

Education for the global economy links schooling to the interests of the business community and international corporations. In fact, by the twenty-first century most Americans seemed to accept business as a natural partner in the control of schools. In the 1990s, few people questioned President George Bush and the National Governors' Association statement: "Parents, businesses, and community organizations will work together to ensure that schools are a safe haven for all children." Why would business be considered a logical partner in this objective? Why was there no mention of unions or churches? In fact, why was there no mention of participation by all the citizens who pay taxes to support schools?

The extensive and often unquestioned involvement of business in American schools has increased at a rapid rate and has made economic goals the number one priority of public schools. A February 1, 1990, article in the business section of *The New York Times* opened, "When it comes to reforming the nation's schools, these days the leading radicals are likely to be wearing pinstriped suits and to come from oak-paneled boardrooms rather than the ivy-covered walls of academia." After detailing business involvement in shaping the curriculum, managerial methods, and organization of the nation's schools, the article states, "The impetus behind the corporate embrace of education reform is concern about the quality of the American labor pool."

Business involvement in schools raises a number of issues. It is not necessarily true that what is good for American business is good for American schools and students. The primary concern of business is the maximization of profits. This can mean several things with regard to public schools. First, a major business expense is taxes. Businesses have a stake in reducing taxes, including taxes that support public schools.

Questions can also be raised regarding financial donations made directly by businesses to public schools. Often, adopt-a-school programs involve some kind of business contribution to an adopted school. Obviously, a direct donation to a public school gives the contributor some influence over school programs. On the other hand, if the same money came to the school through taxes there would be greater public determination of school programs. If businesses have the money to give to schools, they have enough money to be taxed to support schools. Giving money directly to schools increases business influence over education at the expense of control exercised by citizens through the government.

Business profits also depend on the quality and expense of workers. Although businesses want educated workers, they also want workers who are compliant and loyal to the company. Should public schools emphasize the development of habits that will meet the requirements of business?

Also, business has a stake in keeping wages down. Wages often depend on the supply of labor. In business, the ideal situation for hiring is a large pool of applicants that will allow business to pay the lowest wages and select the best workers. Obviously, this situation does not help the workers. For example, in the 1950s, business put pressure on the schools to educate more scientists and engineers and by the late 1960s there was a surplus of scientists and engineers, which caused low wages and unemployment. This situation worked to the advantage of the employer but not the employee.

## ISSUES ABOUT HUMAN CAPITALISM

The new global demands on education raise the following questions about treating students as human capital:

- Should schools emphasize a broad liberal education or preparation for a career?
- In a labor market based on educational attainment, will inequality of educational opportunity cause economic stratification?
- Will educational inflation defeat efforts to reduce inequalities in wealth and income?
- Should economic opportunities be based on high-stakes tests?

The first question was widely debated in the twentieth century. It can be argued that a broad liberal education enhances the joys of learning and thinking and provides the intellectual tools and knowledge for making decisions about the quality of one's life. In contrast, preparation for a career provides only a narrow education, which limits the ability to think about the broad issues related to the quality of life and happiness. Does education for a career produce corporate drones?

The second question relates to the wide variation in the quality of schools in the United States. The quality of teachers, the availability of textbooks and educational materials, class size, the quality of scientific laboratories and computer equipment, and counseling and preparation for college admissions vary among poor rural school districts, wealthy suburban school districts, private schools, and poor urban school districts. If the ability to compete in the labor market depends on the quality of education, then some school graduates will be more advantaged than others. Does this mean that a greater dependence on education for jobs will ensure that the children of the rich remain rich while the children of the poor remain poor?

The issue of educational inflation could defeat any plan designed to use increased educational opportunities as a means of reducing inequalities in wealth and income. What happens if everyone has a college degree?

# CONCLUSION

The school will continue to be used in efforts to solve social, political, and economic problems. It is easier for politicians to blame schools for social and economic problems than to try to directly correct these problems. By relying on the school, issues are shifted from an economic and social level to a personal level. "Reform the individual rather than society" is the message of those who trust the school to end crime, poverty, broken families, drug and alcohol abuse, and myriad other social troubles.

Now the focus is on the role of the school in a global economy. This focus emphasizes the school's role in economic development. Fortunately or unfortunately, students are viewed as human resources whose primary value is their potential contribution to economic growth and productivity. But is economic expansion a worthy goal if the quality of life is not improved? Doesn't education in and of itself improve the quality of an individual's life by opening new possibilities to thinking and learning?

## *Suggested Readings and Works Cited in Chapter*

BAILEY, BETH L. *From Front Porch to Back Seat: Courtship in Twentieth-Century America.* Baltimore: Johns Hopkins University Press, 1988. *A history of twentieth-century dating, including high school dating.*

BENNETT, WILLIAM J. *The De-Valuing of America: The Fight for Our Culture and Our Children.* New York: Simon & Schuster, 1992. *Bennett attacks multicultural education and defends the teaching of European traditions in American culture.*

BERLOWITZ, MARVIN J., and FRANK E. CHAPMAN. *The United States Educational System: Marxist Approaches.* Minneapolis: Marxist Educational Press, 1980. *This collection of articles provides an introduction to Marxist interpretations of the education system in the United States.*

BEST, AMY L. *Prom Night: Youth, Schools, and Popular Culture.* New York: Routledge, 2000. *A historical and sociological study of the high school prom.*

BORJA, RHEA. "Pledge of Allegiance in the Legal Spotlight." *Education Week* (10 July 2002). *This article details the 2002 court decision that declared the phrase "one nation, under God" a violation of the ban on a government-established religion.*

CONANT, JAMES. *The American High School Today.* New York: McGraw-Hill, 1959. *This major study of the conditions and goals of the American high school had an important impact on shaping the future direction of the high school.*

CREMIN, LAWRENCE. *The Republic and the School.* New York: Teachers College Press, 1957. *This is a good selection of Horace Mann's writings taken from his reports to the Massachusetts Board of Education and a good introduction to the social and political purposes of American education.*

DELFATTORE, JOAN. *What Johnny Shouldn't Read: Textbook Censorship in America.* New Haven: Yale University Press, 1992. *Delfattore discusses the Hawkins County, Tennessee, protest by Evangelical Christians over the content of school textbooks. Her book also covers other major censorship conflicts.*

EGAN, TIMOTHY. "In Bid to Improve Nutrition, Schools Expel Soda and Chips." *New York Times on the Web* (20 May 2002). *Story of recent attempts to wean students from snack and junk foods.*

EHMAN, LEE H. "The American School in the Political Socialization Process." *Review of Educational Research* 50 (Spring 1980): 99–119. *This is a summary of studies on the political socialization of American schoolchildren.*

GOODLAD, JOHN I. *A Place Called School.* New York: McGraw-Hill, 1984. *Goodlad uses a great deal of data to analyze the functioning of the American educational system in this detailed study of what actually happens in American schools.*

GORDAN, DAVID. *Fat and Mean: The Corporate Squeeze of Working Americans and the Myth of Managerial "Downsizing."* New York: The Free Press, 1996. *Gordan provides a good analysis of the increasing differences in income among U.S. workers.*

GREENBERG, DAVID. "History Lesson: The Pledge of Allegiance." http://www.slate.msn.com (28 June 2002). *This article provides a history of the Pledge of Allegiance from its origin in 1892 to the present.*

HOLMES, STEVEN. "School Reform: Business Moves In." *The New York Times* (1 February 1990): D2, D8. *This is a good survey of business involvement in public schools.*

JOHNSON, DIRK. "Chicago Schools to Require Community Service for Graduation." *The New York Times* (1 September 1998), http://www.nytimes.com.

JOHNSTON, ROBERT. "Chicago Parents Get Report Cards on Involvement." *Education Week on the Web* (8 November 2000). *This article discusses the experiment of teachers grading parents.*

KAESTLE, CARL. *Pillars of the Republic: Common Schools and American Society, 1780–1860.* New York: Hill and Wang, 1983. *This is currently the best history of the common school movement.*

KATZ, MICHAEL. *The Irony of Early School Reform.* Boston: Beacon Press, 1968. *This is an important study of the early relationship between social reform and education.*

LAZERSON, MARVIN, and W. NORTON GRUBB. *American Education and Vocationalism: A Documentary History, 1870–1970.* New York: Teachers College Press, 1974. *This good collection of documents deals with vocational education and the relationship between the school and the economy.*

LEE, GORDON. *Crusade Against Ignorance: Thomas Jefferson on Education.* New York: Teachers College Press, 1961. *This collection of statements by Jefferson on education has a good introductory essay.*

LIND, MICHAEL. *Up from Conservatism: Why the Right Is Wrong for America.* New York: The Free Press, 1996. *Lind argues that the conservative claim that public schools are failing is a hoax designed to cover up the increasing disparities in wealth and income.*

McCARTY, DONALD, and CHARLES RAMSEY. *The School Managers: Power and Conflict in American Public Education.* Westport, CT: Greenwood, 1971. *This book discusses the liberal and conservative divisions over report cards.*

National Commission on Excellence in Education. *A Nation at Risk.* Washington, DC: U.S. Government Printing Office, 1983. *The report and recommendations of this commission had a major impact on discussions about the American school.*

National Education Association. "Report of the Committee on Character Education of the National Education Association." Washington, DC: U.S. Government Printing Office, 1926. *This report recommended the teaching of sex education in high schools.*

"No Child Left Behind Act of 2001." Public Law 107–110 (8 January 2002). Washington, DC: U.S. Government Printing Office, 2002.

PERKINSON, HENRY. *The Imperfect Panacea: American Faith in Education, 1865–1965.* New York: Random House, 1968. *This is a study of attempts to use the school to solve major social problems in the United States.*

PORTNER, JESSICA. "Baltimore Plan to Offer Teenagers Norplant Raises Ethical, Medical, Legal Questions." *Education Week* (16 December 1992): 1, 13. *This article discusses the Baltimore plan to provide Norplant contraceptives in school clinics.*

QUINDLEN, ANNA. "Indivisible? Wanna Bet?" *Newsweek* (15 July 2002): 64. *Quindlen argues that the phrase "under God" in the Pledge of Allegiance violates the original intention of its author Francis Bellamy and the First Amendment.*

RODMAN, HYMAN; SUSAN LEWIS; and SARALYN GRIFFITH. *The Sexual Rights of Adolescents.* New York: Columbia University Press, 1984. *This book provides information on the legal, social, and psychological aspects of adolescent sexuality.*

SHAPIRO, LAURA. *Perfection Salad: Women and Cooking at the Turn of the Century.* New York: Random House. *A history of the role of home economics in the development of American cuisine.*

SPRING, JOEL. *Education and the Rise of the Global Economy.* Mahwah, NJ: Lawrence Erlbaum Associates, Inc., 1998. *This is a study of the effect of the global economy on education in the United States and other nations and the internationalization of educational policies.*

_____. *Globalization and Educational Rights: An Intercivilizational Analysis.* Mahwah, NJ: Lawrence Erlbaum Associates, Inc., 2001. *This book analyzes the meaning of educational rights in the context of Confucian, Islamic, Hindu, and Western civilizations.*

_____. *The American School: 1642–2000.* New York: McGraw-Hill Companies, Inc., 2000. *This history of U.S. schools emphasizes multiculturalism and critical thinking.*

_____. *The Universal Right to Education: Justification, Definition, and Guidelines.* Mahwah, NJ: Lawrence Erlbaum Associates, Inc., 1998. *This book provides a justification and definition of the right to education as provided for in the Universal Declaration of Human Rights.*

STAGE, SARAH, and VIRGINIA VINCENTI, eds. *Rethinking Home Economics: Women and the History of a Profession.* Ithaca: Cornell University Press, 1997. *A collection of essays on the history of home economics.*

Task Force on Education for Economic Growth. *Action for Excellence.* Denver: Education Commission of the States, 1983. *Presents recommendations made by a task force composed primarily of state governors and leading businesspeople.*

Task Force on Teaching as a Profession. *A Nation Prepared: Teachers for the 21st Century.* New York: Carnegie Corporation of New York, 1986. *This important report calls for the restructuring of the teaching profession and the establishment of a national teacher certification board.*

TIMPANE, MICHAEL. *Corporations and Public Education.* Report distributed by Teachers College, Columbia University, 1981. *This was a study conducted for the Carnegie Corporation on the growing links between public schools and business.*

TOMASKY, MICHAEL. *Left for Dead: The Life, Death and Possible Resurrection of Progressive Politics in America.* New York: The Free Press, 1996. *Tomasky discusses the failure of progressive politics to deal with the increasing economic plight of American workers.*

## CHAPTER 2

# Education and Equality of Opportunity

From the nineteenth century to the present America's democratic ideology has promised equal opportunity for all citizens. Equality of opportunity means that all members of a society are given equal chances to enter any occupation or social class. It does not mean that everyone will have equal incomes and equal status. Equality of opportunity has been the answer to questions about the meaning of equality in the 1776 American Declaration of Independence proclamation that "All men are created equal."

In *The Pursuit of Equality in American History,* J. R. Pole argues that an emphasis on equality of opportunity was America's way of balancing the ideal of equality with a society riddled with inequality. Since the American Revolution, the ideal of equality was seriously compromised by the denial of women's rights, slavery, legal racial segregation, exploitation of Native Americans, and differences in wealth and status. Even many of the signers of the Declaration of Independence, including Thomas Jefferson, owned enslaved Africans and later denied U.S. citizenship to Native Americans. Did the Declaration's statement of equality exclude women since women did not gain the right to vote until the twentieth century? Apparently, given the historical circumstances, the phrase "All men are created equal" applied only to white men at the time of the signing of the Declaration. Limiting full citizenship rights to white men was highlighted by the Naturalization Act of 1790. Passed by the U.S. Congress, this legislation restricted the granting of citizenship to "free white persons" only. Under this law, Native Americans were excluded from citizenship because they were classified as domestic foreigners. Until the 1940s and 1950s, this 1790 law was used to deny citizenship to Asian immigrants.

In the United States, the dilemma over the meaning of equality was resolved by emphasizing equality of opportunity in gaining economic rewards. Ideally, equality of opportunity should result in a social system in which all members occupy their particular positions because of merit and not from family wealth, heredity, or special cultural advantages. One way of thinking about equality of opportunity is as a contest where everyone is competing for jobs and income. To provide everyone with an equal chance in the competition, all participants should begin at the same starting line. During the contest, some people will earn more wealth than others.

In the 1830s, Horace Mann declared equality of opportunity through schooling as the great balance wheel of society that would reduce tensions between the rich and poor. By believing that the school could give everyone an equal opportunity to achieve wealth and power, one could ignore blatant social, economic, and political inequalities. Faced with obvious inequalities, people could now argue, "Hey, everyone is given a chance to get ahead. Those without money or power just didn't work hard enough. They had all the chances. They could have done well in school and gotten into a good college." This reasoning stabilized the social system by shifting the causes of inequality onto the shoulders of the individual. People seeking rectification of unequal conditions could call for more and better schools rather than demanding major political and economic changes. Schools promised to be the gateway to equal opportunity.

There are three major models for explaining the relationship between schools and equality of opportunity. I call these the common school model, the sorting machine, and high-stakes testing. After describing these models, I will examine the evidence on the contribution of schools to equality of opportunity.

## THE COMMON SCHOOL MODEL

In the common school model illustrated in Figure 2–1 everyone receives an equal and common education. Theoretically, this will ensure that everyone begins the economic race on equal footing. Children from all social backgrounds attend school where they receive an education that will prepare them to compete on equal terms in the economic system. Upon graduation, all students have an equal chance to succeed; thus, competition for socioeconomic standing occurs outside the schoolhouse.

Historically, common schools were supported in the nineteenth century because of a belief that differences of social class and special advantages were to disappear, as everyone was given an equal chance to get an equal education. During the 1830s, workingmen's parties advocated the establishment of publicly supported common schools and the end of the pauper schools that were the only free schools up to that time. It was asserted that with public schools for the poor and private schools for the middle class and the rich, education reinforced social differences and doomed the children of the poor to a perpetual lower-class status. Only common schools could provide for equality of opportunity.

The most extreme statements came from one faction of the New York Workingman's Party. This group argued that sending students to a common school would not in itself eliminate differences in social background, because the well-to-do child would return from school to a home richly furnished and full of books, whereas the poor one would return to a shanty barren of books and opportunities to learn. School, in the opinion of these workingmen, could never

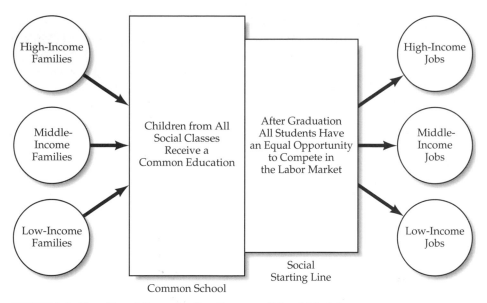

FIGURE 2–1. Equality of Opportunity: Common School Model

eliminate these differences. Their solution was that all children in New York should be removed from their families and placed in state boarding schools where they would all live in the same types of rooms, wear the same types of clothes, and eat the same food. In this milieu, education would truly allow all members of society to begin the race on equal terms. This extreme solution to the problem did not receive wide support, and debates about it eventually led to the collapse of the New York Workingman's Party.

The common school model is plagued by differences in family backgrounds. Children with parents who read to them and expose them to a variety of cultural events are probably better prepared to learn than children whose parents are illiterate. Also, wealthy parents can provide their children with special advantages such as tutors and learning aids, while poor parents might have to struggle just to feed their children. After graduation, children might receive uneven support in pursuing a career.

## THE SORTING MACHINE

In the sorting machine model, as depicted in Figure 2–2, the school attempts to overcome the role of family background in providing for equality of opportunity. Theoretically, equality of opportunity is guaranteed by the impartial decisions of teachers, counselors, and standardized tests. Students from all social backgrounds enter school where they are classified and placed in ability groups and tracks that will lead to appropriate jobs. The result is that students receive unequal and different educations. Some students graduate with vocational

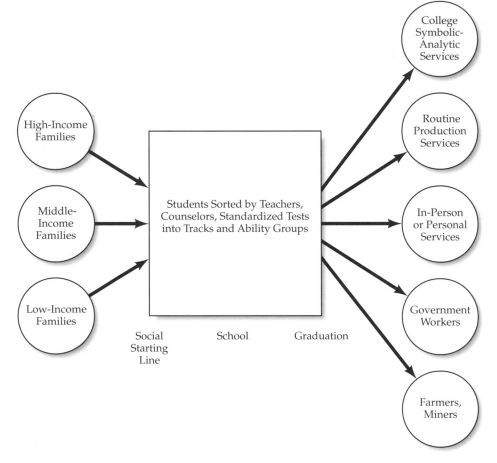

FIGURE 2–2. Equality of Opportunity: Sorting Machine Model

training while others prepare to enter college. In this model, competition for so-cial positions takes place in the school.

In the late nineteenth and early part of the twentieth century, the develop-ment of intelligence tests provided another means of organizing schools so as to provide equality of opportunity. Some people argued that intelligence tests could be an objective measure to decide one's best place in society. The French psychologist Alfred Binet, who wanted to find a method of separating children with extremely low levels of intelligence from those with normal intelligence levels, developed the first intelligence test in the early 1900s. The assumption of the test was that an inherited level of intelligence existed and could be mea-sured independent of environmental factors such as social class, housing con-ditions, and cultural advantages.

In the United States, the intelligence-test movement spread rapidly. Intelli-gence tests seemed to furnish a scientific means to achieve equality of opportunity based on individual ability. Individuals were given an equal chance to develop their particular level of intelligence.

Intelligence tests thus justified a hierarchical social structure based on intelligence. Within this framework democracy was viewed as a social system in which all people were given an equal chance to reach a level in society that corresponded to their individual level of intelligence.

The major problem in linking measured intelligence to equality of opportunity is the cultural bias of tests. In addition, there is the issue of whether an inherited native intelligence exists or whether intelligence is determined by early learning. Those believing in the existence of inheritable intelligence feel that test results accurately reflect social-class differences. Alfred Binet contended that the reason the poor did not do well on intelligence tests was that they had lower levels of intelligence and, moreover, that was why they were poor. More recently, psychologist Arthur Jensen argued that existing tests accurately measure inherited intelligence and that differences in performance by certain racial and social groups are accurate. On the other hand, there are those who believe in the existence of inherited intelligence but feel that the questions asked on existing tests reflect the cultural and social bias of the dominant middle class in the United States. The poor, and certain racial groups, do poorly on existing tests because many test questions deal with things that are not familiar to those groups. Within this framework, the solution to the problem is the creation of an intelligence test that is free of any cultural bias.

*Source:* Reprinted with special permission of North America Syndicate.

Another approach to the problem is the complete rejection of the idea of inherited intelligence and the acceptance of the view that intelligence and abilities are primarily a result of environment. This is the famous nurture versus nature debate. Those who see nurture as more important argue that differences in measured intelligence between social and racial groups primarily reflect differences in social conditions. The poor grow up in surroundings limited in intellectual training: an absence of books and magazines in the home; poor housing, diet, and medical care; and lack of peer-group interest in learning all might account for their poor performance on intelligence tests. This approach suggests that the school can act positively to overcome differences caused by social and cultural conditions.

Most recently, school programs have tried to overcome inequalities caused by differences in preparation for school learning. The argument for equality of opportunity is placed in the culture-of-poverty argument described in Chapter 1. Head Start and early childhood education programs are designed to counteract the supposedly poor learning opportunities of the children of the poor, and compensatory education is designed to provide special instruction in reading and other skills to offset disadvantages in preparation for formal schooling.

## THE HIGH-STAKES TESTING MODEL

The high-stakes testing model is an advanced variation on the sorting machine model (see Figure 2–3). A "high-stakes test" refers to an examination that determines a person's future academic career and job opportunities. High-stakes testing begins in elementary school, where the results determine promotion from one grade to another. High-stakes tests then determine graduation from high school; admission to undergraduate, graduate, and professional schools; and professional licenses and employment credentials. In Chapter 7, I analyze the educational ramifications of high-stakes testing.

Imagine a society where complete regulation of employment is based on high-stakes testing. Tests are the basis for issuing diplomas, assessment certificates for job skills, and licenses. Educational institutions become well-oiled machines processing children using a variety of tests and training to receive a particular credential for a job ranging from child care provider to auto mechanic to real estate salesperson to accountant to college professor. When applying for any job, people are asked to submit proof of their qualifications. This proof would be their credential. A society organized around high-stakes testing is advantageous to employers because they are presented with immediate evidence of a person's abilities to perform a job.

Throughout the twentieth century there existed many forms of high-stakes testing used for granting licenses for careers ranging from medical to beautician. Most of these licenses required a combination of educational achievement and state testing such as attending medical school and then taking a state examination. However, from the 1980s into the twenty-first century the labor market has been swamped with calls for greater testing and certification. Consider the history of the licensing of teachers. In the nineteenth century, a person applying for a teaching position was simply evaluated by a local school board

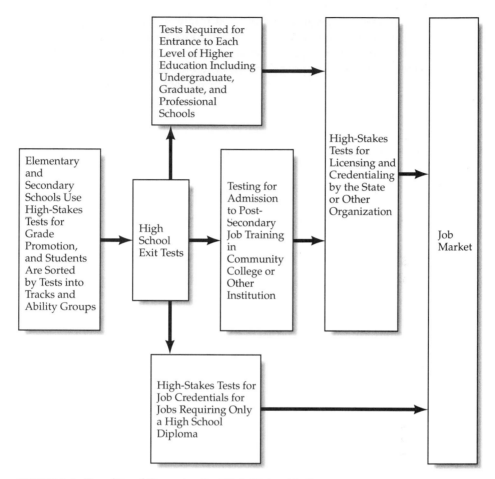

FIGURE 2–3. Equality of Opportunity: High-Stakes Testing

using whatever method it felt adequate. Then in the early twentieth century, state governments required local school systems to hire only those teachers licensed by the state. To obtain these licenses teachers had to take college courses in education. In the second half of the twentieth century, state governments began to require both college courses and the passing of a state examination. Today, the U.S. is rapidly on the path to requiring the passage of a national teaching examination for permanent licensing.

In the twenty-first century, most global school systems are test driven. In the U.S., life-determining standardized testing begins in elementary school and extends into the workplace. Most states now require passing a state test before receiving a high school diploma. Of course, standardized testing does not end in high school but extends through a person's college career. Test centers and test courses exist for the sole purpose of preparing people to take tests. It is now a test-happy world!

In a society organized around high-stakes testing, people can undergo a variety of examinations to gain credentials that provide proof of their ability to perform a job. For instance, some employers might just be interested in a job applicant having a high school or a college diploma. Another employer might want to see a college transcript to ensure the applicant received a particular type of education, such as engineering. Another employer might want to see a diploma plus test scores qualifying the applicant for the job. Another employer might want a diploma, test scores, and a licence.

In a society organized around high-stakes tests, the school becomes a crucial institution for determining economic success. To ensure equality of opportunity, the school must give everyone an equal chance to succeed. Is this possible?

## EDUCATION AND INCOME

Before exploring the problems facing schools in providing equality of educational opportunity, I would like to examine the actual relationship between schooling and income. Studies show that years of schooling are associated with income levels. These findings suggest that achievement in school is the road to economic success. However, a comparison of educational attainment, gender, and race suggest that other social factors effect the role of schools in determining personal income.

To demonstrate the relationship between schooling and income I am using statistics provided by the U.S. Census Bureau and the National Center for Education Statistics. Most of the statistics used in this chapter are taken from the 2000 U.S. Census. However, some of the numbers are taken from older census reports because of differences in analysis. The most recent analysis of education and income published by the U.S. Census Bureau is Jennifer Day and Eric Newburger's *The Big Payoff: Educational Attainment and Synthetic Estimates of Work-Life Earnings*, which uses census surveys from 1998, 1999, and 2000.

**TABLE 2–1. Educational Attainment and Average Annual and Estimated Lifetime Earnings**

| Educational Attainment | Annual Earnings of Full-Time Workers 25 to 64 Years Old in 1999 Dollars | Estimated Lifetime Earnings of Full-Time Workers in 1999 Dollars |
| --- | --- | --- |
| Not high school graduate | $23,400 | $1.0 million |
| High school graduate | 30,400 | 1.2 |
| Some college | 36,800 | 1.5 |
| Associate's degree | 38,200 | 1.6 |
| Bachelor's degree | 52,200 | 2.1 |
| Master's degree | 62,300 | 2.5 |
| Doctoral degree | 89,400 | 3.4 |
| Professional degree | 109,600 | 4.4 |

*Source:* This table is adapted from Figures 1 and 3 of Jennifer Day and Eric Newburger, *The Big Payoff: Educational Attainment and Synthetic Estimates of Work-Life Earnings* (Washington, DC: U.S. Bureau of the Census, July 2002), pp. 2, 4.

**TABLE 2–2.  Educational Attainment and Estimated Lifetime Earnings of Full-Time, Year-Round Workers by Sex and Educational Attainment**

| Educational Attainment | Women: Estimated Lifetime Earnings in 1999 Dollars | Men: Estimated Lifetime Earnings in 1999 Dollars |
|---|---|---|
| Not high school graduate | $0.7 million | $1.1 million |
| High school graduate | 1.0 | 1.4 |
| Some college | 1.2 | 1.7 |
| Associate's degree | 1.3 | 1.8 |
| Bachelor's degree | 1.6 | 2.5 |
| Master's degree | 1.9 | 2.9 |
| Doctoral degree | 2.5 | 3.8 |
| Professional degree | 2.9 | 4.8 |

*Source:* This table is adapted from Figure 6 of Jennifer Day and Eric Newburger, *The Big Payoff: Educational Attainment and Synthetic Estimates of Work-Life Earnings* (Washington, DC: U.S. Bureau of the Census, July 2002), p. 6.

As demonstrated in Table 2–1, there is a steady and sharp increase in annual and lifetime income for each stage of educational attainment. In 1999 dollars, a person without a high school diploma could expect to receive an annual income of $23,400 as compared to an annual income of $109,600 for a person with a professional degree. The lifetime differences are startling with a respective difference of $1 million versus $4.4 million. Even some college increases lifetime earnings compared to a high school graduate by $300,000 ($1.5 million lifetime earning for a person with some college versus $1.2 million for a high school graduate). And, of course, there is a major difference between the annual and lifetime earnings of high school graduates (annual $30,400 and lifetime $1.2 million) and those with bachelor's degrees (annual $52,200 and lifetime $2.1 million).

## GENDER, EDUCATIONAL ATTAINMENT, AND INCOME

Can schools provide equality of opportunity? Are there bias factors in society that limit the ability of schools to ensure everyone an equal chance to attain wealth? Consider these questions in the context of differences between male and female income at the same levels of educational attainment.

Table 2–2 shows the income differences according to educational attainment for full-time, year-round workers, as given in Jennifer Day and Eric Newburger's study. First, it should be noted that incomes for both women and men rise steadily with each advance in educational attainment. Second, there is about the same percentage difference in earnings for each level of educational attainment. As shown in Table 2–2, the lifetime earnings for a female high school graduate are $1 million while for a female with a bachelor's degree, $1.6 million. For men, a high school graduate can expect lifetime earnings of $1.4 million and for those holding a bachelor's degree $2.5 million. Comparing women and men's earnings, a man with a high school diploma will earn

**TABLE 2–3. Educational Attainment and Women's Estimated Lifetime Income as a Percentage of Men's Estimated Lifetime Income for Full-Time, Year-Round Workers**

| Educational Attainment | Women's Estimated Lifetime Income as a Percentage of Men's Estimated Lifetime Income |
| --- | --- |
| Not high school graduate | 63 |
| High school graduate | 71 |
| Some college | 70 |
| Associate's degree | 72 |
| Bachelor's degree | 65 |
| Master's degree | 65 |
| Doctoral degree | 65 |
| Professional degree | 60 |

*Source:* This table is adapted from Figure 6 of Jennifer Day and Eric Newburger, *The Big Payoff: Educational Attainment and Synthetic Estimates of Work-Life Earnings* (Washington, DC: U.S. Bureau of the Census, July 2002), p. 6.

$400,000 more in a lifetime than a woman with a high school diploma. A man with a bachelor's degree will earn $900,000 more in a lifetime than a woman with a bachelor's degree.

At all levels of educational attainment men earn more than women. And it is important to emphasize that these income differences are for full-time, year-round workers. In other words, the differences cannot be attributed to women working part time or taking time from work to raise children.

One day, the owner of the coffee shop down the street from my house posted a notice:

WOMEN'S INCOMES ARE 68% OF MEN'S INCOMES
COFFEE: 68 CENTS FOR WOMEN
1 DOLLAR FOR MEN

I don't know where the owner got the number "68%" but it is close to the percentages provided in Table 2–3. Notice that for each level of educational attainment, women earned from 60 to 72 percent of men's income.

## CLOSING THE GAP BETWEEN MEN'S AND WOMEN'S INCOMES

The above differences in income between men and women indicate the existence of bias in the job market. However, the political and social activism since the nineteenth century is closing the gap. These changes, as indicated in Table 2–4, highlight the importance of the struggle for social justice. Things can change and they can improve. It just takes continued effort over a long period of time.

To demonstrate the improving economic situation for women, Jennifer Day and Eric Newburger compare differences in income by age cohort group. The assumption is that there will be higher levels of income discrimination among

**TABLE 2–4. Women's Income as a Percentage of Men's Income by Age Group and Educational Attainment: 1997–1999**

| Educational Attainment | Women's Income as a Percentage of Men's Income by Age Group | | | | | | | |
|---|---|---|---|---|---|---|---|---|
| | 25 to 29 | 30 to 34 | 35 to 39 | 40 to 44 | 45 to 49 | 50 to 54 | 55 to 59 | 60 to 64 |
| High school only | 78 | 69 | 69 | 66 | 67 | 65 | 65 | 71 |
| Bachelor's only | 81 | 72 | 73 | 64 | 62 | 59 | 58 | 60 |

*Source:* This table is adapted from Figure 5 of Jennifer Day and Eric Newburger, *The Big Payoff: Educational Attainment and Synthetic Estimates of Work-Life Earnings* (Washington, DC: U.S. Bureau of the Census, July 2002), p. 5.

older workers than among younger workers who have been more affected by the struggle for equal pay for equal work. In Table 2–4, these comparisons are made between age groups for high school and college graduates.

As indicated in the table, the incomes for the younger age group of women (25 to 29) are considerably closer to male incomes in that age group than between women and men in the older group (60 to 64). In the younger group, women with high school and bachelor's degrees earn 78 and 81 percent, respectively, of men's income in the same age group as compared to 71 and 60 percent, respectively, in the older group. These younger women have significantly benefitted in income from the equal rights struggles of their parents.

The most significant improvement has been in the salaries of college-educated women. In the youngest age group (25 to 29) women with bachelor's degrees earn 81 percent of men's incomes for the same age and educational level while for the older group (60 to 64) it is only 60 percent.

## RACE, EDUCATIONAL ATTAINMENT, AND INCOME

The question I am exploring is whether schools can provide an equal opportunity to pursue wealth or income. From the above discussion of income differences between men and women with the same levels of education we see that bias factors in the labor market limit the ability of schools to provide equality of opportunity. Racial differences point to another labor market bias. Table 2–5 indicates differences in lifetime income between people of differing races with the same levels of educational attainment.

It is important for educators to understand how racial classifications are made in Table 2–5. Teachers and school administrators need to understand the problems students might face regarding their own racial self-identification. Table 2–5 uses data analyzed by Day and Newburger who use the racial classifications of "white, non-Hispanic," "black," "Hispanic," and "Asian and Pacific Islander." In Chapter 3, I will discuss the complexities in defining these terms. For instance, what does it mean to be "white, non-Hispanic," "black," "Hispanic," or "Asian" when many Americans are of mixed ancestry?

**TABLE 2–5.  Estimated Lifetime Earnings by Educational Attainment, Race, and Hispanic Origin, in 1999 Dollars**

| Educational Attainment | Estimated Lifetime Earnings | | | |
|---|---|---|---|---|
| | White, Non-Hispanic | Black | Hispanic (of any race) | Asian and Pacific Islander |
| Not high school graduate | $1.1 million | $0.8 million | $0.9 million | $0.8 million |
| High school graduate | 1.3 | 1.0 | 1.1 | 1.1 |
| Some college | 1.6 | 1.2 | 1.3 | 1.3 |
| Associate's degree | 1.6 | 1.4 | 1.5 | 1.4 |
| Bachelor's degree | 2.2 | 1.7 | 1.8 | 1.7 |
| Advanced degree | 3.1 | 2.5 | 2.6 | 3.1 |

*Source:* This table is adapted from Figure 7 of Jennifer Day and Eric Newburger, *The Big Payoff: Educational Attainment and Synthetic Estimates of Work-Life Earnings* (Washington, DC: U.S. Bureau of the Census, July 2002), p. 7.

The census data used in Table 2–5 are based on self-identification. In other words, people are asked what they consider to be their race. For instance, the U.S. Census in its official "Definitions and Explanations" defines "white, non-Hispanic" as: "Respondents who selected their race as White and indicated that their origin was not one of the Hispanic origin subgroups of Mexican, Puerto Rican, Cuban, Central or South American." There are many people in these Hispanic subgroups who identify themselves as "white" because their ancestors were primarily European.

At almost every level of educational attainment, "white, non-Hispanic" had higher estimated work-life earnings. The exception is for "advanced degrees" with "white, non-Hispanic" and "Asian and Pacific Islanders" having equal work-life earnings of $3.1 million. Otherwise there are significant differences. For instance, "white, non-Hispanics" with Bachelor's degrees earned an estimated $2.2 million during the work-life, while "blacks" and "Hispanics" with the same educational attainment earned $1.7 million.

Comparisons of income for those with the same levels of educational attainment but of different genders and races seem to indicate that to achieve the goal of equality of opportunity, we must remove the gender and racial biases in the labor market. But let's back up a minute: Is there really equality of opportunity *within* the educational system?

## ARE STUDENTS TREATED EQUALLY? THE ISSUE OF SOCIAL CLASS

Rather than providing equality of opportunity, does the school reproduce and reinforce social-class differences? In other words, does family income determine educational success and, consequently, the student's future income?

To answer these questions requires an understanding of the distribution of U.S. family incomes and a definition of social class based on family income. As

**TABLE 2–6. Social Class by Mean Household Income, 2000 Census**

| Social Class | Percentage or Quintile | Mean Household Income of Each Quintile in 2000 (adjusted dollars) |
|---|---|---|
| Upper | Highest 20% | $141,621 |
| Upper-middle | Fourth 20% | 65,727 |
| Middle | Third 20% | 42,359 |
| Lower-middle | Second 20% | 25,331 |
| Lower | Lowest 20% | 10,188 |

*Source:* Adapted from U.S. Bureau of the Census, *Money Income in the United States: 2000* (Washington, DC: U.S. Printing Office, September 2001), p. 8.

**TABLE 2–7. Share of Total Household Income by Year and Social Class**

| Social Class | 1970 | 1980 | 1990 | 2000 |
|---|---|---|---|---|
| Upper | 43.3% | 43.7% | 46.6% | 49.6% |
| Upper-middle | 24.5 | 24.9 | 24 | 23 |
| Middle | 17.4 | 16.9 | 15.9 | 14.8 |
| Lower-middle | 10.8 | 10.3 | 9.6 | 8.9 |
| Lower | 4.1 | 4.3 | 3.9 | 3.6 |

*Source:* Adapted from U.S. Bureau of the Census, *Money Income in the United States: 2000* (Washington, DC: U.S. Printing Office, September 2001), p. 21.

indicated in Table 2–6, the U.S. Census Bureau divides household incomes into 20 percent groupings. I will identify the top 20 percent according to household income as the upper class and the bottom 20 percent as the lower class. The middle class is the 20 percent between the top 40 percent and bottom 40 percent. The U.S. Census Bureau defines a household as consisting "of all people who occupy a housing unit. A house, an apartment or other group of rooms, or a single room, is regarded as a housing unit, . . . A household includes the related family members and all the unrelated people, if any, such as lodgers, foster children, wards or employees who share the housing unit."

As indicated in Table 2–6, the mean middle-class household income in 2000 was $42,359 as compared with a lower-class mean income of $10,188 and an upper-class income of $141,621. Using the preceding definition of social class, Table 2–7 indicates the increasing income inequalities between social classes based on the share of household income held by each social class.

The table shows that income inequality is increasing, with the upper-class share of total household income growing by 6.3 percent from 1970 to 2000 while the percentage of total household income for all other social classes declined. Why? U.S. Bureau of the Census explains, "Increasing income inequality is believed to be related to changes taking place in the labor market and in the composition of the households in the United States." The composition of households is an important factor with a decline in married couple households and an increase in single-parent and nonfamily households, which typically have lower incomes.

A jump in the number of people living in poverty contributed to increase income inequalities. In 2002, the "official poverty" thresholds were $18,104 for a family of four, $14,128 for a family of three, $11,569 for a family of two, and $9,039 for an individual. According to the U.S. Census Bureau, the percentage of people living below the poverty threshold increased from 11.3 percent in 2000 to 11.7 percent in 2001. In 2001, there were 32.9 million Americans who were classified as poor.

The labor market's contribution to income inequality is the result of increasing wages paid to well-educated or high-skilled workers and declining wages for poorly educated or low-skilled workers. Workers now compete in an international labor market. U.S. companies will move if they can find cheaper labor and production costs in another country. U.S. workers must compete with the wages paid in other countries. This results in a decline in real wages for unskilled labor in the United States.

## EDUCATION, SOCIAL CLASS, AND SCHOOL DISTRICTS

Does the social class of students' families influence their educational opportunities? In the nineteenth century, Horace Mann dreamed of achieving equality of opportunity by giving rich and poor children an equal education. Mann believed this could be achieved by mixing children from all social classes in the same school to create a common school for all. Has this been achieved?

Far from being common schools, public schools today are sharply divided by social class. Census statistics show an American population divided by social class into separate school districts with the sharpest division being between suburban and central city school districts. The U.S. Census Bureau's *Money Income in the United States: 2000* reports: "High-income households tended to be family households that include two or more earners residing in the suburbs of a large city." Table 2–8 shows the findings of the 2000 census on differences in income by residential areas.

The difficulty of achieving Mann's dream of a common school for the rich and poor is indicated by the family income differences between suburban and

**TABLE 2–8. Differences in Median Household Income by Residence**

| Residence | Median Household Income (in 2000 dollars) |
|---|---|
| Suburban-metropolitan area | $50,262 |
| Central city-metropolitan area | 36,987 |
| Rural-outside metropolitan area | 32,837 |

*Source:* Adapted from U.S. Bureau of the Census, *Money Income in the United States: 2000* (Washington, DC: U.S. Printing Office, September 2001), p. 2.

**TABLE 2–9. Current Expenditures per Student by Poverty Level of School District**

| Children in School District Below the Poverty Level | Expenditures per Student, 1996–1997 |
| --- | --- |
| Less than 5.0% | $6,622 |
| 5.0–14.9% | 5,728 |
| 15–24.9 | 5,311 |
| 25.0–34.9 | 5,870 |

*Source:* Adapted from National Center for Educational Statistics, *The Condition of Education 2001* (Washington, DC: U.S. Printing Office, 2001), p. 177.

central city areas—$50,262 and 36,987, respectively. Most parents choose housing based on the quality of education offered by the local school district. There is a direct relationship between the cost of housing in a school district and the amount of money that school districts spend per student. School districts are primarily funded by local property taxes. The more expensive the property, the more money local schools can raise in taxes to support their schools. Depending on state laws, approximately 44 to 47 percent of school revenues come from local sources with the rest coming from state and federal sources. The federal government's contribution, depending on the state, can vary from 6 to 8 percent.

Some major differences exist between suburban school districts. The best way of calculating differences between school districts is by family income. Table 2–9 compares expenditures per students by the percentage of children attending school who come from families with incomes below the poverty level. These figures are from the National Center for Education Statistics' *The Condition of Education 2001* based on 1996–1997 data.

Table 2–9 shows a dramatic difference in educational spending per student between wealthier school districts (those with less than 5.0 percent of children living below the poverty level) and poorer school districts (those with 15 to 24.9 percent of children living below the poverty level). School districts with 25.0 to 34.9 percent of children living in poverty actually spend $599 more per student than districts with 15 to 24.9 percent living in poverty. The difference is the result of additional funds from state and local governments for programs targeting children from low-income families. Even with additional funds, school districts with the lowest percentage of poor children spend $752 more per student.

## EDUCATION, SOCIAL CLASS, AND REAL ESTATE BROKERS

Some parents use reports of test scores and college attendance rates when shopping for a new home. Where do home buyers get their information on schools? They usually get the data from real estate brokers or online services. For instance, the data I use in the next section is taken from the Yahoo! real estate website http://list.realestate.yahoo.com. Using this website, home buyers can collect information on schools, neighborhood characteristics, and housing for anyplace in the United States. Some might consider the website the best guide to quality public education in the United States.

Obviously, most parents checking school data supplied by real estate agents will want to buy in communities that have the best schools. Competition for housing in these communities then drives up the price of houses. The result is to increase the social-class differences between school districts. It becomes more difficult for low- or medium-income families to afford housing in school districts with high educational ratings.

As an example of differences in real estate ratings of school districts, I will compare four neighboring suburban school districts in the New York metropolitan area—Scarsdale, Bronxville, Yonkers, and Mount Vernon. Real estate agents divide Yonkers, the largest of these four suburbs, into four different school areas to highlight differences between neighborhoods.

## SHOPPING FOR A PUBLIC SCHOOL

Imagine that you and your spouse are setting out to buy a house and that your primary concern is settling in an area with good schools. Your dream is for your children to attend college and, thereby, gain access to high-paying jobs. Recognizing the important influence of peers on your children's academic future, you want to live in a community where most students plan to attend college. In other words, you want the best for your children.

Also, you want to live within a reasonable distance of your workplaces. You examine a map and find that the best locations are a group of suburban communities sharing common borders, namely, Scarsdale, Bronxville, Yonkers, and Mount Vernon. You contact a real estate agent serving these communities and request information on schools, residents, and housing costs.

Of course, your household income is a factor in shopping for a new home. Both you and your spouse have had some college and both of you earn the estimated annual income for workers with some college, which, according to Table 2–1, is $36,800. Your total household income of $73,600 places you in the upper middle class which has, according to Table 2–6, a mean household income of $65,727.

Using the Yahoo! real estate website, the local real estate agent organizes Tables 2–10 and 2–11 to give you an overview of the four communities. Examining Table 2–10, you and your spouse are surprised by the academic disparities among these four bordering communities. After high school graduation, 97 percent of the students in Scarsdale and 99 percent in Bronxville attend college while the college attendance rate of graduates in Yonkers and Mount Vernon ranges from 25 to 50 percent. Also, Scarsdale and Bronxville can claim 33 and 6 National Merit Finalists, respectively, while the total for Yonkers and Mount Vernon is only 1. An examination of mean SAT scores reveals that in Scarsdale and Bronxville the range is from 611 to 666, while in Yonkers and Mount Vernon the range is 391 to 462.

**TABLE 2–10. School and Community Data for Scarsdale, Bronxville, Yonkers, and Mount Vernon**

| School District | Graduates Attending 4-Year College | National Merit Finalists | Mean SAT Scores, Math | Mean SAT Scores, Verbal | Percent College or Better | Median Household Income | Average Household Total Consumer Expenditures |
|---|---|---|---|---|---|---|---|
| Scarsdale | 97% | 33 | 666 | 620 | 77.66% | $126,777 | $120,319 |
| Bronxville | 99 | 6 | 630 | 611 | 75.94 | 104,619 | 102,670 |
| Yonkers 1 | 50 | 0 | 416 | 403 | 27.1* | 65,031* | 46,796* |
| Yonkers 2 | 38 | 1 | 462 | 452 | same | same | same |
| Yonkers 3 | 25 | 0 | 419 | 420 | same | same | same |
| Yonkers 4 | 37 | 0 | 402 | 391 | same | same | same |
| Mount Vernon | 43 | 0 | 444 | 429 | 26.39 | 63,609 | 44,990 |

*The Yahoo! real estate site does not provide Yonkers's demographic data by school district. Data are average for all of Yonkers.
*Source:* http://list.realestate.yahoo.com.

**TABLE 2–11. Cost of Living and Housing in Bronxville, Scarsdale, Mount Vernon, and Yonkers (National Average = 100)**

| Community | Cost of Living | Single-Family Home Sale Price Index |
|---|---|---|
| Scarsdale | 325 | 1399 |
| Bronxville | 277 | 1677 |
| Yonkers | 126 | 324 |
| Mount Vernon | 121 | 323 |

*Source:* http://list.realestate.yahoo.com.

You and your spouse are convinced from the data supplied by your real estate agent that the best public schools for your children are in Scarsdale and Bronxville. These school systems prepare students for college. In addition, your children will be surrounded by a college-oriented peer group. After noting that the percentage of college graduates living in Scarsdale and Bronxville is 77.66 and 75.94, respectively, while it is only 27.1 in Yonkers and 26.39 in Mount Vernon, you decide that Scarsdale and Bronxville are the communities where you both want to shop for a home.

Both of you are impressed by the high income levels in these communities, with the median household income in Scarsdale and Bronxville being $126,777 and $104,619, respectively. The average annual consumer expenditures for these communities are $120,319 and $102,670, respectively. You realize that you will never be able to compete with most of your neighbors regarding ostentatious displays of wealth such as expensive cars and clothes. Also, your children might face self-image problems when attending school, particularly high school, because of their more-affluent peers. Still, these school systems promise to be gateways to economic success for your children.

The hopeful vision of your children's future begins to dim as you start looking at real estate prices in the two communities. As indicated in Table 2–11, the price of single-family houses in Scarsdale is nearly 14 times the national average and in Bronxville nearly 17 times the national average. The cheapest house listed in Scarsdale is $710,000 for 4 bedrooms and 3 bathrooms and in Bronxville it is $849,000 for 5 bedrooms and 3.5 bathrooms (these were the cheapest houses listed on the Yahoo! website on August 13, 2002).

All dreams of buying houses in these two communities end when you calculate the monthly payments on these two homes. Assuming a 10 percent down payment and 7 percent interest on a 30-year mortgage, the $710,000 house in Scarsdale will require a down payment of $71,000 and mortgage payments will be $4,251 per month, or $51,015 per year. The $849,000 house in Bronxville will require a down payment of $84,900 and mortgage payments of $5,083.58 monthly, or $61,002.96 per year.

Since your annual household income is $73,600, you cannot afford to make these monthly mortgage payments and, in addition, pay property taxes, buy food and clothing, own an automobile, or take a vacation. In fact, given your household income, you probably would be unable to secure a mortgage for the purchase of either of these two houses. Your next choice is to seek housing in Yonkers or Mount Vernon.

## SAVAGE INEQUALITIES

Residential segregation into rich and poor school districts seriously compromises Horace Mann's dream of mixing the children of the rich and poor in the same schoolhouse to receive an equal education. This is particularly true as income becomes more dependent on educational achievement. Those with already high incomes will be able to buy houses in school districts that promise to provide their children with an education geared for high-income jobs. In this manner, a family can pass on its educational advantages to its children. The reverse might be true for low-income families where educational disadvantages are passed on from generation to generation.

Jonathan Kozol's *Savage Inequalities: Children in America's Schools* is a classic study of residential and educational inequalities. Kozol's book is designed to shock the reader by presenting the most extreme differences in public school systems. The book opens with a description of the economically depressed East St. Louis school system. Taken on a tour of the local high school, Kozol meets frustrated vocational education teachers who are unable to prepare their students for the world of work because of antiquated and broken shop equipment. The high school science teacher shows Kozol a physics lab where the lab stations have empty holes that once contained pipes. Balance scales and other lab equipment are either broken or outdated. The biology lab has no laboratory tables. The lack of tables did not seem to matter since the school district could not

"Miss, I'm finding it hard to concentrate with the
rats nibbling at my books."

*Source:* www.Cartoonstock.com

afford to buy dissecting kits. The chemistry lab, Kozol is informed, is not used because it is considered unsafe. The school has no VCRs and, therefore, is unable to use any of the latest visual-aid material.

A major problem contributing to the low quality of education in financially strapped school districts is the lack of a regular teaching force. Because of low salaries and poor working conditions, many urban school districts are unable to retain good teachers and must rely on substitute teachers. Consequently, many students spend idle time in classrooms as they face a steady stream of substitute teachers. In Chicago, more than a quarter of the teachers are low-paid substitutes. In addition, there is even a shortage of substitute teachers. On an average morning in the Chicago schools, 190 classrooms are without teachers. One high school student complained to Kozol that he had been in a class for an entire semester and there still was not a regular teacher. A student in an auto mechanics class said that he hadn't even learned to change a tire because the substitute teacher only wanted them to sit quietly.

One way the teacher shortage is handled is to increase the number of required study halls. So, many students find themselves sitting idly in classes managed by substitute teachers who do not know the subject matter of the course and then spend more idle time attending two or three study halls. No wonder many of these students do not feel that it is worthwhile to go to school.

In Camden, New Jersey, Kozol found student learning hindered by both poor health conditions and poor school facilities. Learning is difficult for children who come to school sick. Often, poorer school districts have a flood of students with medical and dental problems that their parents cannot afford to correct. The Camden school nurse complained to Kozol about children coming to school with rotting teeth and chronic and untreated illnesses. They sit in class in a state of discomfort unable to really pay attention to the classwork. Even if they could pay attention, they would be receiving an inadequate education. A typing teacher showed Kozol a typing room full of 10-year-old manual typewriters. The training in this class, she reflected, was completely out of touch with the world of word processing and computers. Buying computers is out of the question when the Camden school district can barely pay its teachers.

Kozol found savage inequalities even within the same school district. In New York City, he uncovered disconcerting differences between public schools in the poorer sections of the Bronx and a public school in the wealthy Riverdale section of the Bronx. At one school in the Bronx, he found classes being conducted in a former rollerskating rink with no windows. Although the school's capacity is 900, more than 1,300 children attend. A shortage of textbooks requires students to share social studies books. Because of a lack of classroom space, two first grade classes share the same classroom, with a blackboard being used as a divider. In some parts of the school, Kozol found four classes taking place within the same undivided space. On the top floor of the school, Kozol encountered 59 students and 4 adults of a bilingual class and a regular sixth grade class sharing a classroom that in a suburban school would be assigned to 20 students.

In contrast to the conditions in this school, an elementary school in the Riverdale section of the Bronx allows gifted students to have access to a school planetarium. At this school, class sizes are kept to around 22. Each classroom has a computer. Classes have in-class research centers stocked with up-to-date sources. The school does not depend on substitute teachers. Whereas in other areas of the Bronx students find themselves being forced to sit idly, students at the Riverdale school are engaged in constant learning activities that emphasize the use of reason and critical thinking.

Besides certain privileged urban schools, savage inequalities become most apparent when comparing schools with low per-student expenditures to schools in wealthy suburban districts and elite private schools. In contrast to Chicago schools, where students must worry about having a regular teacher and textbooks, New Trier High School, which serves wealthy Chicago suburban communities, provides 4-year courses in six foreign languages and elective courses ranging from the literature of Nobel winners to computer languages. The school even operates its own licensed television station. The average class size is 24. Each freshman is assigned an adviser who remains the student's counselor through graduation. Each counselor has only 24 students to advise as compared with Chicago schools, where counselors advise an average of 420 students. In contrast to the problems facing students in the Camden school district, the nearby wealthy Cherry Hill suburban school district offers fourteen different courses in its physical science department and eighteen biology electives. In Princeton, New Jersey, students are provided with music suites and computer-equipped subject-related study halls. Besides having up-to-date equipment, a large variety of courses, and a dedicated teaching staff, elite private schools such as Exeter maintain class sizes of about 13. The obvious cause of these savage inequalities is difference in community wealth. The New Trier district has approximately $340,000 of taxable property for each child while the Chicago schools have approximately $70,000 per student.

## CENTRAL CITY SCHOOLS

A frequently mentioned educational disparity occurs between schools in the central areas of large cities and those in surrounding suburban areas. A 1996 National Center for Education Statistics report found that fewer urban students than poor children in rural areas completed high school. What is the educational disadvantage of city living?

Jeanne Griffith, acting commissioner of the center, explained, "We found that in about half the things we looked at—the problems in urban schools were due to poverty. But in the other half, there was something about being in an urban setting that contributed even more." According to the center, the poor academic performance of urban students from low-income families is often a result of:

- Attending schools with large enrollments.
- Attending schools with high rates of teacher absenteeism.
- Attending schools with safety problems.
- Attending schools with high discipline rates.
- Transferring schools more frequently.
- Living in single-parent homes.
- Watching at least three hours of television a day.
- High rates of teenage pregnancy.
- Exposure to crime, including murder.

As Brenda Chaney, a Boston reading teacher states, "Too many of my students have seen murders. One student last year had to move because his brother had gotten shot (fatally) by a gang and they were worried he would get shot, too."

## SOCIAL CLASS AND "AT-RISK STUDENTS"

During the last century many terms were used to characterize students who might have academic problems including "disadvantaged," "urban," and "culturally deprived." The latest descriptor is "at-risk." Many students classified as at-risk experience few academic problems. Being at-risk is only an indication of potential academic problems. The National Center for Education Statistics found that 35 percent of students with risk factors finished high school and enrolled in a 4-year college or university within two years of high school graduation.

Poverty is high on the list of factors that put students at-risk. The report of the National Center for Education Statistics, *The Condition of Education 2002*, lists the factors that might indicate that a student is at-risk of academic failure. In this list, the Center for Educational Statistics uses socioeconomic status (SES) rather than the U.S. Census Bureau's income classifications. The socioeconomic status of students is determined by parental education level, parental occupation, family income, and household items. In the following list of at-risk factors, low socioeconomic status refers to students from the bottom 25 percent of households on a socioeconomic scale. These are families in which the parents have minimum levels of educational attainment, low income, and poor job status. The report's list of at-risk factors are:

- Being in the lowest socioeconomic status.
- Changing schools two or more times from grades 1 to 8 (except for transitions to middle school or junior high school).
- Having average grades of C or lower from grades 6 to 8.
- Being in a single-parent household during grade 8.
- Having one or more older siblings who left high school before completion.
- Being held back one or more times from grades 1 to 8.

The potential for academic failure increases with an increase in the number of risk factors in a student's life. In other words, the student who is most at-risk of academic failure has the lowest socioeconomic status, frequently changes schools, receives low grades from the sixth to eighth grade, has siblings who are high school dropouts, and fails one or more grades. Table 2–12 indicates the accumulative effect of risk factors on college attendance as analyzed in the report *The Condition of Education 2002*. Those students without any risk factors were more than four times (63.5 percent) as likely to go to college as those students with three or more risk factors (14.0 percent). Almost 50 percent of those with three or more risk factors would never enroll in a postsecondary institution, which in a society where income is linked to educational attainment means that they will probably continue in the same socioeconomic status as their parents.

**TABLE 2–12. Risk Factors and Attendance at 4-Year College or University**

| Number of Risk Factors | Percentage of All Students | Percentage Attending 4-Year College or University | Never Enrolled in Postsecondary Institution |
|---|---|---|---|
| None | 42.2 | 63.5 | 12.2 |
| One risk factor | 32.2 | 45.1 | 23.8 |
| Two risk factors | 16.3 | 27.0 | 38.7 |
| Three or more risk factors | 9.3 | 14.0 | 49.2 |

*Source:* National Center for Education Statistics, *The Condition of Education 2002* (Washington, DC: U.S. Printing Office, 2002), p. 77.

# POVERTY AMONG SCHOOL-AGED CHILDREN

Poverty becomes an at-risk factor when a child's parents have a low level of educational attainment. This is why socioeconomic status, which includes parents' level of educational attainment, is used to determine at-risk factors. For instance, highly educated parents might be living in poverty because of a personal choice. The poor writer or artist is a persistent occurrence in our society. While growing up in poverty, these children might benefit from a love of learning displayed by their parents. However, in many situations poverty contributes to educational disadvantages when combined with other risk factors. The National Center for Education Statistics study, *The Condition of Education 2002*, reports:

- 15 percent of all children 5 to 17 years old live in households where the annual income is below the poverty level.
- 29 percent of school-aged children in central cities live in poverty.
- 13 percent of school-aged children in suburbs live in poverty.

# THE END OF THE AMERICAN DREAM: SCHOOL DROPOUTS

Savage inequalities are reflected in dropout rates by social class and race. Certainly, in today's global labor market, dropping out of secondary school almost guarantees a low-income job. Table 2–13 indicates dropout rates according to social class. Born into a lower social class, a student is 22.1 percent more likely to drop out of school and perpetuate the low-income status of her/his family. When you compare Table 2–13 with Table 2–14 you find that if you are

**TABLE 2–13. Dropout Rate by Social Class, 1996**

| Social Class of Family | Percent of Dropout Rate | Percent of All Dropouts |
|---|---|---|
| Upper (top 20% income) | 2.6 | 5.2 |
| Middle (includes upper-middle, middle, and lower-middle) | 10.8 | 56.1 |
| Lower (bottom 20%) | 22.1 | 38.7 |

*Source:* National Center For Education Statistics, "Dropout Rates in the United States, 1996," http://nces.ed.gov/.

**TABLE 2–14. Dropout Rate by Race/Ethnicity in 1996, 2000**

| Year | Total | White | Black | Hispanic |
|---|---|---|---|---|
| 1996 | 11.1% | 7.3% | 13.0% | 29.4% |
| 2000 | 10.9 | 6.9 | 13.1 | 27.8 |

*Source:* National Center for Education Statistics, *The Condition of Education 2002* (Washington, DC: U.S. Printing Office, 2002), p. 164.

Hispanic, male, and from a lower-class family, then your chances of dropping out are even higher.

The consequence of these savage inequalities is the perpetuation of social-class differences. A child attending an impoverished school district is receiving less of an opportunity to gain an education than students in elite suburban and private schools. Without a broad range of electives in humanities and science, regular teachers, and advisers with small student loads, children in impoverished school districts are not being prepared for college or to enter high-paying jobs. Even if they go to college, the graduates of the East St. Louis, Chicago, and Camden schools will have difficulty competing with their better-prepared counterparts from Scarsdale and Bronxville.

## TRACKING AND ABILITY GROUPING

*Tracking,* primarily a practice of the high school, separates students into different curricula such as college preparatory, vocational, and general. *Ability grouping* places students in different classes or in groups within the same classroom based on their abilities. These abilities are usually determined by a combination of a teacher assessment of the student and standardized tests.

The United States, with its emphasis on individual differences, uses ability grouping more often than other countries. A 1991 study found that the use of ability grouping in math classes in the United States was two-thirds higher than in other countries. In lower secondary school grades, 56 percent of math classes used ability grouping. England reported the highest use of ability grouping with 92 percent of math classes grouped in the lower secondary grades.

Often, the family income of students parallels the levels of ability grouping and tracking. That is, the higher the family income of the students, the more likely it is that they will be in the higher ability groups or a college-preparatory curriculum. Conversely, the lower the family income of the students, the more likely it is that they will be in the lower ability groups or the vocational curriculum.

Studies show the existence of this condition in the American public schools from the 1920s to the present. One of the first major studies of social-class differences in relationship to adolescent culture and the high school was conducted in a small town in Indiana by a team of sociologists headed by A. B. Hollingshead. Their findings, which they titled *Elmtown's Youth,* can still be found duplicated in many high schools throughout the country. The Hollingshead study divided the population of Elmtown into five social classes. The tracks, or courses of study, at Elmtown's high school were college preparatory, general, and commercial. When the social-class origins in each track were determined, it was found that children from social classes 1 and 2 concentrated on college-preparatory courses (64 percent) and ignored the commercial courses. Class 3s were found mainly in the general courses (51 percent), with 27 percent in college preparatory and 21 percent in commercial. Class 4s slipped down the hierarchical scale of curricula; only 9 percent were in college preparatory, 58 percent were in general, and 33 percent were in commercial. Only 4 percent of class 5s were in the college-preparatory curriculum, whereas 38 percent were in commercial, and 58 percent were in the general curriculum.

Sometimes teacher expectations are linked to the perceived social class of the student. The most famous study of the tendency to live up to expectations is Robert Rosenthal and Lenore Jacobson's *Pygmalion in the Classroom*. In the first part of the study, a group of experimenters was given a random selection of rats and told that certain rats came from highly intelligent stock. The rats labeled as coming from highly intelligent stock tended to do better than the other rats, though they were randomly grouped. The two psychologists tested their results in a school to see if teacher expectations would affect student performance. After giving students a standardized intelligence test, they gave teachers the names of students whom they called late bloomers and told the teachers to expect a sudden spurt of learning from them. In fact, the names of these students were selected at random from the class. A year later the intelligence tests were administered again. The scores of the supposed late bloomers were compared with those of other children who received scores on the original test similar to the supposed late bloomers. It was found that those students who were identified to teachers as late bloomers made considerable gains in their intelligence-test scores when compared with students not designated as late bloomers.

The principal inference of this study is that teacher expectations can play an important role in determining the educational achievement of the child. This might be a serious problem in the education of children of poor and minority groups, where teachers develop expectations that these children will either fail or have a difficult time learning. Some educators, such as teacher and educational writer Miriam Wasserman, argue that teacher expectations are a major barrier to educational success for the poor and for certain minority groups.

Wasserman, in her case study of the New York school system, *The School Fix: NYC, USA,* relates the issue of teacher expectations to what she calls the "guidance approach to teaching." The guidance approach means that when planning instructional units, the teacher tries to take into account the student's family background, social life, and problems outside school. On the surface this sounds like good educational practice in relating teaching methods and materials to the background and needs of the student. In practice, Wasserman discovered the tendency to label all students from poverty areas as having learning problems, as not being interested in school, and as probably not succeeding in school. Teachers tended to provide material that was not very challenging to students so labeled or explained their own failure to teach the student in terms of the student's background.

In further investigation of this problem, Wasserman interviewed students from poverty backgrounds who had been successful in school. She found that these students believed the major element in their successful educational career was having a teacher who was primarily interested in the student's learning and who emphasized and demanded high-quality work. These teachers had high expectations for their students, expectations that were not influenced by the social-class backgrounds of the students.

According to a 1996 report by educational researcher Dennis Carlson, tracking underwent significant change in the 1990s. Many vocational programs were collapsed into a basic skills curriculum, causing a major division between students enrolled in basic skills tracks and those enrolled in college-preparatory tracks.

The combination of the classification of students according to abilities and curriculum and the expectation of teachers and other school officials seems to contribute to the social-class divisions of the surrounding society being reflected in the placement and treatment of students in the school. In addition, it has been found that in terms of educational achievement, the differences between children from different social classes become progressively greater from the first grade through high school.

## SHOULD TRACKING AND ABILITY GROUPING BE ABOLISHED?

In 1992, with the backing of Governor William Weld and the Commissioner of Education Robert Antonucci, the Massachusetts Department of Education began an active campaign to eliminate grouping by academic ability in local schools. Since the 1920s the separation of students by academic ability has been criticized because the result is often separation by socioeconomic class and race. In 1985 these practices again became an important issue with the publication of Jeannie Oakes's *Keeping Track: How Schools Structure Inequality.* As the name of the book suggests, Oakes documented the use of grouping by academic ability as a means of fostering social inequality. By 1993 the debate over grouping by academic ability had reached the point that, in the words of educational researcher Robert Slavin, "Whenever anybody holds a meeting on this topic, it is packed to the rafters." The National Education Association adopted a resolution in 1992 condemning the use of academic tracking as a means of segregation by social class, race, and gender.

Opponents of tracking and ability grouping argue that these practices primarily promote inequality without benefitting the fast or slow learner. An analysis of the National Education Longitudinal Study concluded that a group of eighth graders separated by academic ability and studied for two years showed few benefits from the practice. In this analysis, separation by ability worsened the educational achievement of low achievers and did nothing for high achievers.

While criticizing academic ability grouping that results in discrimination by social class, race, and gender, supporters argue that the practice makes it easier for teachers and it allows high achievers to progress at a more rapid rate. Teachers of gifted and talented classes are particularly upset at the idea of ending academic ability grouping. A defender of ability grouping, Peter D. Rosenstein, the executive director of the National Association of Gifted Children, worries that it has become "politically correct to deny that there are different potentials among children." Supporters might be correct that there are different academic potentials among children, but the reality is that tracking and ability grouping are frequently used as a means of discrimination.

## SOCIAL REPRODUCTION

The discussion so far in this chapter would suggest that schools might play a role in maintaining differences between social classes. This argument is called social reproduction. Simply defined, *social reproduction* means that the schools reproduce the social-class structure of society. Economists Samuel Bowles and Herbert Gintis are the major proponents of the concept of *social reproduction.* They contend that the school causes occupational immobility. This argument completely reverses the idea that the school creates occupational mobility. Bowles and Gintis, in constructing this thesis, accept the findings that mobility rates are consistent throughout Western industrialized countries and that family background is one major factor in determining economic and social advancement. What they argue is that the school is a medium through which family background is translated into occupational and income opportunities.

This translation occurs regarding personality traits relevant to the work task; modes of self-presentation such as manner of speech and dress; ascriptive characteristics such as race, sex, and age; and the level and prestige of the individual's education. Bowles and Gintis insist that the four factors—personality traits, self-presentation, ascriptive characteristics, and level of educational attainment—are all significantly related to occupational success. They also are all related to the social class of the family. For instance, family background is directly related to the level of educational attainment and the prestige of that attainment. Here the economic level of the family determines educational attainment. Children from low-income families do not attain so high a level of education as children from rich families. From this standpoint the school reinforces social stratification and contributes to intergenerational immobility. For ascriptive characteristics such as race, the social advantages or disadvantages of a particular racial group are again related to levels of educational attainment.

Personality traits and self-presentation are, according to Bowles and Gintis, important ingredients in occupational success. These characteristics are a direct product of child-rearing practices and reflect the social class of the family. Also, the economists assert, child-rearing patterns are directly related to the occupation of the head of the family. This argument is based on the work of Melvin Kohn, whose study *Class and Conformity: A Study of Values* found that middle-class parents are more likely to emphasize children's self-direction while working-class parents are more likely to emphasize conformity to external authority.

In other words, working-class families tend to be more authoritarian and violent toward their children than upper-class families. Children are more often punished with beatings in lower-class families than upper-class families. On the other hand, children in upper-class families are often given more freedom to pursue their own interests than children in lower-class families. Working-class parents value obedience, neatness, and honesty; higher-status parents emphasize curiosity, self-control, and happiness. Even when racial and religious divisions are considered, Kohn found that social class still stands out as the more important determinant in child-rearing values. Kohn argues that the most important thing that determines how children are treated in a family is the type of job held by the head of the household. If the head of the household works in a factory or other workplace where they primarily take orders, they will give orders to their children. On the other hand, if the head of the household has a job with a great deal of freedom to make independent decisions, then the children will be granted the same freedom. The more self-direction experienced on the job by the head of the family, the more likely it is that child-rearing patterns will emphasize self-direction. Self-direction on the job is directly related to the social class of the family. Higher-status and higher-income jobs usually involve self-direction; lower-status and lower-income jobs tend to be more routine and require more conformity to imposed rules.

In *Schooling in Capitalist America,* Bowles and Gintis support Kohn's conclusions. Child rearing, they declare, is important in developing personality traits related to entrance into the workforce. Personalities evidencing a great deal of self-direction tend to have greater success in high-status occupations. The differences in child-rearing patterns, the authors state, are reflected in the schools attended by different social classes. Schools with populations from lower-income families tend to be more authoritarian and to require more conformity than schools attended by children from higher-income families. This is often reflected in the differences between educationally innovative schools in high-income suburbs and the more traditional schools in low-income, inner-city neighborhoods. In some cases, parents place pressure on local schools either to be more authoritarian or to allow more self-direction. The nature of this pressure tends to be related to the social class of the parents.

In this manner, Bowles and Gintis argue, the child-rearing patterns of the family are reflected in the way schools treat children. Children from authoritarian families are prepared by authoritarian schools to work at low-paying jobs that do not require independent thinking and decision making. The reverse is true for children coming from upper-income families and schools; they are socialized to high-paying jobs that require independent thinking. In this manner, education reproduces social classes. One problem with the social reproduction argument is the treatment of students as passive recipients of knowledge. But, as the next section on resistance suggests, students are not passive objects that are easily manipulated by school authorities.

## *RESISTANCE*

As educational philosopher Henry Giroux argues, most educational studies assume that students are nonresistant recipients of instruction and that they can be easily managed by the school. Certainly, arguments that schools simply reproduce the social-class structure create an image of submissive students being molded for their place in society. Even the more-effective-schools movement assumes that students can be easily managed to achieve higher test scores. But any teacher will tell you that students are not that easily controlled and manipulated. Many students balk at following instructions, and they go out of their way to make life difficult for teachers. Students have an agenda regarding life that might have little to do with the goals of the school.

Giroux contends that students often resist the plans made by teachers and school administrators. In this case, resistance means the culture developed among students to oppose the goals of teachers and the schools. The pioneer study of this phenomenon is Paul Willis's *Learning to Labour.* Willis studied a group of students from working-class backgrounds who attended an all-male comprehensive high school in an industrial area of England. These students learned to manipulate the environment of the school to make sure that they would have a good time. They created a peer culture that was antischool. Their culture differed sharply from what they called the "ear-'oles." The ear-'oles—students who appeared to do nothing but sit and listen in school—represented the student who conforms to the authority and the expectations of the school. The working-class students resented both the ear-'oles and the authority of the school. They felt that the school was out of touch with real life and had little relationship with the male working-class world that they came from and expected to enter as adults. They took every opportunity to play pranks on school officials, teachers, and ear-'oles. Their culture was a rejection of hopes for upward mobility through schooling and the values of schooling and learning.

Ironically, Willis portrays this antischool culture as preparation for the generalized labor force the students will be entering. The pranks they play in school are similar to the pranks they will later play on the shop floor. The peer culture they develop is similar to the culture of their fathers at work and the culture they will experience when they enter the workforce. This interpretation provides a more complex picture of the interaction between family background and the school. The students create an antischool culture that plays a determining role in ensuring the perpetuation of their working-class status. In Willis's account, the school is not the villain that takes account of family background to reproduce existing social classes. Rather, the culture of the school comes into conflict with the culture of the students.

The antischool culture that developed among these students was not in their best interests. The school did hold out the opportunity for them to gain an education and improve their status in life. In addition, the student culture described in Willis's study is sexist and racist. Given these facts, the notion of an antischool culture should not be romanticized as something to protect.

On the other hand, students do resist school programs that they know are not working in their interests. Some students develop an antischool culture when they note that the real benefits of schooling seem to go to students in the upper curriculum tracks and ability groups. Often, this resistance is exhibited as a general defiance of school authority. In addition, many students develop a sense of rage as they witness their life's chances slipping away. Rage turns to anger, and anger sometimes results in physical violence.

Within this framework, the key to improving the schools for the children of the poor is to understand that school learning is really a function of the interaction between student culture and the school's intentions. Students at many times have reasons for feeling oppressed. Consequently, educational change should be a product of a dialogue between students and school authorities. This dialogue might result in the school adjusting to the culture of students and students adjusting to the culture of the school. One might argue that this is the method for ensuring that the school provides equality of opportunity.

In *Theory of Resistance: A Pedagogy for the Opposition* and his many other writings, Henry Giroux argues that student resistance can be the vehicle for developing an educational method that will empower students and teachers to transform society. I do not have room in this book to cover Giroux's arguments in any depth, but at the end of Chapter 9 there is a brief discussion of critical theory that forms the framework for Giroux's argument. Critical theory suggests that by itself education can never provide equality of opportunity. Not only may the pursuit of equality of opportunity through schooling be a false hope, but it may also distract people from the real issues. It could be that equality of opportunity depends on concrete economic changes in society.

## PARENTAL INVOLVEMENT

"Thirty years of research tells us that the starting point of American education is parent expectations and parental involvement with their children's education, regardless of their station in life, their income level or their educational background," Secretary of Education Richard Riley told the National Press Club in a speech on September 7, 1994, launching a major federal effort to involve families in education. Educators have argued since the nineteenth century that one of the keys to breaking down social-class differences in education is educating families about how they can help their children learn.

Riley based his argument for parental involvement on a study that found that 90 percent of the difference between high and low eighth grade math test scores could be explained by factors within the control of a student's family. These factors were student absenteeism, the variety of reading materials in the home, and excessive television viewing. He also cited studies showing that the single most important factor in a child's eventual success in reading is being read to aloud in early childhood. In other words, the difference between success and failure in reading is often a result of whether family members read books aloud to a student at a young age. Riley suggested that television be limited to two hours a night "even if that means that the remote control may have to disappear on occasion." He urged parents to check their children's homework and to set high expectations.

In Washington, DC, a coalition led by Jesse Jackson asked parents to sign pledges to take their children to school the first day, meet with teachers, pick up report cards, and turn off the television for three hours a night. Also, the Education Department formed a 45-member National Coalition for Parental Involvement in Education to make family participation a top national goal. Working with this coalition are the national PTA, the Boys and Girls' Clubs of America, the National Alliance of Businesses, and the U.S. Catholic Conference. Whether the effort for increasing parental involvement will break down social-class differences in education will be determined in the future. In the next chapter, I explore the question of equality of education versus social transformation in the context of issues related to gender, ethnicity, and race. Related to this question and set of issues is the problem of equal educational opportunity.

## CONCLUSION

Can schools provide equality of opportunity? Or does equality of opportunity depend on economic circumstances outside the power of the school? Does the school reduce social differences or heighten them through ability grouping, tracking, teacher expectations, counseling, and inequalities in school financing? Will the equalizing of school finances ensure an equal education for children from all social classes? These questions reflect the major problems confronting a public school system that professes equal educational opportunity and tries to provide an education that will guarantee equality of opportunity.

### Suggested Readings and Works Cited in Chapter

BOWLES, SAMUEL, and HERBERT GINTIS. *Schooling in Capitalist America.* New York: Basic Books, 1976. *This classic book by two neo-Marxist economists argues that schooling in the United States maintains the existing social-class structure for the benefit of an economic elite.*

DAY, JENNIFER, and ERIC NEWBURGER. *The Big Payoff: Educational Attainment and Synthetic Estimates of Work-Life Earnings.* Washington, DC: U.S. Bureau of the Census, July 2002. *An important study on the relationship between income and educational attainment.*

GIROUX, HENRY. *Theory of Resistance: A Pedagogy for the Opposition.* South Hadley, MA: Bergin and Garvey, 1983. *In this book Giroux criticizes reproduction theorists and presents his theories of resistance.*

HOLLINGSHEAD, A. B. *Elmtown's Youth.* New York: John Wiley, 1949. *This is a classic study of the effect of social class on adolescent life in a small town.*

JENCKS, CHRISTOPHER. *Inequality.* New York: Harper and Row, 1972. *Jencks presents a major study of the effects of family and schooling on inequality.*

KOHN, MELVIN. *Class and Conformity: A Study of Values.* Homewood, IL: Dorsey, 1969. *This is a study of the relationship between child-rearing practices and social class.*

KOZOL, JONATHAN. *Savage Inequalities: Children in America's Schools.* New York: Crown Publishers, 1991. *Kozol details the inequalities in spending per student between school districts and the resulting inequalities in the quality of education.*

National Center for Education Statistics. *The Condition of Education 2001.* Washington, DC: U.S. Printing Office, 2001. *This excellent annual report on the conditions of schools in the United States is an invaluable source for educational statistics.*

———. *The Condition of Education 2002.* Washington, DC: U.S. Printing Office, 2002. *This excellent annual report on the conditions of schools in the United States is an invaluable source for educational statistics.*

———. "Dropout Rates in the United States, 1996." http://nces.ed.gov/. *Cites examples of differences in dropout rates between schools.*

———. "Revenues and Expenditures for Public Elementary and Secondary Education: School Year 1997–98." http://nces.ed.gov/pubs20000/quarterly/summer/2feat/q2-7.html. *Provides valuable information on inequality in school expenditures.*

———. "Student Membership and Current Expenditures per Pupil in Membership for Public Elementary and Secondary Schools, by Function and State: School Year 1997–98." http://nces.ed.gov/. *This is another demonstration of inequality of educational spending.*

OAKES, JEANNIE. *Keeping Track: How Schools Structure Inequality.* New Haven: Yale University Press, 1985. *This book explores the issue of tracking as a source of inequality.*

POLE, J. R. *The Pursuit of Equality in American History: Second Edition,* revised and enlarged. Berkeley: University of California Press, 1993. *This is the best history on the concept of equality in U.S. history and the importance of the idea of equality of opportunity.*

RATTER, MICHAEL, ET AL. *Fifteen Thousand Hours.* Cambridge, MA: Harvard University Press, 1979. *A study of the differences among twelve inner-city schools in London and how those differences are related to behavior and academic achievement.*

REICH, ROBERT. *The Work of Nations: Preparing Ourselves for 21st-Century Capitalism.* New York: Alfred Knopf, 1991. *This study by President Bill Clinton's secretary of labor outlines the educational requirements for jobs in a global economy.*

RIDDLE, WAYNE, and LIANE WHITE. "Expenditures in Public School Districts: Estimates of Disparities and Analysis of Their Causes," 1996. http://nces.ed.gov/. *Presents the differences in spending between schools.*

ROSENTHAL, ROBERT, and LENORE JACOBSON. *Pygmalion in the Classroom: Teacher Expectation and Pupils' Intellectual Development.* New York: Irvington, 1988. *Studies the effects of teacher expectations.*

SPRING, JOEL. *Education and the Rise of the Global Economy.* Mahwah, NJ: Lawrence Erlbaum, 1998. *Spring studies the development of education in the context of global economics.*

STOUT, DAVID. "Recession Cut Incomes and Swelled Poverty Rolls, U.S. Says." *New York Times on the Web.* 24 September 2002. *Summarizes the U.S. Census Bureau's report on the increase in poverty in the U.S.*

U.S. Bureau of the Census. *Money Income in the United States: 2001.* Washington, DC: U.S. Government Printing Office, 2001. *The best source of information about income distribution in the U.S.*

WASSERMAN, MIRIAM. *The School Fix: NYC, USA.* New York: Outerbridge and Dienstfrey, 1970. *The first section of the book has case studies of students who did and did not make it successfully through the New York schools.*

WILLIS, PAUL. *Learning to Labour.* Lexington, MA: D. C. Heath, 1979. *Willis presents a study of the development of an antischool peer culture among working-class students in England.*

Yahoo! Real Estate Website. http://list.realestate.yahoo.com. *Frequently used by home buyers to determine quality of local schools.*

## CHAPTER 3

# Equality of Educational Opportunity:

## Race, Gender, and Special Needs

### THE LAW, RACE, AND EQUALITY
### OF EDUCATIONAL OPPORTUNITY

Equality under the law is the great legal principle underlying the idea of equality of educational opportunity. Everyone should receive equal treatment by the law. No one should receive special privileges or treatment because of race, gender, religion, ethnicity, or wealth. This means that if a government provides a school system, then everyone should be treated equally by that system; everyone should have equal access to that educational system. As Figure 3–1 illustrates, the path to equality of educational opportunity remains a work in progress.

Added in 1868, the Fourteenth Amendment to the Constitution provided for equality under the law. One of the purposes of the Fourteenth Amendment was to extend the basic guarantees of the Bill of Rights into the areas of state and local government. The clause of the amendment that emphasized the principle of equality under the law stated, "No State shall . . . deny to any person within its jurisdiction the equal protection of the laws."

At first glance, "equal protection of the laws" would suggest that if state laws created a school system, then everyone should have equal access. However, the initial interpretation by the U.S. Supreme Court in 1895 was that "equal protection" could also mean "separate but equal." Or, in other words, segregated education based on race could be legal under the Fourteenth Amendment if all the schools were equal.

The separate but equal ruling occurred in the 1895 U.S. Supreme Court decision *Plessy v. Ferguson*. The case involved Homer Plessy, who was one-eighth African American and seven-eighths white. He was arrested for refusing to ride in the colored coach of a train, as required by Louisiana state law. The Supreme Court's decision in this case that segregated facilities could exist if they were equal became known as the separate but equal doctrine.

The 1954 desegregation decision *Brown v. Board of Education of Topeka* overturned the separate but equal doctrine by arguing that segregated education was

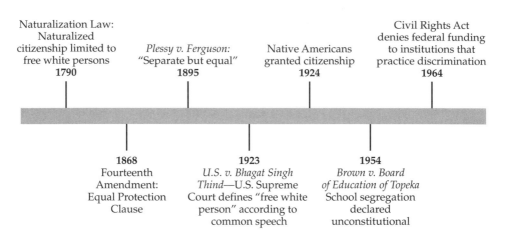

FIGURE 3–1. Time Line of Events Discussed—Equality of Educational Opportunity

inherently unequal. This meant that even if school facilities, teachers, equipment, and all other physical conditions were equal between two racially segregated schools, the two schools would still be unequal because of the racial segregation.

In 1964 Congress took a significant step toward speeding up school desegregation by passing the important Civil Rights Act. About school desegregation, Title VI of the 1964 Civil Rights Act was most important because it provided a means for the federal government to force school desegregation. In its final form, Title VI required the mandatory withholding of federal funds from institutions that practiced racial discrimination. Title VI states that no person, because of race, color, or national origin, can be excluded from or denied the benefits of any program receiving federal financial assistance. It required all federal agencies to establish guidelines to implement this policy. Refusal by institutions or projects to follow these guidelines was to result in the "termination of or refusal to grant or to continue assistance under such program or activity."

Title VI of the 1964 Civil Rights Act was important for two reasons. First, it established a major precedent for federal control of American public schools by making it explicit that the control of money would be one method used by the federal government to shape local school policies. (This aspect of the law will be discussed in more detail in Chapter 7.) Second, it turned the federal Office of Education into a policing agency with the responsibility of determining whether school systems were segregated and, if they were, of doing something about the segregated conditions.

One result of Title VI was to speed up the process of school desegregation in the South, particularly after the passage of federal legislation in 1965 that increased the amount of money available to local schools from the federal government. In the late 1960s southern school districts rapidly began to submit school desegregation plans to the Office of Education.

In the North, prosecution of inequality in educational opportunity as it related to school segregation required a different approach. In the South, school

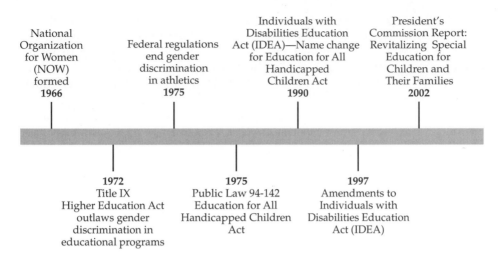

National
Organization
for Women
(NOW)
formed
**1966**

Federal regulations
end gender
discrimination
in athletics
**1975**

Individuals with
Disabilities Education
Act (IDEA)—Name change
for Education for All
Handicapped
Children Act
**1990**

President's
Commission Report:
Revitalizing Special
Education for
Children and
Their Families
**2002**

**1972**
Title IX
Higher Education Act
outlaws gender
discrimination in
educational programs

**1975**
Public Law 94-142
Education for All
Handicapped Children
Act

**1997**
Amendments to
Individuals with
Disabilities Education
Act (IDEA)

segregation existed by legislative acts that required separation of the races. There were no specific laws requiring separation of the races in the North. But even without specific laws, racial segregation existed. Therefore, it was necessary for individuals bringing complaints against northern school districts to prove that the existing patterns of racial segregation were the result of purposeful action by the school districts. It had to be proved that school officials intended racial segregation to be a result of their educational policies.

The conditions required to prove segregation were explicitly outlined in 1974, in the Sixth Circuit Court of Appeals case *Oliver v. Michigan State Board of Education.* The court stated, "A presumption of segregative purpose arises when plaintiffs establish that the natural, probable and foreseeable result of public officials' action or inaction was an increase or perpetuation of public school segregation." This did not mean that individual motives or prejudices were to be investigated but that the overall pattern of school actions had to be shown to increase racial segregation; that is, in the language of the court, "the question whether a purposeful pattern of segregation has manifested itself over time, despite the fact that individual official actions, considered alone, may not have been taken for segregative purposes."

## THE MEANING OF RACE

The question of the meaning of race was highlighted by the original separate but equal case, *Plessy v. Ferguson.* According to the lines of ancestry as expressed at the time, Plessy was one-eighth African American and seven-eighths white. Was Homer Plessy white or black? What was the meaning of the term *white?* Why wasn't Plessy classified as white since seven-eighths of his ancestory was white and only one-eighth was black? Why did the court consider him black?

*Plessy v. Ferguson* highlights the principle that race is a social and legal construction. The U.S. legal system was forced to construct a concept of race because the 1790 Naturalization Law limited naturalized citizenship to immigrants who were free white persons. This law excluded Native Americans from citizenship. This limitation remained until 1952. Because of this law, U.S. courts were forced to define the meaning of white persons. Adding to the legal problem was that most Southern states had adopted the so-called one drop of blood rule which classified anyone with an African ancestor, no matter how distant, as African American. Under the one drop of blood rule, Homer Plessy was considered black.

The startling fact about the many court cases dealing with 1790 law was the inability of the courts to rely on scientific evidence in defining white persons. Consider two of the famous twentieth-century court cases. The first, *Takao Ozawa v. United States* (1922), involved a Japanese immigrant who graduated from high school in Berkeley, California, and attended the University of California. He and his family spoke English and attended Christian churches. A key issue in *Takao Ozawa v. United States* (1922) was whether "white persons" referred to skin color. Many Japanese are fair skinned. The court responded to this issue by rejecting skin color as a criteria. The court stated, "The test afforded by the mere color of the skin of each individual is impracticable, as that differs greatly among persons of the same race, even among Anglo-Saxons, ranging by imperceptible gradations from the fair blond to the swarthy brunette, the *latter being darker than many of the lighter hued persons of the brown and yellow races* [my emphasis]." Rejecting the idea of skin color, the court recognized the term *Caucasian* to define white persons and denied citizenship.

However, the following year the U.S. Supreme Court rejected Caucasian as a standard for defining white persons in *United States v. Bhagat Singh Thind* (1923). In this case, an immigrant from India applied for citizenship as a Caucasian. According to the scientific rhetoric of the time, Thind was a Caucasian. Faced with this issue, the court suddenly dismissed Caucasian as a definition of white persons. The court argued, "It may be true that the blond Scandinavian and the brown Hindu have a common ancestor in the dim reaches of antiquity, but the average man knows perfectly well that there are unmistakable and profound differences between them today." Therefore, rather than relying on a scientific definition as it had in *Takao Ozawa v. United States,* the U.S. Supreme Court declared, "What we now hold is that the words 'free white persons' are words of common speech, to be interpreted in accordance with the understanding of the common man." The court never specified who was to represent this common man. Thind was denied citizenship.

U.S. court histories are filled with disputable efforts to define race. My nineteenth-century ancestors on my father's side were denied U.S. citizenship and were recognized as having only tribal citizenship despite the fact that the majority of their ancestors were European. Until Native Americans were granted U.S. citizenship in 1924, many so-called mixed bloods were limited to tribal citizenship. The confusion over legal racial categories was exemplified by an 1853 California court case involving the testimony of immigrant Chinese witnesses regarding the murder of another Chinese immigrant by one George Hall. The California Supreme Court overturned the murder conviction of George Hall by applying a state law that disallowed court testimony from blacks, mulattos, and Native Americans. California's Chief Justice ruled that the law barring the testimony of Native Americans applied to all "Asiatics" since, according to theory, Native Americans were originally Asians who crossed into North America over the Bering Straits. Therefore, the chief justice argued, the ban on court testimony from Native Americans applied to "the whole of the Mongolian race."

The effect of this questionable legal construction of race was to heighten tensions between different groups of Americans. Many of those classified as African American have European and Native American citizenship. However, because of the one drop of blood rule and legal support of segregation, the possibilities for continuing assimilation and peaceful coexistence between so-called whites and blacks were delayed and replaced by a tradition of hostility between the two groups. The law reduced the chances of evolving into a peaceful multiracial society. It will probably take another century to undo the damage created by the legal construction of race and segregation in the nineteenth and early twentieth centuries.

## WHAT RACE AM I?: RACIAL AND CULTURAL SELF-IDENTIFICATION

In an effort to resolve the problems in defining a person's race, the U.S. Census Bureau calls for self-identification. The Census Bureau asks people to select their race from a "flash card" listing five groups: White, Black, American Indian, Eskimo and Aleut, Asian or Pacific Islander, and Other races. Regarding Hispanic self-identification, the U.S. Census Bureau explains its method: "Respondents were asked to select their [Hispanic] origin (and the origin of other household members) from a 'flash card' listing ethnic origins. People of Hispanic origin, in particular, were those who indicated their origin was Mexican, Puerto Rican, Cuban, Central or South American, or some other Hispanic origin. It should be noted that people of Hispanic origin may be of any race."

Self-identification makes race a matter of cultural choice. Consider a person who has a great-grandmother who was Native American while all other ancestors were of European ancestry. This person might prefer to identify with Native American as opposed to European cultures and, consequently, choose Native American from the U.S. Census Bureau's flash card. Or consider a person who has African, European, and Native American ancestry. This combination of ancestry is typical of many U.S. citizens who identify themselves as black.

The meaning of "white" continues to be a perplexing issue. In *Shades of White: White Kids and Racial Identities in High School,* Pamela Perry investigates white identity in two high schools in California. One high school is racially mixed while the other is predominantly white. Perry defines white students as those of European ancestry who are not Hispanic. Her central question for white students at both schools is: "What does it mean to be white?" Perry summarizes the responses from both schools: "Most believed that to be white meant that you had no culture. . . . Some felt victimized as whites, some felt privileged, many felt both. Some felt 'racist', some felt nonracist, many felt both."

White students said they had no culture, Perry concluded, because they did not recognize that their culture is the standard and dominant culture of the United States. They are unconsciously accepting white culture as the norm. This is exemplified when these white students identify black and Latino students as each having a culture. In identifying separate black and Latino cultures, white students are unconsciously making a distinction between white and other cultures. Feeling that they lack culture sometimes causes white students to envy blacks and Latinos. For example, many white students have adopted the clothing and music styles of black student culture.

Black high school students recognize that white students are imitating their clothing and music styles. One black student commented to Perry, "They'll [white students] be listening to rap music and trying to wear clothes that we wear and overdo it. . . . You're [in reference to white students] trying to be me, but you're getting only the surface."

As an example of differing views regarding cultural exchanges, some black students feel demeaned rather than proud when white students imitate their cultural styles. The reaction of black students is in sharp contrast to the envy some white students have of black culture. One black student describes the reason for white adoption of black styles: "They try to overaccommodate. Or they feel bad that we're structurally lower and so they try to be like that so they can relate to your friends that way." This student intimated that she would feel more comfortable with white students if they acted within their own cultural boundaries.

Many white students distinguish whiteness as lacking any ties to the past. For instance, some white students feel that African American, Native American, and Mexican American students have a conscious relationship to a historical past. This historical past is directly related to a distinctive culture. From the perspective of these white students, black students think about their roots in Africa, Native American students feel linked to their pre-Columbian cultures, and Mexican American students identify with the dominant Mexican culture of the Southwest that existed prior to that territory being conquered by the United States. In contrast, white students did not focus on the cultures of their European ancestry.

Self-identification as a method of defining race results in a focus on cultural differences because of the often and complicated ancestry of American citizens. I find it interesting to ask my college students to identify their race and to discuss the problems associated with self-identification. Sometimes, students who identify themselves as black or white find that they share a common Native American ancestry.

## RACE AND SOCIAL CLASS

Does race or social class determine equal educational opportunity? Take the case of African American Professor Cornell West. While a professor of theology at Princeton University, West, after lecturing on Plato's *Republic,* drove into New

York City for a photo session for his new book. Driving, as he described it, an expensive car and planning to have dinner at an expensive restaurant, West felt the burden of the race line when stepping onto the streets of Manhattan. After parking his car, West tried to hail a taxicab to take him to the photo session. In a simmering rage, West watched taxi after taxi stop for white people while ignoring him. After an hour, a cab finally stopped for him. David Dinkins, the former mayor of New York City, remembers a similar experience. The first black mayor of the city watched as taxis responded to whites while ignoring him. Even the former leader of the city could not escape its racist temperament.

No matter how high a person's status or income, racism is still a problem. However, social class remains important. Opportunities are quite different for an African American growing up in an upper-class household compared with an African American or white child growing up in poverty. Social-class lines are as sharply drawn in the black community as they are in the white community. Therefore, it is important to consider social class as it intersects with race.

As indicated in Table 3–1, wealth is as disproportionately distributed in the African American and Hispanic communities as in the white community. The upper class in the white community commands about the same percentage (49.0 percent) of total white income as the upper class of the African American and Hispanic communities, 50.0 percent and 47.9 percent, respectively. Indeed, the lower class of each racial grouping shares similar small percentages of the total income of their race—white, 3.9 percent; African American, 3.1 percent; Hispanic, 4.1 percent.

Although social class is highlighted by the income distribution within each racial group, race is still a factor in the overall distribution of income in the United States. Table 3–2 indicates these racial differences according to household median income. According to the table, white household incomes and per capita incomes are significantly above those of African Americans and Hispanics with the 2-year average (1999–2000) white median household income at $44,079 as compared with African Americans ($29,644) and Hispanics ($30,831).

**TABLE 3–1. Share of Aggregate Income by Social Class, Race, and Hispanic Origins, 1999**

| Social Class | White | Black | Hispanic |
| --- | --- | --- | --- |
| Upper | 49.0% | 50.0% | 47.9% |
| Upper-middle | 23.1 | 24.0 | 23.4 |
| Middle | 15.0 | 14.7 | 15.2 |
| Lower-middle | 9.1 | 8.3 | 9.5 |
| Lower | 3.9 | 3.1 | 4.1 |

*Source:* U.S. Census Bureau, "Table B–3. Share of Aggregate Income Received by Each Fifth and Top 5 Percent of Households by Race and Hispanic Origin of Householder: 1967 to 1999," *Money Income in the United States— 1999* (Washington, DC: U.S. Printing Office, 2000).

**TABLE 3–2. Median Income of Households by Race and Hispanic Origins, 2-Year Average, 1999–2000**

| Race and Hispanic Origins | Median Income of Households |
| --- | --- |
| White | $44,079 |
| Black | 29,644 |
| Hispanic | 30,831 |

*Source:* U.S. Census Bureau, *Money Income in the United States—2001* (Washington, DC: U.S. Printing Office, 2001), p. 6.

## THE ECONOMICS OF RACISM

What is the economic value of being white instead of African American? In Chapter 2, I discussed differences in lifetime income according to race. Andrew Hacker and his students used a more subjective approach to determine that being white was worth a million dollars a year. In *Two Nations: Black and White, Separate, Hostile, Unequal,* Hacker describes presenting his students with a fictional account of a white person being visited by representatives of an unnamed institution. The white person is informed that a terrible mistake was made and that he should have been born black. Consequently, the person was now going to be given a black skin and facial features but his memory and ideas would remain the same. Since this was a mistake, the person would be offered financial compensation for being made black. The white students were then asked to name what they felt should be the compensation for becoming black. Their answer was $1 million yearly.

## DEFINING RACISM

*Racism* means prejudice plus power. The preceding differences in income based on educational attainment highlight this definition of racism. Racism refers to acts of oppression of one racial group toward another. One form of oppression is economic exploitation.

This definition of racism distinguishes between simple feelings of hostility and prejudice toward another racial group and the ability to turn those feelings into some form of oppression. For instance, black people might have prejudicial feelings toward white people, but they have little opportunity to express those prejudicial feelings in some form of economic or political oppression of white people. On the other hand, prejudicial feelings that white people might have toward blacks can turn into racism when they become the basis for discrimination in education, housing, and the job market. Within this framework, racism becomes the act of social, political, and economic oppression of another group.

When discussions of racism occur in my multicultural education classes, white students complain of a sense of hostility from black students and, consequently, accuse black students of racism. Black students respond that their feelings represent prejudice and not racism because they lack the power to discriminate against whites. The troubling aspect of this response is the implication that if these black students had the power, they would be racist. One black student pointed out that there are situations where blacks can commit racist acts against whites. The black student used the example of the killing of white passengers by a black man on a commuter railroad several years ago. The evidence seemed to indicate that the killer was motivated by an extreme hatred of whites that the newspapers labeled "black rage." This was a racist act, the black student argued, because the gun represented power.

Racism is often thought of as whites oppressing people of color. Of course, there are many problems with this definition. If one parent is black and another white, are their children considered black or white? Can one white-skinned child of this marriage be considered white while one dark-skinned child is considered black? Jake Lamar recalls how the confusion over skin color sparked the development of his racial consciousness at the age of 3. Jake was sitting at the kitchen table when his Uncle Frank commented "about how obnoxious white people were." Jake responded, "But Mommy's white." His uncle replied that his mother was not white but was "just light-skinned." Jake then said that he thought his father, brother, and himself were black while his sister and mother were white. His mother then explained that they had many white ancestors that caused the variation in skin color, but they were still "all Negroes." Thinking back on this incident, Jake Lamar reflected, "Black and white then meant something beyond pigmentation . . . so my first encounter with racial awareness was at once enlightening and confusing, and shot through with ambiguity."

Keeping in mind the complexities of racial classification and the importance of social class, certain generalities can be made about the racial attitudes of whites at the end of the twentieth century. In *Prejudice and Racism,* social psychologist James Jones summarizes the racial attitudes of some whites:

- Whites feel more negatively toward blacks than they do toward Hispanics, Asians, and legal and illegal immigrants.
- Whites perceive blacks as lazy, violent, and less intelligent than Hispanics, Asians, and legal and illegal immigrants.
- Whites believe blacks are receiving more attention from the government than they deserve.
- Whites believe blacks are too demanding in their struggle for equal rights.
- High levels of antiblack racism are correlated with white attitudes that police and the death penalty make streets safe, and with opposition to assistance to the poor.
- Antiblack and anti-Hispanic racism are correlated with whites' opposition to open immigration and multilingualism.

## RACE, SOCIAL CLASS, AND EQUAL EDUCATIONAL OPPORTUNITIES

The Advisory Board for the President's Initiative on Race in *One America in the 21st Century: Forging a New Future* recognized that the problem of equal educational opportunity involves the intersection of social class and race. Wealthy

African Americans, whites, Asians, and Hispanics can choose to live in school districts with adequate and exceptional public schools. In the words of the Advisory Board, "Our concern is that educational opportunities and public services are being restricted to those who live disproportionately in areas of concentrated poverty." The Advisory Board identified the following conditions in areas of concentrated poverty:

- Schools with low expectations and standards.
- Substandard and crumbling school facilities.
- Inadequate public transportation.
- Poorly financed social services.

In addition, the Advisory Board found that students from low-income families were less likely to have access to such educational opportunities and resources as:

- Preschool programs
- High-quality teachers
- Challenging curriculums
- High standards
- Up-to-date technology
- Modern facilities

In the context of the changing U.S. population and existing educational problems, the Advisory Board recommended the following to achieve equal educational opportunity:

1. *Enhance early childhood learning.* Data indicate that racial disparities persist in terms of early childhood learning. For example, 1996 data show that 89 percent of white children ages 3 to 5 were read to three or more times per week compared with 74 percent of black children and 62 percent of Hispanic children . . . efforts could include providing training and services for parents . . . and expanding support for such programs as Head Start, Early Head Start, and Even Start.

2. *Strengthen teacher preparation and equity.* High-quality teachers are too scarce a resource, especially in high-poverty, high-minority communities . . . [action] could include creating incentives to both attract top students to teaching and encourage certified teachers to teach in underserved communities.

3. *Promote school construction.* It is estimated that building and renovating our public schools to adequately serve all students will cost more than $100 billion.

4. *Promote movement from K–12 to higher education.* Efforts must be taken to ensure equal opportunity in higher education and to strengthen the pipeline from K–12 through higher education. Such efforts should include support for partnerships between colleges and K–12 schools that increase expectations by exposing students to future educational opportunities . . . efforts could include increasing the availability of advanced-placement courses in high-poverty, high-minority school districts and providing financial support, such as loans or grants, for college test preparation courses.

5. *Promote the benefits of diversity in K–12 and higher education.* Diversity can promote many benefits that accrue to all students and society, including: improve teaching and learning by providing a range of perspectives that enrich the learning environment; strengthen students' critical-thinking skills by challenging their existing perspectives . . . improve students' preparation for employment . . . and foster the advancement of knowledge by spurring study in new areas of concern.

6. *Provide education and skills training to overcome increasing income inequality that negatively affects lower-skilled and less-educated immigrants.* The high rates of Hispanic high school dropouts suggest . . . there is a clear need for continued English-language training to ensure that limited-English-proficient students can perform and compete in the educational system.

7. *Implement the comprehensive American Indian and Alaska Native education policy.* To meet the particular needs of American Indian and Alaska Native students, we urge . . . improving and expanding educational opportunities.

The Advisory Board's recommendations might have effected the real increase in the number of minority students in college. A 2002 report of the American Council of Education stated that minority student enrollment in colleges and universities jumped by 48 percent in the 1990s. However, the report found that "despite greater numbers of minority students in college, blacks and Latinos lagged behind whites and Asian-Americans in graduating."

In summary, the recommendations for equality of educational opportunity include early childhood education, high-quality teachers in schools serving low-income families, school construction, equal access to higher education, diversity in the classroom, and adequate English instruction for children from non-English-speaking homes.

## TEACHING ABOUT RACISM

The Advisory Board for the President's Initiative on Race was primarily concerned about the intersection of poverty and racial differences. It did not deal directly with the role that schools can play in reducing racism through classroom instruction. A variety of approaches to teaching about racism are available. One excellent book is Beverly Tatum's *Why Are All the Black Kids Sitting Together in the Cafeteria?: A Psychologist Explains the Development of Racial Identity.* Educator and African American activist Beverly Tatum worries about the loss of white allies in the struggle against racism and the hostility she feels from white college students when teaching about racism. Reflecting on her teaching experiences, she writes, "White students . . . often struggle with strong feelings of guilt when they become aware of the pervasiveness of racism. . . . These feelings are uncomfortable and can lead white students to resist learning about race and racism." Part of the problem, she argues, is that seeing oneself as the oppressor creates a negative self-image, which results in a withdrawal from a discussion of the problem. What needs to be done, she maintains, is to counter the guilt by giving white students a positive self-image of whites fighting against racism. In other words, a self-image of whites being allies with blacks in the struggle against racism.

The National Association for the Education of Young Children's "Anti-Bias Curriculum: Tools for Empowering Young Children" is a popular antiracist curriculum for preschool children. This curriculum and related methods of instruction are designed to reduce prejudice among young children regarding race, language, gender, and physical ability differences. The premise of the method is that at an early age children become aware of the connection between power and skin color, language, and physical disabilities. Cited as examples are a 2½-year-old Asian child who refuses to hold the hand of a black classmate because "It's dirty" and a 4-year-old boy who takes over the driving of a pretended bus because "Girls can't be bus drivers."

According to the Anti-Bias Curriculum, research findings show that young children classify differences between people and they are influenced by bias toward others. By the age of 2, children are aware of gender differences and begin to apply color names to skin colors. Between ages 3 and 5, children try to figure out who they are by examining the differences in gender and skin color. By 4 or 5 years old, children engage in socially determined gender roles and they give racial reasons for the selection of friends. Based on these research findings, the advocates of the curriculum believe that prejudice can be reduced if there is conscious intervention to curb the development of biased concepts and activities.

Another antiracist education program is the Teaching Tolerance Project that began after a group of teenage skinheads attacked and beat to death an Ethiopian man on a street in Portland, Oregon, in 1988. After this incident, members of the Southern Poverty Law Center decided it was time to do something about teaching tolerance. Dedicated to pursuing legal issues involving racial incidents and denial of civil rights, the law center sued, for the man's family, the two men who were responsible for teaching violent racism to the Portland skinheads. These two teachers, Tom Metzger, the head of the White Aryan Resistance, and his son, became symbols of racist teachings in the United States. In a broad sense, the Teaching Tolerance Project is designed to provide information about teaching methods and materials that will counter the type of racist teachings represented by Metzger and his son.

Similar to the Anti-Bias Curriculum, the Teaching Tolerance Project primarily defines racism as a function of psychological attitudes, in contrast to an emphasis on racism as a function of economic exploitation. On the inside cover of its magazine *Teaching Tolerance,* tolerance is defined as "the capacity for or the practice of recognizing and respecting the beliefs or practices of others." Within the context of this definition, the project members "primarily celebrate and recognize the beliefs and practices of racial and ethnic groups such as African-Americans, Latinos, and Asian-Americans."

The primary purpose of the Teaching Tolerance Project is to provide resources and materials to schools to promote "interracial and intercultural understanding between whites and nonwhites." There have also been decisions to include material dealing with cultural tolerance, homelessness, and poverty. The Teaching Tolerance Project is only one of many educational attempts to end racism in the United States. The end of racism is essential for the full provision of equality of opportunity and equality of educational opportunity in U.S. society.

# THE FUTURE OF DESEGREGATION

In 1999 Gary Orfield, a long-time advocate of school desegregation, issued a report with the ominous title, "Resegregation in American Schools." The report states, "We are clearly in a period when many policymakers, courts and opinion makers assume that desegregation is no longer necessary. . . . Polls show that most white Americans believe that equal educational opportunity is being provided."

Responding to the report, Chester Finn, a conservative critic of public schools, faulted Orfield for even worrying about school segregation. "Gary Orfield," Finn said, "must be the only American who still thinks that integration for its own sake is an important societal goal." For Finn, "The price of forced busing and other forms of social engineering is too high to pay when there are more urgent crises facing this country's schools."

Orfield's study found that segregation of schools in the South increased from 1988 to 1997 with the number of black students attending majority white schools declining from 43.5 percent to 34.7 percent, as shown in Table 3–3. Hispanic students are now the most segregated group with about 75 percent attending schools with over 50 percent nonwhite students. On the average, white students attend schools that are 81 percent white. Orfield's report concludes, "We are floating back toward an educational pattern that has never in the nation's history produced equal and successful schools."

In response to increased school segregation in Southern states, Gary Orfield, in the summer of 2002, organized a joint conference between Harvard University's Civil Rights Project and the University of North Carolina's Center for Civil Rights. Sean F. Reardon, a professor at Pennsylvania State University, reported that white and black students are now more segregated than in 1990. In addition, the teaching staffs of individual schools are becoming more segregated. Others reported an increase in school segregation in cities throughout the South. Experts at the conference gave the following reasons for increased segregation:

- Recent court decisions outlawing race as a main factor in student assignment.
- Increased residential segregation.
- Increased role of private schools in contributing to segregation.

### TABLE 3–3. Segregation Pattern in Southern Schools

| Year | Percentage of Black Students Attending Majority White Schools in the South |
|------|-----------------------------|
| 1960 | Almost none |
| 1988 | 43.5% |
| 1997 | 34.7 |

*Source:* Ethan Bonner, "Study Finds Desegregation in U.S. Schools," *The New York Times on the Web* (13 June 1999).

Of course, the larger issue is whether racial segregation is still an important issue. Here are some points to consider in answering this question:

- Does school segregation contribute to continuing tensions between racial and ethnic groups?
- Does school segregation result in inequalities in school finances?
- Does school segregation contribute to inequality of educational opportunities?

## *SECOND-GENERATION SEGREGATION*

*Second-generation segregation* refers to forms of racial segregation that are a result of school practices such as tracking, ability grouping, and the misplacement of students in special education classes. Unlike segregation that existed by state laws in the South before the 1954 *Brown* decision, second-generation forms of segregation can occur in schools with balanced racial populations; for instance, all white students may be placed in one academic track and all African American or Hispanic students, in another track.

Nationally, most studies examine the process of great change and no change as integration of schools results in segregation within schools. The collection of studies in Ray Rist's *Desegregated Schools: Appraisals of an American Experiment* describe the subtle forms of segregation that began to occur as white and African American students were placed in integrated schools for the first time. For instance, in one recently integrated school, African American students were suspended for committing the same offenses for which white students received only a reprimand. A teacher in the school complained that, unlike African American students, when white students were sent to the principal's office, they were immediately sent back to class. In this school, equal opportunity to attend the school did not result in equal treatment within the school.

Unequal treatment of different races within the same school is one problem in integrated schools; the establishment of racial boundaries among students creates another. One study in the Rist book describes how racial boundaries were established in a high school in Memphis, Tennessee, after the students of an all-African-American school were integrated with the students of an all-white school. Here, white students maintained control over most student activities. So, when African American students began to participate in athletics and cheerleading, for example, the status of these activities was denigrated by white students. On the other hand, whites maintained control of the student government, ROTC, school clubs, and the staff of the yearbook.

This division of control among student activities reflected the rigid social boundaries that existed in the high school between the two groups. Individuals who crossed these social boundaries had to adapt to the social customs of those on the other side. For instance, African American students changed their style of dress and social conduct to be accepted by white students. African American students who crossed racial lines by making such changes found themselves accused by other African American students of "acting white" and were subsequently rejected by "unchanged" African American students. The same was true of white students who crossed racial boundaries.

The racial boundaries that continue to exist in high schools after integration reflect the racial barriers that continue in the larger society. The social life of a school often reflects the social world outside the school. Integration of a school system can help ensure equality of educational opportunity, but it cannot break down society's racial barriers. Although schools attempt to deal with this problem, its solution requires a general transformation of racial relationships in the larger society.

## THE RECENT STRUGGLE FOR EQUAL EDUCATION FOR WOMEN

Since the nineteenth century, the struggle for racial justice paralleled that of justice for women. Demands for equal educational opportunity pervaded both campaigns for civil rights. In the second half of the twentieth century the drive for equal educational opportunity for women was led by the National Organization for Women (NOW), which was organized in 1966. The founding document of the organization declared, "There is no civil rights movement to speak for women as there has been for Negroes and other victims of discrimination. The National Organization for Women must therefore begin to speak." In NOW's founding document, education is called "the key to effective participation in today's economy . . . [and public schools should educate a woman] to her full potential of human ability."

During its first years of activism, NOW focused on:

- Eliminating discriminatory quotas against women in college and professional school admissions.
- Urging parents, counselors, and teachers to encourage women to pursue higher education and professional education.
- Eliminating discriminatory practices against women in the awarding of fellowships and loans.
- Investigating the problem of female school dropouts.

NOW's activities and that of other women's organizations turned to legal action with the passage of Title IX of the 1972 Higher Education Act. Title IX provided for sexual equality in employment in educational institutions and for sexual equality in educational programs. The legislation applied to all educational institutions, including preschool, elementary and secondary schools, vocational and professional schools, and public and private undergraduate and graduate institutions. A 1983 U.S. Supreme Court decision, *Grove City College v. Bell*, restricted Title IX in its application to specific educational programs within institutions. In the 1987 Civil Rights Restoration Act, Congress overturned the court's decision and amended Title IX to include all activities of an educational institution receiving federal aid.

Armed with Title IX, NOW and other women's organizations placed pressure on local school systems and colleges to ensure equal treatment of women in vocational education, athletic programs, textbooks and the curriculum, testing, and college admissions. Following is a brief chronological list of achievements in providing equality of educational opportunity for women:

- *1972:* Legal action against school systems with segregated courses in home economics and industrial arts.
- *1974:* With backing from NOW, more than 1,000 women's studies departments created on college campuses.
- *1975:* Federal regulations to end sex discrimination in athletics.
- *1976:* Lawsuits regarding female participation in athletics and gender-biased hiring in school administration.
- *1976:* Educational Equity Act authorizes Office of Education to prepare "non-sexist curricula and non-discriminatory vocational and career counseling, sports education, and other programs designed to achieve equity for all students regardless of sex."
- *1983:* Last all-male school in Ivy League, Columbia University, becomes coeducational.
- *1986:* FairTest organized to counter sex bias in high-stakes tests.
- *1996:* Virginia Military Institute and the Citadel become coeducational.

The struggle for equality of educational opportunity is reflected in the following changes in educational programs:

- The number of female medical school graduates increased from 8.4 percent in 1969 to 34.5 percent in 1990.
- The percentage of doctoral and professional degrees awarded women increased from 14.4 percent in 1971 to 36.8 percent in 1991.
- Most discrimination in vocational programs ended.
- Female participation in high school athletics increased from 7 percent in 1972 to 37 percent in 1992 and in college athletics from 15.6 percent in 1972 to 34.8 percent in 1993.

## SEXISM AND EDUCATION

In *Failing at Fairness: How America's Schools Cheat Girls,* Myra and David Sadker summarize current research on educational discrimination against girls. One surprising result of their research and analysis of other data was that girls were equal to or ahead of boys in most measures of academic achievement and psychological health during the early years of schooling, but by the end of high school and college, girls had fallen behind boys on these measurements. On entrance examinations to college, girls scored lower than boys, particularly in science and mathematics. Boys received more state and national scholarships. Women scored lower than men on all entrance examinations to professional schools.

An explanation for the decline in test scores is that girls suffer a greater decline than boys in self-esteem from elementary school to high school. (Of course, an important general question about the following statistics is why both boys and girls decline in feelings of self-esteem.) As a measure of self-esteem, the Sadkers rely on responses to the statement, "I'm happy the way I am." The Sadkers report that in elementary school 60 percent of girls and 67 percent of boys responded positively to the statement. By high school these positive responses declined to 29 percent for girls and 46 percent for boys. In other words, the decline in self-esteem for girls was 31 percentage points as compared with 21 percentage points for boys. Why is there less self-esteem and a greater decline in self-esteem among girls as compared with boys?

To get an answer to the question, the Sadkers asked students how their lives would be different if they suddenly were transformed into members of the opposite sex. Overall, girls responded with feelings that it wouldn't be so bad and that it would open up opportunities to participate in sports and politics. In addition, girls felt they would have more freedom and respect. Regarding self-esteem, girls expressed little regret about the consequences of the sex change. In contrast, boys expressed horror at the idea, and many said they would commit suicide. They saw themselves becoming second-class citizens, being denied access to athletics and outdoor activities, and being racked with physical problems. Concerning self-esteem, and in contrast to girls, boys expressed nothing but regret about the consequences of the sex change.

The Sadkers argue that modes of classroom interaction, the representation of women in textbooks and other educational materials, and the discriminatory content of standardized tests contribute to the lack of self-esteem among girls. In one of their workshops with classroom teachers, the Sadkers illustrate classroom sex bias by asking four of the participants—two men and two women—to act like students in a middle-school social studies classroom. The lesson is about the American Revolution and it begins with an examination of homework. Acting as the teacher, David Sadker perfunctorily tells one woman that two of her answers are wrong and comments to the group on the neatness of the other woman's homework. He tells one man that two of his answers are wrong and, unlike his response to the woman with wrong answers, he urges the man to try harder and suggests ways of improving his answers. David then states to the other man that he failed to do his homework assignment. In contrast to the woman with the neat paper, this man illustrates what the Sadkers call the "bad boy role."

David Sadker then continues the lesson by discussing battles and leaders. All of the Revolutionary leaders are, of course, male. During the lesson he calls on the males twenty times each while only calling on one woman twice and completely ignoring the other woman. The one woman called on misses her question because she is given only half a second to respond. When questioning the men, David Sadker spends time giving hints and probing. At the end of this demonstration lesson, the Sadkers report, one woman commented that she felt like she was back in school. She often had the right answer but was never called on by the teacher.

What this workshop demonstration illustrates, based on the Sadkers' findings on classroom interaction, is that boys receive more and better instruction.

Boys are more often called on by the teacher and boys interact more with the teacher than girls. In a typical classroom situation, if both boys and girls have their hands raised to answer a question, the teacher is most likely to call on a boy. A teacher will spend more time responding to a boy's question than to a girl's question. In other words, girls do not receive equal educational opportunity in the classroom.

In addition, women are not so well represented as men in textbooks. The Sadkers found in 1989 elementary school language arts textbooks that there were from two to three times as many pictures of men as women. In one elementary history text, they found four times as many pictures of men as women. In one 1992 world history textbook, of 631 pages they found only 7 pages related to women. Two of those pages were devoted to a fifth grade female student who made a peace trip to the Soviet Union.

It is most likely that the treatment received by girls in the classroom and in textbooks contributes to their low self-esteem and to their decline, as compared with boys, in performance on standardized tests from elementary school to high school. It seems logical that if less instructional time is spent with girls than boys, then boys would more rapidly advance academically. In addition, without equal representation in textbooks, girls might value themselves less and have less incentive to achieve. Instructional time and representation in textbooks contribute to the glass ceiling of the classroom.

The lowering of self-esteem and content bias may contribute to the significant gender gap in scores on standardized college entrance examinations and entrance examinations to professional schools. For instance, on the widely used Scholastic Aptitude Test (SAT) males score 50 points higher on the math section and up to 12 points higher on the verbal section. It is important to understand that discrimination in standardized testing involves the denial of economic rewards, specifically scholarships and career opportunities.

The content bias and economic value of standardized tests were recognized in a 1989 ruling by a federal judge in New York. The judge ruled that the awarding of New York State scholarships using the SAT discriminated against female students. The case was brought to court by the Girls Clubs of America and NOW. The court argued that the scholarships were to be awarded based on academic achievement in high school and that the SAT was not constructed to test achievement but to determine college performance. The court's decision states, "The evidence is clear that females score significantly below males on the SAT while they do equally or slightly better in high schools."

In this court case, academic achievement was defined according to grades received in high school courses. Interestingly, the Sadkers argue that this apparent paradox between girls' high grades and low standardized-test scores is a result of grade inflation. This grade inflation results from female passivity and their willingness to follow classroom rules. Often, teachers formally and informally incorporate evaluations of student behavior in their academic grading practices. For girls, good behavior can result in good grades.

But the issue of grade inflation still doesn't solve the puzzle of lower performance by girls on tests like the SAT. The Sadkers suggest that one possible reason for the differences in scores between males and females is that the content of standardized tests is biased. Boys are more familiar with organized sports, financial issues, science, wars, and dates. Consequently, test items referring to these areas tend to favor boys. As an example, the Sadkers describe a gifted high school girl who lost her concentration on the preliminary SAT when she encountered an analogy question comparing a "football and a gridiron." The analogy baffled her because she had little knowledge of football.

One possible solution to teacher bias in classroom interaction, the Sadkers suggest, is to have an observer code classroom interaction so that the teacher becomes aware of any possible bias. If teachers are unconsciously favoring boys, then this observation provides the opportunity for them to change their behavior. One teacher told the Sadkers that she distributes two chips to all students. When students want to comment or ask a question, they have to give up one chip. Before the class is over, all students must use their two chips. This guarantees equal participation of all students and ensures that classroom interaction is not dominated by only a few students. In addition, the Sadkers recommend that teachers consciously search for books portraying strong female characters in a variety of occupational and social roles. They point to the work of the National Women's History Project, which since the 1970s has published materials emphasizing women's roles in history. In addition, the Sadkers recommend the use of workshops to heighten teachers' awareness of their own possible sexist behavior and to understand how to find nonsexist educational material for the classroom.

Another possible solution is single-sex education. This would eliminate the problem of female students having to compete with male students for teachers' attention. In classrooms of only girls, teachers would not tend to push girls aside and focus their instructional efforts on boys. In an all-girls school or classroom, female students might receive the equal educational opportunity denied to them in a coed classroom.

Writing in favor of girls' schools, Susan Estrich, professor of law and political science at the University of Southern California, notes that 60 percent of the National Merit Scholarship finalists are boys. Echoing the Sadkers' findings, she reports from a 1992 study of the American Association of University Women, "that even though girls get better grades (except in math), they get less from schools." While she does not dismiss efforts to equalize opportunities for girls in coed schools, she argues that currently single-sex education is working. For instance, in all-girls schools 80 percent of girls take four years of math and science, whereas in coed schools the average is two years of math and science. In Fortune 1000 companies, one-third of the female board members are graduates of women's colleges even though graduates of women's colleges represent only 4 percent of all female college graduates. In addition, graduates of women's colleges earn 43 percent of the math and 50 percent of engineering doctorates earned by all women, and they outnumber all other females in *Who's Who*.

Estrich does see the possibility of offering single-sex classes within a coed institution. She cites the example of the Illinois Math and Science Academy, which experimented with a girls-only calculus-based physics class. Instead of sitting meekly at their desks while boys command all the attention, girls are actively asking and answering questions. In an all-girls algebra class in Ventura, California, the teacher reports spending time building self-confidence along with teaching math. For Estrich, at least at this point in time, all-girls schools are a means for ending sexism in education.

Of course, for an all-girls school or classroom to overcome the problems of sexism completely it would require the maintenance of the same educational expectations as there are for boys and the use of textbooks and other educational materials that provide strong female role models. One of the problems with segregated female education in the nineteenth century was the belief that women did not have the physical and mental stamina to undergo the same academic demands as men. Consequently, to avoid sexism, there should be no watering down of the curriculum in female schools and classrooms. In addition, sex-segregated education would have to avoid the pitfalls of tracking women into a sex-segregated labor market. One of the problems in the development of the high school in the early twentieth century was that it tended to track women into certain occupations. For an all-girls school or classroom to avoid this form of discrimination, there would have to be an emphasis on opening up all career opportunities for women.

There are many critics of proposals for all-female schools. One University of Michigan researcher, Valerie Lee, found that many all-girls classrooms still contained high levels of sexist behavior on the part of the teacher. In one case, a history teacher assigned a research paper and told students that she would provide "major hand-holding" to help the students. Lee argued that the offer of major hand-holding would not occur in a boy's school. In addition, she found male bashing taking place in some all-female schools.

In addition, Lee found boys in all-male schools engaging in serious sexist comments about women. In other words, all-female schools do not do anything about the sexist attitudes of men. In fact, all-male schools might reinforce male sexist behavior. For instance, in a 1994 court case involving a suit by Shannon Faulkner to gain entrance to the all-male military college, The Citadel, one of the witnesses, a 1991 graduate of the school, reported that the word *woman* was used on campus in a derogatory manner "every day, every minute, every hour, [it was] a part of the life there."

Therefore, there is the possibility that single-sex education might result in greater academic achievement for girls while doing nothing about sexist attitudes among men. The academic gains made by women might mean little in a world dominated by sexist males. Also, the courts may not approve of single-sex public schools, because of a decision regarding all-boys African American schools in Detroit. The court argued that the all-boys schools were a violation of the 1954 *Brown* decision that declared as unconstitutional separate but equal schools that were racially segregated.

In 1998, the American Association of University Women (AAUW) released a follow-up report to its earlier charges that public schools were shortchanging girls. The new study found that the number of girls enrolled in algebra, trigonometry, precalculus, and calculus was growing at a faster rate than the number of boys. Probably the most impressive statistic was that the differences between boys and girls was the smallest in the world on international tests in math and science. However, the report found that technology, particularly computer technology, was emerging as the new boys' club. The report found that girls have less exposure to computers inside and outside school and that girls feel less confident about using computers. The gap between boys and girls in computer knowledge and use increases from grades 8 to 11. Only 17 percent of students taking the College Board's Advanced Placement Test in computer science were women.

In reference to the technological gap between males and females, Janice Weinman, the executive director of the Washington-based AAUW said, "This is becoming the new club [computer technology] from which girls are feeling disenfranchised. Consequently, girls are not going to be appropriately prepared for the technology era of the new twenty-first century."

However, there are areas where girls outperform boys. More girls than boys are enrolled in advanced English, foreign language, and art courses. In addition, girls outscore boys by wide margins on reading and writing tests in middle and elementary grades.

*Education Week* reporter Debra Viadero provides the following summary of other findings in the AAUW study:

- In school-to-work programs, which combine challenging academics with vocational training, girls still tend to cluster in traditional female occupations.
- Although girls are taking more advanced-placement courses and getting better grades than boys, their scores on those exams still tend to be lower.
- On large-scale exams, such as the National Assessment of Educational Progress, the top scorers in math and science still tend to be boys.

## STUDENTS WITH DISABILITIES

By the 1960s, the civil rights movement encompassed students with disabilities. Within the context of equality of educational opportunity, students with special needs could only participate equally in schools with other students if they received some form of special help. Since the nineteenth century many of the needs of these students were neglected by local and state school authorities because of the expense of special facilities and teachers. In fact, many people with disabilities were forced to live in state institutions for the mentally retarded or those with mental illness. For instance, consider "Allan's Story," a case history of treatment prior to the 1970s provided by the U.S. Office of Special Education Programs:

> Allan was left as an infant on the steps of an institution for persons with mental retardation in the late 1940s. By age 35, he had become blind and was frequently observed sitting in a corner of the room, slapping his heavily callused face as he rocked back and forth humming to himself.

In the late 1970s, Allan was assessed properly for the first time. To the dismay of his examiners, he was found to be of average intelligence; further review of his records revealed that by observing fellow residents of the institution, he had learned self-injurious behavior that caused his total loss of vision.

Although the institution then began a special program to teach Allan to be more independent, a major portion of his life was lost because of a lack of appropriate assessments and effective interventions. (*Source:* U.S. Office of Special Education, "History: Twenty-Five Years of Progress in Educating Children with Disabilities through IDEA," www.ed.gov/offices/OSERS/OSEP/, 2002.)

The political movement for federal legislation to aid students with disabilities followed a path similar to the rest of the civil rights movement. First, finding themselves unable to change educational institutions by pressuring local and state governments, organized groups interested in improving educational opportunities for students with special needs turned to the courts. This was the path taken in the late 1960s by the Pennsylvania Association for Retarded Children (PARC). PARC was one of many associations organized in the 1950s to aid citizens with disabilities. These organizations were concerned with state laws that excluded children with disabilities from educational institutions because they were considered uneducable and untrainable. State organizations like PARC and the National Association for Retarded Children campaigned to eliminate these laws and to demonstrate the educability of all children. But, as the civil rights movement discovered throughout the century, local and state officials were resistant to change and relief had to be sought through the judicial system.

In *Pennsylvania Association for Retarded Children (PARC) v. Commonwealth of Pennsylvania,* a case that was as important for the rights of children with disabilities as the *Brown* decision was for African Americans, PARC objected to conditions in the Pennhurst State School and Hospital. In framing the case, lawyers for PARC focused on the legal right to an education for children with disabilities. PARC, working with the major federal lobbyist for children with disabilities, the Council for Exceptional Children (CEC), overwhelmed the court with evidence on the educability of children with disabilities. The state withdrew its case, and the court enjoined the state from excluding children with disabilities from a public education and required that every child be allowed access to an education. Publicity about the PARC case prompted other lobbying groups to file 36 cases against different state governments. The CEC prepared model legislation and lobbied for its passage at the state and federal levels.

# PUBLIC LAW 94–142: EDUCATION
# FOR ALL HANDICAPPED CHILDREN ACT

In 1975, Congress passed Public Law 94–142, the Education for All Handicapped Children Act that guaranteed equal educational opportunity for all children with disabilities. In 1990, Congress changed the name of this legislation to Individuals with Disabilities Education Act (IDEA). The major provisions in Public Law 94–142 were to provide for equal educational opportunity for all children with disabilities. This goal included the opportunity for all children with disabilities to attend regular school classes. As stated in the legislation, "All children with disabilities [should] have available to them . . . a free appropriate public education which emphasized special education and related services designed to meet their unique needs."

## WRITING AN IEP

One of the issues confronting Congress during legislative debates was that of increased federal control over local school systems. Congress resolved this problem by requiring an individual education plan (IEP) be written for each student with disabilities. This reduced federal control since each IEP would be written in local school systems. IEPs are now a standard part of education programs for children with disabilities. Public Law 94–142 requires that an IEP be developed for each child jointly by the local educational agency and the child's parents or guardians. This gives the child or the parents the right to negotiate with the local school system about the type of services to be delivered.

Teachers, school administrators, and parents work together to arrive at an IEP statement. It is important that school officials and teachers understand the regulations governing the writing of IEPs. As provided for in the original legislation, an IEP includes:

1. A statement of the present levels of educational performance of such child.
2. A statement of annual goals, including short-term instructional objectives.
3. A statement of the specific educational services to be provided to such child, and the extent to which such child will be able to participate in regular educational programs.
4. The projected date for initiation and anticipated duration of such services.
5. Appropriate objective criteria and evaluation procedures and schedules for determining, on at least an annual basis, whether instructional objectives are being achieved.

## WHICH CHILDREN HAVE DISABILITIES?

The category of "learning disability" created a continuing controversy in determining which children should be classified as disabled. Some critics of special education, as I discuss in a later section on the report of President George W. Bush's Commission on Excellence in Special Education, think the learning disabilities category is too broad and includes children who have not received adequate classroom instruction in reading. This controversy is caused by federal regulations defining disabilities.

Of course, any legislation must define its target population. According to federal regulations, the following federal regulation identifies children who are considered disabled:

"the term child with a disability means a child evaluated . . . as having:

1. Mental retardation;
2. Hearing impairment including deafness;
3. A speech or language impairment;
4. A visual impairment;
5. Serious emotional disturbance;
6. An orthopedic impairment;
7. Autism;
8. Traumatic brain injury;
9. A specific learning disability;
10. Deaf-blindness; [or]
11. Multiple disabilities."

In addition, federal regulations provide specific definitions of each one of these disabilities.

## INTEGRATING CHILDREN WITH DISABILITIES INTO THE REGULAR CLASSROOM

The 1975 Education for All Handicapped Children Act called for the integration of children with disabilities into regular classes. Similar to any form of segregation, the isolation of children with disabilities often deprives them of contact with other students and denies them access to equipment found in regular classrooms, such as scientific equipment, audiovisual aids, classroom libraries, and computers. Full inclusion, it is believed, will improve the educational achievement and social development of children with disabilities. Also, it is hoped, bias against children and adults with disabilities decreases because of the interactions of students with disabilities with other students. The integration clause of The Education for All Handicapped Children Act specified that:

> to the maximum extent appropriate, handicapped children, including children in public or private institutions or other care facilities, are educated with children who are not handicapped, and that special classes, separate schooling, or other removal of handicapped children from the regular educational environment occurs only when the nature or severity of the handicap is such that education in regular classes with the use of supplementary aids and services cannot be achieved satisfactorily.

The term "inclusion" is the most frequently used word to refer to the integration of children with disabilities into regular classrooms. The phrase "full inclusion" refers to the inclusion of all children with disabilities.

In 1990, advocates of full inclusion received federal support with the passage of the Americans with Disabilities Act. This historic legislation bans all forms of discrimination against the disabled. The Americans with Disabilities Act played an important role in the 1992 court decision *Oberti v. Board of Education of the Borough of Clementon School District,* which involved an 8-year-old, Rafael Oberti, classified as educable mentally retarded. U.S. District Court Judge John F. Gerry argued that the Americans with Disabilities Act requires that people with disabilities be given equal access to services provided by any agency receiving federal money, including public schools. Judge Gerry decided that Rafael Oberti could manage in a regular classroom with special aides and a special curriculum. In his decision, Judge Gerry wrote, "Inclusion is a right, not a privilege for a select few."

The 1997 Congressional amendments to this legislation, now called the Individuals with Disabilities Education Act, emphasized the importance of including children with disabilities in regular classes. In the text of the 1997 Amendments, it was claimed that since the passage of the original legislation research demonstrated that inclusion in regular classes had improved the academic performance of children with disabilities. In the words of the Amendments, "Over 20 years of research and experience has demonstrated that the education of children with disabilities can be made more effective by . . . having high expectations for such children and ensuring their access in the general curriculum to the maximum extent possible."

During Congressional hearings leading to the passage of the 1997 Individuals with Disabilities Education Act Amendments, there were complaints that appropriate educational services were not being provided for more than one-half of the children with disabilities in the United States. Also, more than 1,000,000 of the children with disabilities in the United States were excluded entirely from the public school system and were not educated with their peers. In addition, there were complaints that many disabilities were going undetected.

The inclusion of children with disabilities in regular classrooms created a new challenge for regular teachers. Classroom teachers, according to the legislation, were to be provided with "appropriate special education and related services and aids." The legislation specified that teachers should receive extra training to help children with disabilities. In the words of the legislation, school districts must provide: "high-quality, intensive professional development for all personnel who work with such children in order to ensure that they have the skills and knowledge necessary to enable them to meet developmental goals." Also, teacher education programs were to give all student teachers training in working with students with disabilities.

## AN INCLUSION SUCCESS STORY

In the July 10, 2002, issue of *Education Week*, Allison Shelley tells the story of Down syndrome student Chris Vogelberger, whose first experience with inclusion was in a third grade classroom. During the first year, his spoken-language abilities increased by two years. Now attending middle school, Chris has a full-time assistant, Debbie Beiling, whom he calls Bean.

His daily lessons are loaded onto his iMac laptop by the school's special education resource teacher. His iMac lessons are modified versions of what the teacher will be presenting in class. During class instruction, the regular teacher can focus on the rest of the class while Chris works on his laptop. At times, the teacher directly helps him begin one of the modified lessons. For instance, in science class as other students are learning about the periodic table and properties of metals and nonmetals, Chris is studying the parts of the atom. In language arts, he studies words on flash cards.

Most importantly, Chris is learning to interact with other students and other students are learning to accept him. He has developed a circle of friends. One of those friends, Dan O'Connell, told reporter Allison Shelley, "I've had a better year with him here. I started out the school year thinking that everyone would be perfect in a sense, the way that they would talk and act. But then I found out that people can really be different. You learn how to deal better with everyone."

Praising the idea of inclusion, Chris's mother said, "He will not be living in a special education world. He'll be living in our world."

## THE INCLUSION DEBATE

While Chris Vogelberger's story is a model of successful inclusion, There has been sharp criticism of the concept. The lack of trained classroom teachers and the availability of aides and special education resources make inclusion difficult. Of course, lack of adequate funding underlies all.

One of the strongest critics of inclusion is the American Federation of Teachers (AFT), one of the major teachers unions. The organization's resolution on "Inclusion of Students with Disabilities" complains that teachers and support staff are not receiving adequate training for educating children with disabilities in regular classrooms. The teachers union charges that inclusion is just a method for reducing costs in local school districts because separate special education classrooms could be eliminated. Also, the resolution expresses concern about the extra burden inclusion places on classroom teachers. Consequently, the union declares,

> Resolved that the AFT oppose inclusion—that is, any movement or program that has the goal of placing all students with disabilities in general education classrooms regardless of the nature or severity of their disabilities, their ability to behave or function appropriately in the classroom, or the educational benefits they and their general education peers can derive.

In contrast to the AFT, the National Association of State Boards of Education supports full inclusion in its report *Winners All: A Call for Inclusive Schools*. The report calls for a fundamental shift in the provision of services for students with disabilities. As the report envisions the full-inclusion process, rather than teaching in a separate classroom, special education teachers would provide their services in regular classrooms by team-teaching with the regular teacher or providing other support.

The idea of inclusion is resisted by some parents who believe that separate special education classrooms provide important benefits for their children. For instance, twenty parents of children with disabilities attending the Vaughn Occupational High School in Chicago carried signs at the board of education meeting on September 7, 1994, reading "The board's inclusion is exclusion."

The parents were protesting the board's decision to send their children to neighborhood schools for inclusion in regular classrooms. Traditionally, Vaughn provided vocational training for students with disabilities. The students would hold low-level jobs at McDonald's, an airline food service company, and a glass-installation business.

The board's action regarding the Vaughn students was the result of a 1992 complaint by the Illinois State Board that Vaughn students were not spending time with nondisabled peers. The state board threatened to remove all federal and state funds from the school district if the students were not included in regular classrooms. Martha Luna complained about the decision because it denied her 15-year-old son, Tony, vocational training to meet his needs. Ms. Luna stated, "I know Tony won't go to college so I don't expect that, just for him to learn everyday living and work skills."

Reflecting the AFT complaint about the extra burden inclusion places on classroom teachers, a survey found that over 70 percent of practicing teachers object to including students with disabilities in their classrooms. The West Virginia Federation of Teachers released a survey of 1,121 teachers showing that 87 percent did not believe that inclusion helped general education students and 78 percent did not believe that inclusion helped students with disabilities. A survey of teachers in Howard County, Maryland, reports that 64 percent of middle school teachers believe "that inclusion detracts from their ability to fully serve the needs of the general student population." Only 21 percent believed inclusion benefitted children with disabilities. The complaints about inclusion are occurring as the proportion of disabled students receiving their education in regular classrooms increases. In 1991, for instance, 32.8 percent of disabled students were receiving their educations in regular classrooms. By 1995, the figure had risen to 44.5 percent.

The preceding figures indicate the complications in implementing inclusion programs. Following is a list of objections by teachers to inclusion programs:

- Disabled students are moved into regular classrooms without any support services.
- Experienced teachers have never received training in teaching students with disabilities or in teaching in an inclusive classroom.
- School districts implementing inclusion policies do not provide adequate training for general education teachers.
- Education schools do not provide prospective teachers with a basic knowledge of learning disabilities or situations they are likely to confront in inclusive classrooms.
- General education teachers are often excluded from the individualized education plan (IEP) team.
- Parents of nondisabled students worry that their children's education will be compromised in inclusive classrooms.

The preceding issues contain their own solutions, which include (1) more education and training for experienced and future teachers, (2) adequate support services for teachers in inclusive classrooms, (3) teacher participation on the individual planning team, and (4) education of parents about inclusive classrooms. Model full-inclusion schools and teacher education programs do exist that address the preceding issues. Teachers and administrators at the Zachary Taylor Elementary School, a suburban Washington, DC, community, operate a model full-inclusion school that they believe is improving the academic and social performance of disabled students and has made other students more caring and tolerant. Syracuse University, in response to the problem of inadequately prepared teachers, instructs general education and special education teachers together. At the end of four years, both groups receive dual certification. In answer to worried parents of students in general education, John McDonnell, chair of the special education department at the University of Utah, states, "There really has been no effect on the educational progress of kids without disabilities by including kids with disabilities at the classroom level."

## PRESIDENT GEORGE W. BUSH'S COMMISSION ON EXCELLENCE IN SPECIAL EDUCATION

In its 2002 report, "Revitalizing Special Education for Children and Their Families," President George W. Bush's Commission on Excellence in Special Education decries the condition of special education despite over 25 years of federal involvement. The Commission lists the following problems regarding students with disabilities:

- Young people with disabilities drop out of high school at twice the rate of their peers.
- Enrollment rates of students with disabilities in higher education are still 50 percent lower than enrollment among the general population.
- Most public school educators do not feel well prepared to work with children with disabilities. In 1998, only 21 percent of public school teachers said they felt very well prepared to address the needs of students with disabilities, and another 41 percent said they felt moderately well prepared.

In addition, the Commission is particularly concerned with the classification "specific learning disabilities" whose numbers have grown by 300 percent since 1976. The Commission report claims that 80 percent are classified as learning disabled because they do not know how to read. As a result, out of the total population of children with disabilities, the Commission maintains, 40 percent "are there because they weren't taught to read." The reading difficulties may not be their only area of difficulty, but it's the area that resulted in special education placement.

The Commission also worried about racial bias in special education placements, particularly in the areas of mental retardation. The Commission's report contends that African American children are overrepresented among those children classified mentally retarded and emotionally disturbed. This overrepresentation illustrates another form of second-generation segregation for children who received insufficient reading instruction.

In addressing these problems, the Commission made the unique recommendation of using federal funds designated for children with disabilities to provide parents whose children are in failing schools with vouchers that would allow them to transfer to another public school or private school. From the perspective of the Commission, vouchers would give parents greater power to control their child's educational future. As I discuss in Chapter 6, there exists a heated debate about school voucher plans.

The Commission report reiterates the concept of equality of educational opportunity for students with disabilities and the importance of inclusion. The Commission report expresses concern about many instances of local school's segregating children with disabilities from the general population. The Commission report declares: "We affirm our commitment to the fundamental belief that children with all types of disabilities must be included to the maximum extent appropriate in their school community."

Of course, the key to any improvement in education and the education of children with disabilities is the training of future teachers. The Commission's recommendations went beyond concerns with just the proper preparation of classroom teachers for inclusion and the education of special education teachers. The Commission called for the recruitment of candidates with high levels of verbal ability for teacher education. In addition, they suggested that prospective teachers major in the subject they are planning to teach and receive instruction in the school curriculum they are expected to transmit.

Adequate teacher training, proper classification of students, and provision of equipment and teachers for inclusion require greater investment of local, state, and federal funds. The lack of funding is an ongoing problem for the education of children with disabilities. However, Chris Vogelberger's story demonstrates how the struggle for equality of educational opportunity has improved the condition of human beings. Sixty years ago, people with Down syndrome might have spent their entire lives in state institutions cut off from the rest of society.

## CONCLUSION

Unequal educational opportunities continue to plague American schools. Even though the civil rights movement was able to overturn laws requiring school segregation, second-generation segregation continues to be a problem. Differences between school districts in expenditures per student tend to increase the effects of segregation. Many Hispanic, African American, and Native American students attend schools where per student expenditures are considerably below those of elite suburban and private schools. These reduced expenditures contribute to unequal educational opportunity that, in turn, affects a student's ability to compete in the labor market.

However, the advances resulting from the struggle for equal educational opportunity highlight the importance of political activity in improving the human condition. In and out of the classroom, teachers assume a vital role in ensuring the future of their students and society. In the areas of race, gender, and children in disabilities, there have been important improvements in education since the nineteenth century. The dynamic of social change requires an active concern about the denial of equality of opportunity and equality of educational opportunity.

## Suggested Readings and Works Cited in Chapter

American Federation of Teachers. "Resolution on Inclusion of Students with Disabilities." www.aft.org/about/resolutions/1994/inclusion.html. *This is the teachers union's resolution giving reasons for rejecting the idea of inclusion.*

ANYON, JEAN.   *Ghetto Schooling: Political Economy of Urban Educational Reform.* New York: Teachers College Press, 1997. *This book demonstrates how the combination of politics and economics creates segregated and underfunded urban schools.*

BRONNER, ETHAN.   "Study Finds Desegregation in U.S. Schools." *The New York Times on the Web* (13 June 1999). *This report presents the study by Gary Orfield, "Resegregation in American Schools."*

Commission on Excellence in Special Education. "Revitalizing Special Education for Children and Their Families, 2002." Washington, DC: Department of Education, 2002. *The report of George W. Bush's commission on special education which recommended the use of federal funds (including vouchers) for students with disabilities.*

ESTRICH, SUSAN.   "For Girls' Schools and Women's Colleges, Separate Is Better." *The New York Times Magazine* (22 May 1994): 39. *Estrich argues against coeducation.*

"Feminist Chronicles." http://www.now.org. *NOW gives its official account of its struggle for equal opportunity and equal educational opportunity for women.*

HACKER, ANDREW.   *Two Nations: Black and White, Separate, Hostile, Unequal.* New York: Charles Scribner's Sons, 1992. *This is a study of racial divisions in the United States.*

HELLER, CAROL, and JOSEPH HAWKINS.   "Teaching Tolerance: Notes from the Front Line." *Teachers College Record* (Spring 1994): 1–30. *Presents a history and description of the Teaching Tolerance Project.*

IDEA '97 Regulations. www.ideapractices.org/law/regulations/regs/SubpartA.php. *These are the federal regulations issued in 1997 that regulate the education of children with disabilities.*

IGNATIEV, N., and JOHN GARVEY.   *Race Traitor.* New York: Routledge, 1996. *This important book for antiracist education is based on the idea of the importance of reconstructing "whiteness."*

KLUGER, RICHARD.   *Simple Justice.* New York: Random House, 1975. *Kluger provides a good history of Brown v. Board of Education and the struggle for equality.*

LAMAR, JAKE.   *Bourgeois Blues: An American Memoir.* New York: Plume Books, 1992. *This autobiography deals with the racism encountered by an upper-class African American.*

LEMANN, NICHOLAS.   *The Promised Land: The Great Black Migration and How It Changed America.* New York: Vintage Books, 1991. *This is a definitive history of African American migration from the South to the urban North.*

LOPEZ, IAN F. HANEY.   *White by Law: The Legal Construction of Race.* New York: New York University Press: 1996. *Discusses legal cases involved in defining the legal meaning of "white."*

MANEGOLD, CATHERINE.   " 'Save the Males' Becomes Battle Cry in Citadel's Defense against Woman." *The New York Times* (25 May 1994): A4. *This article tells the story of a female student's struggle to enter an all-boys school.*

MEIER, KENNETH; JOSEPH STEWART, JR.; and ROBERT ENGLAND.   *Race, Class, and Education: The Politics of Second-Generation Discrimination.* Madison: University of Wisconsin Press, 1989. *This book studies the politics of second-generation segregation.*

"National Organization for Women's 1966 Statement of Purpose" (adopted at the Organizing Conference in Washington, DC, October 29, 1966). http://www.now.org. *This historic document establishes the foundation for the participation of women in the civil rights movement.*

"Opening Doors in Education." http://www.feminist.org. *Lists the educational accomplishments of the women's movement.*

ORFIELD, GARY. *The Reconstruction of Southern Education: The Schools and the 1964 Civil Rights Act.* New York: Wiley-Interscience, 1969. *Orfield presents a study of the desegregation of southern schools following the passage of the 1964 Civil Rights Act.*

RICHARD, ALAN. "Researchers: School Segregation Rising in South." *Education Week on the Web* (11 September 2002). *Report on the conference about the rise of school segregation in the South.*

RIST, RAY. *Desegregated Schools: Appraisals of an American Experiment.* New York: Academic Press, 1979. *This book provides many examples of second-generation segregation.*

SACK, JOETTA. "Side by Side." *Education Week* (25 March 1998). http://www.edweek.org. *This extensive article discusses the objections, problems, and solutions for creation of inclusive schools and classrooms.*

SCHEMO, DIANA JEAN. "Report Finds Minority Ranks Rise Sharply on Campuses." *The New York Times on the Web* (23 September 2002). *Summary of American Council on Education report on increased minority students on college campuses.*

SCHNAIBERG, LYNN. "Chicago Flap Shows Limits of 'Inclusion,' Critics Say." *Education Week* (5 October 1994): 1, 12. *This article describes parent protest about inclusion in Chicago.*

SHELLEY, ALLISON. "Brave New World." *Education Week* (10 July 2002). *The story of Down's syndrome student Chris Vogelberger's inclusion in regular classes.*

SMOTHERS, RONALD. "In Pupil 'Tracks,' Many See a Means of Resegregation." *The New York Times* (18 February 1990): E5. *Smothers reports on how the use of tracking as a means of second-generation segregation caused a school boycott in Selma, Alabama.*

SMYLIE, MARK. "Reducing Racial Isolation in Large School Districts: The Comparative Effectiveness of Mandatory and Voluntary Strategies." *Urban Education* 17, no. 4 (January 1983). *This is a good analysis of the different types of school desegregation plans.*

TATUM, BEVERLY DANIEL. *Why Are All the Black Kids Sitting Together in the Cafeteria?* New York: Basic Books, 1997. *This landmark book on antiracist education discusses methods of creating positive antiracist models for white students.*

U.S. Census Bureau. "Current Population Survey (CPS)—Definitions and Explanations." http//www.census.gov/population/www/cps/cpsdef.html. *This is a guide to the racial and other terms used in the collection of the census.*

U.S. Office of Special Education Programs. "History: Twenty-Five Years of Progress in Educating Children with Disabilities Through IDEA, 2001." www.ed.gov/offices/OSERS/OSEP. *This document provides a history of federal legislation for children with disabilities beginning with the passage of Public Law 94–142.*

VIADERO, DEBRA. "'Full Inclusion' of Disabled in Regular Classes Favored." *Education Week* (30 September 1992): 11. *This is a report on the court case Oberti v. Board of Education of the Borough of Clementon School District, which involves full inclusion.*

_____. "NASBE Endorses 'Full Inclusion' of Disabled Students." *Education Week* (4 November 1992): 1, 30. *This article discusses the report supporting full inclusion of students with disabilities. The report* Winners All: A Call for Inclusive Schools *was issued by the National Association for State Boards of Education.*

_____. "Some Progress, But Gaps Remain." *Education Week* (14 October 1998), http://www.edweek.org. *This article summarizes the American Association of University Women's 1998 report on inequities faced by girls in public schools.*

_____. "Va. Hamlet at Forefront of 'Full Inclusion' Movement for Disabled." *Education Week* (18 November 1992): 1, 14. *This article describes the implementation of a full-inclusion plan in a community in Virginia.*

WALSH, MARK.   "Judge Finds Bias in Scholarships." *Education Week* (15 February 1989): 1, 20. *This article describes the court ruling that found the awarding of scholarships by using test scores to be biased against female students.*

WEST, CORNELL.   *Race Matters.* New York: Vintage Books, 1994. *This set of essays empha-sizes the continuing importance of race in social relationships in U.S. society.*

WILSON, WILLIAM J.   *The Declining Significance of Race: Blacks and Changing American In-stitutions.* Chicago: University of Chicago Press, 1979. *This book argues that social class is a more important factor than race in determining equality of opportunity among African Americans.*

WOLLENBERG, CHARLES.   *All Deliberate Speed: Segregation and Exclusion in California Schools, 1855–1975.* Berkeley: University of California Press, 1976. *This is a good his-tory of segregation in California. It includes a discussion of the important court decision re-garding Mexican Americans,* Mendez et al. v. Westminster School District of Orange County, *and of the segregation of Asian Americans.*

# CHAPTER 4

# Student Diversity

The U.S. student population will increasingly be more diverse with regard to race, ethnicity, and language as a result of changes in U.S. immigration laws. Since the 1970s, large numbers of new immigrants to the United States made the education of differing ethnic and language groups a major issue. In Los Angeles, New York City, and cities scattered across the country, neighborhoods identified with emigrants from particular South American, Caribbean, Asian, and Central American countries sprang up in the 1970s. In New York City, a traditional home for new immigrants, a Spanish Yellow Pages telephone directory was issued in the 1980s, and most advertising on the subway system is now in Spanish. Throughout New York, emigrants from South Korea took over greengrocer businesses and opened manicure salons, while other emigrant groups took over newspaper stands and restaurants. In the Brighton Beach section of Brooklyn, the presence of Jewish emigrants from Russia can be seen in the ethnic goods in stores and the foreign titles in bookstores.

The new wave of immigration into the United States since the 1970s was made possible by the Immigration Act of 1965. Before 1965, immigration was determined by the ethnic quota section of the 1924 Immigration Act. Under the 1924 act, passed during a period of extreme racism, the annual quota of a national group allowed to immigrate to the United States was determined by the percentage to which the total U.S. population in 1920 comprised that group. The openly stated purpose of the 1924 immigration legislation was to limit immigration of nonwhite populations.

As a consequence of the 1924 Immigration Act, the depression of the 1930s, and World War II, immigration to the United States declined from the late 1920s through the early 1950s. Immigration began to increase again in the 1950s and underwent a dramatic change after passage of the 1965 Immigration Act. Before 1965, the proportion of emigrants from Europe remained approximately constant compared with those from Asia and the rest of the Americas. But after 1965, the proportion of emigrants from Europe dramatically declined and the proportion from Asia and the Americas dramatically increased.

Between the late 1960s and the twenty-first century, the largest number of immigrants each year came from Mexico. In recent years, more emigrants have arrived from Asian sources, although Mexico continues to provide more than any other single country. In 1969, the order of immigrant sources to the United

States was Mexico, Italy, the Philippines, Canada, and Greece. By 1973, Canada and Greece dropped off the list, which then read Mexico, the Philippines, Cuba, Korea, and Italy. Two years later Italy was replaced by China-Taiwan. Through the rest of the 1970s, the proportion of emigrants from Asia and the Pacific steadily increased. In 1980, the top five sources of immigrants were Mexico, Vietnam, the Philippines, Korea, and China-Taiwan.

During the 1980s, the Asian population of the United States grew by 70 percent from 3.8 million in 1980 to 6.5 million in 1988. One-third of the Asian population settled in California. Asian immigrants represented many nationalities and language groups. At least 80 percent of the Asian immigrants in the 1980s came from China, Taiwan, Hong Kong, Vietnam, Cambodia, Laos, the Philippines, Japan, South Korea, and Micronesia. Most of the Asian immigrants have higher professional and educational training than earlier groups.

The primary reasons for immigration since the 1970s are economic, political, and familial. The 1965 Immigration Act established a preference system that favored family ties. In the distribution of immigration visas, preference is given to spouses, children, and siblings of U.S. citizens. Also, preference is given to professionals and persons of exceptional ability who will benefit the U.S. economy and to skilled workers who are needed in the economy. Finally, preference is given to political refugees. Table 4–1 indicates the foreign-born population of the United States and the year of entry.

As indicated in Table 4–1, the largest immigration into the United States took place after 1980 with 64 percent of the foreign-born population entering during that period. The highest percentage of foreign-born (27.1 percent) are from Mex-

**TABLE 4–1. Country of Origin and Year of Entry into the United States of Foreign-Born Population, March 1998**

| Country of Origin | Number of Foreign-Born (in thousands) | Percent of Foreign-Born |
|---|---|---|
| Mexico | 7,119 | 27.1% |
| Cuba | 914 | 3.5 |
| Dominican Republic | 635 | 2.4 |
| El Salvador | 723 | 2.8 |
| Great Britain | 622 | 2.4 |
| China and Hong Kong | 1,022 | 3.9 |
| India | 722 | 2.7 |
| Korea | 589 | 2.2 |
| Philippines | 1,207 | 4.6 |
| Vietnam | 989 | 3.8 |
| Elsewhere | 11,738 | 39.3 |
| Came to the United States | | |
| Before 1970 | 4,812 | 18.3 |
| 1970 to 1979 | 4,605 | 17.5 |
| 1980 to 1989 | 8,236 | 31.3 |
| Since 1990 | 8,628 | 32.8 |

*Source:* U.S. Census Bureau, *"March 1998 Current Population Survey,"* http://www.census.gov/.

ico. Many Mexicans legally enter the United States because of family ties with Mexican Americans. Many of these Mexicans, along with those entering the country illegally, are poorly educated and escaping harsh economic conditions. In contrast to the Mexican immigration, the large Cuban and Vietnamese immigration of the 1970s fell under the political refugee preference category of the 1965 legislation. Many of these refugees were from the professional and business classes.

The preference given to professionals is resulting in the immigration of many medical doctors and other highly educated workers. Most often, foreign professionals immigrate because of higher salaries in the United States. For instance, by the mid 1970s more than half of the interns in municipal hospitals in New York City were immigrant Asian doctors. By 1976, about 40 percent of all Filipino doctors practiced in the United States. The most dramatic case was in 1972 when almost the entire graduating class of a new medical school in Thailand chartered a plane and flew to the United States.

As indicated in Table 4–2, immigration is rapidly changing the racial/ethnic composition of the U.S. population. There will be a dramatic decline by 2050

**TABLE 4–2. Resident Population of the United States: Estimates by Race and Hispanic Origin**

| Race/Ethnicity | July 1, 1990 | July 1, 2000 | July 1, 2035 | July 1, 2050 |
|---|---|---|---|---|
| White, not Hispanic population (in thousands) | 188,581 | 197,061 | 210,100 | 207,901 |
| White, not Hispanic percentage of total | 75.6% | 71.8% | 58.6% | 52.8% |
| Black, not Hispanic population (in thousands) | 29,397 | 32,568 | 47,393 | 53,555 |
| Black, not Hispanic percentage of total | 11.8% | 12.2% | 13.2% | 13.6% |
| American Indian, Eskimo, Aleut, not Hispanic population (in thousands) | 1,802 | 2,054 | 3,044 | 3,534 |
| American Indian, Eskimo, Aleut, not Hispanic percentage of total | 0.7% | 0.7% | 0.8% | 0.9% |
| Asian and Pacific Islander, not Hispanic population (in thousands) | 7,084 | 10,584 | 25,281 | 32,432 |
| Asian and Pacific Islander, not Hispanic percentage of total | 2.8% | 3.9% | 7.1% | 8.2% |
| Hispanic origin (of any race) population (in thousands) | 22,575 | 31,366 | 72,639 | 96,508 |
| Hispanic origin (of any race) percentage of total | 9.1% | 11.4% | 20.3% | 24.5% |

*Source:* U.S. Bureau of the Census, *"Population Estimates,"* http://www.census.gov/.

in the population that is white (not Hispanic) from 75.6 to 52.8 percent. During the same period, the Hispanic population will increase dramatically from 9.1 to 24.5 percent of the population, and the Asian and Pacific Islander percentage will increase from 2.8 to 8.2. The black (not Hispanic), American Indian, Eskimo, and Aleut will remain about the same percentage of the population. However, in 1990, the black (not Hispanic) was higher (11 percent) than the Hispanic percentage (9.1 percent), while by the year 2035 this relationship will be reversed with (black, not Hispanic) at 13.2 percent and Hispanic at 20.3 percent of the total population.

## IS IT HISPANIC OR LATINO?

Throughout this chapter I use the term *Hispanic* because it is used by the U.S. Census Bureau which also makes a distinction between white Hispanic and nonwhite Hispanic. A student in my college class complained when police checked a box on a form that indicated he was white Hispanic. He insisted that he was Latino.

One idea is that Spanish usage creates a common identity of being Hispanic or Latino. This identity is strengthened in struggles to gain recognition for bilingual education programs in U.S. public schools. Under the subtitle "Languages of Latino Self-Formation," Juan Flores and George Yudice contend, "the conditions for identity-formation, in all its dimensions . . . have been largely provided by the struggle over how to interpret language needs." However, the language issue is complicated by the fact that many of those labeled as Hispanic or Latino, such as Mayan Americans from Guatemala, arrived in the U.S. speaking only their native tongues and without a knowledge of Spanish. The existence of non-Spanish-speaking Native American groups throughout Mexico, Central America, and South America complicates the problem of defining Hispanic and Latino.

Another complicating factor is the meaning of Hispanic in context of the commemoration of El Dia de la Raze (The Day of the Race) when, on October 12, 1492, Columbus landed in the Antilles. For some, this date represents the birth of the Hispanic people as a new hybrid race created from a mixture of Africans, Europeans, and Native Americans. Within the framework of "La Raza," Hispanic refers to most Mexican, Central American, Caribbean, and South American peoples, including French-speaking Haitians, Portugese-speaking Brazilians, and English-speaking Trinidadians. However, the concept of La Raza excludes those Native Americans who have no African or European ancestors and those of European ancestry who live south of the United States and have no African or Native American forebears. Theoretically, the concept of La Raza would also include under the heading Hispanic the many U.S. citizens who are descended from enslaved Africans brought to the U.S. who also have European and Native American ancestors.

The term Hispanic can also be traced to the early nineteenth century when Simon Bolivar, the liberator of South America from Spanish rule, dreamed of a pan-American republic that would extend from the tip of South America up the west coast of what is now the United States (during Bolivar's time California was part of Mexico). In this sense, Hispanic encompasses all peoples living in areas not under the control of the United States or Canada.

The terms Latino and Latin America also have their origin in dreams of a pan-American union. The term *Latin America* was coined by Chilean author Francisco Bilbao in 1858 to distinguish between the supposedly cold and rigid temperament of Anglo-Saxons and the hypothetically warm and light-hearted souls of others living in the Americas. Also, the use of the word *Latin* broke the direct connection with Spain. Rather than Spanish America it was now Latin America. For this reason, many people prefer the term *Latino* because Hispanic is associated with Spanish cultural imperialism.

Latin America, as opposed to Spanish America, encompasses all speakers of Latin-based languages including Portugese-speaking Brazilians and French-speaking Haitians. However, similar to the problems encountered with the term Hispanic, Native American peoples who do not speak French, Spanish, or Portuguese are not theoretically included in the terms Latino or Latin America. In addition, at least technically, French-speaking Canadians would have to be called Latinos.

The U.S. Census Bureau continues to use the term Hispanic despite the difficulties in defining the term and the preference of some people to be identified as Latino or Latina. Using the term Hispanic, the 1990 U.S. Census reported the four largest groups constituting more than 80 percent of Hispanic Americans by country of origin as, in descending order, Mexican American (61.5 percent), Puerto Rican American (12.2 percent), Cuban American (4.8 percent), and Dominican American (2.4 percent).

## THE CHANGING POPULATION OF U.S. SCHOOLS

The changing population of the United States will result in dramatic changes in the school-age population. The meaning of majority and minority groups as legal classifications will be transformed. The majority population is often considered to be white; however, the U.S. Census Bureau projects that by the year 2040 the majority of school-age children will be members of minority groups.

The major changes in the school-age population are identified in the report of the Advisory Board for the President's Initiative on Race, *One America in the 21st Century: Forging a New Future*. The report makes the following predictions:

- By the year 2005, Hispanics, who may be of any race, are projected to be the largest minority group in the United States.
- By the year 2050, about 50 percent of the U.S. population will comprise Asians, non-Hispanic blacks, Hispanics, and American Indians.

The 2000 report of the U.S. Census Bureau projects that these population changes will have the following impact on the school-age population of the United States:

I. Percentage of school-age population that is non-Hispanic white
   A. In 2000—65 percent.
   B. In 2020—56 percent.
   C. In 2040—less than 50 percent.
II. Changes in Hispanic school-age population
   A. Between 2000 and 2020 the percentage of the Hispanic school-age population will increase by 60 percent.
   B. By 2025 nearly 25 percent of the school-age population will be Hispanic.
III. Percentage of school-age population that is Asian and Pacific Islander
   A. In 2000—4 percent.
   B. In 2025—6.6 percent.
IV. The percentage of school-age children who are black and Native American will remain stable.

Educational issues regarding this changing population are directly related to residential patterns and educational attainment of immigrants. Of fundamental importance for the future funding of public schools and the provision of equal educational opportunity is the fact that most African Americans, Asians, and Hispanics are living in central cities. According to the Advisory Board for the President's Initiative on Race:

- Blacks, Asians, and Hispanics are more likely to live in central cities of metropolitan areas than are non-Hispanic whites or American Indians.
- A large percentage of non-Hispanic whites and Asians live in suburbs. The fraction living in suburbs has increased since 1970.

In addition, immigrant populations bring with them a variety of educational backgrounds. The Advisory Board emphasized the following:

- On the average, Asian immigrants are highly educated and have high incomes.
- Hispanic immigrants, along with immigrants from some Asian countries, have relatively low average levels of educational attainment and income.

Overall, the picture presented by the Advisory Board is a growing gap between the educational advantages of the suburbs and the educational problems of the central cities with changes in the population. These problems are related to the intersection of social class and race.

## EDUCATIONAL EXPERIENCES OF IMMIGRANTS TO THE UNITED STATES

Immigrant groups arrive with a variety of educational backgrounds. For instance, studies of Chinese immigrants in New York City found a vast range of educational achievement. Those living in Chinatown arrived with primarily working-class backgrounds and limited exposure to formal learning. One study found that the roughly 85 percent of Chinatown residents in New York,

Boston, and San Francisco had not attended secondary school. The children of these immigrants often struggle in school because of language problems. On the other hand, many wealthy and well-educated Chinese immigrants, who in New York tend to live outside Chinatown, often send their children to elite universities. The educational level of immigrants reflects their social-class backgrounds. In the case of the Chinese, some come from peasant backgrounds with little access to higher education; on the other hand, some come from professional classes and are engineers and college teachers. Therefore, the educational needs of immigrants must be assessed according to their social and educational backgrounds. These backgrounds vary widely within each immigrant group and between immigrant groups. For the purposes of this discussion, I am going to focus on variations among Asian-Pacific immigrants; however, similar differences exist among immigrants from other areas, particularly countries of the Commonwealth of Independent States.

Table 4–3 indicates variations in social-class backgrounds as defined by employment. As you can see, a significant percentage of Asian Indian and Chinese immigrants are well-educated professionals. Despite the high percentages of professionals, however, at least 18 percent of Asian Indians and 31 percent of Chinese immigrants come from low-income service and laborer backgrounds. In contrast, only 8 percent of Cambodians are professionals, while 40 percent have service and laborer backgrounds.

These variations in employment backgrounds are reflected in levels of educational achievement as indicated in Table 4–4. Again, there is a wide variation in educational attainment within and between immigrant groups. As indicated in Table 4–4, 39 percent of Asian Indians immigrate with bachelor's, doctorate, or professional degrees. If master's degrees had been included, the table would have indicated that 59 percent of Asian Indian immigrants have some form of college degree. Despite this high level of educational attainment, there are still 15 percent of Asian Indians who immigrate with less than a high school education. Cambodian immigrants have a low level of educational attainment with 64 percent having less than a high school education. Among Chinese immigrants there is almost an even split between those with a bachelor's, professional, or doctorate degree (26 percent) and those with less than a high school education (29 percent).

Knowledge of English is an important factor for immigrant occupational and educational success. Again, proficiency in English varies between and

### TABLE 4–3. Occupational Attainment of Asian-Pacific Islanders

| Occupation | Asian Indian | Cambodian | Chinese | Korean | Pacific Islander |
|---|---|---|---|---|---|
| Professional | 28% | 5% | 19% | 13% | 6% |
| Service | 8 | 18 | 19 | 17 | 16 |
| Laborer | 10 | 32 | 12 | 13 | 18 |

*Source:* Adapted from Meyer Weinberg, *Asian-American Education: Historical Background and Current Realities* (Mahwah, NJ: Lawrence Erlbaum Associates, Inc., 1997), p. 5.

**TABLE 4–4. Selected Levels of Educational Attainment of Asian-Pacific Immigrants**

| Educational Attainment | Asian Indian | Cambodian | Chinese | Korean | Pacific Islander |
|---|---|---|---|---|---|
| Doctorate or professional | 14% | 1% | 6% | 5% | 1% |
| Bachelor's degree | 25 | 5 | 20 | 22 | 6 |
| High school diploma | 12 | 12 | 15 | 25 | 31 |
| Less than high school | 15 | 64 | 29 | 20 | 32 |

*Note:* Columns do not add up to 100 percent because figures for "some college" and "master's degree" were not included.
*Source:* Adapted from Meyer Weinberg, *Asian-American Education: Historical Background and Current Realities* (Mahwah, NJ: Lawrence Erlbaum Associates, Inc., 1997), p. 7.

within immigrant groups as indicated in Table 4–5. The level of English proficiency among Asian Indian immigrants is a result of policies imposed by British colonialists that made English a major language in India and the key to success in Indian higher education. Despite the fact that among Indian immigrants 57 percent speak English very well, 18 percent speak English well, and 16 percent speak only English (for a total of 91 percent), there are still 9 percent who have difficulty with English. In contrast, 42 percent of Cambodian immigrants and 31 percent of Chinese immigrants do not speak English well or at all. These variations in social class, educational achievement, and English proficiency highlight the importance of not casting an immigrant population into a single mold.

**TABLE 4–5. English Proficiency of Asian-Pacific Immigrants**

| English Proficiency | Asian Indians | Cambodian | Chinese | Korean | Pacific Islander |
|---|---|---|---|---|---|
| Very well | 57% | 24% | 32% | 29% | 43% |
| Well | 18 | 31 | 32 | 28 | 20 |
| Not well | 7 | 32 | 22 | 23 | 10 |
| Not at all | 2 | 10 | 9 | 5 | 5 |
| Speak only English | 16 | 3 | 5 | 15 | 25 |
| Total | 100 | 100 | 100 | 100 | 100 |

*Source:* Adapted from Meyer Weinberg, *Asian-American Education: Historical Background and Current Realities* (Mahwah, NJ: Lawrence Erlbaum Associates, Inc., 1997), p. 8.

## IMMIGRANT LANGUAGES

Unfortunately, numbers were not available in 2000 for the percentage of families with school-age children who spoke non-English languages. However, the U.S. Department of Education report *The Condition of Education 2000* did pro-

TABLE 4–6.  **Language Spoken at Home by Hispanic Students: Percentage Distribution of Hispanic Students in Grades K–12, by Language Spoken at Home and Grade, 1999**

| Grade Enrolled | Spoke Mostly English at Home (%) | Spoke English and Spanish Equally at Home (%) | Spoke Mostly Spanish at Home (%) | Spoke English and Other Language Equally/ Spoke Other Language (%) |
|---|---|---|---|---|
| K–5 | 54.8% | 16.2% | 28.2% | 0.8% |
| 6–8 | 58.2 | 20.1 | 20.6 | 1.0 |
| 9–12 | 61.5 | 15.9 | 22.4 | 0.2 |

*Source:* Adapted from "Table 6–2: Language Spoken at Home by Hispanic Students: Percentage Distribution of Hispanic Students in Grades K–12, by Language Spoken at Home and Grade: 1999," *The Condition of Education 2000* (Washington, DC: U.S. Printing Office, 2000).

vide information about the language spoken at home by Hispanic students. Table 4–6 indicates the number of Hispanic students who spoke mostly English at home, who spoke English and Spanish equally at home, and who spoke mostly Spanish at home. The problematic nature of the classification Hispanic is indicated by the column titled "spoke English and other language equally/spoke other language," which reflects immigrants from Central and South America who speak Native American languages and French.

As shown in the table, almost 50 percent of the students classified as Hispanic speak Spanish with their families. Some of these families were bilingual with Spanish and English being used equally in the household. Approximately 20 to 28 percent of Hispanic students spoke only Spanish at home. There are several ways of interpreting these figures. One interpretation is to emphasize the value of being bilingual. Throughout the century, the schools have stressed the importance of learning a non-English language, particularly Spanish. Another interpretation is that the learning of English in school is not strengthened by the language of the family for about 20 to 28 percent of Hispanic students. This is a problem that has always faced non-English-speaking immigrant students.

The teaching of English in U.S. public schools is complicated by the variety of immigrant languages. While recent statistics do not exist on the variety of languages spoken at home, Table 4–7 does provide some guide to language diversity in U.S. schools. Table 4–7 also indicates changing language patterns in the United States. The most notable changes are the percentage declines in families speaking European languages (German, Italian, Polish, and Greek) and the percentage increases in families speaking Spanish and Asian languages. The increase in French use in the family is probably a reflection of immigration from French-speaking Caribbean islands, such as Haiti. The most dramatic percentage increases are Chinese (+109 percent), Vietnamese (+161 percent), Hindi (+155 percent), and Korean (+135 percent) but Spanish remains the most often used language at home other than English.

**TABLE 4–7. Top 15 Languages Other Than English Spoken at Home, 1990 and 1980 (numbers in thousands)**

| Language | 1990 | 1980 | Percent Change, 1980–1990 |
|---|---|---|---|
| Spanish | 17,345 | 11,116 | 56% |
| French | 1,930 | 1,609 | 20 |
| German | 1,548 | 1,587 | –2 |
| Chinese | 1,319 | 631 | 109 |
| Italian | 1,309 | 1,618 | –19 |
| Tagalog (Filipino) | 843 | 452 | 87 |
| Polish | 723 | 821 | –12 |
| Korean | 626 | 266 | 135 |
| Vietnamese | 507 | 195 | 161 |
| Portuguese | 431 | 352 | 22 |
| Japanese | 428 | 336 | 27 |
| Greek | 388 | 401 | –3 |
| Arabic | 355 | 217 | 63 |
| Hindi (Urdu) | 331 | 130 | 155 |
| Russian | 242 | 173 | 40 |

*Source:* U.S. Bureau of the Census, *"We Asked . . . You Told Us Language Spoken at Home,"* http://www.census.gov/.

Spanish is nine times more frequently spoken in the home than French (including Creole), which is the second most common non-English language used in the home. Regarding regional distribution of language groups, New Mexico has the largest percentage (36 percent) of non-English-language speakers in the home followed by California, with 31 percent. Only five other states have 20 percent or more—Texas, Hawaii, New York, Arizona, and New Jersey.

Illustrating the plight of some immigrants are the 50,000 Mayans who in the 1980s fled rape, torture, and murder during the civil war in Guatemala. They are descendants of the Mayan civilization that constructed pyramids and monuments throughout Central America and had a written language. Few English speakers know the Mayan language. Consequently, many Mayans attend immigration proceedings without the aid of an interpreter. In addition, Mayans do not want to attract attention to their indigenous heritage because, according to *The New York Times* reporter, Christian Berthelsen, "their indigenous heritage . . . can be a target for condescension from Latino peers who ridicule them for being 'Indios' or 'ignorant'." So at immigration hearings, many Mayans are unable to follow the proceedings, which are interpreted into Spanish, but the judges assume they speak Spanish and understand what is happening.

These problems are being overcome with the organization of Mayavision, which now provides interpreters. For instance, after Rosario Lucas fled Guatemalan guerillas in 1994 to join her husband in California, she struggled with asylum forms that were written in Spanish. In 1997, she received the help of an interpreter from Mayavision. She told Christian Berthelsen, "I'm feeling

**"Come on, come on—don't you understand English?"**

*Source:* www.Cartoonstock.com

real happy, because somebody's coming to help me in my language. I can understand him and I can explain my case to him. If he understands me, and he can tell everything I'm saying to the judge, I can answer all the questions the judge is going to ask me."

Political power will resolve the issues of discrimination and Americanization for most immigrant groups. Those groups that can organize sufficient political power will have the schools serve their needs. Those who are unable to exercise political power must accept whatever programs are developed within the schools. In this context, achieving equality of educational opportunity is primarily a political issue.

## ARE U.S. TEACHERS PREPARED FOR LANGUAGE DIVERSITY?

A major problem for schools is finding teachers who are trained to teach students who have limited English proficiency (LEP). As indicated in Table 4–8, nationally only 29.5 percent of teachers of LEP students have LEP training. This figure varies between regions with the West having 47.3 percent of teachers of LEP students with training in LEP, while only 11.6 percent of teachers in the Midwest have this training. According to the National Center for Education Statistics, "When children with little or no previous exposure to the English language enter the public schools, they are often unable to profit fully from English-language-based instruction. Exceptionally high dropout rates have been reported for these students.

Another problem is the potential cultural clash between a predominantly white teaching staff and a student body with high percentages of cultural minorities, as reflected in Table 4–9. While 91.8 percent of public school teachers are white, only 66.1 percent of students are white. While only .03 percent of

**TABLE 4–8. Percentage of Public School Teachers with LEP Training and with LEP Students in Their Classes, by Region, 1993–1994**

| Region | Percentage of Teachers |
|---|---|
| Northeast | 21.5% |
| Midwest | 11.6 |
| South | 29.0 |
| West | 47.3 |
| National | 47.3 |

*Source:* National Center for Education Statistics, "Are Limited English Proficient (LEP) Students Being Taught by Teachers with LEP Training?" (December 1996), http://www.ed.gov/NCES.

**TABLE 4–9. Enrollment and Teacher Characteristics in Public Elementary and Secondary Schools in the U.S., Fall 1993**

| | Percent Distribution of Students | Percent Distribution of Teachers |
|---|---|---|
| Total | 100% | 100% |
| White | 66.1 | 91.8 |
| Black | 35.8 | .03 |
| Hispanic | 12.7 | .03 |
| Asian or Pacific Islander | 3.6 | .013 |
| American Indian/ Alaskan Native | 1.1 | .003 |

*Source:* National Center for Education Statistics, "1995 Digest of Education Statistics," Tables 44 and 66, http://www.ed.gov/NCES.

teachers are black, 35.8 percent of the students are black. As the Asian immigration increases with 3.6 percent of the student population classified as Asian or Pacific Islander, only .013 percent of the teachers are Asian or Pacific Islander. The "whiteness" of the teaching force might ensure the domination of Eurocentric culture in public schools.

## MEXICAN AMERICAN STUDENTS AND U.S. SCHOOLS

Following the time line depicted in Figure 4–1, in this section I discuss the educational experiences of Mexican Americans as the largest group in the Hispanic/Latino/Latina population. Public schools have not provided a warm haven for these students. Popular Anglo American writers in the nineteenth century argued that the mixture of Spanish conquerors and Native Americans resulted in "wretched hybrids and mongrels [who were] in many respects actually inferior to the inferior race itself." At the time, Anglo Americans classified Spanish as nonwhite and an inferior race. Some American leaders envisioned, as stated by representative William Brown, "the Anglo Saxon race, like a mighty flood [spreading over] all Mexico." This flood of Anglo Saxons, Brown hoped, would eventually cover all of Central and South America, creating republics whose "destinies will be guided by Anglo Saxon hands."

Considering Mexican Americans and other Hispanic Americans as U.S. citizens was a serious issue in 1848 with the ending of the Mexican-American War and the ratification of the Treaty of Guadalupe Hidalgo. Today, few U.S. citizens are aware of the importance of this war for the territorial expansion of the United States and the disaster for Mexico in losing almost one-half of its total territory. At the war's conclusion, the United States added territory that included major parts of the future states of California, Colorado, New Mexico, Nevada, Arizona, Utah, and Texas.

The 1848 Treaty of Guadalupe Hidalgo did provide for the granting of U.S. citizenship to the former Mexican citizens who lived in the areas conquered by the United States. Despite the treaty's provisions for citizenship, citizenship rights were abridged throughout the Southwest through limitations placed on voting rights and segregation in public accommodations and schooling. Courts wrestled with the issue of racial classification. In 1897, Texas courts ruled that Mexican Americans were not white. In California, Mexican Americans were classified as Caucasian until 1930 when California's Attorney General Webb categorized them as Indians. He argued, "The greater portion of the population of Mexico are Indians." Therefore, according to the California school code, Mexican Americans were segregated based on the provision the "governing board of the school district shall have power to establish separate schools for Indian children, excepting children of Indians . . . who are the descendants of the original American Indians of the U.S." Classified as Indians, Mexican Americans were not considered "the original American Indians of the U.S."

The attitude of racial, religious, and cultural superiority—which provided motivation for the United States to take over Mexican land and fueled hostilities between the two countries throughout the nineteenth and twentieth centuries—was reflected in the treatment both of the Mexicans who remained after the U.S. conquest and of later Mexican immigrants, many of whom were lured to the United States to become farm laborers. Segregated schools, housing, and discrimination in employment became the Mexican American heritage. Reflecting the attitude of the Mexican government toward the anti-Mexican feelings in the United States, the president of Mexico, General Porfirio Díaz, was reported to have remarked in the latter part of the nineteenth century: "Poor Mexico! So far from God and so close to the United States."

The conquered Mexican population was greatly concerned by the mandate that English was to be spoken in the schools. In 1856, two years after the Texas legislature established public schools, a law was passed requiring the teaching of English as a subject. In 1870, at the height of the cowboy era, the Texas legislature passed a school law requiring English to be the language of instruction in all public schools. The same attempt to eradicate Spanish occurred in the conquered territory of California. The California Bureau of Instruction mandated in

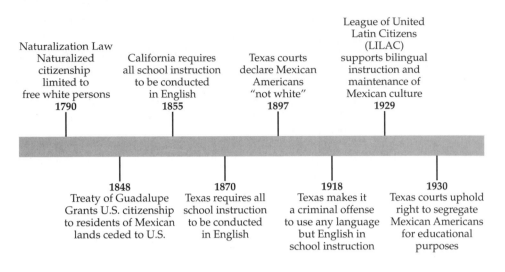

League of United
Latin Citizens
(LILAC)

Naturalization Law
Naturalized     California requires     Texas courts     supports bilingual
citizenship     all school instruction     declare Mexican     instruction and
limited to     to be conducted     Americans     maintenance of
free white persons     in English     "not white"     Mexican culture
**1790**     **1855**     **1897**     **1929**

**1848**     **1870**     **1918**     **1930**
Treaty of Guadalupe     Texas requires all     Texas makes it     Texas courts uphold
Grants U.S. citizenship     school instruction     a criminal offense     right to segregate
to residents of Mexican     to be conducted     to use any language     Mexican Americans
lands ceded to U.S.     in English     but English in     for educational
     school instruction     purposes

FIGURE 4–1. Key Decisions Affecting Mexican American Students in U.S. Schools

1855 that all school classes be conducted in English. In *The Decline of the Californios: A Social History of the Spanish-Speaking California 1846–1890*, Leonard Pitt writes about the English-only requirement in public schools: "This linguistic purism went hand in hand with the nativist sentiments expressed in that year's legislature, including the suspension of the publication of state laws in Spanish."

Mexican Americans in the last half of the nineteenth century tried to escape the anti-Mexican attitudes of public school authorities by attending either Catholic schools or nonsectarian private schools. In California, some members of the Mexican community were interested in providing a bilingual education for their children. They wanted their children to improve their ability to read and write Spanish and become acquainted with the cultural traditions of Mexico and Spain, while at the same time learning to speak English. In some places, such as Santa Barbara, California, local Mexican leaders were able to bypass the state requirement on teaching in English and were able to maintain a bilingual public school. But in most places, bilingual instruction could be had only through schools operated by the Catholic church.

The patterns of discrimination and segregation established in the nineteenth century were accentuated during the great immigration of Mexicans into the United States in the early twentieth century. Between 1900 and 1909, a total of 23,991 Mexicans immigrated to the United States. Between 1910 and 1919 this figure increased dramatically to 173,663, and between 1920 and 1929 the number rose to 487,775.

Anglo attitudes about the education of the children of immigrant Mexicans involved two conflicting positions. On the one hand, farmers did not want children of their Mexican laborers to go to school because school attendance meant that they were not available for farmwork. On the other hand, many public officials wanted Mexican children in school so that they could be Americanized.

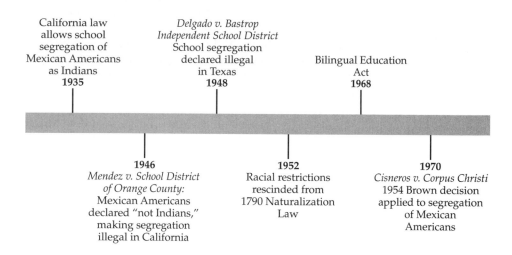

California law
allows school
segregation of
Mexican Americans
as Indians
**1935**

*Delgado v. Bastrop
Independent School District*
School segregation
declared illegal
in Texas
**1948**

Bilingual Education
Act
**1968**

**1946**
*Mendez v. School District
of Orange County:*
Mexican Americans
declared "not Indians,"
making segregation
illegal in California

**1952**
Racial restrictions
rescinded from
1790 Naturalization
Law

**1970**
*Cisneros v. Corpus Christi*
1954 Brown decision
applied to segregation
of Mexican
Americans

In addition, many Mexican families were reluctant to send their children to school because of the loss of the children's contribution to the family income.

These conflicting positions represent the two methods by which education can be used as a method of social control. One is to deny a population the knowledge necessary to protect its political and economic rights and to economically advance in society; the other is segregation. Farmers wanted to keep Mexican laborers ignorant as a means of assuring a continued inexpensive source of labor. As one Texas farmer stated, "Educating the Mexicans is educating them away from the job, away from the dirt." Reflecting the values of the farmers in his district, one Texas school superintendent explained, "You have doubtless heard that ignorance is bliss; it seems that is so when one has to transplant onions. . . . So you see it is up to the white population to keep the Mexican on his knees in an onion patch or in new ground. This does not mix very well with education." A school principal in Colorado stated, "Never try to enforce compulsory attendance laws on the Mexicans. . . . The banks and the company will swear that the labor is needed and that the families need the money." Therefore, according to Guadalupe San Miguel, Jr., in *"Let All of Them Take Heed": Mexican Americans and the Campaign for Educational Equality in Texas, 1910–1981*, one of the most discriminatory acts against the children of Mexicans was the nonenforcement of compulsory school laws. A survey of one Texas county in 1921 found only 30.7 percent of Mexican school-age children in school. In another Texas county in the 1920s, school authorities admitted that they enforced school attendance on Anglo children but not on Mexican children. San Miguel, Jr., quotes one school authority from this period: "The whites come all right except one whose parents don't appreciate education. We don't enforce the attendance on the whites because we would have to on the Mexicans." One school superintendent explained that he always asked the local school board if they wanted the Mexican children in school. Any enforcement of the compulsory education law against the wishes of the school board, he admitted, would probably cost him his job.

Those Mexican children who did attend school faced segregation and an education designed, in a manner similar to the programs applied to Indians, to rid them of their native language and customs. School segregation for Mexican children spread rapidly throughout Texas and California. The typical pattern was for a community with a large Mexican school population to erect a separate school for Mexican children. For instance, in 1891 the Corpus Christi, Texas, school board denied admission of Mexican children to their Anglo schools and built a separate school.

In *Chicano Education in the Era of Segregation,* Gilbert Gonzalez finds that the typical attitude in California schools was reflected in the April 1921 minutes of the Ontario, California, Board of Education: "Mr. Hill made the recommendation that the board select two new school sites; one in the southeastern part of the town for a Mexican school; the other near the Central School." Gonzalez reports that a survey conducted in the mid 1930s found that 85 percent of the districts investigated in the Southwest were segregated. In *All Deliberate Speed: Segregation and Exclusion in California Schools, 1855–1975,* Charles Wollenberg quotes a California educator writing in 1920: "One of the first demands made from a community in which there is a large Mexican population is for a separate school." A Los Angeles school official admitted that pressure from white citizens resulted in certain neighborhood schools being built to contain the majority of Mexican students.

Mexican Americans experienced many years of segregation in schools before winning a series of important legal cases. The first major case occurred in Ontario, California, in 1945, when Mexican American parents demanded that the school board grant all requests for transfer out of segregated Mexican schools. When the board refused this request, Gonzalo Mendez and William Guzman sued for violation of the Fourteenth Amendment to the Constitution. The school board responded to this suit by claiming that segregation was not based on race or national origins but on the necessity of providing special instruction. In other words, the school district justified segregation on the basis that Mexican American children required special instruction because they came from homes where Spanish was the spoken language.

In 1946 a U.S. District Court ruled in *Mendez et al. v. Westminster School District of Orange County* that the only possible argument for segregation was the special educational needs of Mexican American children. These needs involved the issue of learning English. Completely reversing the educational justification for segregation, the judge argued that "evidence clearly shows that Spanish-speaking children are retarded in learning English by lack of exposure to its use by segregation." Therefore, the court ruled segregation was illegal because it was not required by state law and because there was no valid educational justification for it.

Heartened by the Mendez decision, the League of United Latin American Citizens (LULAC), the Mexican American equivalent of the NAACP, forged ahead in its legal attack on segregation in Texas. With support from LULAC, a group of parents in 1948 sued the Bastrop Independent School District, charging that local school authorities had no legal right to segregate children of Mexican descent and that segregation was solely because the children were of Mexican descent. In *Delgado v. Bastrop Independent School District,* the court ruled that segregating Mexican American children was illegal and discriminatory. The ruling required that the local school district end all segregation.

Although the *Mendez* and *Delgado* decisions did hold out the promise of ending segregation of Mexican Americans, local school districts used many tactics to avoid integration, including manipulation of school district lines, choice plans, and different forms of second-generation segregation. For instance, the California State Department of Education reported in 1966 that 57 percent of the children with Spanish surnames were still attending schools that were predominantly Mexican American. In 1973, a civil rights activist, John Caughey, estimated that two-thirds of the Mexican American children in Los Angeles attended segregated schools. In *All Deliberate Speed,* Wollenberg estimates that in California by 1973 more Mexican and Mexican American children attended segregated schools than in 1947.

In 1970, Mexican Americans were officially recognized by the federal courts as an identifiable dominated group in the public schools in a Mexican American Legal Defense and Education Fund (MALDEF) case, *Cisernos v. Corpus Christi Independent School District.* Central to the case was whether the 1954 school desegregation decision could be applied to Mexican Americans. The original *Brown* decision dealt specifically with African Americans who were segregated by state and local laws. In his final decision, Judge Owen Cox ruled that blacks and Mexican Americans were segregated in the Corpus Christi school system and that Mexican Americans were an identifiable dominated group because of their language, culture, religion, and Spanish surnames.

Despite years of struggle, many Mexican Americans still feel their demands for equality of educational opportunity have not been met. In the fall of 1994, the Latino Education Coalition in Denver, Colorado, threatened to call a student strike if the school district did not hire more bilingual education teachers, involve Latino parents in policy decisions, and increase the number of Latino students going on to college. The threat was reminiscent of 1969, when 3,000 Latino students went on strike against the Denver school district because of high dropout rates, low academic achievement, and the district's failure to be sensitive to cultural differences. It would appear that only steady political pressure can ensure equality of educational opportunity.

## ASIAN AMERICAN STUDENTS AND U.S. SCHOOLS

Similar to Mexican Americans, Asian Americans did not receive a warm welcome by many Anglo American citizens. They were not eligible for citizenship because the 1790 Naturalization Act limited naturalized citizenship to "free white persons." Children born in the U.S. of Asian immigrant parents were U.S. citizens by birth. Figure 4–2 presents a time line of the Asian Americans' struggle in the U.S. school system.

The first Chinese immigrants arrived in California in the 1850s to join the gold rush. In search of the Golden Mountain, these first arrivals were free laborers who paid their own transportation to the gold fields of California. By 1852, there were about 20,000 Chinese immigrants in California. By the 1860s,

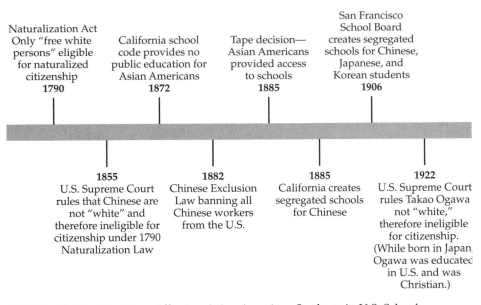

FIGURE 4–2. Key Decisions Affecting Asian American Students in U.S. Schools

approximately 16,000 Chinese immigrants were working in the California gold fields. But as mining profits decreased, the Chinese immigrants found themselves without enough money to return to their homeland. Searching for work, these Chinese immigrants were hired to build the transcontinental railroad at wages that were about one-third less than would have been paid to white workers. In addition, Chinese workers filled low-wage jobs and built the agricultural industry in California. Racial hostility was highlighted in 1871 with the lynching of 22 Chinese men by Los Angeles mobs.

Japanese immigrated at a later date because a 1639 Japanese law forbade travel to foreign countries. Circumstances began to change in 1868 when Hawaiian planters were able to recruit 148 Japanese contract laborers and 100 laborers were signed up for work in the California silk industry in 1869. By 1884, the Japanese government allowed open recruitment by Hawaiian planters. Between 1885 and 1920, as many as 200,000 Japanese immigrated to Hawaii and 180,000 to the U.S. mainland. Adding to the Asian population were 8,000 Koreans who immigrated, primarily to Hawaii, between 1903 and 1920. Between 1907 and 1917, when immigration from India was restricted, 6,400 Asian Indians came to the United States. In 1907, Filipinos, who incidentally were citizens of the U.S.-captured Philippine Islands, were recruited as laborers. By 1930, there were 110,000 Filipinos settled in Hawaii and 40,000 on the mainland.

The white-only provisions of the 1790 Naturalization Act and other laws necessitated U.S. courts to deal with the racial classification of Asian Americans. In the nineteenth century, California laws simply classified as Mongolian those immigrants from northern and southern Asia, southeast Asia, and India. Later, despite the wide-ranging cultural and language differences between these regions, European Americans used the term *Asian* in reference to immigrants and their descents

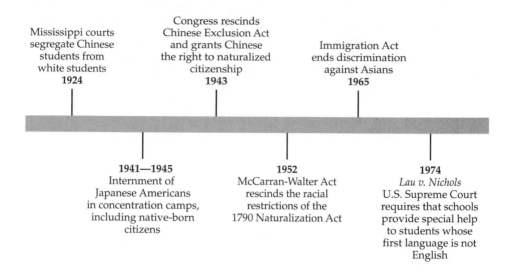

Mississippi courts segregate Chinese students from white students
**1924**

Congress rescinds Chinese Exclusion Act and grants Chinese the right to naturalized citizenship
**1943**

Immigration Act ends discrimination against Asians
**1965**

**1941—1945**
Internment of Japanese Americans in concentration camps, including native-born citizens

**1952**
McCarran-Walter Act rescinds the racial restrictions of the 1790 Naturalization Act

**1974**
*Lau v. Nichols*
U.S. Supreme Court requires that schools provide special help to students whose first language is not English

from these differing areas. Unfortunately, while *Asian American* is now commonly used in the United States, the term tends to conceal the differences between countries and peoples, such as Korea, Japan, China, Cambodia, Indonesia, and India.

Confusion over the legal status of Asians was exemplified by the 1855 case of Chan Yong. A federal district court in California ruled that under the 1790 Naturalization Act citizenship was restricted to whites only and, consequently, immigrant Chinese, such as Chan Yong, were not eligible for U.S. citizenship.

The combination of court rulings and restrictive citizenship laws were used to deny Asian ownership of land. In the 1920s, laws were passed in California, Washington, Arizona, Oregon, Idaho, Nebraska, Texas, Kansas, Louisiana, Montana, New Mexico, Minnesota, and Missouri denying the right to own land to individuals who were ineligible for U.S. citizenship. The purpose of these laws was to deny land ownership to Asians.

Naturalization laws and court rulings underwent rapid change during World War II. Prior to the outbreak of hostilities against Japan, most Anglo Americans seemed to operate from the position that all Asians were the same and that it was difficult to discern physical differences. However, during World War II, China was a U.S. ally while Japan was the enemy. Consequently, popular media, including radio, movies, newspapers, and magazines, depicted Chinese, in contrast to images presented earlier in the century, as "hardworking, brave, religious, intelligent, and practical," while Japanese were depicted as "treacherous, sly, cruel, and warlike."

As a result of wartime conditions, the ban on naturalization of Chinese was ignored and between 15,000 and 20,000 Chinese American men and women joined all branches of the military. In 1943, Congress rescinded the Chinese Exclusion Law and granted Chinese immigrants the right to become naturalized citizens but established a limited immigration quota for Chinese of only 105 each year. Naturalization rights were not extended to immigrants from India and the Philippines until 1946, with each country being given a limited quota of 100 per year.

In contrast to the treatment of Chinese, Japanese American citizenship status was completely ignored with the internment in concentration camps of more than 100,000 Japanese Americans during World War II. Many of these Japanese Americans were U.S. citizens because they had been born in the United States.

Why were Japanese Americans interred in concentration camps but not the descendants of other U.S. enemies, such as German and Italian Americans? Because "the Occidental eye cannot rapidly distinguish one Japanese resident from another" argued three lawyers working for the U.S. Justice Department. Adding to the demands to place Japanese citizens in concentration camps were the conclusions of the U.S. government report on the bombing of Pearl Harbor, which called the Japanese an "enemy race" and claimed that despite many generations in the United States their "racial affinities [were] not severed by migration." The report recommended the removal of all people of Japanese ancestry from coastal areas of the United States.

The citizenship issue for Asian Americans was finally resolved in 1952 when the McCarran-Walter Act rescinded the racial restrictions of the 1790 Naturalization Act. It had taken over 160 years for U.S. leaders to decide that naturalized citizenship would not be restricted to whites. The Japanese American Citizens League played an active role in eliminating the white-only provisions in immigration laws. A Japanese American Citizens League member, Harry Tagaki, commented after the passage of the McCarran-Walter Act, "The bill established our parents as the legal equal of other Americans; it gave the Japanese equality with all other immigrants, and that was a principle we had been struggling for from the very beginning."

The educational experiences of Asian Americans have paralleled their public image in the United States. By public image, I mean the representation of Asian Americans that appears in the popular press and media that is dominated by European Americans. In his study of the portrayal of Asian Americans in U.S. popular culture, Robert Lee identified five major images of Asians—"the coolie, the deviant, the yellow peril, the model minority, and the gook." As he points out, each image, including that of the model minority, has presented some threat to "the American national family."

Prior to World War II, educational discrimination and segregation resulted from the images held by many European Americans of Asian Americans as the coolies, deviants, and yellow peril. The coolie image was that of the servile Asian worker who was willing to work endless hours at low wages and accept substandard living conditions; this image was considered a threat to the standard of living of the white working-class family. The deviant image was that of the Chinese opium den and Asian sexual freedom and was considered a threat to the morality of the white family. The yellow peril image was that of Asian immigrants overrunning the United States.

The image of Asians as the model minority evolved during the civil rights movement of the 1960s and 1970s. In the popular mind of European Americans, Asians were not only the model minority but also the model students. This image is strikingly different from earlier images of coolie and yellow peril. However, European Americans used the model minority image to criticize African Americans and Hispanics. As writer Frank Chin said in 1974 regarding the model minority image, "Whites love us because we're not black."

Ironically, the stereotype of a model minority student has caused many educators to overlook the educational problems encountered by many Asian American students in U.S. schools. Part of the problem is the tendency for non-Asians to lump all Asian Americans together. In fact, Asian Americans represent a broad spectrum of different cultures and nations including, as Valerie Ooka Pang indicates in her article "Asian American Children: A Diverse Population," "Cambodian, Chinese, East Indian, Filipino, Guamian, Hawaiian, Hmong, Indonesian, Japanese, Korean, Laotian, Samoan, and Vietnamese . . . [and] smaller Asian American groups within the category of all other Asians." According to U.S. Census classification there are sixteen of these smaller Asian American groups.

The diversity of Asian Americans also reflects a wide range of adjustment to conditions in the United States. Most non-Asians think of Asian Americans as successful entrepreneurs and professionals who were model students while in school and quickly moved up the economic ladder after graduation. In fact, a report issued in 1994 by the Asian Pacific American Public Institute and the Asian American Center suggests that many Asian Americans face a difficult economic life in the United States. For instance, according to the report, while 8 percent of households nationally received public assistance in 1991, 77 percent of Cambodian and Laotian households in California received public assistance. The report states that Cambodians, Vietnamese, and Laotians have the highest rate of welfare dependency of any racial or ethnic group in the United States. For all Asian Americans the per capita income in 1990 was $10,500, which was less than the $12,000 per capita income for non-Hispanic whites. Or, another way of viewing the economic differences in the Asian American community, according to the report, is to consider that for every Asian American family earning more than $75,000, there is an Asian American family earning less than $10,000 a year. Although a third of Asian Americans have college degrees, 23 percent of those Asian Americans over the age of 25 have less than a high school diploma. A quarter of all families in Chinatown in New York City are living below the poverty line.

While economic figures highlight the plight of many Asian Americans, history points out the educational discrimination encountered by Asian American students. In *All Deliberate Speed*, Charles Wollenberg tells the story of the denial of equal educational opportunity to Asian Americans in California schools. With cries of yellow peril coming from the European American population, the state superintendent of public instruction in California, William Welcher, pointed out in 1884 that the state constitution called Chinese "dangerous to the well-being of the state" and, therefore, argued that San Francisco did not have "to undergo the expense of educating such people." Denied a public education for his daughter, Joseph Tape, an Americanized Chinese, challenged the decision in court. Judge

Maguire of the municipal court ruled that since the daughter, Mamie, was an American citizen she could not be denied equal educational opportunity according to the Fourteenth Amendment to the U.S. Constitution. In addition, Judge Maguire argued that it was unjust to tax Chinese for the support of a school system that excluded Chinese children. State superintendent Welcher reacted angrily to the decision, declaring it a "terrible disaster" and asked, "Shall we abandon the education of our children to provide that of the Chinese who are thrusting themselves upon us?"

In reaction to the court decision, the California State Assembly passed legislation allowing school districts to establish segregated schools for Mongolians. This legislation empowered the San Francisco Board of Education to establish a segregated school for Asians. The courts affirmed this action in 1902, when Wong Him challenged the requirement of attending a segregated institution. Eventually, pressure from the Chinese American community brought an end to segregation. In 1921, Chinese American educator Mary Bo-Tze Lee challenged the segregation policy by showing that Chinese students scored as well as white students on IQ tests. As the Chinese population dispersed through the city, traditionally white schools were forced to open their doors to Chinese students. A study in 1947 found that formal school segregation had ended but that the original segregated Commodore Stockton School was still 100 percent Chinese.

Because Asian American students are stereotyped as model minority students, those students with educational problems are often neglected. Teachers simply assume all Asian Americans will do well in school. On the other hand, many non-Asian educators resent the achievement of some Asian Americans. In 1987, *Time* called Asian Americans the "new whiz kids." *Time* reported that Asian Americans comprised 25 percent of the entering class at the University of California at Berkeley, 21 percent at the California Institute of Technology, 20 percent at the Massachusetts Institute of Technology, and 14 percent at Harvard. *Time* also reported in 1987 that because of quota systems many qualified Asian Americans were being refused admission to major universities.

The largest number of complaints centered on the admission policies of the University of California at Berkeley. *Time* quotes the cochairperson of the Asian American Task Force on University Admissions, Alameda County Superior Court Judge Ken Kawaichi, as stating that university administrators envision a campus that "is mostly white, mostly upper-class with limited numbers of African Americans, Hispanics and Asians. One day they looked around and said, 'My goodness, look at this campus. What are all these Asian people doing here?' Then they started tinkering with the system."

## NATIVE AMERICAN STUDENTS AND U.S. SCHOOLS

Traditionally, as depicted in Figure 4–3, the U.S. government attempted to destroy the languages and cultures of Native American tribes. These policies were not reversed until the civil rights movement of the 1950s and 1960s. The initial attempt by the U.S. government to destroy the cultures and languages of Native Americans was spearheaded by Thomas McKenney, the first head of the Office of Indian Affairs. In 1819, he convinced the U.S. Congress to pass the Civilization Fund Act which authorized the president to "employ capable persons of good moral character, to instruct them [Indians] in the mode of agriculture suited to their situation; and for teaching their children in reading, writing, and arithmetic." Reflecting on his effort to gain approval of the legislation, McKenney wrote, "I did not doubt then, nor do I now, the capacity of the Indian for the highest attainments in civilization, in the arts and religion, but I was satisfied that no adequate plan had ever been adopted for this great reformation." The Civilization Act funded Christian missionaries to educate Native Americans. Typical of missionary attitudes was Reverend James Ramsey's speech at a Choctaw school in 1846. Ramsey described his initial lecture to students and trustees in the following words: "I showed them [on a map] that the people who speak the English language, and who occupied so small a part of the world, and possessed the greatest part of its wisdom and knowledge; that knowledge they could thus see for themselves was power; and that power was to be obtained by Christianity alone." Then he told them that the key to their success would be to continue the practice of establishing religious schools. In this way, they could share in the glory of Anglo-Saxon culture and Christianity.

As white settlers moved into western lands in the latter part of the nineteenth century, leaders in the U.S. government were forced to reconsider their relationships to tribes and their attempts to "civilize" Indians. First, there was the problem of land on which to settle displaced tribes. Unlike in the 1820s and 1830s, there was a realization that white settlement would eventually cover most of the continent. In 1858, Commissioner of Indian Affairs Charles E. Mix, in his annual report, declared that the U.S. government had made several serious errors in dealing with the southeastern tribes, including "the assignment to them of too great an extent of country, to be held in common." Holding large tracts of land in common, according to Commissioner Mix, limited the attempts to civilize the Indian because it prevented Indians from learning the value of separate and independent property. The reservation system combined with education was considered by the U.S. government as the best method of dealing with the "wilder tribes." Once concentrated in reservations where they could be controlled, the tribes would be compelled to remain until they proved themselves to be civilized.

In 1867, Congress created an Indian Peace Commission to deal with the warring tribes. The Peace Commission advocated different methods for the education and civilization of Indians and placed emphasis on the role of education in converting Indians to civilization. Nathaniel Taylor, Chairman of the Peace Commission, told Crow Indians at Fort Laramie: "Upon the reservations you select, we . . . will send you teachers for your children." According to Jon Reyhner and Jeanne Eder, this promise was embodied in the Treaty of Fort Laramie with the Sioux and their allies.

The members of the Peace Commission were not entirely satisfied with the traditional attempts to educate Indians, particularly with regard to language. The Indian Peace Commission report of 1868 stated that differences in language were a major source of the continuing friction between whites and Indians; therefore, an emphasis on the teaching of English would be a major step in reducing hostilities and civilizing Native Americans. In the words of the report:

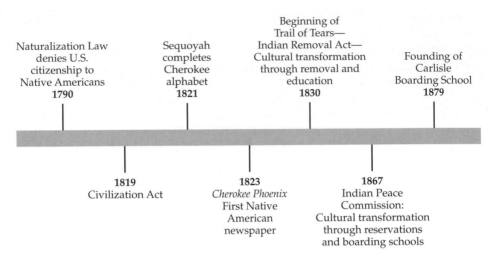

FIGURE 4–3. Key Decisions Affecting Native American Students in U.S. Schools

"Through sameness of language is produced sameness of sentiment and thought; customs and habits are moulded [sic] and assimilated in the same way, and thus in process of time the differences producing trouble would have been gradually obliterated."

The first off-reservation boarding school was the Carlisle Indian School, established in Carlisle, Pennsylvania, in 1879. The founder of the school, Richard Pratt, wanted to instill the work ethic in Indian children and as he told a Baptist group, he wanted to immerse "Indians in our civilization and when we get them under [hold] them there until they are thoroughly soaked." The slogan for the Carlisle Indian School reflected the emphasis on changing the cultural patterns of Indians: "To civilize the Indian, get him into civilization. To keep him civilized, let him stay."

Pratt attacked the tribal way of life as socialistic and contrary to the values of civilization. Reflecting the values of economic individualism, Pratt complained about missionary groups who did not "advocate the disintegration of the tribes and the giving to individual Indians rights and opportunities among civilized people." He wrote to the Commissioner of Indian Affairs in 1890, "Pandering to the tribe and its socialism as most of our Government and mission plans do is the principal reason why the Indians have not advanced more and are not advancing as rapidly as they ought."

Between the founding of the Carlisle Indian School in 1879 and 1905, twenty-five nonreservation boarding schools were opened throughout the country. It is important to emphasize the nonreservation location of the boarding schools because of the educational philosophy that Indian children should be removed from family and tribal influences.

Teaching English was an important issue for both nonreservation boarding schools and schools on reservations. The attitude of many white educators in

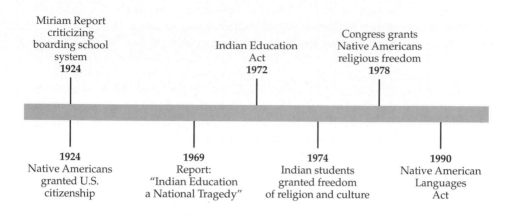

the latter part of the nineteenth century was that elimination of tribal languages and the learning of English would lead to the absorption and practice of white values by Indians. In the Annual Report of the Commissioner of Indian Affairs in 1887, Commissioner J.D.C. Adkins ordered the exclusive use of English at all Indian schools. Adkins pointed out that this policy was consistent with the requirement that only English be taught in public schools in territories acquired by the United States from Mexico, Spain, and Russia.

In 1889, U.S. Commissioner of Indian Affairs Thomas J. Morgan wrote a bulletin on Indian Education that outlined the goals and policies of Indian schools. The bulletin was distributed by the U.S. Bureau of Education with an introduction written by the commissioner of education, William T. Harris. In the introduction, Harris praised what he called "the new education for our American Indians," particularly the effort "to obtain control of the Indian at an early age, and to seclude him as much as possible from the tribal influences." Harris singled out the boarding school as an important step in changing the character of American Indians and argued that it was necessary to save the American Indian, but, he wrote, "We cannot save him and his patriarchal or tribal institution both together. To save him we must take him up into our civilization."

With regard to instruction in English, Morgan stressed in the bulletin, "Only English should be allowed to be spoken, and only English-speaking teachers should be employed in schools supported wholly or in part by the Government." Also, the general principles stressed the importance of teaching allegiance to the U.S. government. As an added note, Morgan stressed the importance of bringing together the members of many different tribes in boarding schools as a means of reducing antagonisms among them.

Morgan also advocated early childhood education as a method of counteracting the influence of the Indian home. Similar to the boarding school, early childhood education would help to strip away the influences of Indian culture and language. Morgan stated, "Children should be taken at as early an age as possible, before camp life has made an indelible stamp upon them."

The conditions in boarding schools lived up to Morgan's edict: "In the sweat of their faces must they eat bread." During the 1920s, a variety of investigators of Indian schools were horrified by the conditions they found. At the Rice Boarding School in Arizona, Red Cross investigators found that children were fed "bread, black coffee, and syrup for breakfast; bread and boiled potatoes for dinner; more bread and boiled potatoes for supper." In addition to a poor diet, overcrowded conditions contributed to the spread of tuberculosis and trachoma.

Using a paramilitary form of organization, boarding schools were supported by the labor of the students. As early as the fifth grade, boys and girls attended classes for half the day and worked for the other half. As part of the plan to teach agricultural methods, children raised crops and tended farm animals. The paramilitary organization was reflected in the constant drilling of students. The children were given little time for recreation. They were awakened at 5 A.M. and marched to the dining room, then marched back to the dormitories and classrooms. At the Albuquerque Indian School, students marched in uniforms with dummy rifles. For punishment children were flogged with ropes, and some boarding schools contained their own jails. In the 1920s, anthropologist Oliver La Farge called the Indian schools "penal institutions—where little children were sentenced to hard labor for a term of years to expiate the crime of being born of their mothers."

It was a result of the boarding schools and the long history of attempts to destroy their cultures that led Native Americans to demand control of the education of their children and restoration of their cultural heritage and languages to the curriculum. The demand for self-determination by Native Americans received consideration in government decisions after the election of John F. Kennedy in 1960. The Kennedy administration advocated Indian participation in decisions regarding federal policies. Kennedy's secretary of interior, Stewart Udall, appointed a Task Force on Indian Affairs that, in its 1961 report, recommended that Native Americans be given full citizenship and self-sufficiency.

As a result, the Rough Rock Demonstration School was created in 1966. Established on a Navajo reservation in Arizona, the school was a joint effort of the Office of Economic Opportunity and the Bureau of Indian Affairs. One major goal of the demonstration school was for Navajo parents to control the education of their children and to participate in all aspects of their schooling. Besides tribal control, the Rough Rock Demonstration School attempted to preserve the Navajo language and culture. In contrast to the attempts to destroy native cultures and languages that took place in the nineteenth and early twentieth centuries, both Navajo and English were taught to prepare children to live in both cultures.

Based on the assumption that Native American tribes shared a common set of values and interests, a pan-Indian movement developed in the United States. Pan-Indian organizations, such as the American Indian Movement (AIM) and the Indians of All Tribes, led demonstrations demanding self-determination. In 1969, members of the Indians of All Tribes seized Alcatraz Island in San Francisco Bay calling attention to the plight of Native Americans and demanding that the island, which Indians had originally sold to the federal government for $24 worth of beads, be made an Indian cultural and education center. In 1972, AIM organized a march on Washington, DC, called the Trail of Broken Treaties. Members of the march seized the Bureau of Indian Affairs and hung a large sign at its entrance declaring it the American Indian Embassy.

It was in this climate of civil rights activism and political support for Indian self-determination that the U.S. Senate Committee on Labor and Public Welfare issued in 1969 the report *Indian Education: A National Tragedy—A National Challenge.* The report opened with a statement condemning previous educational policies of the federal government: "A careful review of the historical literature reveals that the dominant policy of the Federal Government toward the American Indian has been one of forced assimilation . . . [because of] a desire to divest the Indian of his land." After a lengthy review of the failure of past educational policies, the report's first recommendation was for "maximum participation and control by Indians in establishing Indian education programs." In its second recommendation, the report called for maximum Indian participation in the development of educational programs in federal schools and local public schools. These educational programs were to include early childhood education, vocational education, work-study, and adult literacy education.

The congressional debates resulting from the report eventually culminated in the passage of the Indian Education Act in 1972. The declared policy of the legislation was to provide financial assistance to local schools to develop programs to meet the special educational needs of Native American students. In addition, the legislation created a federal Office of Indian Education.

In 1974, the Bureau of Indian Affairs issued a set of procedures for protecting student rights and due process. In contrast to the brutal and dictatorial treatment of Indian students in the boarding schools of the late nineteenth and early twentieth centuries, each Indian student was extended the right "to make his or her own decisions where applicable." And, in striking contrast to earlier deculturalization policies, Indian students were granted "the right to freedom of religion and culture."

The most important piece of legislation supporting self-determination was the 1975 Indian Self-Determination and Education Assistance Act, which gave tribes the power to contract with the federal government to run their own education and health programs. The legislation opened with the declaration that it was "an Act to provide maximum Indian participation in the Government and education of Indian people; to provide for the full participation of Indian tribes in programs and services conducted by the federal government."

The Indian Self-Determination and Education Assistance Act strengthened Indian participation in the control of education programs. The legislation provided that a local school district receiving funds for the education of Indian students that did not have a school board composed of mostly Indians had to establish a separate local committee composed of parents of Indian students in the school. This committee was given the authority over any Indian education programs contracted with the federal government.

The principles embodied in the Indian Self-Determination and Education Assistance Act of 1975 were expanded upon in 1988 with the passage of the

Tribally Controlled Schools Act. Besides the right to operate schools under a federal contract as provided in the 1975 legislation, the Tribally Controlled Schools Act provided for outright grants to tribes to support the operation of their own schools.

Title VII of the No Child Left Behind Act of 2001 addressed the Native American Educational issues by emphasizing instruction in English rather than maintaining Native American languages. Native American language usage, according to this legislation, would simply be a means for learning English. In addition, the legislation stressed the importance of educating Native American teachers and counselors to serve in local communities.

## CONCLUSION

Important questions regarding culture and language are raised by the diversity of the student population. The history of Mexican American, Asian American, and Native American schooling highlights serious issues regarding the responsibility of the schools to preserve language and cultural traditions. Consider the following set of questions:

- Should public schools consciously attempt to eradicate the language of non-English-speaking students in a manner similar to that used with Mexican American and Native American students?
- Should public schools attempt to preserve the home language of non-English-speaking students?
- Should the public schools consciously attempt to change or Americanize the culture of immigrant students?
- Should public schools preserve the cultures of immigrant, Native American, and Mexican American students?

### Suggested Readings and Works Cited in Chapter

COLEMAN, MICHAEL C.   *Presbyterian Attitudes toward American Indians, 1837–1893.* Jackson: University of Mississippi Press, 1985. *This is a good history of missionary attempts to change Native American cultures.*

Committee on Labor and Public Welfare, U.S. Senate 91st Congress, 1st Session. *Indian Education: A National Tragedy—A National Challenge.* Washington, DC: U.S. Government Printing Office, 1969. *This is the report that set the stage for recent efforts in Indian education.*

DONATO, RUBEN.   *The Other Struggle for Equal Schools: Mexican Americans during the Civil Rights Era.* Albany: State University of New York, 1997. *This is the best study of the Mexican American civil rights movement and its impact on education.*

FOX, GEOFFREY.   *Hispanic Nation: Culture, Politics, and the Constructing of Identity.* Tucson: University of Arizona Press, 1996. *I relied on this book for my discussion of the meaning of Hispanic and Latino/Latina.*

GONZALES, MANUEL.   *Mexicanos: A History of Mexicans in the United States.* Bloomington: Indiana University Press, 1999. *Gonzales provides a good introductory history of Mexican Americans.*

LEE, ROBERT G. *Orientals: Asian Americans in Popular Culture.* Philadelphia: Temple University Press, 1999. *This is an important study of the popular image of Asian Americans in the United States.*

LOW, VICTOR. *The Unimpressible Race: A Century of Educational Struggle by the Chinese in San Francisco.* San Francisco: East/West Publishing, 1982. *This is the book to read to understand racism and segregation of Chinese in California.*

NAKANISHI, DON T., and TINA YAMANO NISHIDA, eds. *The Asian American Educational Experience.* New York: Routledge, 1995. *This is an excellent collection of articles on Asian American education.*

National Center for Education Statistics. "Are Limited English Proficient (LEP) Students Being Taught by Teachers with LEP Training?" (December 1996), http://www.ed.gov/NCES. *Brings to light the lack of training for U.S. teachers to educate LEP students.*

_____. *The Condition of Education 2000.* Washington, DC: US Printing Office, 2000. *This is an excellent source of statistics on school conditions at the beginning of the twenty-first century.*

PANG, VALERIE OOKA. "Asian American Children: A Diverse Population." *The Educational Forum* (Fall 1990): 49–66. *This is a good discussion of diversity in the Asian American population in the United States.*

PRUCHA, FRANCIS PAUL. *Documents of United States Indian Policy.* Lincoln: University of Nebraska Press, 1990. *This volume contains reprints of all the important laws, court cases, and reports affecting Indian education.*

REYHNER, JON, and JEANNE EDER. *A History of Indian Education.* Billings: Eastern Montana College, 1989. *The authors provide a short introduction to the history of Indian education.*

SAN MIGUEL, GUADALUPE, JR. *"Let All of Them Take Heed": Mexican Americans and the Campaign for Educational Equality in Texas, 1910–1981.* Austin: University of Texas Press, 1987. *This is a good history of the events and court cases surrounding efforts by Mexican Americans to end segregation.*

SZASZ, MARGARET. *Education and the American Indian: The Road to Self-Determination, 1928–1973.* Albuquerque: University of New Mexico Press, 1974. *Szasz provides a good history of the revolution in Native American education in the twentieth century.*

TAKAKI, RONALD. *A Different Mirror: A History of Multicultural America.* Boston: Little, Brown and Company, 1993. *This is the single best history of multiculturalism in the United States.*

_____. *Strangers from a Different Shore: A History of Asian Americans.* New York: Penguin Books, 1989. *Takaki writes an excellent history of Asian Americans.*

U.S. Census Bureau. "March 1998 Current Population Survey." http://www.census.gov/.

_____. "Population Estimates." http://www.census.gov/. *Lists population projections into the next century.*

_____. "We Asked . . . You Told Us Language Spoken at Home." http://www.census.gov/. *Provides statistics on non-English-speaking households in the United States.*

WEINBERG, MEYER. *Asian American Education: Historical Background and Current Realities.* Mahwah, NJ: Lawrence Erlbaum Associates, Inc., 1997. *Weinberg presents an excellent history of the Asian American educational experience in the United States.*

WOLLENBERG, CHARLES M. *All Deliberate Speed: Segregation and Exclusion in California Schools, 1855–1975.* Berkeley: University of California Press, 1976. *This is a landmark study of segregation in the education of Asian Americans, Mexican Americans, and Native Americans in California.*

## CHAPTER 5

# Multicultural
# Education

In multicultural education a distinction is made between *dominant, dominated,* and *immigrant* cultures. The dominant culture is the prevailing culture, which is European American in the United States. This is the culture brought to the colonies and the United States by immigrants from Europe and modified by the social and political conditions in America. Traditionally, the curriculum of public schools has been based on European American traditions. In this sense, European American culture is the dominant culture of public schools.

Dominated cultures refer to groups who were forcefully incorporated into the United States. For instance, African Americans were forcefully brought to the United States as slaves, and their African American cultures were changed by the domination of European American culture to produce an African American culture. Native American tribes were conquered by the United States. Mexican Americans living in the Southwest were forcefully made part of the United States with the signing in 1848 of the Treaty of Guadalupe Hidalgo. The Spanish-American War of 1898 resulted in the forceful annexation of Puerto Rico to the United States. Puerto Ricans are another dominated culture that the U.S. government tried to change through educational policies designed to replace Puerto Rican culture and Spanish with European American culture and English.

Immigrant cultures refer to the *first generation* of groups who freely decided to come to the United States. First generation refers to adults and children who are born in another country and then immigrate to the United States. European American immigrants are included in this category. Immigrants have a variety of educational, cultural, and linguistic backgrounds. The diversity of immigrant languages and cultures presents a complex problem for school teachers. In *The Inner World of Immigrant Children* Christina Igoa provides questions designed to help teachers do research into the educational background of immigrant children. I strongly recommend that all teachers of immigrant children read Igoa's invaluable book. Igoa's list of questions includes the following:

- Were the children schooled or unschooled before they came into the country?
- Was their education fragmented?

- Are the children dependent on the teacher for learning? Do they have any independent learning skills?
- Did they learn English abroad?
- How much of their own language did they learn, orally and in writing, receptively and productively?
- What is the educational attainment of their parents?

## *DOMINATED CULTURES: JOHN OGBU*

Anthropologist John Ogbu concludes that the historical experience of dominated groups resulted in the development of a basic distrust of the major institutions in American society. For instance, a history of forced subjugation and slavery, segregation, discrimination, and harassment by police and government officials left many members of the African American community with the feeling that the government works primarily to benefit European Americans. This general distrust of institutions includes public schools. Segregation and second-generation segregation have left many African Americans feeling that public schooling is organized to keep African Americans at the bottom rungs of America's social and economic system. Mexican Americans and Puerto Ricans encountered the hostility of segregation and second-generation segregation as well as attempts to keep them from speaking Spanish.

Many Native Americans feel a strong hostility toward schools because of the deculturalization programs they experienced in government-operated boarding schools. For instance, Mick Fedullo, in his wonderful book on Indian education, *Light of the Feather: Pathways Through Contemporary Indian America*, recounts a discussion with an Apache bilingual education teacher, Elenore Cassadore, about Apache attitudes toward schools. As she tells Fedullo, many Apache parents were sent to Bureau of Indian Affairs' boarding schools where they "came to believe that their teachers were the evil ones, and so anything that had to do with 'education' was also evil—like books." Now, she explains, they only send their children to school because of compulsory-education laws. "But they tell their kids not to take school seriously. So, to them, printed stuff is white-man stuff."

According to Ogbu, these historical conditions created a *cultural frame of reference* among dominated groups that is quite different from that of many immigrants and European Americans. Cultural frames of reference refer to the manner in which people interpret their perceptions of the world. A person's cultural frame of reference is formed, in part, by his or her family's historical experience. For instance, an African American child might not have witnessed a lynching of a black person by a white mob, but knowledge of these incidents might be passed on to the child through the recounting of family history and experience in the United States. A Mexican American child might not have experienced discrimination in employment, but he or she might frequently hear about it through family conversations. The history told by families and a person's experiences play a major role in shaping one's cultural frame of reference.

Differences in cultural frames of reference can result in differing interpretations of the same event. For instance, a European American might perceive a school as an institution that is benign and helpful. In contrast, a member of a dominated group might perceive a school as an institution not to be trusted. The actions of a disgruntled waiter in a restaurant might be interpreted through the cultural frame of reference of a European American as resulting from the waiter not feeling good about his job. On the other hand, the cultural frame of reference of African Americans, Native Americans, Mexican Americans, and Puerto Ricans might lead members of these groups to interpret the waiter's actions as hostile and prejudicial.

Also, differences in cultural frames of reference can result in differences in action in particular situations. For instance, in the preceding example, a European American might give little attention to the actions of a disgruntled waiter. On the other hand, members of a dominated group might act in a hostile manner to what they perceive to be the prejudicial actions of the waiter.

Low academic achievement, Ogbu argues, results from dominated cultures holding negative feelings about schools. Ogbu identifies six ways this can occur:

1. Some members of dominated groups believe that they must act white to succeed in school. This feeling is exemplified by the previous quotation from the Apache teacher.
2. Some students from dominated cultures may fear that doing well in school will symbolize a rejection of their own culture.
3. Peer pressure against acting white might result in students actually avoiding academic achievement.
4. The feelings of hostility some students from dominated cultures might feel toward school can result in conflicts with European American administrators, teachers, and other students. Of course, these conflicts might be in response to real feelings and actions displayed by school officials and other students.
5. Conflicts with school personnel and other students can heighten distrust of school and a rejection of school rules. The open rejection of school rules leads to suspension, expulsion, and other forms of school punishment.
6. Some students from dominated cultures might begin school disillusioned about their ability to achieve. This can result in little effort being put into academic work.

These six reactions to school cause, according to Ogbu, *low academic effort syndrome* and *counteracademic attitudes and behaviors.* Low academic effort syndrome refers to lack of effort in doing schoolwork, which results from peer pressure, conflict, and disillusionment. Counteracademic attitudes and behaviors refer to actions that are hostile toward the school and its rules.

Obviously, many students from dominated groups succeed in school and they do not display a low academic effort syndrome or adopt counteracademic attitudes and behavior. Despite their success in school, many of these students still interpret their educational experience through a cultural frame of reference that is quick to note prejudice and unfair treatment. This type of cultural frame of reference can be found in Jake Lamar's autobiography *Bourgeois Blues: An American Memoir*. Although his father was a successful businessperson who could afford to live in wealthy neighborhoods in New York City and send his children to elite private schools, Jake discovered that racism was still a major factor in his life. Richard Rodriguez interprets his academic success through the cultural frame of reference of a Mexican American in his autobiography *Hunger of Memory: The Education of Richard Rodriguez*. Important in understanding the problems of students from dominated cultures is the pain Rodriguez felt as his academic success widened the gap between him and his family culture.

It is important to remember that many students of dominated cultures do succeed in school and in the economic life of the United States. Advocates of multicultural education programs argue that educational programs supporting cultural diversity can help students from dominated cultures who might be experiencing low academic effort syndrome and exhibiting counteracademic attitudes and behaviors. These multicultural programs are described in the next section.

## EMPOWERMENT THROUGH MULTICULTURAL EDUCATION: JAMES BANKS, SONIA NIETO, AND CRITICAL PEDAGOGY

Leaders of the multicultural education movement, such as James Banks, Christine Sleeter, Carl Grant, and Sonia Nieto, are concerned with empowering oppressed people by integrating the history and culture of dominated groups into public school curricula and textbooks. In general, their goal is to reduce prejudice, eliminate sexism, and equalize educational opportunities.

Empowerment is concerned with ethnic studies and raising consciousness. Within this context, the term *empowerment* means providing the intellectual tools for creating a just society. Usually the concept of empowerment is contrasted with benevolent helping, such as welfare programs, family assistance, and other forms of aid. These programs, it is argued, keep people in a state of dependence. Empowerment gives people the ability to break out of these dependent states.

Ethnic studies can empower dominated and oppressed immigrant cultures by creating an understanding of the methods of cultural domination and by helping to build self-esteem. For instance, the study of African American, Native American, Puerto Rican, Hawaiian American, and Mexican American histories serves the dual purpose of building self-esteem and empowerment. In addition, the empowerment of women and people with disabilities involves, in part, the inclusion of their histories and stories in textbooks and in the curriculum.

As one aspect of social empowerment, ethnic studies have influenced textbooks and classroom instruction in the United States. The ethnic studies movement resulted in the integration of content into the curriculum dealing with dominated and immigrant cultures, women, and people with disabilities.

Multicultural educator James Banks worries that many school districts consider content integration as the primary goal of multicultural education. He states, "The widespread belief that content integration constitutes the whole of multicultural education might . . . [cause] many teachers of subjects such as mathematics and science to view multicultural education as an endeavor primarily for social studies and language arts teachers."

The best example of multicultural education for empowerment is Sonia Nieto's *Affirming Diversity: The Sociopolitical Context of Multicultural Education.* Growing up as a Puerto Rican in New York City, Nieto felt the tension between the language and culture of her family and the language and culture of the school. The school made her feel that there was something deficient with her background. She states, "We learned to feel ashamed of who we were, how we spoke, what we ate, and everything else that was 'different' about us." For Nieto, the goal of multicultural education should be to bridge the gap between the culture of the family and the culture of the school so that children of immigrant and dominated families do not have to suffer the pain and shame that she experienced. In her words, "Our society must move beyond causing and exploiting students' shame to using their cultural and linguistic differences to struggle for an education that is more in tune with society's rhetoric of equal and high-quality education for all students."

Multiculturalism for social empowerment attempts to maintain cultural identity while promoting values of social justice and social action. In her book, Nieto presents a chart displaying the seven characteristics of this form of multicultural education.

1. The school curriculum is openly antiracist and antidiscriminitory. An atmosphere is created where students feel safe about discussing sexism, racism, and discrimination. In addition, the curriculum includes the history and cultural perspectives of a broad range of people. Students are taught to identify and challenge racism in society.
2. Multicultural education is considered a basic part of a student's general education, which means that all students become bilingual and all students study different cultural perspectives.
3. Multiculturalism should pervade the curriculum and be included in all aspects of the curriculum and in the general life of the school, including bulletin boards, lunchrooms, and assemblies.
4. Multicultural education is considered important for all students.
5. Schools should teach social justice by preparing students to overcome racism and discrimination against various cultures.
6. Learning should emphasize asking questions why, how, and what if. When these questions are asked regarding issues of social injustice they can lead to a questioning of the very foundations of political and economic institutions. This makes multicultural education a combination of content and "process."
7. Multicultural education should include critical pedagogy as the primary method of instruction. With critical pedagogy, in Nieto's words, "students and teachers are involved in a 'subversive activity' and decision making and social action skills are the basis of the curriculum."

In the framework of this approach to multicultural education, critical pedagogy helps students to understand the extent to which cultures can differ. In addition, these differences are to be affirmed and given equal treatment. Also, critical pedagogy will help students to understand cultural domination and how they can end it.

Missing from multicultural education for social empowerment is an analysis of the intersection of different cultures. It is assumed that an understanding of oppression and discrimination will provide a common theme in critical pedagogy that will prepare all students to struggle for social justice. But there are important and deep differences in values between cultures. Does social justice mean giving a person an opportunity to achieve within the framework of English or Native American values? Or, does it mean creating a whole new set of values for the world?

## EDUCATING FOR ECONOMIC POWER: LISA DELPIT

Lisa Delpit is more interested in directly instructing children of dominated groups in the culture of power. She believes that advocates of multicultural education often fail to reveal to children the requirements for economic advancement. She does not reject the importance of critical thinking, but she does think children should be directly told about the standards for acceptable speech and behavior for social mobility.

Working at the University of Alaska, she criticized what she called liberal educators for primarily focusing on native culture while instructing native Alaskans. These liberal educators, she claimed, were damaging students by not preparing them for success in the broader society. She was also critical of traditional instructors for ignoring native traditions. From her perspective, traditional culture needed to be considered when preparing students to achieve in the real world.

Delpit encountered the same issues when working with teachers of black children in Philadelphia schools. White teachers often thought they knew what was best for black students. Usually this meant some form of progressive instruction designed to enhance critical thinking and imagination. While not denying the importance of these goals, Delpit found white teachers neglecting the instruction of black students in standard English. One complaining black parent told her, "My kids know how to be black—you all teach them how to be successful in the white man's world." Several black teachers suggested to Delpit that the "'progressive' educational strategies imposed by liberals upon black and poor children could only be based on a desire to ensure that the liberals' children get sole access to the dwindling pool of American jobs."

According to Delpit, there are five important aspects that need to be addressed when preparing dominated children for access to power.

1. "Issues of power are enacted in classrooms." It is important to examine, Delpit argues, the power of teachers and government over students, textbook

publishers, and curriculum developers. This examination can be considered preparation for understanding the exercise of power in the world of work.

2. "There are codes or rules for participating in power; that is, there is a 'culture of power'." In the classroom, this means direct instruction in linguistic forms and presentation of self, including ways of talking, writing, dressing, and interacting.

3. "The rules of the culture of power are a reflection of the rules of the culture of those who have power." For Delpit, the culture of the school is the culture of the middle and upper classes. Therefore, it is important for children from dominated groups to participate and learn school culture.

4. "If you are not already a participant in the culture of power, being told explicitly the rules of that culture makes acquiring power easier."

5. "Those with power are frequently least aware of—or least willing to acknowledge—its existence. Those with less power are often most aware of its existence." From Delpit's perspective, white liberal educators are uncomfortable admitting they are part of the culture of power. On the other hand, students from dominated groups are aware of white power and they would like the parameters of power clearly stated.

## *ETHNOCENTRIC EDUCATION*

In *ethnocentric education* subjects are taught from the perspective of a particular culture. Obviously, this is what U.S. public schools have always done. The curriculum of public schools is organized around the cultural frame of reference of European Americans, while the curriculum of new ethnocentric schools is organized around the cultural frames of reference of African Americans, Native Americans, and Hispanics.

The purpose of these new ethnocentric schools is twofold. First, these schools want to overcome among some children of dominated cultures the resistance to schooling that results in low academic effort and counteracademic attitudes and behaviors. Second, these schools want to preserve the cultural traditions of each dominated group. The preservation of culture is considered important because of what are believed to be some shortcomings of European American culture. For instance, many Native Americans feel that European Americans show little respect for nature and that they are primarily concerned with the control of nature. The result of these attitudes is massive environmental destruction. What Native American culture can contribute is an understanding of how to live with nature and an attitude that shows respect for nature and desires its preservation.

The concern with student resistance to schooling and with preservation of culture resulted in the establishment of Afrocentric schools. In 1990, a proposal for the establishment of an Afrocentric school for black males in Milwaukee was quickly followed by similar proposals in Detroit, Minneapolis, and New York. In February 1991, a Hispanic-centered school was proposed for the Denver public school system.

The proposal for a Hispanic school was advanced by the advocacy group Latin American Research and Service Agency. As reported in an Associated Press article, "Hispanic Schools," the executive director of the organization, Audrey Alvardo, argues, "What our children need is a school that works, and they need it now." In Denver, Hispanic students are the fastest-growing part of the school population, making up nearly 40 percent. Hispanic students have the highest dropout rate of any ethnic students and are among the lowest-scoring students on college entrance examinations. Alvardo states, "Not only do Hispanic youths enter school slightly behind their white counterparts, but they continue to fall further and further behind as they go through school."

The proposals for Hispanic and Afrocentric schools are designed to redirect resistance cultures and build student self-esteem. A major source of inspiration for ethnocentric schools comes from the work of Jawanza Kunjufu, president of the Chicago-based African American Images. African American Images serves as a publishing house for Kunjufu's books and other books and videos focused on the teaching of African American culture. African American Images also offers a model curriculum: "SETCLAE: Self-Esteem Through Culture Leads to Academic Excellence." The stated goals of the curriculum are to improve academic achievement, discipline, and school climate while transmitting racial pride and enhancing students' knowledge of culture and history and its significance to contemporary living.

Kunjufu's discussion of the experience of African American students is similar to that of John Ogbu. Kunjufu argues that for most African American students, being successful in school means acting white. Kunjufu exemplifies this situation by an exchange between African American students about two other academically successful African American students in his book *To Be Popular or Smart: The Black Peer Group:*

> "Girl, she thinks she's something, making the honor roll."
> "I know, she's beginning to act like Darryl. They both think they're white, joining the National Honor Society."

One of the effects of American slavery, Kunjufu argues, is the public characterization of African Americans as intellectually inferior. The expectation of intellectual inferiority eroded the confidence in academic success among black youth. In addition, having been stripped of their cultural heritage, slaves internalized white ideals about beauty and culture. Consequently, later black resistance to domination involved the creation of a culture that opposed certain white ideals. Kunjufu found that when black teenagers are asked, How do you act black? they respond with cultural issues. From their perspective, being black is speaking black English, listening to rap and rhythm and blues, and attending parties. On the other hand, being white is considered by black students as speaking standard English, listening to rock and classical music, and going to museums.

Kunjufu found the same pattern among black college students. Recalling his own years in college in his book *To Be Popular or Smart*, Kunjufu states he was almost ostracized by his fellow black students when he joined the college debating society. What saved him from cultural exclusion was being an athlete, liking to dance, and "talking the talk." On the other hand, white students made comments such as "You're different" and "You're not like the rest of them." Out of the 1,000 African Americans in his entering class, only 254 graduated. In Kunjufu's words, "Many of them flunked out while pledging, roller skating, partying, talking in the cafeteria or dormitories, playing ball or records, and getting high."

Through this concern about the development of a self-destructive resistance culture among African American students, Kunjufu advocates the teaching of an Afrocentric curriculum for breaking cultural stereotypes. He wants African American students to know that African Americans have a long history of learning and creativity. He wants them to understand that within African American cultural traditions it is all right to be *black* and to be an intellectual. He wants them to realize that studying hard and learning is not being white, but follows the best traditions of African American culture.

In addition, he wants black students to understand that there is an Afrocentric way of viewing the world that is different from that of a Eurocentric view. Molefi Kete Asante, chairperson of the Department of African American Studies at Temple University and one of the proponents of an Afrocentric curriculum, argues that Afrocentricity is a transforming power involving five levels of awareness. On the first four levels of this transforming experience individuals come to understand that their personality, interests, and concerns are shared by African American people around the world. Afrocentricity is achieved on the fifth level when a people struggle against foreign cultures that dominate their minds. At this stage, Asante argues in his book *Afrocentricity*, "An imperative of will, powerful, incessant, alive, and vital, moves to eradicate every trace of powerlessness. Afrocentricity is like rhythms; it dictates the beat of your life."

By purging images given by white culture of African Americans as stupid and powerless, African American students can, according to the arguments of those advocating Afrocentricity, gain a new image of themselves as people of ability and power. In this sense, Afrocentricity is considered a curriculum of empowerment. In addition, the students lose the lenses that filter the world through a white Eurocentric perspective and replace them with a set of Afrocentric lenses.

Therefore, ethnocentric curriculums in the United States create a cultural battle at two levels. At one level, an ethnocentric curriculum is an attempt to give equal value to different cultural traditions. At the second level, it means purging a Eurocentric view of the world from Native American, Hispanic, and African American children's minds and replacing it with a different cultural frame of reference. The purpose of this cultural battle is to empower Native American, Hispanic, and African American children so that they believe they can succeed in the world and so that they are not self-destructive. From this perspective, getting ahead in the economic and social system is not a matter of being white but of learning to believe in oneself and one's cultural traditions.

Ethnocentric education is one method for helping children from dominated groups succeed in school. Another method is bilingual education. Bilingual education, as I discuss in the next section, is particularly important for Native Americans, Mexican Americans, and Puerto Ricans because of the conscious attempt by public schools in the past to destroy their languages.

## BILINGUAL EDUCATION AND ENGLISH LANGUAGE ACQUISITION: NO CHILD LEFT BEHIND

The No Child Left Behind Act of 2001 transforms the original goals of the bilingual education movement. Bilingual education is a means for protecting minority languages while teaching English to non-English speakers. It is part of the effort to protect language and cultural rights. Some Americans object to public schools protecting minority languages and believe the primary goal should be the acquisition of English.

The No Child Left Behind Act clearly places the federal government's support on the side of English acquisition as opposed to bilingual education. One part of the legislation is titled "English Language Acquisition, Language Enhancement, and Academic Act." This part of the legislation symbolically changes the name of the federal government's Office of Bilingual Education to the Office of English Language Acquisition, Language Enhancement, and Academic Achievement for Limited English Proficient. Its shorter title is simply the Office of English Language Acquisition. The Director of Bilingual Education and Minority Languages Affairs is now called the Director of English Language Acquisition.

To understand the significance of these changes, we need to consider the arguments *for* bilingual education. Bilingual education refers to teaching a person to be proficient in the use of two languages. For instance, Native American students can be taught to be proficient in the use of their own native languages and English, while a Mexican American or Puerto Rican child can be taught to be proficient in Spanish and English.

In addition, there are several specific types of a bilingual education, including *maintenance bilingual, transitional bilingual,* and *two-way bilingual.* As the term suggests, maintenance bilingual programs are designed for students to maintain the ability to speak, read, and write in their native language while learning English. For instance, a student might enter school speaking only Spanish with little knowledge of English. The ability to speak Spanish does not necessarily mean that the child knows how to read and write in Spanish. Similarly, most English-speaking students entering school do not know how to read and write in English. During the early years, maintenance bilingual education programs conduct classes in the language of the student while also teaching English. Therefore, during the period when students are learning English, they are also learning the content of the curriculum, including how to read and write, in their native tongue. This avoids the problem of learning being delayed until students know English. After learning English, students continue to receive lessons in both their native languages and in English.

One of the strongest arguments for maintenance bilingual education is that students are better able to learn English if they know how to read and write in their native language. In *Affirming Diversity* Sonia Nieto argues that children who know how to read and write in their native language will be more successful in school than children whose language is neglected by the school and who do not become literate in their native tongue.

In contrast, transitional bilingual does not have the goal of making the student literate in two languages. The student's native tongue is used in class until the student learns English. After the student learns English, classes are taught only in English. Two-way bilingual programs include both English-speaking and non-English-speaking students. By conducting class in two languages, English-speaking students can learn the language of the non-English speakers, while the non-English speakers learn English. The goal is for all students to become bilingual in English and another language.

Of course, language is linked to culture. Many Mexican Americans, Puerto Ricans, and Native Americans believe that maintenance bilingual education programs are essential for the retention of their cultures. As discussed earlier in this chapter, many deculturalization programs were directed at stamping out the use of Spanish and Native American languages. In addition, a person's cultural frame of reference is directly related to attitudes regarding the use in the United States of languages other than English. The issue of cultural perspective is highlighted in Humberto Garza's comment regarding a requirement that Los Altos, California, city employees speak only English on the job. Garza is quoted by Rosalie Pedalino Porter in her book *Forked Tongue: The Politics of Bilingual Education:* "Those council people from Los Altos should be made to understand that they are advocating their law in occupied Mexico [referring to the U.S. conquest of Mexican territory, including California]. . . . They should move back to England or learn how to speak the language of Native Americans."

Garza's remarks reflect the political explosiveness of bilingual education issues. In fact, the bilingual education movement was born during the civil rights upheavals of the 1960s. During the 1960s, Mexican Americans protested for Spanish in schools and the teaching of Mexican American history and culture. In 1968, Mexican American students boycotted four East Los Angeles high schools, demanding bilingual programs, courses in Mexican American history and culture, and the serving of Mexican American food in school cafeterias. In addition, students demanded the hiring of more Spanish-speaking teachers and the firing of teachers who seemed anti–Mexican American.

The school boycotts in Los Angeles attracted the attention of the newly formed La Raza Unida. La Raza Unida was formed in 1967, when a group of Mexican Americans boycotted federal hearings on the social conditions of Mexican Americans and started their own conference. At the conference, La Raza Unida took a militant stand on the protection of the rights of Mexican Americans and the preservation of their culture and language. As quoted by Guadalupe San Miguel, Jr., in his book *"Let All of Them Take Heed": Mexican Americans and the Campaign for Educational Equality in Texas, 1910–1981,* the statement drafted at the first conference proclaimed: "The time of subjugation, exploitation, and abuse of human rights of La Raza in the United States is hereby ended forever." La Raza Unida's statement on the preservation of culture and language reflected the growing mood in the Mexican American community that public schools needed to pay more attention to dominated cultures and languages. The statement drafted at the first conference affirmed "the greatness of our heritage, our history, our language, our traditions, our contributions to humanity and our culture."

Politicians responded to Mexican American and Puerto Rican demands for the preservation of Spanish in the schools. Senator Ralph Yarborough of Texas, believing that he would lose the 1970 election to a wealthy and conservative Democrat, decided that Hispanic support was crucial for his coalition of blacks, Mexican Americans, and poor whites. To win Hispanic support, Yarborough, after being appointed to a special subcommittee on bilingual education of the Senate Committee on Labor and Public Welfare, launched a series of hearings in major Hispanic communities.

The testimony at these hearings came primarily from representatives of the Mexican American and Puerto Rican communities, and not educational experts or linguistic theorists. The hearings concluded in East Harlem, with Senator Edward Kennedy and Bronx Borough President Herman Badillo decrying the facts that there were no Puerto Rican principals and only a few Puerto Rican teachers in the New York City school system.

Yarborough supported bilingual legislation that focused on students whose "mother tongue is Spanish." The legislation included programs to impart knowledge and pride about Hispanic culture and language and to bring descendants of Mexican Americans and Puerto Ricans into the teaching profession. The legislation was clearly designed to win political support from the Hispanic community in Texas. Yarborough's efforts resulted in the passage of the previously mentioned Bilingual Education Act of 1968.

Native Americans along with Mexican Americans and Puerto Ricans welcomed the idea of bilingual education. On the other hand, some members of the Republican Party joined a movement opposing bilingual education and supporting the adoption of English as the official language of the United States. The movement for making English the official language was led by an organization, U.S. English, founded in 1983 by S. I. Hayakawa, a former Republican senator.

Some educators now argue that bilingual education is necessary for the growing Asian population in the United States. In *Myth or Reality: Adaptive Strategies of Asian-Americans in California,* Henry Trueba, Li Rong Lilly Cheng, and Kenji Ima advocate bilingual education for Asian Americans who are having difficulty learning English. They contend that many Asian immigrants are never able to enter mainstream classrooms because they never learn English. Consequently, many Asian Americans drop out of school before graduation. These Asian American dropouts often go unnoticed because of the academic success of other Asian American students. According to their study, Asian immigrants who received no prior training in English before coming to the United States are most at risk for dropping out of school. The importance of prior training in English for academic success is highlighted by the argument "that the higher academic performance of Asians in contrast with Hispanics is consistent with the fact that 31 percent of Asians had trained in English before their arrival . . . in contrast with only 3 percent for Hispanics."

In addition, certain Asian immigrants come from areas with oral traditions and they have little exposure to written materials in their own language. This is particularly true of children from the Pacific Islands, Laotian rural groups, and Montagnards from Vietnam. This lack of exposure to a written language is a major obstacle to learning English. These students, it is argued, have difficulty differentiating between the written language forms of the classroom and oral language forms.

But even Asian American students who are successful in school continue to have language problems. At both the undergraduate and graduate levels in college, Asian Americans are predominantly in engineering, physical sciences, mathematics, and computer sciences. "Asian students," the authors write, "pursue occupations they perceive as having higher status and ones in which communicative language skills are less required." Choosing fields requiring little communicative skills limits Asian American choices in the job market.

While bilingual education remains a controversial issue, many non-English-speaking students are served primarily by English as a Second Language (ESL) programs. Although the teachers of these programs might speak the language of the students, the primary purpose of ESL classes is to teach students English so that they can learn the content of instruction in English. Unlike bilingual education programs, no attempt is made to teach reading and writing in the native language of the students.

The differences between bilingual and ESL education programs highlight the bicultural aspects of bilingualism. The general goal of ESL is the learning of English and, as a result, the gaining of knowledge about European American culture. On the other hand, Mexican Americans, Native Americans, and Puerto Ricans advocate bilingualism to retain both the student's native language and culture while learning English and European American culture.

The bitter fights over language policies are exemplified by voter response to California's Proposition 227, which severely limited the use of bilingual education as a method for teaching English. The election can be considered a gauge of public opinion regarding bilingual education. Table 5–1 summarizes an exit poll on Proposition 227 conducted on June 2, 1998, and reported by the *Los Angeles Times/Washington Edition*. A yes vote on Proposition 227 can be considered a vote against bilingual instruction as a method for teaching English.

Political attitudes, as is the case regarding most educational issues, were the primary factor in differentiating attitudes about bilingual education. As indicated in Table 5–1, 77 percent of those identifying themselves as Republicans and conservatives voted against bilingual education by voting yes for Proposition 227. In contrast, 53 percent of Democrats and 64 percent of liberals voted for bilingual education by voting no on Proposition 227. There are also sharp racial and ethnic differences in support of bilingual education. Sixty-seven percent of white voters voted for Proposition 227, while 63 percent of Latino vot-

**TABLE 5–1. Exit Poll on California Proposition 227 Conducted on June 2, 1998**

| Category | % of All Voters | % Yes on 227 | % No on 227 |
|---|---|---|---|
| Sex | | | |
| Male | 52% | 64% | 36% |
| Female | 48 | 57 | 43 |
| Race/ethnicity | | | |
| White | 69 | 67 | 33 |
| Black | 14 | 48 | 52 |
| Latino | 12 | 37 | 63 |
| Asian | 3 | 57 | 43 |
| Political affiliation | | | |
| Democrat | 48 | 47 | 53 |
| Independent | 6 | 59 | 41 |
| Republican | 40 | 77 | 23 |
| Political philosophy | | | |
| Liberal | 20 | 36 | 64 |
| Moderate | 43 | 59 | 41 |
| Conservative | 37 | 77 | 23 |

*Source:* "Exit Polls on the June 2nd Vote on Proposition 227," *Los Angeles Times/Washington Edition* (4 June 1998), http://www.latimes.com/.

ers voted against it. The 37 percent of the Latino population that voted for Proposition 227 indicates a division among Spanish speakers about the best way to learn English. However, a majority of Latinos did indicate their approval of bilingual education.

## ENGLISH LANGUAGE ACQUISITION ACT OF 2001

In 2001, a majority of Congress and President George W. Bush opposed bilingual education and stood firmly for the principle that the primary objective of U.S. schools should be the teaching of English without any attempt to preserve minority languages. The one limited exception was for Native Americans and Puerto Ricans. While recognizing programs designed to maintain Native American languages and Spanish, the major thrust, the legislation states, of these programs had to be English proficiency. The legislation declares that

> programs authorized under this part that serve Native American (including Native American Pacific Islander) children and children in the Commonwealth of Puerto Rico may include programs . . . designed for Native American children learning and studying Native American languages and children of limited Spanish proficiency, except that an outcome of programs serving such children *shall be increased English proficiency among such children* [my emphasis].

The English Language Acquisition Act's nine major purposes clearly spell out the antibilingual education agenda. As the Office of Bilingual Education becomes the Office of English Acquisition, the goals focus on learning English in the context of state academic standards and high-stakes testing. The first stated purpose of the legislation crystallizes the English language acquisition objectives: "(1) to help ensure that children who are limited English proficient, including immigrant children and youth, attain English proficiency, develop high levels of academic attainment in English, and meet the same challenging State academic content and student academic achievement standards as all children are expected to meet." The rest of the eight legislative purposes support this first goal, including (2) preparation for learning core academic subjects; (3) developing language instructional programs for limited English proficient students; (4) designing instructional programs that prepare limited English proficient children to enter all-English instruction settings; (5) continuing English instruction for limited English proficient children; (6) designing language instruction programs for the parents and communities of limited English proficient children; and (7) streamlining the grant programs for English language acquisition.

The eighth purpose gives the federal government supervisory power to ensure that states comply with the intent of the legislation. Even if a state government supports bilingual education, it is now faced with the problem of having to refuse any federal money granted under this legislation. The legislation requires that state governments measure English proficiency. The eighth purpose clearly states that the federal government will "hold State educational agencies, local educational agencies, and schools accountable for increases in English proficiency and core academic content knowledge of limited English proficient children by requiring—(A) demonstrated improvements in the English proficiency of limited English proficient children each fiscal year." The ninth and final purpose uses the language of "scientifically based research" to ensure that schools do not use bilingual education methods to teach English proficiency.

The larger question is whether politicians and the federal government should ever have been involved in the struggle to protect minority languages. The English Language Acquisition Act of 2001 replaces the goals and programs of the Bilingual Education Act of 1968. Will some future federal legislation resurrect federal involvement in bilingualism? Imagine the waste of time and money in replacing the Office of Bilingual Education with the Office of English Language Acquisition! Of course, there will continue to be a struggle between the advocates of English-only and those wanting to protect minority languages. This issue will persist in debates about American education.

## BICULTURAL EDUCATION: IS THIS THE ANSWER?

*Bicultural education* provides another method of dealing with the resistance to schooling exhibited by students from dominated cultures. Biculturalism means being able to function in another culture without losing ties to one's original culture. Currently, biculturalism is an important part of Native American education. Until the 1960s and 1970s, federal policies for Indian education were premised on the idea that deculturalization had to take place before the Native American could function in the world of the European American. In contrast to these policies, biculturalism is designed to help Native American youth function in the world of the dominant culture without having to sacrifice traditional Indian cultures.

One of the important advocates of biculturalism for Native Americans is educator and poet Mick Fedullo. The central feature of Fedullo's approach to biculturalism is easing Indian children into the use of English by having them do creative writing on themes relevant to Indian culture. In this manner, learning English does not serve as a tool of deculturalization, but it serves to express cultural pride. Indian children can cross over into the use of English without feeling they are betraying their cultural heritage. Through student publications and the creation of calendars using student poetry, Fedullo makes students proud of their culture and their ability to write in English. In addition, Fedullo helps Indian students to understand the cultural differences between Native Americans and European Americans. One of his most striking lessons was given to Apache students on the subject of prejudice against Indians. The lesson opened with a brief discussion of the meaning of the word *prejudice* and quickly moved on to the question of the types of prejudice encountered by the Apache students. The first issue raised by the students was being stared at by whites in the local town. In the cultural world of these Apache students, being stared at is a sign of hostility and prejudice. As Fedullo led the students through the discussion, the students began to realize that being stared at is not necessarily a result of hostility and prejudice. Some whites might be staring because of curiosity and interest, while others might truly be hostile. The lesson left the students with less apprehension and greater understanding about crossing the border into white culture. In this lesson, Fedullo did not ask the Apache students to abandon their cultural rules that staring is impolite and aggressive, but he helped them understand that white society functions under different cultural rules.

As Fedullo introduces Indian students to the dominant culture, he constantly reminds them that there is nothing wrong with their cultural traditions and that these traditions do not have to be abandoned to function in the world of the dominant culture. For instance, Fedullo accompanied a group of Apache students from the Apache reservation in Arizona to Spokane, Washington. It was the first time many of these students had visited a city, and they were in awe of such things as parking meters and escalators. One of the major events on the trip was eating in an expensive restaurant. Before going to the restaurant, Fedullo prefaced his instructions on table etiquette by explaining that there were many ways of conducting oneself at a meal. For instance, reservation manners require that at Indian feasts children and younger adults do not approach the food until after the elders are served. Also, Fedullo explained to the children that the manners they were teaching the children were appropriate for restaurants but not for all situations.

The destructive consequences of European Americans failing to learn to be bicultural are well illustrated in Fedullo's story about the anger Navajo students felt toward a new counselor who, for Navajo culture, was too probing and aggressive in his questioning. By unknowingly breaking the rules of Navajo culture, the counselor gained nothing but the hatred and scorn of the students.

The consequences of not receiving a bicultural education are also well illustrated in the previously mentioned autobiography by Richard Rodriguez. The autobiography describes Rodriguez's education from elementary school to his eventual graduate work in one of the temples of European American culture—the British Museum. Throughout the autobiography, he describes his increasing alienation from the Mexican American culture of his family as he absorbed the dominant European American culture. He is never taught how to move between the two cultural worlds and to appreciate the long history of Mexican American culture. His education involves the subtraction of one culture and its replacement by another. Bicultural education would have made European American culture an addition to his existing cultural framework rather than requiring a subtraction of his Mexican American heritage.

## GLOBALIZATION: LANGUAGE AND CULTURAL RIGHTS

The issues surrounding language and culture of the schools are present in most of the world's nations. Most nations are now multicultural and multilingual. As a result, there has been a call for international recognition of language and cultural rights. A longtime champion of these international rights, Tove Skutnabb-Kangas proposes a universal covenant protecting linguistic human rights as part of the protection of cultural rights. Key to her proposal is the definition of a mother tongue. A mother tongue, she writes, can be distinguished as "the language one learned first (the language one has established the first long-lasting verbal contacts in)" or "the language one identifies with/as a native speaker of; and/or the language one knows best."

Of fundamental importance to Tove Skutnabb-Kangas's Universal Covenant of Linguistic Human Rights is the stress on bilingual education if the student's language is not the official national language or the language of global culture and economics, which at this time is English. Bilingualism resolves the problem of maintaining the mother tongue and associated culture, while ensuring that the student has access to the world's knowledge. According to her Universal Covenant, everybody has the right to

- Identify with his/her mother tongue(s) and have this identification accepted and respected by others.
- Learn the mother tongue(s) fully, orally (when physiologically possible) and in writing.
- Profit from education mainly through the medium of his/her mother tongue(s) and within the state-financed educational system.
- Use the mother tongue in most official situations (including schools).

In reference to other languages, the covenant states that those "whose mother tongue is not an official language in the country where s/he is resident . . . [have the right] to become bilingual (or trilingual, if s/he has 2 mother tongues) in the mother tongue(s) and (one of) the official language(s) (according to her own choice)." Additionally, "any change . . . [in] mother tongue . . . [should be] voluntary (includes knowledge of long-term consequences) . . . [and] not imposed."

Applied to the United States, this covenant would mean that students whose mother tongues were not English would have the right to receive instruction in their mother tongues but would not have to exercise that right. In other words, students could choose to be instructed in English. The covenant also guarantees that all children will learn English, the dominant language of the United States. Essentially, students would have the right to a bilingual education if they wanted.

Some constitutions of other nations specifically recognize language rights. For instance, the Italian Constitution states, "The Republic shall safeguard linguistic minorities by means of special provisions." The Indian Constitution provides specific protection for minority language rights. The Indian Constitution states:

> 350. **Facilities for instruction in mother-tongue at primary stage.** It shall be the endeavor of every State and of every local authority within the State to provide adequate facilities for instruction in the mother-tongue at the primary stage of education to children belonging to linguistic minority groups.

Should the government be required to provide classes in a mother tongue that is spoken by only one or two students in a community? Realistically, the educational rights of minority languages can only be exercised when there is a sufficient number of students speaking a language. This is particularly a problem in a country with a high number of immigrants like the United States. Considering this problem an international agreement on language rights might state:

> Everyone has a right to an education using the medium of his/her mother-tongue within a government-financed school system when the number of students requesting instruction in that mother-tongue equals the average number of students in a classroom in that government-financed school system.

Of equal importance is learning the dominant or official language of society. Therefore, an addition to the right to learn minority languages might state:

> Everyone has the right to learn the dominant or official language of the nation. The government-financed school system will make every effort to ensure that all students are literate in the dominant or official language of the country.

Cultural rights are an important issue for indigenous peoples such as Native Americans. The United Nation's International Labor Office defines indigenous peoples as "tribal peoples in independent countries whose social, cultural and economic conditions distinguish them from other sections of the national community, and whose status is regulated wholly or partially by their own customs or traditions." In addition, the definition includes those groups who identify themselves as indigenous. This definition of indigenous includes, for example, Native Americans and Hawaiians in the United States, Aborigines in Australia, Mayans in Guatemala, Maoris in New Zealand, and Hmongs in Laos. The World Commission on Culture and Development estimates that in 1995, indigenous peoples composed 7 percent of the population of China and India (80 and 65 million, respectively). In the Americas, the largest numbers of indigenous peoples are in Peru (8.6 million) and Mexico (8 million). In Africa, the number is 25 million. The international group Worldwatch estimates that there are at least 300 million indigenous people worldwide and that between 4,000 and 5,000 of the 6,000 world languages are spoken by indigenous peoples.

A Draft Declaration of Indigenous Peoples Rights has been proposed to the United Nations. The declaration asserts, with regard to human rights and development,

> That the indigenous peoples have been deprived of their *human rights and fundamental freedoms,* resulting . . . in their colonization and dispossession of their lands, territories, and resources, thus preventing them from exercising, in particular, *their right to development in accordance with their own needs and interests* [my emphasis].

Regarding the right to education, the declaration asserts that indigenous children have a right to education in their own language and according to cultural practices. Article 15 states:

> Indigenous children have the right to all levels and forms of education of the State. All indigenous peoples also have this right and the right to establish and control their educational systems and institutions providing education in their own languages, in a manner appropriate to their cultural methods of teaching and learning.

Recognition of these rights in the United States would guarantee that Native Americans would have the right to operate their own schools according to the principles of their cultures and using their languages.

## *CONCLUSION*

The struggle over issues of language and culture will continue as dominated groups struggle for equality of opportunity and as new immigrant groups adjust to American society. On a global scale, issues of multicultural, ethnocentric, bicultural, and bilingual education will become increasingly important with the development of a global economy and the internationalization of the labor force. The United States is not the only country confronting these issues. Many European American countries have begun multicultural education programs because of the influx of foreign workers.

In the United States, a central conflict will continue between those who want to maintain the supremacy of English and European American traditions and dominated cultures whose members want to protect and maintain their cultural traditions. Many Native Americans, African Americans, and Hispanics reject the image of European American culture at the head of a dinner table ruling over other cultures. In addition, many immigrant groups might not be willing to give up their cultural traditions to a European American model. But whatever the conclusion of this conflict, American public schools will never be the same after the impact of the cultural and language demands of dominated groups and after the adjustment of educational programs to meet the needs of the new immigrants.

The discussion of multiculturalism generates the following set of questions:

- Should public schools teach a common culture to all students? Should that common culture be based on a Eurocentric culture?
- Should English be the official language of the United States?
- Should students have the right to learn their mother tongue and the dominant language?
- Should students have the right to receive instruction in their own culture?
- Should the major goal of instruction about different cultures be the teaching of appreciation of other cultures?
- Should public schools teach non-Eurocentric cultural traditions to maintain those cultural traditions?
- Should multicultural education attempt to change the dominant culture by incorporating values from other cultures?

## Suggested Readings and Works Cited in Chapter

ASANTE, MOLEFI KETE. *Afrocentricity*. Trenton, NJ: Africa World Press, Inc., 1988. *This is an important discussion of the philosophy of Afrocentricity.*

BANKS, JAMES. "Multicultural Education: Historical Development, Dimensions, and Practice." In *Review of Research in Education 19*, edited by Linda Darling-Hammond. Washington, DC: American Educational Research Association, 1993, pp. 3–50. *This article is an excellent introduction to the development of the field of multicultural education.*

DELPIT, LISA. *Other People's Children: Cultural Conflict in the Classroom.* New York: The New Press, 1995. *Delpit provides a strong argument for utilizing a student's culture to prepare him/her for success in the economic power structure of the United States.*

"Exit Polls on the June 2nd Vote on Proposition 227," *Los Angeles Times/Washington Edition* (4 June 1998). http://www.latimes.com/. *Provides results of voting on bilingual issue in California.*

FEDULLO, MICK. *Light of the Feather: Pathways Through Contemporary Indian America.* New York: William Morrow, 1992. *Fedullo provides a beautiful description of the development of bicultural education among Native Americans.*

IGOA, CHRISTINA. *The Inner World of the Immigrant Child.* Mahwah, NJ: Lawrence Erlbaum Associates, Inc., 1995. *This is an invaluable guide to instructing immigrating children and dealing with their educational and psychological problems.*

KUNJUFU, JAWANZA. *Countering the Conspiracy to Destroy Black Boys.* Chicago: African American Images, 1985. *This book provides a strong argument for the necessity of an Afrocentric curriculum.*

———. *To Be Popular or Smart: The Black Peer Group.* Chicago: African American Images, 1988. *This is a discussion of the attitudes of African American youth regarding education.*

LAMAR, JAKE. *Bourgeois Blues: An American Memoir.* New York: Penguin, 1992. *This powerful contemporary autobiography details the racism encountered by an upper-middle-class African American.*

NIETO, SONIA.   *Affirming Diversity: The Sociopolitical Context of Multicultural Education.* White Plains, NY: Longman, Inc., 1992. *This is a good introduction to issues in multicultural education.*

OGBU, JOHN.   "Class Stratification, Racial Stratification, and Schooling." In *Class, Race, & Gender in American Education,* edited by Lois Weis. Albany: State University of New York Press, 1988, pp. 163–183. *In this article, Ogbu outlines his basic theory for the development of resistance to schooling among dominated cultures in the United States.*

PORTER, ROSALIE PEDALINO.   *Forked Tongue: The Politics of Bilingual Education.* New York: Basic Books, 1990. *Porter attacks maintenance bilingual education programs. The book is a good introduction to the controversy surrounding bilingual education.*

Public Law 107–110, 107th Congress, Jan. 8, 2002 [H.R. 1]. "No Child Left Behind Act of 2001." Washington, DC: U.S. Printing Office, 2002. *Federal legislation contains the English Acquisition, Language Enhancement, and Academic Achievement Act which overturns the 1968 Bilingual Education Act.*

RODRIGUEZ, RICHARD.   *Hunger of Memory: The Education of Richard Rodriguez.* New York: Bantam Books, 1982. *This is an important autobiography of the emotional and social struggles of a successful Mexican American student.*

"SETCLAE: Self-Esteem Through Culture Leads to Academic Excellence." Chicago: African American Images, 1991. *This is a model Afrocentric curriculum.*

SPRING, JOEL.   *Education and the Rise of the Global Economy.* Mahwah, NJ: Lawrence Erlbaum Associates, Inc., 1998. *This book describes the process of globalization of education through colonialism and current economic policies.*

_____. *Globalization and Educational Rights: An Intercivilizational Analysis.* Mahwah, NJ: Lawrence Erlbaum Associates, Inc., 2000. *This book discusses educational rights in the context of Confucian, Moslem, Hindu, and Western civilizations and as provided for in the constitutions of the world's nations. The book offers a statement of educational rights that could be included in national constitutions.*

_____. *The Universal Right to Education: Justification, Definition, and Guidelines.* Mahwah, NJ: Lawrence Erlbaum Associates, Inc., 2000. *This book provides a justification for the universal right to education provided by the Universal Declaration of Human Rights. The books discusses cultural, language, and child rights. It provides examples of human rights teaching.*

TRUEBA, HENRY et al.   *Myth or Reality: Adaptative Strategies of Asian-Americans in California.* New York: Falmer Press, 1993. *This is a study of Asian American adjustments to social life in California.*

# PART TWO

# Power and Control in American Education

## CHAPTER 6

# Local Control, Choice, Charter Schools, and Commercialism

## LOCAL CONTROL, CHOICE, CHARTER SCHOOLS, AND COMMERCIALISM

The No Child Left Behind Act of 2001 provides money for parents with children in low-performing schools to choose another public school for their children. This school choice plan will supposedly give parents greater power to determine their children's education. The No Child Left Behind Act, which I will analyze in more detail later in this chapter in "School Choice," is one of many proposals for changing the balance of power over the control of education. Others include site-based management, home schooling, and charter schools. This chapter will deal with these issues along with the role of local school boards. These topics reflect a fundamental question about who or what agency should control the education of America's children. In the next section, I will explore the problems in answering this question.

## THE EDUCATION CHAIR

One way of thinking about the problem of control is to imagine yourself sitting in what I will call the *education chair*. Imagine that at a flick of a lever this chair has the power to shape your morality, to control your behavior, and to teach you any subject. This education chair can be considered a public school that works. After all, the goals of public schooling include moral instruction, shaping behavior, and transmitting knowledge.

Now the question is, who should control this education chair? In other words, who should decide your morality, behavior, and knowledge? You? Your parents? Your professor of education? Elected officials? How you answer this question will reflect the political values you have regarding the control of public schools.

Currently, the debate over who should control education has ranged from the business community to religious organizations to minority parents. Many groups have a stake in the outcomes of public schooling. The business community wants graduates with knowledge and behaviors that conform to its needs. Some religious organizations want schools to teach their versions of morality. In fact, a major controversy in recent years has involved fundamentalist Protestant churches accusing the public schools of teaching a morality that is destructive to their religious principles. Minority parents complain that public schools are damaging to their children because they teach the culture and values of the white elite.

Understanding the concept of representation is important for answering the question of who should control American education. The United States is primarily composed of representative forms of government; that is, people elect government officials to represent them on school boards, in state legislatures, and in Congress. In only a few situations, such as voting on local property taxes, are decisions made by the direct vote.

While reading this chapter, you should keep in mind the following questions:

- Who should decide what knowledge is of most worth to be taught in public schools?
- Do you think public schools should let parents decide what should be taught to their children?
- Should parents receive government funding to send their children to a private secular school, a religious school, or a for-profit school?
- Do you think the government should only finance parental choice of public schools?
- Should state charter school laws finance private secular schools, religious schools, or for-profit schools?

## SCHOOL BOARDS

Traditionally, community members exercised their control over public schools by electing representatives to local school boards. In turn, the school board appoints the superintendent of schools who functions as the chief executive officer of the school district. Usually, the superintendent of schools works out of the central office of the school district. School principals report directly to the central office and the superintendent.

This traditional district organization is criticized for its lack of responsiveness to the desires of parents. School board members are criticized as not being representative of the interests of the parents. The central office and superintendent are criticized for being bureaucratic barriers to any real change in the school district. As I will discuss later in this chapter, home schooling, school choice, and charter schools are promoted as giving power to parents when faced with unrepresentative school boards and an entrenched bureaucratic structure in the central office.

Criticisms of school boards not being representative of parental desires touch upon a basic problem in representative governments such as those in the

United States. The issue involves the concepts of *trustee* and *delegate* representation. Most school boards operate on the principle of trustee representation. Trustee forms of representation are premised on the idea that decisions, particularly about social institutions such as schools, should be removed from the immediate control of the general population. For instance, a school board member acting as a trustee would make decisions based on what he or she believes is good for the public. These types of decisions might often be contrary to what the public actually wants. The public interest or general good as defined by the board member might not represent the true wishes of the public.

A delegate form of representation reflects the actual desires of the voters. Decision making is based on what the representative believes the public wants. This form of representation is preferred by those who believe that social institutions should function according to what people want and not based on the representative's personal interpretation of the public good. It is argued that those who try to make decisions based on a set of beliefs about what constitutes the public good cannot separate their own beliefs from the decision-making process.

Most school board elections in the United States are organized around the concept of trustee representation to limit public participation in direct control of school board affairs. This is accomplished through at-large and nonpartisan elections. In at-large elections a person running for the school board must be elected by the entire voting population of a school district. This means a person must have enough money and organizational support to campaign throughout the school system. In contrast, during the nineteenth century the voting districts for many school board elections were confined to limited geographical areas within a school district. In such situations a person did not need a great deal of financial backing to campaign within a small area and could win elections based on neighborhood contacts. This method of election made it easier for the average person to win elections to the school board. It can be argued that at-large elections favor trustee forms of representation, while the other types of election favor delegate forms of representation because there is more direct contact between the elector and the elected.

Nonpartisan elections also favor the election of elites to school boards. In *Nonpartisan Elections and the Case for Party Politics,* Willis Hawley argues that nonpartisan elections create a partisan bias in favor of Republicans. In this argument he is associating Republicans with community elites. Nonpartisan means that regular political parties cannot nominate and campaign for a particular candidate. When this is the case, Hawley argues, informal networks begin to operate to select and provide support for candidates. These informal networks are generally composed of civic-business clubs such as the Chamber of Commerce, Kiwanis Club, Rotary, and other luncheon-service clubs.

In the twentieth century boards of education were criticized for their elite membership. In other words, their membership primarily is drawn from the professional and business groups in the local community. This is not so true in rural areas, where there is often heavy representation from the farm community. Most boards of education in the United States are composed of white male professionals or businesspeople. The representation from this group on boards of education is out of proportion to their actual numbers in the population so it does not reflect the social composition of the local community.

Some educators view the elite nature of school boards as a positive asset to the local school district. Joseph M. Cronin in his history *The Control of Urban Schools* found that educators during the early part of the twentieth century believed it was important to have successful and well-educated men on the school board because this social group was more knowledgeable and more interested in education than the rest of the population. In fact, the limited size and centralization of urban school boards were designed to limit public participation in school affairs to the social leaders of the community. Opposition to this trend came from organized labor, which felt that board membership drawn from only one sector of the community would result in the domination of school policy by certain political and economic views.

## WHO KNOWS THEIR SCHOOL BOARD MEMBERS?

Ask people in your community to name the members of the local school board. Most frequently, you will be greeted with a shrug of the shoulders and a curious smile. Even parents who are deeply interested in their child's education will frequently be unable to identify school board members. Yet board members continue to play an important role in shaping policies that affect teachers and students. Why is there such low visibility for board members? Is this related to the nature of school board elections?

The linkage between the school board and the community power structure is important for understanding the actions of board members; it is also important for understanding the relationship between the board and the school administration. To be effective and for job protection the superintendent of schools must have a cooperative and friendly board of education. Therefore, school administrators favor school board members who have successful business or professional backgrounds.

In *The School Managers: Power and Conflict in American Public Education*, Donald McCarty and Charles Ramsey provide a classification of the relationships between community power structures, school boards, and administrative styles. They assume that the type of community power structure determines the nature of the school board and the administrative style of the superintendent. They divide community power structures into the following:

1. Dominated
2. Factional
3. Pluralistic
4. Inert

In dominated communities majority power is exercised by a few persons or one person. Usually, these people are part of the community's economic elite, though sometimes they could be leaders of ethnic, religious, or political groups.

**TABLE 6–1. Community Power Structures, School Boards, and Superintendents**

| Power Structures | Types of School Boards | Superintendent Styles |
|---|---|---|
| Dominated | Dominated | Functionary |
| Factional | Factional | Political |
| Pluralistic | Pluralistic | Adviser |
| Inert | Sanctioning | Decision making |

Factional communities are usually characterized by two factions competing for power. Very often these factions differ in values, particularly religious values. Pluralistic communities have a great deal of competition among a variety of community interest groups with no single group dominating school policies. And in inert communities, there is no visible power structure and there is little display of public interest in the schools.

Table 6–1 indicates the types of school boards and superintendent styles classified by McCarty and Ramsey.

In a dominated community, the local elite controls access to membership on the school board and, consequently, controls school board policies. To retain his or her position, the superintendent must follow the wishes of the community elite. McCarty and Ramsey studied one dominated community where a superintendent protested his firing by a school board acting against the wishes of the local power elite. In response to the situation, the community elite met in the offices of a local bank and decided, to avoid community conflict, to let the superintendent be fired. Simultaneously, they decided the school board had gotten out of control. The most respected member of the elite group was made the chair of the school board's nomination committee, and the committee's membership was selected to ensure elite control. (Traditionally, those recommended by the nomination committee were elected to the school board without opposition.) Finally, the leading members of the community kept a close watch on the nominating committee for several years to ensure the selection of candidates they approved.

In a factional community, the survival of a superintendent depends on his or her ability to function as a political strategist balancing the concerns of each community faction. In a factional community studied by McCarty and Ramsey, the major competing groups were permissive Jewish and conservative Catholic populations. The two groups represented almost equal populations in the school district, and the control of the school board shifted from group to group in each highly contested election. The campaigns were very emotional, with each group accusing the other of undermining the quality of education. When McCarty and Ramsey arrived in the community, liberals on the school board had lost their majority to conservatives who immediately fired the superintendent. The fired superintendent, according to McCarty and Ramsey, failed as a political strategist because he appeared to favor the previous liberal majority.

The competition among a variety of groups in a pluralistic community results in constantly shifting coalitions on the school board. In the community studied by McCarty and Ramsey, a dispute over a bond issue created a coalition of Catholics, the Chamber of Commerce, and a labor union in opposition, and Protestant churches and the PTA in support. The superintendent in this community played the role of the professional adviser. On the bond issue, his support was given in professional statements about the need for additional classrooms and more teachers. In the role of a professional adviser to a pluralistic board, the superintendent should move cautiously to avoid adverse community reaction to proposals for change.

Finally, inert communities give most of the power over school issues to the superintendent. McCarty and Ramsey describe inert communities as ideologically homogeneous and without a sense of purpose. In most situations, the composition of the board is indirectly controlled by the superintendent. Board members turn to the superintendent for leadership and decision making. Sometimes, McCarty and Ramsey report, the superintendent claimed that board members accepted 99 percent of his or her proposals. Very seldom in inert communities does the board turn to leaders outside the school system for advice on educational matters.

In all four of these categories, superintendents prefer school board members who have successful business or professional backgrounds. In *Governing American Schools,* Zeigler and Jennings found that board members from lower socioeconomic groups are more involved in administrative detail than those from higher socioeconomic groups. For the superintendent, board-member involvement in administrative details can restrict the actions of the administrative staff. Usually, superintendents prefer board members to restrict their activities to general educational policies.

The major objection to the elitist composition of American school boards is that they do not reflect the interests and opinions of all members of the community. Basic disagreements over educational policy can occur among social groups. For instance, higher-status groups in a community may give strong support to a vocational program for lower-status children, whereas lower-status groups may disapprove of this type of program because they want a college preparatory program for their children to provide upward mobility. Which group is right here is not important for this discussion. What is important is that fundamental differences among social groups can exist over educational policy; however, the social composition of school boards and their linkage to the informal power structures of local communities are not reflected in debates among school board members.

## EDUCATIONAL BUREAUCRACY

Is bureaucracy bad? In earlier times, bureaucracies were seen as a means of protecting the public good from corrupt politicians and special interests. Bureaucrats are supposed to be public servants. From this perspective, school administrators, local superintendents, and educators serving in state and federal governments are supposed to be dedicated to serving the interests of the public and child. In local school districts, the educational bureaucracy is identified with the central office staff, which is usually composed of an administrative staff that deals with the overall organization of the school system's curriculum, financial matters, personnel policies, and all programs that affect any of the schools within a district. As for the control of local education, the central office staff is very important because it often controls the lines of communication among the building principals and teachers, and the superintendent.

Critics of educational bureaucracies claim that they are self-serving and resistant to change and improvement. Critics argue that the major goal of bureaucracy is to expand its numbers, protect its members, and gain increasing amounts of revenue. Arguments supporting site-based management, home schooling, choice, charter schools, and privatization usually attack the power of the educational bureaucracy. The goals of these plans are to give individual schools more autonomy by breaking the hold of the bureaucratic structure.

## SITE-BASED MANAGEMENT

Many states require individual public schools to have some form of *site-based management*. The goal is to increase teacher, parent, and community involvement in school governance. It is believed that this participation will improve the quality of individual schools. Ideally, site-based management involves school administrators, teachers, parents, and community members in decision making about the school budget, curriculum, and school activities. A survey conducted in the 1990s found that 56 percent of the schools in the United States had some form of site-based management. The numbers varied from state to state. For example, 86 percent of the schools in West Virginia report site-based management while only 22 percent of Nebraska schools have this form of decision making.

Site-based management is a means of strengthening the leadership role of teachers. Placed on site-based management teams, teachers can exert greater influence over important educational decisions. In its 2001 report, *Leadership for Student Learning: Redefining the Teacher as Leader,* the Institute for Educational Leadership contends that "there are at least ten areas, all of them having an impact on teacher-student relationships, where teacher involvement is actually essential to the health of a school." Participation on site-based management teams provides teachers with the opportunity to influence decisions in these 10 areas. The Institute for Educational Leadership lists the following issues that should involve teacher management:

1. Choosing textbooks and instructional materials.
2. Shaping the curriculum.
3. Setting standards for student behavior.
4. Deciding whether students are tracked into special classes.
5. Designing staff development and in-service programs.
6. Setting promotion and retention policies.
7. Deciding school budgets.

**TABLE 6–2. Percentage of Public Schools Whose Site-Based Management Team Was Composed of Various Individuals and Groups**

| Participant on Site-Based Management Team | Percentage of Teams with This Participant |
|---|---|
| Principal/vice principal | 96% |
| Teachers/department heads | 95 |
| Parents | 79 |
| Community representative | 37 |
| Students | 28 |
| Superintendent of district | 21 |

*Source:* National Center for Education Statistics, "How Widespread Is Site-Based Decisionmaking in the Public Schools?" (Washington, DC: U.S. Printing Office, December 1966), p. 2.

8. Evaluating teacher performance.
9. Selecting new teachers.
10. Selecting new administrators.

The U.S. Department of Education's example of the operation of site-based management in a suburban district just outside of Grand Rapids, Wyoming, includes many of the above recommended areas for teacher management. In 1987, Wyoming adopted a law requiring site-based management in individual schools. In this suburban district, each school is governed by a School Improvement Committee. School Improvement Committees consist of four teachers, a paraprofessional (such as a teacher's aide), a representative of the community, and the school principal. Each member of the committee has an equal vote. While serving on the committee, members receive an orientation to the operation of the school, seminars on state and federal programs and regulations, and workshops on leadership. The School Improvement Committee makes decisions about instruction, curriculum, the school budget, and personnel.

Nationally, as indicated in Table 6–2, most site-based management teams are composed of school administrators, teachers, and parents. The participation

**TABLE 6–3. Percentage of Public Schools Reporting Selected Functions of Their Site-Based Management Teams**

| Function of Site-Based Management Team | Percentage Performing This Function |
|---|---|
| Considers parent and community input on curriculum and student discipline issues | 83% |
| Aids principal in budget and spending issues | 66 |
| Confers on school personnel issues | 34 |

*Source:* National Center for Education Statistics, "How Widespread Is Site-Based Decisionmaking in the Public Schools?" (Washington, DC: U.S. Printing Office, December 1966), p. 2.

of students is a more controversial issue. As indicated in Table 6–2, student participation only occurs on 28 percent of site-based management teams.

What type of issues are dealt with by site-based management teams? Table 6–3 indicates that teams primarily deal with the individual school curriculum, student discipline, and the budget. Only a small percentage deal with school personnel issues such as the hiring and firing of staff.

## HOME SCHOOLING

Home schooling is one answer for parents who want to take charge of their children's education. Parents can dodge the control of an unrepresentative school board and school bureaucracy by educating their children at home; however, most states do regulate home schooling to some extent.

In 2000, the Home School Legal Defense Association reported 1.7 million home schoolers in the United States. "Put another way," the organization claimed, "there are more home school students [than all the public school students] in Wyoming, Vermont, Delaware, North Dakota, Alaska, South Dakota, Rhode Island, Montana, and Hawaii—combined." Home schooling is so popular that in 2000 Amazon.com, the online bookseller, announced the opening of a special bookstore for home schoolers. The Home School Legal Defense Association also claimed in 2000 that "home-schooled students scored higher than their traditionally educated peers on the ACT, one of the nation's two major college-entrance exams, for the third consecutive year."

Home schooling is now a global movement. Writing for *The Washington Times,* Andrea Billups reports, "Home schooling is rapidly expanding worldwide as families abroad search for options to guide their children's education amid growing concerns over lax educational standards and increasing violence in government-run schools." The Home School Legal Defense Association claims that its has been contacted by home educators from 25 countries for information on legalization of home schooling. Christopher J. Klicka, senior lawyer at the Home School Legal Defense Association, traveled to Germany and Japan in the summer of 2000 to work with families to gain legal protection.

Home schooling represents a rejection of traditional arguments for public schooling. Originally, common school reformers believed that all children should attend public schools where they would learn to get along with others and learn a common morality and culture. Public schools were to educate good citizens. Public schools were to create a community spirit. By the twentieth century, schools required certified teachers based on the belief that good teachers needed to be trained.

Home schooling tosses all these arguments out the window. By educating their children at home, home schooling advocates reject the belief that children should obtain a common morality and culture through the public schools. In fact, many fundamentalist Christian parents, a major source of support for home schooling, feel that public schools are both immoral and irreligious. They don't want their children exposed to the values taught by public schools. Others, such as politically liberal parents, home school their children because they reject the conservative economic and political philosophy of public schools. Some choose home schooling because of what they perceive to be the factorylike instruction of public schools.

Home schooling raises the issue of parental competence as teachers. Teachers' unions and members of the educational establishment believe this is a basic flaw. Can you trust parents to be good teachers? Do good teachers require special training and certification?

Another frequently asked question is whether home schoolers develop social skills. The Home School Legal Defense Association provides the following answers to this question:

- Home school support groups organize field trips, teaching co-ops, and tutoring services.
- Home-schooled youngsters are active in community sports, scouting, church activities, political volunteering, community service, and more.
- Home schoolers are taken to museums, parks, libraries, and other educational institutions.

James Dobson, a columnist for *The Washington Times*, writes,

> The great advantage of home schooling, in fact, is the protection it provides to vulnerable children against the wrong kind of socialization. When children interact in large groups, the strongest and most aggressive children quickly intimidate the weak and vulnerable. I am absolutely convinced that bad things happen to immature and "different" boys and girls when they are thrown into the highly competitive world of other children.

Laws governing home schooling vary between states. Table 6–4 provides examples of legal requirements in selected states. As shown, Illinois provides the maximum freedom among the four states with no requirements for testing, record keeping, teacher qualifications, or giving notice to school authorities. According to the Home School Legal Defense Association, in Illinois you simply have to declare your home a private school and follow the subject matter requirements. Home schoolers in Illinois are not obligated to report to local authorities. In contrast, New York requires home schoolers to file a notice with the local superintendent of schools, maintain attendance records, and report standardized test scores.

With regard to the controversial issue of teacher qualifications, none of the four states requires parents to be certified teachers. California law simply specifies "capable of teaching." Ohio law only requires a high school diploma. In addition, Ohio allows the home schoolteacher, who is without a high school diploma, to "work under a person with a baccalaureate degree until child's test scores show proficiency or parent earns diploma." Illinois requires no qualifications for home schooling teachers and New York simply requires "competent."

Although home schoolers see themselves at war against the monopoly of public schooling over control of their children's education, choice opens another possible door to parental power.

**TABLE 6–4. Laws Governing Home Schooling in Selected States**

|  | California | Illinois | Ohio | New York |
|---|---|---|---|---|
| Compulsory school age | Between 6 and 18 | Between 7 and 16 | Between 6 and 18 | Between 6 and 16 |
| Legal option to home schooling | Qualify as private school | Operate home school as a private school | Establish and operate a home school | Establish and operate a home school |
| Attendance required | None | 176 days per year | 900 hours per year | Equivalent of 180 days |
| Subjects required | Same as the public schools and in the English language | School subjects along with honesty, justice, kindness, and moral courage | Language arts geography, U.S. and Ohio history, government, math, health, physical education, fine arts, first aid, and science | Grades K–12: patriotism and citizenship, substance abuse, traffic safety, fire safety, and regular school subjects |
| Teacher qualifications | Must be "capable of teaching" | None | Must have a high school diploma | Must be "competent" |
| Notice | File an annual required affidavit with the local superintendent between Oct. 1 and Oct. 15 | None | Submit annual notice of intent with local superintendent | File annual notice with local superintendent |
| Record keeping required | Maintain an attendance register | None | None | Maintain attendance records |
| Testing required | None | None | Options: Standardized test scores, written narrative, approved alternative assessment | File an annual assessment based on standardized test |

*Source:* Home School Legal Defense Association, http://www.hslda.org.

*Source:* Jeff Parker/*Florida Today.* Reprinted with permission of Cagle Cartoons, Inc.

## *SCHOOL CHOICE*

From the 1960s to the No Child Left Behind Act of 2001, school choice has been touted as the answer to many school problems. The original 1960s proposal by economist Milton Friedman is very similar to the choice provisions of the No Child Left Behind Act of 2001. Both Friedman's proposal and this recent legislation provide parents with children in low-performing schools the opportunity to send their children to another public school. Milton Friedman's original proposal called for the government to give parents monetary vouchers that could be used to purchase an education for their children at any school. Parents would give the vouchers to the school that enrolled their child. The school would then turn the voucher over to the government for reimbursement. Vouchers are another method for distributing tax dollars to schools. As a free market economist, Friedman blamed the poor quality of public schools on the lack of competition. Also, he argued that impoverished parents are often trapped in poor school systems because they cannot afford to move to the school districts with better schools.

The free market aspects of Friedman's plan appealed to many school reformers. The assumption of free market economics is that competition will produce the best products. Free market advocates argue that if parents can choose between schools, then schools will be forced to improve to remain competitive. Schools are like any other product in the marketplace. If a large number of parents don't choose a particular school then that school would be forced to either change or shut down. If the school that is least attractive to parents wants to survive it will probably model itself after a school that is attractive to parents or create an entirely new educational package. Imagine the production of cars: if no one buys a particular car model, then the company must either discontinue the model or improve it.

Of course, schools differ from automobiles in that they are produced by the government and by private groups. The mix of public and private schools adds another dimension to choice plans. Should the government only issue vouchers that can be redeemed at public schools? Or, should the government issue vouchers that can be redeemed at both public and private schools? The answers to these questions are reflected in the following plans:

1. *Public School Choice.* Under this type of choice plan, students are free to choose any public school in their district or in the state. Traditionally, students are assigned to schools in their districts and if they wish to attend school in another district, then they are often required to pay tuition.
2. *Public-Private Choice.* Students can choose between a public or private school with the tuition at the private school being paid for by a government or privately issued voucher. Traditionally, students have the choice of private and public schools without government support. Government support of private school choice, some argue, provides the opportunity for children from low-income families to attend private schools.

Many supporters of religious schooling and free market advocates support the public-private model of choice. Supporters of private Catholic schools argued from the nineteenth century that it is unfair that they should pay for the education of public school students while paying for their children to attend a religious school. In addition, Catholics and Protestant fundamentalists complain that the moral values taught in public schools are destructive of the values of Christianity and that their only choice is to send their children to private religious schools. The rapid growth of private Catholic schools occurred in the nineteenth and early twentieth centuries, while privately operated fundamentalist Protestant schools grew rapidly in the latter half of the twentieth century.

In 1990, the choice idea received support from the work of two political scientists, John Chubb and Terry Moe. In their book *Politics, Markets & America's Schools,* they argue that a major hindrance to student achievement is the existence of large bureaucracies that control local schools. They maintain that bureaucracies work against the basic requirements of effective school organizations by imposing goals, structures, and requirements. Bureaucracies do not allow, according to Chubb and Moe, principals and teachers to exercise their professional expertise and judgment and deny them the flexibility needed to work effectively together to ensure student achievement. Chubb and Moe argue that schools controlled by competition in a free market have less bureaucracy and, consequently, promote student achievement.

The two teachers' unions are leading opponents of voucher systems that include religious schools. Union leadership argues that government money used

to finance vouchers for religious schools reduces the money available for the support of public schools. In 2000, the American Federation of Teachers (AFT) issued the following fact sheet that was highly critical of vouchers:

- California Voucher Measure Would Benefit Affluent: California's ballot proposal to give $4,000 vouchers for students to attend private or religious schools will be a $3 billion windfall to affluent parents whose children already attend private schools, says a study released by the Policy Analysis for California Education (PACE).
- Study's Pro-Voucher Findings Now in Doubt: A study released in August [2000] touting the effectiveness of vouchers in improving student achievement among African American students is now under a cloud. The study, authored by researcher Paul E. Peterson of Harvard University, reported that voucher students in New York City, Dayton, Ohio, and Washington, DC, outscored students who had applied for vouchers but did not get them. But in its September 15 edition, *The New York Times* reports that the company that gathered research for the New York City portion of the study, Mathematica Policy Research of Princeton, NJ, has taken the unusual step of issuing a statement challenging the study's claims.
- Milwaukee Voucher Program Overcharges Taxpayers Millions: A new study by the People for the American Way Foundation (August 2000) shows that a flaw in the formula for voucher funding in Wisconsin has cost the state's taxpayers an extra $11 million in a single year—at a time when

the public school system is cutting programs and staff to close a $32 million budget shortfall for the 2000–2001 school year.

• Vouchers vs. Small Class Size: Comparing Costs, Effects and Public Support—Given limited resources, what education reforms have the best chance of improving student achievement, especially for low-income children? This new AFT analysis compares two very different education approaches and concludes that small class size trumps vouchers in terms of results, costs, and public support.

## NATIONAL PUBLIC SCHOOL CHOICE PLAN: NO CHILD LEFT BEHIND ACT OF 2001

Originally, Republican supporters wanted to include in the No Child Left Behind Act a provision for parents of children in low-performing schools to receive a voucher that could be used to send their children to a private school. Democratic opposition forced this provision to be stripped from the legislation. In its final form, the legislation provided federal funds to pay for the transportation and related costs if parents of children in low-performing schools wanted to transfer them to another public school in the same school district.

In effect, the No Child Left Behind Act forced a limited plan for public school choice on the nation's school districts. The actual wording of this revolutionary federal mandate for public school choice and the qualifications for student participation in the program are stated in the legislation as:

> (E) PUBLIC SCHOOL CHOICE.—
> (i) IN GENERAL.—In the case of a school identified for school improvement [low-performing school] under this paragraph, the local educational agency shall, not later than the first day of the school year following such identification, provide all students enrolled in the school with the option to transfer to another public school served by the local educational agency . . . that has not been identified for school improvement [low-performing]. . . .
> (ii) RULE.—In providing students the option to transfer to another public school, the local educational agency shall give priority to the lowest achieving children from low-income families.

The No Child Left Behind Act encountered unexpected problems in its provision of money to parents of children in failing schools to choose another public school within the same school district. In the fall of 2002, the approximately 3.5 million children eligible for the choice plan either could not find room in another public school or their parents did not want to place them in a school outside their neighborhood. Consequently, only a few parents applied for the choice vouchers.

The problem of space was particularly acute in urban areas. In Baltimore there were 30,000 students in failing schools and only 194 spaces in classrooms in nonfailing schools. In addition, only 347 out 30,000 applied for these spaces. In Chicago, parents of 2,425 students of the 145,000 students in failing schools applied for transfers but there was only room for 1,170.

Some argue that part of the problem is a result of school districts not preparing for the exercise of choice. Paul Houston, director of the American

Association of School Administration, said that local school systems needed to adjust budgets, find more space for students in better performing schools, and hire extra teachers for these schools. The basic problem in transferring students from low-performing schools to other schools is the lack of money. While federal money is set aside to pay for transportation and other costs associated in transferral, no additional money is allocated to the well-performing schools to pay for more spaces.

## PUBLIC-PRIVATE CHOICE PLAN: THE STATE OF OHIO'S PILOT PROJECT SCHOLARSHIP PROGRAM

In Chapter 10, I will explore the legal issues in the U.S. Supreme Court ruling, *Zelman v. Simmons-Harris,* which deals with the Cleveland public-private choice plan. In this section, I will describe the plan and the issues that prompted the court case. The State of Ohio's Pilot Project Scholarship Program provides tuition aid vouchers to families residing in the Cleveland City School District. These vouchers can be used to attend any accredited private school or public schools in other school districts adjacent to the Cleveland City School District. The dollar amount of the tuition aid voucher is determined by the financial need of the family. Families below 200 percent of the poverty line could receive 90 percent of private school tuition up to $2,250. The legislative justification for the program is that educational choice of private schools increases the educational opportunities of children from poor families. It is also hoped the voucher plan will improve the test scores of the 90 percent of Cleveland's ninth graders who failed Ohio's basic proficiency test.

In reality, Cleveland parents are limited in choice to private schools. School districts surrounding Cleveland refuse to accept Cleveland students under the voucher program. Limited to private schools, Cleveland parents primarily use the vouchers to send their children to Catholic schools. In fact, 96 percent of the state-funded vouchers are redeemed at parochial schools. The public funding of religious schools resulted in the U.S. Supreme Court cases discussed in Chapter 10.

## CHARTER SCHOOLS

Charter schools represent another method of bypassing unrepresentative school boards and educational bureaucracy. The idea was first proposed by educator Ray Budde in the 1970s and then promoted by AFT President Albert Shanker in the 1990s. Minnesota and California had the first charter school laws in 1991 and 1992, respectively. State charter school legislation mushroomed in the 1990s and by 2002 there were 580,000 children enrolled in nearly 2,400 charter schools in 37 states.

The basic charter school structure involves some local agency applying to the state to receive a charter to operate as a school at public expense. The governmental relationship is directly between a charter school and the state agency responsible for granting charters. This allows a charter school to operate outside the control of the state educational bureaucracy and the local school board and its bureaucracy. Consequently, a charter school is free to experiment with different methods of instruction and school organization.

The No Child Left Behind Act provided $300 million in aid to local and state governments to support charter schools. Charter schools were also listed as an optional choice for parents with children in low-performing schools. The legislation provided an official federal government definition of a charter school. As noted in the definition below, charter schools are public schools. They are different from regular public schools in that they are, as stated in section (A) below, "exempt from significant State or local rules." This exemption is supposed to foster innovative teaching, curriculum, and school organization. Also, as stated in section (B), a charter school can be developed as a new public school or created from "an existing public school." According to federal legislation, as stated in section (F), they cannot charge tuition. Charter schools, per sections (E) and (G), cannot be affiliated with a religious institution and they cannot discriminate on the basis of age, race, gender, religion, ethnic origin, or disability. In addition, according to section (L), charter school students must take any state-required tests.

The No Child Left Behind Act of 2001 states:

(1) CHARTER SCHOOL.—The term "charter school" means a public school that—
　　(A) in accordance with a specific State statute authorizing the granting of charters to schools, is exempt from significant State or local rules that inhibit the flexible operation and management of public schools, but not from any rules relating to the other requirements of this paragraph;
　　(B) is created by a developer as a public school, or is adapted by a developer from an existing public school, and is operated under public supervision and direction;
　　(C) operates in pursuit of a specific set of educational objectives determined by the school's developer and agreed to by the authorized public chartering agency;
　　(D) provides a program of elementary or secondary education, or both;
　　(E) is nonsectarian in its programs, admissions policies, employment practices, and all other operations, and is not affiliated with a sectarian school or religious institution;
　　(F) does not charge tuition;
　　(G) complies with the Age Discrimination Act of 1975, title VI of the Civil Rights Act of 1964, title IX of the Education Amendments of 1972, section 504 of the Rehabilitation Act of 1973, and part B of the Individuals with Disabilities Education Act;
　　(H) is a school to which parents choose to send their children, and that admits students on the basis of a lottery, if more students apply for admission than can be accommodated;
　　(I) agrees to comply with the same Federal and State audit requirements as do other elementary schools and secondary schools in the State, unless such requirements are specifically waived for the purpose of this program;

(J) meets all applicable Federal, State, and local health and safety requirements;

(K) operates in accordance with State law; and

(L) has a written performance contract with the authorized public charter-ing agency in the State that includes a description of how student per-formance will be measured in charter schools pursuant to State assess-ments that are required of other schools and pursuant to any other assessments mutually agreeable to the authorized public chartering agency and the charter school.

Autonomy and freedom from bureaucratic controls are the major reasons for the founding of charter schools according to the U.S. Department of Educa-tion report, *The State of Charter Schools 2000*. This report states, "Nearly two-thirds of newly created charter schools seek to realize an alternative vision of schooling and an additional one-quarter of newly created schools were founded primarily to serve a special target population of students." In addi-tion, the report affirms, "More than one-third of preexisting public schools re-port that they converted to charter status in order to gain autonomy from dis-trict and state regulations."

Charter school laws vary widely from state to state. Some states allow a va-riety of agencies to charter schools while others allow only a single state agency to grant charters. In some states only public schools are allowed to convert to charter schools while in other states the establishment of new schools is al-lowed along with public school conversions. States vary in their requirements for charter school compliance with state education regulation. Most states granted automatic waivers to most of the state education code. In a few states, charter schools must follow most of the state education code.

An example of charter school legislation is the first charter school law passed in Minnesota in 1991. This law specifies that only licensed teachers can apply to local school boards to establish charter schools. In addition, proposals for charter schools must be approved by the state department of education. To maximize their autonomy, the only power given to local school boards is to en-sure that a charter school fulfills the outcome of its original charter. Otherwise, school board members and administrators are not allowed to interfere in the operation of the charter school. Under this law, the first charter school to be ap-proved was the Bluffview Montessori School that operated for three years as a private school before deciding to seek public support.

*The State of Charter Schools 2000* reported the following characteristics of charter schools:

- Most charter schools are small—the median enrollment in all charter school sites is 137 students per school.
- Many charter schools have nontraditional grade configurations, with some being ungraded while others house K through 12 or K through 8.
- About 70 percent of charter schools are newly created.
- Newly created charter schools, with a median enrollment of 128 students, are smaller, on average, than converted preexisting public schools.
- About 10 percent are conversions from preexisting private schools.

- The median student-to-teacher ratio for charter schools, 16 to 1, was slightly lower than the ratio for all public schools, 17 to 1.

## Examples of Three Charter Schools

The following is a description of three charter schools that are separated by philosophy and geography. They represent the startling contrasts that exist between charter schools around the country.

Located in San Diego, California, High Tech High was opened in 2000 to solve the labor shortage in high-tech industries. Executives from Qualcomm and other high-tech industries spent three years planning the school, with Qualcomm donating $3 million to the project. The long-range plan is to establish nine other High Tech Highs around the country.

High Tech High opened in September 2000 with 200 ninth and tenth grade students selected by lottery from 1,000 applications. At the school, the student's day is broken into two parts with one part focusing on independent work and the other stressing group work. Each student is given a workstation similar to what adults have in the workplace. Students develop digital portfolios that can be displayed online or on a CD-ROM.

Across the United States from High Tech High, students at the Bronx Preparatory Charter School begin each hour with a recitation of school rules. Before entering classes, students line up in the hallway with their heads aligned with that of the student they are behind. After class, the students assume the same positions with their right feet on a green tape. A teacher then marches them to their next classroom. In each classroom, the students open their identical color-coded binders to the first page and trace the words of the school rules with their fingers while reading them aloud.

"Structure creates peace of mind," said Marina Bernard Damiba, principal of the school, which educates 100 fifth and sixth graders from poor black and Hispanic families. "Remember, the kids we're teaching, this may be the only place they get it."

In 2002, *Education Week* featured a model charter school organization in Minnesota called the EdVisions Cooperative. EdVisions Cooperative is a nonprofit collective of 100 teachers and other educational professionals who operate seven charter schools in Minnesota and one in Wisconsin. The basic principle of the organization is that teachers should be democratically empowered to operate schools. The organization operates democratically to manage instruction, to evaluate instructors, to evaluate the academic program, and to hire and fire staff. Under Minnesota's charter school law, each of the EdVisions Cooperative schools receives $6,000 per student from the state.

The guiding philosophy of the EdVisions Cooperative is that teachers should have complete control over the teaching and learning that goes on in schools. In other words, traditional school administrators, such as principals, are not present in these charter schools. EdVisions claims that it saves 10 percent in normal operating costs by dispensing with the traditional administrative structure. In opposition to traditional administrative control of a school's curriculum and teaching, the selection of textbooks, and the hiring and firing of teachers, it is believed by the EdVisions Cooperative that teachers can make better decisions about these educational issues.

*Education Week's* reporter Julie Blair quotes David Greenberg, the lead teacher at El Colegio Charter School in Minneapolis and a member of the cooperative, "This model allows people to be leaders in areas in which they excel. You have control in the hands of the people who need it to deliver education to students who need it." In his former teaching job, Greenberg commented, "The most important decision I made was when to hold yearbook day. Here, we decide if we want to hire another art teacher or buy another computer."

Ms. Sage-Martinson told reporter Julie Blair, "The opportunities are endless. My last job was great, but it was a dead end. I'd teach and teach and teach, but have no say in what I taught."

While EdVisions Cooperative is a model for teacher empowerment, the American Federation of Teachers issued a sharply critical 2002 report on charter schools. This report reversed the organization's early support of the charter school movement.

## *"DO CHARTER SCHOOLS MEASURE UP?":* *2002 REPORT OF THE AMERICAN FEDERATION OF TEACHERS*

In 2002, the American Federation of Teachers issued a scathing report on the charter school movement. The report admits, "The American Federation of Teachers (AFT) supported the creation of educationally strong charter schools from their inception. We believed that innovative schools could be a boon to public education."

Essentially, the AFT report argues that the charter school movement is a distraction from the real business of improving public schools. In general, the report states that charter schools are selective in recruiting students, fail to meet high academic standards, and erode the rights of teachers as employees.

The report claims that charter schools contribute to racial and ethnic isolation of students by failing to educate high-cost students at the same rate as regular public schools. Consequently, these high-cost students remain in regular schools rather than transferring to charter schools. The report defines high-cost students as "low-income, English Language learners, and special education students."

In addition, the report states that charter school teachers are less experienced, lower paid, and receive inferior benefits and pensions compared to regular public school teachers. The report admits that surveys show that charter school teachers "are most satisfied with education-related and colleague-related issues." On the other hand, these teachers complain about salaries and workload.

Charter schools are not improving student achievement according to the report. More importantly, the report claims that charter schools have not lived up to the expectation of experimenting with new curricula and instructional methods. "Rather than bring new ideas to education," the report contends, "the charters sometimes import existing programs from schools outside the district in which they operate."

The AFT's strongest criticism was directed at charter schools operated by for-profit corporations. In the next section, I will examine these for-profit educational corporations in more detail. The AFT's criticism of for-profit charter schools includes the following:

- They enroll few students with disabilities and spend little money on special education.
- They spend more on administration and less on instruction.
- They do not innovate but use a standardized school design, curriculum, and technology package provided by the company.
- Teachers are disgruntled about the lack of professional opportunities for advancement.
- Teachers complain about not being involved in school decision making.

## FOR-PROFIT SCHOOLS AND CHARTERS

Education is big business and charter schools open the door to investment by for-profit corporations. In many states, for-profit companies, meaning companies that earn a profit for their owners, can apply for state charter school status. In fact, some public school districts are now contracting for-profit companies to manage their schools. Some education companies are going global. In 2000, Nobel Learning Communities, a large for-profit operator of secondary and elementary private schools in the United States, announced the formation of a partnership with South Ocean Development Corp., which owns seven precollegiate private schools and two colleges in China. Already operating 162 private schools in the United States, Nobel hopes through its new partnership to open for-profit preschools and an international school in China.

The two teachers' unions are highly critical of the for-profit education movement. The NEA's report *Can Corporate Management Solve the Challenges Facing America's Public Schools?* asserts, "Corporate management of public schools has not improved students' academic performance in any of the four cities in which it's been tried." The union report concludes: "Education is not simply another economic good or service. The learning of a nation's children is of concern to the entire nation. And while business can and should play a role in education, communities and the school boards that represent them must retain control over the future of America's public schools. Instead of corporate takeovers, school systems should seek to fully engage their communities and build cooperation among school staff, parents, and all concerned groups and citizens."

The AFT criticizes for-profit companies for their packaged and standardized designs. In a report for the Center for Education Research, Analysis, and Innovation, Gerald Bracey writes, "An increasing number of . . . schools have been turned over to for-profit educational management organizations such as

Mosaica Education, based in San Rafael, California. Yet Mosaica and other such companies appear to have schools that resemble each other in cookie-cutter fashion, eliminating the very diversity and innovation that these charter schools' founders had envisioned."

In addition, Bracey argues, for-profit schools such as Edison, TesseracT, and Sabis provide alternative programs to existing public schools while tolerating no diversity within a school. He cites the case of an Edison school in San Francisco where half the teachers planned not to return for the 2000–2001 school year. Supposedly, teachers felt demeaned because they were required to follow a tightly controlled educational plan. "They literally give you a script with what you're supposed to say," one teacher complained.

While teachers are complaining about the rigid formulaic teaching prescribed by for-profit educational companies, businesspeople, according to *The New York Times* reporter Edward Wyatt, are turning the "$700 billion education sector into the 'next health care'—that is, transforming large portions of a fragmented, cottage industry of independent, nonprofit institutions into a consolidated, professionally managed, money-making set of businesses that include all levels of education." Leading the pack of for-profit corporations are Christopher C. Whittle's Edison Schools Inc. and the University of Phoenix, the largest private and for-profit university in the United States. In 2002, the Edison Schools Inc. operated 150 public schools with a student enrollment over 84,000. Referring to the corporate trend to contract with outside companies to handle some of their operations, Guilbert C. Hentschke, dean of the Rossier School of Education at the University of Southern California, told reporter Wyatt, "Now, in a sense, you've got that same process in schools, where districts are entering agreements for outsourcing, contracting for services and chartering new schools."

Reflecting recent trends, a conference was convened in New York City in June 2002 to discuss the "site-based education market." The conference featured presentations from major education companies, including Edison and National Heritage. Mergers are another aspect of recent trends. In 2001, Mosaica Education Inc. of New York City acquired Boston-based Advantage Schools Inc. In 2002, Chancellor Academies Inc. acquired Beacon Education Management, Inc.

Some of these companies simply offer services to nonprofit public schools rather than actually operating for-profit schools. These services include advice and materials in such areas as administration and curriculum to operate a charter school. Charter schools can simply buy a complete administrative plan and organized curriculum. Other companies sell consulting services for accounting and payroll.

Similar to McDonald's, KFC, and other fast-food franchises, some education companies have standardized all aspects of their schools. For instance, National Heritage Academies Inc. uses a cookie-cutter building design with simple frame buildings. The president of National Heritage, Peter Ruppert, told *Education Week* reporter Mark Walsh, "We build very bright, learning-conducive buildings, but they are not the Taj Mahal by any means."

National Heritage is one of the few education companies to actually earn a profit. The company was found by J. C. Huizenga, a cousin of the founder of Blockbuster Video. National Heritage schools focus on the teaching of a Christian moral code along with a back-to-basics curriculum. The curriculum appeals to conservative Christians. One reason for the profitability of National Heritage is that the company avoids low-income neighborhoods and builds in affluent suburbs. In addition, Gary Miron, a research associate at the Evaluation Center at Western Michigan University, argues that the company's profitability is a result of it being "streamlined for profit." In 2000–2001, the company reported revenues of $77.8 million from 27 schools serving 11,400 students. In 2002, it predicted revenues of over $100 million from the operation of 28 for-profit charter schools serving 14,000 students. "Our vision is to some day have 2000 schools," Ruppert told reporter Walsh. "More than 85 percent of charters are run by folks without a management company. That alone says there is still a huge opportunity."

## EDISON SCHOOLS INC.: A TALE OF AN EDUCATION COMPANY IN SEARCH OF PROFIT

Edison Schools Inc. is the most well-known and largest of the for-profit school companies. It operates charter schools and is contracted by school boards to manage schools. In 2002, the company signed a contract with the Philadelphia school system to manage 20 of its elementary and middle schools. This number is in addition to the other 150 public schools it operates across the country. Despite the size of its operation, Edison Schools has been unable to earn a profit for its shareholders. (It is a public company traded on the NASDAQ stock exchange.) In 2002, according to *The New York Times* financial service, the value of its stock dropped from $21.68 a share to $0.22 a share. In the previous year, the company reported a total revenue of $375.8 million with earnings per share of $–0.81. One reason for its lack of profitability is its $27.9 million debt.

The history of Edison Schools Inc. provides insight into the world of for-profit education. Moving in the world of the rich and famous, Benno Schmidt, while president of Yale in 1990, encountered entrepreneur Chris Whittle at a party in the ultraexclusive Hamptons section of Long Island. That meeting, according to Whittle, led him to the decision to hire Schmidt to head his school privatization scheme, called the Edison Project. Lured from Yale in 1992 with a salary around $1 million, Benno Schmidt applied his elite private school background (St. Bernard's in New York City and Exeter) to designing private schools that were to be nationally franchised. When Whittle was unable to raise enough money to support this scheme, the Edison Project decided to operate charter schools for profit.

Edison Schools received help in their efforts to enter the charter school market when the company was contacted by Governor William F. Weld of Massachusetts. Weld was an advocate of for-profit and charter schools. According to *New York* magazine reporter James Traub, "Governors William Weld of Massachusetts and Buddy Roemer of Colorado contacted [the president of Edison

Schools Inc., Benno] Schmidt in the fall of 1992 to say that they would like to find a way to bring Edison into the public schools in their states. Both states went on to pass 'charter school' laws that permit states and school systems to award contracts to . . . private contractors."

Whittle and Schmidt's monied backgrounds and desires for profits caused NEA president Keith Geiger to warn delegates to the 1994 convention of the "merchants of greed, [who] mask their money-hungry motives with phrases like 'school' choice." In 1994, the Wichita, Kansas, school board signed a contract with the Edison Project to operate two of its elementary schools and a middle school. Similar agreements were reached with school boards in Greeley, Colorado; Hawaii; Austin, Texas; Mount Clemens, Michigan; Dade County, Florida; and Bridgeport, Ohio. In addition, Massachusetts awarded the Edison Project the right to run three charter schools in Boston, Worcester, and Lowell starting in the fall of 1995. These schools would be operated for a profit.

By 1998, the Edison Project claimed operation of 51 schools nationwide with a student enrollment of more than 23,000. Even more impressive was the projected annual earnings of $126 million. Consequently, the Edison Project was not having difficulty finding backers. J. P. Morgan, the influential Wall Street financial institution, invested $20 million, Invest AB put up $20 million, Chris Whittle gave $10 million to the investment pot, and others invested another $6 million. A total of $56 million provided a healthy sum for Edison to compete for new schools to operate.

With this financial backing, the Edison Project in the fall of 1998 entertained and paid the lodging for many (some school districts do not allow board members and administrators to accept free lodging) of the 200 school board members and school administrators attending a 2½-day Edison sales promotion at the luxurious Broadmoor resort in Colorado Springs. "This is an opportunity for those considering [a contract with Edison] to meet all sorts of Edison representatives in one place," Christopher Whittle told the group. One potential customer, Gene Buinger, the superintendent of the Bibb County, Georgia, schools, told *Education Week* reporter Mark Walsh that he made the trip to talk to superintendents and principals in districts that had already contracted with the Edison Project. "So far," Buinger said, "everyone I've talked to has been very satisfied."

In contrast to Buinger's upbeat statement, a representative from the NEA, Heidi Stevens, complained, "This was a real sales conference. The purpose wasn't anything but to attract new clients. I would have found it more convincing if there was more discussion of the warts." Those warts, according to her, are problems with special education services, difficulty adapting to Edison's design, and differing interpretations of test results from Edison sites.

At the meeting, Christopher Whittle announced some more twists in the for-profit school movement. One is the creation of a private foundation, Edison Foundation, that will funnel additional money into school districts that sign contracts. The model for this is the Fisher Family Foundation, which gave $25 million to school districts in California that signed contracts with Edison.

Another development is profit-sharing with teachers and principals. "Educators in this country have essentially had to take a vow of poverty," Whittle said. In 1998, teachers in a Dade County, Florida, elementary school operated by Edison were signed on to a profit-sharing plan. The move was applauded by teacher union officials. "The basic idea is to give teachers a broader sense of ownership in the enterprise in which they are the key professionals," said Benno Schmidt. "They are not giving up anything, but we want them to participate if Edison does well." Praising the plan, the executive vice president of the United Teachers of Dade, Local 1974 of the AFT, Pat Tornillo said it was "the first time in the history of American education that teachers have become direct economic stakeholders in the public schools where they work."

In 2002 things began to sour for the Edison Schools when their shares plunged on the NASDAQ. Most of Edison's schools were not showing a profit. In order to escape financial ruin the company borrowed $40 million from Merrill Lynch and from School Services Inc., an affiliate of the investment firm Leeds Weld & Co. The money was to be used, in part, to finance its August 2002 agreement to manage 20 elementary and middle schools in Philadelphia for five years. This was less than half the 45 schools Edison campaigned to manage. Edison spent $1 million in its effort to convince Philadelphia officials that it should manage their schools.

The growing involvement of financial institutions in public schooling is highlighted by the loans used to finance Edison's management of Philadelphia schools. Thirty million dollars came from Leeds Weld & Co. In 1997, the former governor and sponsor of for-profit charter schools in Massachusetts, William Weld, became a principal in Leeds Weld & Co. Currently, Leeds Weld & Co. is the nation's largest private equity fund focused on investing in the education and training industry. Former Secretary of Education Lamar Alexander is on the advisory board. In 2001, Weld also became a member of the Medsn's Board of Directors. Medsn makes its money by providing online education to health care professionals and organizations. In 2002, Jonathan Newcomb, former CEO of Simon & Schuster (a major publisher of textbooks), joined Leeds Weld & Co.

While Edison Schools was entangled in a financial web some of its ventures were failing. Two weeks after signing the contract with the Philadelphia schools, the superintendent of the Dallas school system recommended ending the district's contract with Edison to manage seven of its elementary schools. The reasons were poor performance of the schools and the school district's financial problems. The contract with Edison cost the district $39 million in the 2001–2002 school year. The school district rated three of the seven schools as low-performing and the other four as acceptable.

## The Edison Design

The charge of cookie-cutter educational programs seems substantiated by a quick trip to the Edison Schools Inc. website, http://www.edisonschools.com. However, a standardized school design does not mean educational failure. In fact, the design could be defended as the best method for delivering educational services. The curriculum is organized around specific learning standards. According to the guiding principles of Edison's curriculum, "A world-class education must also be taught to clear and demanding standards. Accordingly, each field of Edison's curriculum is guided by student academic standards that specify what students must know and be able to do to satisfy the expectations of each academy."

Not only is student learning standardized by "student academic standards," but the school day is also tightly regulated and mapped out. The school day begins at 6:30 A.M. with a before-school program for children who need to be dropped off prior to the actual beginning of instruction and ends at 4:00 P.M. Each time slot is carefully calibrated for teaching a particular subject so that every student in a particular grade in every Edison school might be learning the same thing at the same time.

For instance, the Edison School design plan calls for most elementary students to arrive at 7:30 A.M. and see as they are entering the school a "colorful mural in the school entranceway, which depicts all eight [Edison] core values; Wisdom, Justice, Courage, Compassion, Hope, Respect, Responsibility, and Integrity." The standardized mural design and mottoes could be compared to the standardized designs found in fast-food franchises such as McDonald's or Burger King. At 8:00 A.M., students meet at their "home-base" to discuss news and school activities. At 8:30 A.M. begins 90 minutes of "The Whole School is Reading." Students are grouped by reading ability rather than by grade level for the focused reading time. The rest of the day is scheduled for the study of subjects such as science and social studies. At 3:30 P.M. time is devoted to character education, which is also integrated into other subjects. In this standardized character education program, students, according to the Edison website, "really do internalize the core values that are at the heart of the curriculum."

Are standardized school designs employed by for-profit corporations the future vision for American public schools? Similar to other business designs ranging from The Home Depot to Pizza Hut, will parents be able to identify school curricula by logos on buildings? Will education become a competition between brand names?

## COMMERCIALISM IN SCHOOLS

Advertising is creeping into every aspect of American life from tiles on supermarket floors to flashing commercials in elevators. Why not public schools? Alex Molnar, author of the best-selling book, *Giving Kids the Business: The Commercialization of America's Schools,* and head of the University of Wisconsin's Center for the Analysis of Commercialism in Education, tells the story of the Colorado Springs School District 11 which signed an exclusive contract with Coca-Cola. The school district agreed that it would only receive financial benefits from the contract if students consumed at least 70,000 cases of Coke products. Worried that students wouldn't consume enough Coke, the district's central office issued a memo to school principals: "Allow students to purchase and consume products throughout the day. Locate machines where they are accessible to the students all day." Accompanying the memo was a list of Coke products, a calendar of promotional events, and an offer to install extra outlets for vending machines.

On September 14, 2000, the U.S. General Accounting Office released a report on the commercialization of U.S. schools. The report stated, "In-school marketing has become a growing industry. Some marketing professionals are increasingly targeting children in schools, companies are becoming known for their success in negotiating contracts between school districts and beverage companies, and both educators and corporate managers are attending conferences to learn how to increase revenue from in-school marketing for their schools and companies." The General Accounting Office found the following:

- About 25 percent of the nation's middle schools and high schools now show Channel One, a broadcast of news features and commercials.
- Two hundred school districts have signed exclusive contracts with soft-drink companies to sell their beverages in schools.
- Students using computers in classrooms are being offered incentives to enter personal data—names, addresses, information on personal habits—which will then be sold to advertisers.
- A math textbook published in 1995 by McGraw-Hill and approved for use in about fifteen states names Gatorade, Sega and Sony video games, and Nike sneakers in its word problems.
- Zap Me offers schools free computers with screens that include continuously flashing ads.

Schools are invaded by other forms of advertising with fast-food chains supporting reading and other educational programs, commercial advertising appearing at athletic events, and credit card companies offering to teach money management skills. Corporations distribute educational materials bearing their logos to classroom teachers.

A clear example of the commercialization of schools is Pizza Hut's BOOK IT! This is a national reading incentive program that began in 1984 with an enrollment of 200,000 elementary school students. By the 1998–1999 school year, 22 million children in 895,000 classrooms were enrolled. Under the program, children who achieve their monthly reading goals are rewarded with a Personal Pan Pizza and a button from the manager of the local Pizza Hut restaurant. Achieving six-month goals earns an All-Star Medallion at a local Pizza Hut restaurant. In 1998, the BOOK IT! beginners program was started for preschool and kindergarten students with the monthly Personal Pan Pizza award. In 1999, this beginners program was active in 20,000 kindergarten classrooms and day care centers around the country.

BOOK IT! is a win-win program. Children, particularly preschool and kindergarten children, are usually escorted by their parents to the local Pizza Hut restaurant. Do the parents simply sit and watch their child eat a Personal Pan Pizza or do they also buy the child a drink and pizzas and drinks for themselves? It is possible that the parents might spend more than the cost of the award. In fact, Pizza Hut might actually make money by giving the award while implanting their brand name in the child's mind. In addition, Pizza Hut gets free help for their advertising campaign from the local school system. Principals and teachers enroll the students in the program, and teachers set monthly goals, verify completion of reading assignments, and mark wall charts to monitor children's progress toward their Personal Pan Pizza.

Should schools engage in these forms of commercialization? Or, are schools just mimicking the commercialization that is taking over every other aspect of living? Paralleling the growth of for-profit schooling, the commercialization of education holds out the possibility of a world where there are no borders between education, business, and consumption.

## CONCLUSION

After considering the power and politics of local school boards, site-based management, choice, charter schools, privatization, and commercialization you should again imagine that you are sitting in the education chair and answering the following questions:

- Who should control the switch?
- Should it be controlled by a team of teachers, administrators, and community members engaged in site-based management?
- Should the options for throwing the switch be determined by petitioners for charter schools?
- Should the switch be controlled by parental choice?
- Should an elected school board control the switch?
- Should it be controlled by the educational bureaucracy?
- Should it be controlled by for-profit companies?

Whatever your answers, the important thing is for you to understand that the political structure of education determines the content of education that in turn directly affects what a student learns. Often, students never question the reasons for being subjected to a particular curriculum or textbook. The content of learning in public schools is determined by a political process. But local politics of education is only one part of the process.

### Suggested Readings and Works Cited in Chapter

American Federation of Teachers, "Do Charter Schools Measure Up?: The Charter School Experiment After 10 Years." http://www.aft.org. *The American Federation of Teachers' 2002 report criticizing charter schools. Also, this website should be searched for updated information on school choice, home schooling, charter schools, and privatization.*

Associated Press. "Dallas Official Wants to End Edison Deal." *The New York Times on the Web* (17 August 2002). *Dallas superintendent complains about failure of Edison-managed schools to increase performance of students.*

BILLUPS, ANDREA. "Home-School Movement Goes Global." *The Washington Times* (19 September 2000). http://www.hslda.org.

_____. "Home Schoolers No. 1 on College-Entrance Test." *The Washington Times* (22 August 2000). http://www.hslda.org.

BLAIR, JULIE. "Doing It Their Way: Teachers Make All Decisions at Cooperative Venture." *Education Week* (27 July 2002). http://www.edweek.org. *This article features Minnesota's EdVisions Cooperative, which establishes charter schools based on teacher control.*

Bloomberg News. "Edison Reaches Contract on Philadelphia Schools." *The New York Times on the Web* (1 August 2002). *News story about contract reached by Edison to manage 20 elementary and middle schools in Philadelphia.*

BRACEY, GERALD. "Charter Schools." This was written for and distributed by the Center for Education Research, Analysis, and Innovation (12 October 2000). http://www.uwm.edu/Dept/CERAI.

Commercialism in Education Research Unit. http://www.asu.edu/educ/epsl. *This cite is organized by Alex Molnar to maintain a continual analysis of the commercialization of public schools.*

Center for Education, Research, Analysis, and Innovation. http://www.uwm.edu/Dept/CERAI. *This center conducts original research and provides independent analyses of research and policy information. It is an important source of information on school choice, charter schools, and privatization.*

Center for Educational Reform. http://www.edreform.com. *This website is an important source for information about school choice and charter schools.*

_____. "What the Research Reveals About Charter Schools." http://www.edreform.com. *This report summarizes 53 research-based studies on charter schools.*

CHUBB, JOHN E., and TERRY MOE. *Politics, Markets & America's Schools.* Washington, DC: The Brookings Institution, 1990. *This important study of the relationship between political control and student achievement supports choice as a means of improving student achievement.*

CRONIN, JOSEPH N. *The Control of Urban Schools.* New York: Free Press, 1973. *This is a history of the control of American schools and an exploration of the major issues surrounding the relationships among the public, school board members, and professional staff.*

Edison Project, http://www.edisonproject.com. *This website provides ongoing information about Edison school projects and financial reports.*

*Education Week. This excellent weekly newspaper contains news about local, state, and federal politics of education.*

HAWLEY, WILLIS D. *Nonpartisan Elections and the Case for Party Politics.* New York: John Wiley, 1973. *This is a study of the effects of nonpartisan elections.*

HAYS, CONSTANCE L. "New Report Examines Commercialism in U.S. Schools." *The New York Times on the Web* (14 September 2000). *Summarizes the General Accounting Office Report on commercialization of public schools.*

Home School Legal Defense Association. http://www.hslda.org. *This is the best source for information on the home schooling movement.*

Institute for Educational Leadership. *Leadership for Student Learning: Redefining the Teacher as Leader.* Washington, DC: Institute for Educational Leadership, 2001. *This report advocates the strengthening of teacher leadership roles in schools.*

McCARTY, DONALD, and CHARLES RAMSEY. *The School Managers: Power and Conflict in American Public Education.* Westport, CT: Greenwood, 1971. *This is a study of the different types of community power structures and the resulting style of boards of education and school superintendents.*

MOLNAR, ALEX. *Giving Kids the Business: The Commercialization of America's Schools.* Boulder: Westview Press, 1996. *This is the best introduction to the corporate invasion of American public schools.*

NATHAN, JOE. *Charter Schools: Creating Hope and Opportunity for American Education.* San Francisco: Jossey-Bass, 1996. *Nathan describes the struggle for charter schools and provides help in organizing a charter school.*

National Center for Education Statistics. "How Widespread Is Site-Based Decisionmaking in the Public Schools?." Washington, DC: U.S. Printing Office, December 1966, p. 2. *Provides information on the extent and activity of site-based management in the U.S.*

National Education Association. "Charter Schools: A Tool for Reform," http://www. nea.org. *Gives the NEA's policy statement on charter schools. Also, this website should be searched for updated information on school choice, home schooling, charter schools, and privatization.*

PRIMACY, DAVID. "Leeds Weld Markets $500 Million Fund IV." www.ventureeconom-ics.com (18 March 2002). *A news story from Thomson Venture Economics of Leed Weld & Co., a major investor in Edison Schools and other for-profit education projects, about the Leed Weld's hiring of Simon and Schuster CEO.*

Public Law 107–110, 107th Congress, Jan. 8, 2002 [H.R. 1]. "No Child Left Behind Act of 2001." Washington, DC: U.S. Printing Office, 2002. *This federal legislation contains important provisions supporting public school choice and charter schools.*

*Rethinking Schools: An Urban Educational Journal Online.* www.rethinkingschools.org. *This is an important source of information on urban school reform, including school choice, charter schools, and multicultural education.*

SPRING, JOEL. *Educating the Consumer-Citizen: A History of the Marriage of Schools, Advertising, and Media.* Lawrence Erlbaum Associates, 2003. *Provides a history of the commercialization of schools and American society.*

TIERNEY, JOHN. "THE BIG CITY Voucher Issue Casts Light on a Paradox." *The New York Times on the Web* (3 November 2000). *This article supports school choice by parents of children in failing schools.*

U.S. Department of Education. "Site-Based Management: Wyoming Public School." http:www.ed.gov/pubs/Paraprofessionals/wyoming.html. *Provides an example of site-based management at work.*

_____. "The State of Charter Schools 2000." http://www.uscharterschools.org.

WALSH, MARK. "Businesses Flock to Charter Frontier." *Education Week on the Web* (22 May 2002). *This article surveys the operation of the major companies trying to make a profit from the development of charter schools, including National Heritage Academies Inc.*

_____. "Education Inc." *Education Week on the Web* (4 October 2000). *This article describes Nobel Learning Communities Inc.'s planned investment in for-profit schools in China.*

_____. "Edison Outlines Strategies to Reassure Wall Street." *Education Week on the Web* (7 August 2002). *Provides an analysis of Edison Schools Inc.'s financial maneuvering.*

WEINER, REBECCA. "San Diego Charter School a Model for Technology Leaders." *The New York Times on the Web* (1 November 2000). *This provides a description of the founding and operation of High Tech High charter school.*

WILGORIN, JODI. "School Days Are Rule Days in Bronx Charter Classrooms." *The New York Times on the Web* (30 October 2000). *Provides a description of the Bronx Preparatory Charter School.*

WYATT, EDWARD. "Educational Company Says Its Scores Rise." *The New York Times on the Web* (10 August 2000). *Edison Schools report that test scores in its schools are improving.*

_____. "Investors Are Seeing Profits in Nation's Demand for Education." *The New York Times on the Web* (4 November 1999). *This is an important article on investment in for-profit education companies.*

_____. "Union Study Finds For-Profit Schools No Better." *The New York Times on the Web* (19 October 2000). *The AFT disputes an Edison school report that its test scores are improving in comparison to traditional public school students.*

www.uscharterschools.org. *This is the official website on charters operated by the U.S. Department of Education.*

ZEIGLER, L. HARMON, and M. KENT JENNINGS. *Governing American Schools: Political Interaction in Local School Districts.* North Scituate, MA: Duxbury, 1974. *This is a major national study of local boards of education.*

## CHAPTER 7

# Power and Control at the State and National Levels:

## High-Stakes Testing, School Violence, the Reading and Math Wars, and Private Foundations

The No Child Left Behind Act of 2001 opens the door to the high-stakes testing model of equality of opportunity discussed in Chapter 2. The legislation orders the use of high-stakes testing and it requires states to create academic standards that would determine what is taught in local schools. The legislation also stipulates national testing. In addition, the legislation ensures that all the nation's schools will use one particular method to teach reading.

Essentially, the No Child Left Behind Act of 2001 creates a nationalized school system with variations being allowed in academic standards and the content of state tests. However, these variations are reduced by the requirement that every other year a sample of fourth and eighth graders in each state must take national tests administered by the National Assessment of Educational Progress. The results of these national tests will be compared to the tests created by each state. In other words, the National Assessment of Educational Progress tests could have a determining effect on the construction of state tests.

What is the academic power of standards and tests besides supporting the high-stakes model of equality of opportunity? First, state academic standards determine what will be taught in the classroom. For instance, state science standards establish the content of instruction in science. Second, state high-stakes tests ensure that teachers teach the content specified in the state's academic standards. The state tests are constructed around the state's academic standards. If students do poorly on high-stakes tests then teachers and school administrators are blamed. Consequently, both teachers and administrators are motivated to ensure that classroom instruction complies to academic standards and provides students with the specific knowledge and skills required by the tests.

How can the federal government exert this type of control over local schools when the U.S. Constitution does not mention education and, therefore, education is a power entrusted to the states? Most state constitutions give legal responsibility to the state government to control local schools. A school district is a legal creation of the state, and local school boards exercise powers granted explicitly by the state legislature.

# LOCAL, STATE, AND FEDERAL SCHOOL REVENUES

Federal power over local schools seems out of proportion to the amount of financial aid it provides local schools. The federal share of education spending is considerably below that of state and local communities. The maximum amount of federal education revenues was only 9.4 percent in 1977–1978. Table 7–1 provides a history of revenue sharing in the support of elementary and secondary education. As indicated in the table, in 1919–1920 the majority of revenue came from local sources (83.2 percent) with the state governments providing 16.5 percent and the federal government only 0.3 percent. This proportion changed over time with significant increases in state revenues and significant decreases in local revenues so that by 1998–1999 state governments were providing 48.7 percent of the revenues for elementary and secondary education and local revenues represented 44.2 percent. By 1998–1999, the federal share was only 7.1 percent.

The data in Table 7–1 provide a history of the changing relationships between local, state, and federal involvement in education. Between 1945 and 1965, the state proportion of educational revenues increased because of the classroom and teacher shortage created by the post-World War II baby boom. In the 1950s, there was a massive school building program to accommodate the increased student population caused by the baby boom. From the 1970s to the present, states have been pressured to equalize funding between school districts; this has resulted in greater state aid to low-revenue school districts. In addition, state programs for low-performing students and students with disabilities have increased state funding. And, of course, state departments of education have expanded as state academic standards and state high-stakes tests were created.

**TABLE 7–1. Revenues for Public Elementary and Secondary Education, by Source of Funds: 1919–1920 to 1998–1999**

| School Year | Percentage from Federal | Percentage from State | Percentage from Local |
|---|---|---|---|
| 1919–1920 | 0.3% | 16.5% | 83.2% |
| 1945–1946 | 1.4 | 34.7 | 63.6 |
| 1955–1956 | 4.6 | 39.5 | 55.9 |
| 1965–1966 | 7.9 | 39.1 | 53.0 |
| 1972–1973 | 8.7 | 39.7 | 51.6 |
| 1977–1978 | 9.4 | 43.0 | 47.6 |
| 1982–1983 | 7.1 | 47.9 | 45.0 |
| 1987–1988 | 6.3 | 49.5 | 44.1 |
| 1992–1993 | 7.0 | 45.8 | 47.2 |
| 1998–1999 | 7.1 | 48.7 | 44.2 |

*Source:* U.S. Department of Education, National Center for Education Statistics, *Statistics of State School Systems; Revenues and Expenditures for Public Elementary and Secondary Education; and Common Core of Data surveys,* May 2001.

The increase in federal funding from 1.4 percent in 1945–1946 to 8.7 percent in 1972–1973 was a result of the Cold War and the War on Poverty. The Cold War sparked greater federal involvement in science, math, and language programs in order to strengthen national defense against the Soviet Union. The 1950s can be characterized as a war between U.S. and Soviet school systems with each trying to educate the best scientists and engineers for development of military technology. In the mid 1960s, the federal government launched its War on Poverty programs with funds going to local schools for the education of low-performing students. These programs continue to exist.

The federal share of education revenues declined from its all-time high of 9.4 percent in 1977–1978 to 6.3 percent in 1987–1988. This was a result of the Reagan Administration's position that the problem with schools was not the lack of money but the lack of academic standards. The Reagan Administration, as I discuss later in this chapter, ushered in the present era of high-stakes tests and academic standards.

## CATEGORICAL AID: THE SOURCE OF FEDERAL POWER

During the 1950s, there was a debate about whether the federal government should give money to local school systems and let them determine how to spend the money or whether the federal government should specify how the money should be used. With the passage of the major Cold War education legislation, the National Defense Education Act (NDEA), Congress targeted funds for specific purposes, such as improving mathematics, science, and foreign language instruction. The next major federal educational legislation, the 1965 Elementary and Secondary Education Act (ESEA), also tied education to national policy objectives; in this case it was the War on Poverty. Funds were targeted for reading and arithmetic programs that would supposedly provide equality of educational opportunity for students from low-income families.

The targeting of federal funds for specific programs became known as *categorical aid*. Rather than providing federal funds to be used at the discretion of local school officials, categorical aid requires the implementation of specific programs. Of course, local school officials can refuse federal aid because the federal government has no direct control over local school districts. But who is going to refuse federal money? Once a school district or state accepts federal money, then federal control is present. This process is called *indirect control* since the federal power over education is made possible by local or state acceptance of a federal program.

Indirect control is exemplified by Title VI of the 1964 Civil Rights Act, which applies to federal education legislation. Any school agency receiving federal funds must comply with Title VI, which requires the mandatory withholding of federal funds from institutions practicing racial, religious, or ethnic discrimination. Title VI states that no person, because of race, color, or national origin, can be excluded from or denied the benefits of any program receiving federal financial assistance. Also, any education agency receiving federal funds must comply with Title IX of the 1972 amendments to the Higher Education Act. Title IX states: "No person in the United States shall, on the basis of sex, be excluded from participation in, be denied the benefits of, or be subjected to discrimination under any education program or activity receiving Federal Assistance."

Another indirect method of control is the use of persuasion. President Reagan's last secretary of education William Bennett would use his office as a bully pulpit to harangue educators to change their educational practices. In addition, the type of educational research funded by the federal government indirectly influences the future of American schools.

In summary, the federal government exerts considerable indirect influence over education by

- Providing federal money to support a particular educational program (categorical aid).
- Attaching federal regulations to federal programs, such as the Republican proposal requiring states to enact state testing programs as a requirement for receiving federal money.
- Using federal agents to influence educational practices or to create model programs.
- Forcing schools to comply with civil rights legislation to receive federal money.
- Researching.

I hypothesize, based on my knowledge of contemporary education events, the following rank-order federal branches and agencies having the most influence over federal education policies:

1. Congress
2. President
3. Secretary of Education
4. Staff of the Department of Education

The following nongovernmental groups exert important influence on federal education policies:

1. Teachers' unions and other education associations.
2. Business leaders.
3. Special interest groups (Christian Coalition, People for the American Way, etc.).
4. Private think tanks (Free Enterprise Institute, Brookings Institute, Hudson Institute, etc.).
5. Educational research organizations.

## INCREASING STATE INVOLVEMENT IN SCHOOLS

While the federal government influence over local school is out of proportion to constitutional dictates and revenue provided to local schools, the increase in state control follows the mandates of most state constitutions. In the early years of the nineteenth century public schools, state departments of education remained small and confined their activities to collecting statistics related to education and promoting good schools and teacher training. In the late nineteenth and early twentieth centuries, states expanded their role in education with the passage of compulsory-education laws and laws requiring specific curriculum content in the schools. Over the years these curriculum requirements expanded in many states to cover a great deal of the course content offered in local school districts. Teacher-certification requirements also increased and became more complex. Because of the enforcement requirements of these laws, state educational bureaucracies grew steadily in the twentieth century.

In the 1960s, as the federal government became more involved in schooling, federal money expanded state educational bureaucracies by funneling federal money and programs through the state government to local school districts. This widening of state power over education carried with it seeds of controversy. For some, an expanded state-controlled education enterprise signaled the collapse of local control of education. For others, state control of education appeared necessary for the improvement of schools. And, as I discussed previously, state governments attempted to equalize spending between school districts.

Then in the 1980s and 1990s, governors, including Bill Clinton in Arkansas and George W. Bush in Texas, focused their political campaigns on educational issues. The result was a state-initiated school reform movement that called for statewide testing of public school students. Since testing required academic standards for measurement, state governments entered the business of establishing academic standards for each grade level. State testing measured the success of students in achieving these academic standards. The result of the process was greater state control over school curriculum and the actual content of instruction.

Today, most states exercise the following major functions regarding education:

- Establishing academic standards and curriculum guidelines for local school districts.
- Testing students for achievement of academic standards.
- Testing teachers as part of the licensing procedure.
- Licensing of teachers.
- Enacting laws that affect the content of instruction (these laws vary with some states requiring the teaching of patriotism, free enterprise, drivers' education, and other educational topics).
- Providing funds to local school districts.

Researchers Catherine Marshall, Douglas Mitchell, and Frederick Wirt rank-ordered the following parts of state government regarding their influence over state education policies:

1. The state legislature.
2. The chief state school officer and senior members of the state department of education.
3. The governor and executive staff.

4. The legislative staff.
5. The state board of education.

Concerning the influence on state educational policymakers in government by groups outside government, Marshall, Mitchell, and Wirt listed the following groups by order of importance:

1. Teachers' unions and other education associations.
2. Noneducation groups (business leaders, taxpayers' groups).
3. Lay groups (PTAs, school advisory groups).
4. Educational research organizations.
5. Producers of educational materials.

## HIGH-STAKES TESTS AND ACADEMIC STANDARDS AS PART OF STATE AND FEDERAL SCHOOL REFORM

High-stakes tests can be a driving force in a school system. The New York School Chancellor Joel Klein announced near the opening of the 2002–2003 school year that district superintendents would receive bonuses up to $40,000—about a quarter of their base salaries—if test scores improved in their districts. School principals were already receiving bonuses for improved scores in their schools.

How did the high-stakes testing model of equality of opportunity capture the imagination of some politicians and educators? Part of the answer is in the argument made by the 1983 report *A Nation at Risk* that national success in a global economy depended on the quality of the education system.

In the 1980s, Japan and the Japanese system of testing became a model for many Americans who were concerned about the conclusions of *A Nation at Risk*. Not only did the report evaluate U.S. education in a global context but its also globalized educational policy. *A Nation at Risk* blamed public schools for America's difficulties in competing in world markets with Japan and West Germany. The allegedly poor academic quality of American public schools was seen as the cause of lower rates of productivity than those of Japan and West Germany, as well as of the declining lead of the United States in technological development. The report states, "If only to keep and improve on the slim competitive edge we still retain in world markets, we must rededicate ourselves to the reform of the educational system for the benefit of all." The report went on to exhort states and local communities to increase academic standards, improve the quality of teachers, and reform the curriculum.

Testing is the key to Japanese control of the curriculum and tracking students into different educational programs based on national economic need. The result is an examination system that determines the life chances of students. Students engage in *juken senso* or "examination preparation war." Besides regular school preparation for the examinations, parents send their children to private cram schools, called jukus. These privately operated neighborhood schools operate outside the hours of regular schools so parents may send their children there in the evenings or on Saturdays or Sundays. In addition, there are commercially published practice tests and drill books.

Compare the above description of Japanese cram schools to the current U.S. scene. In the United States, private companies, such as Kaplan, the Sylvan Learning Centers, the Princeton Review, and others, act as cram schools for test preparation. Some public schools offer test preparation courses for both state and college admission examinations. Some public school teachers follow scripts while teaching to the test. Some summer schools are now devoted to preparing students to pass state tests.

Is the knowledge in standardized tests politically neutral? A test for grades K through 12 resulted in a bitter struggle between the governor of California, the state legislature, and educators. The storm over the test, originally called the California Learning Assessment System test and later the California Comprehensive Assessment System, erupted in early 1994 when Alice Walker and the liberal group People for the American Way objected to state education officials removing two of Ms. Walker's stories from the test. State officials removed one story, "Roselily," because of objections from a conservative group, Traditional Values Coalition, that the story about a Christian woman in rural Mississippi married to a Muslim was antireligious. Beverly Sheldon, research director for the conservative group, argued that the test would influence the values of students. They removed the other story by Alice Walker because a member of the state board of education considered it hostile to meat eating. The People for the American Way objected to the removal of the stories because it sent "a chilling message across the country of the threat to educational freedom and constitutional rights posed by extremist pressure groups."

By May of 1994 hundreds of people were turning out for school board meetings to support or protest the test. Some protests were about a rumored question on the test about a barber contemplating slitting a customer's throat. A Los Angeles school board member, Sue Stokka, objected to the test not emphasizing basic skills. A superior court judge issued a temporary restraining order against giving the test in the San Bernardino school district after the conservative Rutherford Institute sued. The school board in the Antelope Valley Union High School District voted not to give the test.

By September of 1994 the test was a major political issue, with Governor Pete Wilson (who was running for re-election in November) threatening to veto a reauthorization of the testing program. Governor Wilson objected to the test program when a study found that men, Latinos, and Asian Americans were underrepresented in the groups that developed the test questions. A new legislative bill called for the exclusion of all questions related to personal beliefs regarding family life, sex, and religion.

The political turmoil over the California testing program highlights the political quality of knowledge. It raises fundamental questions regarding content of tests. This is an important issue as the United States adopts national standards and tests.

It wasn't just the Japanese model that created the testing mania among politicians and educators, it was also the idea of accountability. Leon Lessinger's

1970 book *Every Kid a Winner: Accountability in Education* popularized the idea of accountability. Lessinger wanted to balance public control with expert control by educators. He pointed out that in a hospital, patients and the community in general do not and should not participate directly in decisions regarding medical treatment or surgery because these are areas of decision making that require expert knowledge and training. In his opinion, users of medical services had the right to complain, but decisions about how to deal with the complaint should remain in the hands of medical experts. He felt that the same model was applicable to education. Modern schooling, he maintained, was based on professional knowledge gained through research and study. The average member of the community does not have the training necessary to make correct educational decisions. Like the hospital clientele, the community has the right to complain but does not have the right or the knowledge to make decisions regarding the resolution of complaints. Only the educational expert should be entrusted with decision-making power.

Lessinger believed that schools should report their accomplishments and failures to the public. This public accounting of the results of schooling was the heart of the accountability movement. Lessinger envisioned the creation of a national educational accounting firm operated by educational engineers who would measure educational results by the use of achievement tests and report the results to the public. He assumed that these results would provide the public with expert data that could be used to express approval or criticism of the accomplishments of the school system. As the accountability movement spread in the early 1970s, states and local communities began to require schools to publish achievement test scores annually. The use of test scores to measure the schools' success kept power in the hands of educational experts. In the schools, students found themselves taking an increasing number of achievement tests in order to satisfy the requirements of accountability.

The combination of accountability and the Japanese model is very appealing to politicians. First, the emphasis on tests and high academic standards shifts the burden of educational reform from spending more money on schools to the idea of "getting tough with students." The approach implies that the problem is students and teachers not working hard enough in schools. High-stakes tests that determine promotion from grade to grade, high school graduation, and the evaluations for teachers, principals, and other school administrators will, it is assumed, cause students, teachers, and school administrators to focus on academic learning.

There is concern that standardized tests cannot be objective in measuring student learning. There are such things as test skills which can be learned. In fact, many private agencies offer courses in test-taking. Also, the wording of questions can reflect particular cultural knowledge. I remember being stumped on a question in a standardized math test because I did not know the meaning of a word. I excelled at math but missed this test item because of my limited cultural knowledge. Writing in *Education Week*, test expert W. James Popham contends:

> If you were to review the actual items in a typical standardized achievement test, you'd find many items whose correct answer depends heavily on the socioeconomic status of a child's family. There are also many items that measure

the verbal, quantitative, or spatial aptitudes that children inherit at birth. Such items are better suited to intelligence tests. Clearly items dependent either on the affluence of a student's family or on a child's genetic inheritance are not suitable for evaluating schools.

The testing approach shifts the discussion from the conditions of learning to motivation to learn. By conditions of learning, I mean students having well-trained teachers, complete sets of textbooks, small classes, and school buildings in good repair. The threat of failure on high-stakes tests will, it is assumed, overcome any major obstacles to learning. According to this reasoning,

- Fear of failure will cause students to study.
- Worried about their evaluations by school administrators, teachers will focus on instruction to keep their students from performing poorly on high-stakes tests.
- Worried about their evaluations, principals will work to ensure that teachers prepare students for high-stakes tests.
- Worried about their jobs and public images, superintendents will work to ensure that each school receives high test scores by preparing principals and teachers to ready their students for testing.

Finally, many argue that if money is going to be invested in education, then there must be some means of measuring its effectiveness. Of course, tests provide the easiest measure to report. Test results can be published in local newspapers or distributed by state agencies. But accountability based on test scores can potentially contribute to greater inequality between school districts. Some states, such as California, are now reporting test scores as an incentive for schools to improve. However, the reporting of scores has a direct effect on the housing market. Real estate agents, as I discussed in Chapter 2, are reporting that home buyers are arriving at their offices with lists of school test scores to use in selecting houses. Obviously, school districts reporting high test scores will be the most attractive to home buyers with school-age children. The effect is to drive up home prices in school districts with high test scores.

## NO CHILD LEFT BEHIND: HIGH-STAKES TESTING AND ACADEMIC STANDARDS

No Child Left Behind Act of 2001 mandates a schedule, target populations, and reporting procedures for high-stakes testing and academic standards. The schedule is:

1. By 2002–2003, states must provide annual report cards containing
   a. Student achievement scores
   b. Performance by school district
2. By 2002–2003, school districts must provide annual report cards containing
   a. Districtwide scores
   b. School-by-school scores

*Source:* John Trever/*Albuquerque Journal*

3. In 2002–03, biennial assessments begin using the National Assessment of Educational Progress for fourth and eighth grade reading and mathematics
4. By 2005–2006, each state will have academic standards in mathematics, reading or language arts for all public elementary and secondary school children; and standards in other subjects selected by the state
5. Beginning in 2005–2006, each state will have academic standards in science for all public elementary and secondary school children
6. By 2005–2006, states must begin administering annual statewide tests in reading and mathematics for grades 3 through 8
7. By 2007–2008, states must implement science tests once during elementary, middle, and high school

Theoretically, all of this test data is to spur school improvement by identifying low- performing schools and motivating teachers and school administrators to achieve state standards. The combination of state report cards for each school district and district report cards for each school results in every level of school administration and all teachers being judged by student performance.

Also, to highlight any possible discrimination of schools and school districts, states must make available to the public a list of elementary and secondary schools receiving funds for school improvement because they have, according to state standards, been failing for two years. This public list must include "the percentage of students in each school from families with incomes below the poverty level." In addition, the state must report students "by race, ethnicity,

**"I feel like I'm ahead of the game . . . I got better grades than my school did!"**
*Source:* Bruce Beattie/Copley News Service

gender, disability status, migrant status, English proficiency, and status as economically disadvantaged."

However, state and local report cards might increase economic and racial segregation. Real estate agents will be able to easily use this data to identify for clients high- and low-achieving school districts anyplace in the country. Many parents will be motivated to move to high-performing school districts resulting in a rise of housing prices and rents. Racial and ethnic reporting could result in greater racial and ethnic segregation in housing and schools.

Of course, one objective of the reporting is to allow parents in schools that have not shown improvement in two years the choice of sending their children to another public school. The major problem in executing this part of the plan is the lack of space in other public schools to accommodate students from failing schools. There are other parts of the law besides the choice plan that are designed to help children in failing schools. These include the following:

- Low-performing schools that do not improve in two years will receive technical assistance from the school district for school improvement.
- After three years of no improvement the school will be required to offer parent supplemental education services including private tutoring.
- After four years of no school improvement the district must replace some staff and adopt a new curriculum.
- After five years of no school improvement the school would be completely reorganized with an alternative governance structure such as reopening as a charter school.

Realistically, parents would avoid buying or renting in an area where they might have to send their child to a school that has publically be identified as having shown no improvement in two to four years. Family income will determine whether parents can avoid these low-performing schools. The result could be the residential concentration of academically low-performing students.

The triumph of the high-stakes testing model might be the identification of test scores by a person's residence. Imagine telling someone that you went to school in community X and, consequently, they know because of state and district report cards that you probably had a high score on state tests. State and local report cards would give everyone an economic and social rating.

## THE BACKLASH TO HIGH-STAKES TESTING

Getting tough with tests does not guarantee school improvement. A nationwide study conducted in 2000 by the Rand Corporation on the factors that contribute to higher test scores found a wide disparity in performance between states for students from socioeconomically similar families. Texas topped the list, with students scoring an average of 11 percentile points higher than their counterparts in last-ranked California. Most studies show that social class is the best predicator of school success and test performance. One would assume that test scores for people in the same social class would be the same between states. The discovered variation suggested that there were other important factors affecting test performance. By comparing state education programs and test results, the Rand study found that the following factors were key to high test performance:

- Higher expenditures per student.
- Smaller class sizes.
- Less teacher turnover.
- More public prekindergarten.
- Higher teacher satisfaction with classroom resources.

Interestingly, teacher salaries, experience, and level of education had little impact on student performance.

The Rand study demonstrates why low-income students do so poorly on high-stakes tests. Large numbers of low-income students are in school districts with high teacher turnover, few classroom resources, crowded classes, and low expenditures per student. Kati Haycock, director of the Education Trust, a Washington group focused on disadvantaged students, argues that the Rand study confirms a truth too many people want to ignore: "Poor children achieve at lower rates because we give them an inferior education. With targeted investments and high expectations, we can close the achievement gap once and for all."

So high-stakes tests have the potential of branding low-income students as failures. It is difficult to learn in school districts where there is little continuity in instruction because of high teacher turnover. It is also difficult to learn in large classrooms which make discipline rather than learning the major concern of teachers. It is difficult to learn with a lack of classroom resources. Essentially, the Rand study suggests that rather than improving schools, high-stakes testing just provides another way of labeling students.

The other major criticism of high-stakes examinations is that they primarily focus on lower-order thinking skills. The result is that in schools struggling to improve test performance, teachers emphasize lower-order as opposed to higher-order thinking skills. This compounds the problem for children from low-income families. They seldom are given projects and independent work designed to enhance critical thinking. Instead, their teachers follow scripted lessons for improving performance on tests.

In 1999, Walter Haney became concerned about the ability of schools that emphasized lower-order thinking skills to begin teaching higher-order skills. Haney became worried about this issue after encountering a statement by the Texas Commissioner of Education that it would only take two to three years for schools to shift their focus from tests emphasizing lower-order skills to higher-order thinking. He sent the following question to a group of top-ten American educators: "How long would it likely take for this large school system [Texas] to shift from having 80–90% of teachers teaching basic skills, to having 80–90% of teachers teaching the more advanced skills?" The response ranged from 2 to 20 years. Professor Henry Levin suggested that the change in instruction would take two to five years with the implementation of "continuous staff development, continuous support and technical assistance, administrative encouragement, intrinsic and extrinsic incentives, public information on results, and a culture of commitment. Add to this the transformation of local teacher training programs, careful selection of new teachers, and a strong public relations campaign, and things will move." However, Levin made the gloomy prediction, "No district has ever been able to achieve these conditions. Further, this will be competing with basic skills testing that is often high stakes and high visibility promoted by the states."

After studying the Texas school system, Haney came to the following conclusions:

1. Texas schools are devoting a huge amount of time and energy preparing students specifically for TAAS (Texas Assessment of Academic Skills).
2. Emphasis on TAAS is hurting more than helping teaching and learning in Texas schools.
3. Emphasis on TAAS is particularly harmful to at-risk students.
4. Emphasis on TAAS contributes to retention in grade and dropping out of school.

High-stakes testing also has a negative effect on teachers. Eighty-five percent of respondents agreed with Haney that

> It has also been suggested that the emphasis on TAAS is forcing some of the best teachers to leave teaching because of the restraints the tests place on decision making and the pressures placed on them and their students.

One teacher commented, "Mandated state TAAS testing is driving out the best teachers who refuse to resort to teaching to a low-level test!"

Haney concluded:

Texas . . . shows us the hazards of high stakes testing. It is, of course, possible to impose a "whips and chains" test-based accountability system on schools. Yet the Texas miracle story shows us the need to return standardized testing to its rightful place, as a source of potentially useful information to inform human judgment, and not as a cudgel for implementing education policy.

Other critics of high-stakes testing worry about the time devoted to test preparation in schools and how tests are being used to determine real estate values. Janyce Speier, a leader of the Potomac, Maryland, PTA said, "I find teachers are frustrated with the amount of time they spend on testing and would rather be with their kids doing other things. I salute accountability, but maybe you push the envelope too far." Jerry Weast, the superintendent of the school district, condemned the popular use of test scores. "These tests," he said, "were never designed for setting real estate values or for politicians to use as a way to lever their campaigns."

Professional organizations are also concerned about the widespread reliance on high-stakes tests. In 1999 the National Council of Teachers of English passed a resolution expressing concern about the effect of testing on classroom learning, the curriculum, teachers' work life, and children from low-income families. The resolution stated, "High-stakes testing often harms students' daily experience of learning, displaces a more thoughtful and creative curriculum, diminishes the emotional well-being of educators and children, and unfairly damages the life-improving chances of members of vulnerable groups." The resolution called upon state legislators to repeal laws that provide for significant consequences, such as retention of students in the same grade, denial of high school diplomas, and teacher and administrator evaluations.

At its 2000 national meeting, the National Council of Teachers of English also debated a Test Takers Bill of Rights which stated:

Resolved, that the National Council of Teachers of English, in conjunction with other professional and public policy organizations and learned societies, develop a Test Takers Bill of Rights that addresses such issues as:

- the right to insist that standardized tests be adopted through an open, public process that considers the design and appropriateness of the test;
- the right to know before the test date the form that any given test will use;
- the right to have assurance that a high-stakes test has been aligned with the standards of the curriculum;
- the right to experience a challenging curriculum that is not constrained by any given test;
- the right to know how the results of the test will be used;
- the right to arrange accommodations for documented learning differences and/or unforeseeable circumstances;
- the right to display competencies through various means;
- the right to an open process of review of test items and results;
- the right to challenge test scores and have them changed if they are incorrect;
- the right to a process that corrects tests and/or individual items found to be invalid or unreliable.

Be it further resolved, that NCTE encourages decision-making groups at the district, state, and federal levels to adopt the Test Takers Bill of Rights in order to protect students, parents, teachers, and the general public.

## CHEATING ON HIGH-STAKES TESTS

Cheating is likely as high-stakes testing is used to evaluate teachers and school administrators. With a state government that claims its educational miracle is based on accountability by high-stakes testing, Texas has been the scene of widespread cheating. Administrators and teachers have been accused of erasing student answers and adding correct answers. In 2000 the Houston public schools fired a teacher and reprimanded two principals after test tampering was discovered. In Austin, Texas, school officials were accused of raising state accountability ratings through test tampering. One Austin staff member was forced to resign. An elementary school teacher was fired after it was discovered the teacher used an answer key to change student answers. In addition, Austin school officials changed student-identification numbers so that students with low scores would not be factored into the school system's accountability ratings.

In Rhode Island, state education officials were forced to cancel the administration of English and mathematics tests for 2000 when it was discovered that many teachers had kept copies of the previous year's exams to use with students as part of the test preparation. The problem was that both years' exams contained the same questions. "It became clear that the scope of the breach was extensive," said Commissioner of Education Peter J. McWalters, "and that the assessment results would be invalid."

Also in 2000 officials at one of the best schools in affluent Potomac, Maryland, were accused of cheating—the school's principal resigned and a teacher was suspended. The principal was accused of allowing students extra time to complete state examinations, coaching them on questions, and changing incorrect answers. In Fairfax County, Virginia, charges were brought against a middle school teacher for improper coaching of students for state examinations.

In 1999, teachers and administrators in 32 schools in New York City were accused of erasing wrong answers and doing corrective editing on student answer sheets. A total of 47 principals, teachers, and staff members were implicated in the scandal. Examples of cheating included a seventh grade teacher who left a sheet of answers to a citywide math test near a pencil sharpener and then urged students to sharpen their pencils while she was out of the room. A fourth grade teacher discovered an essay question concerning Cubist art on the state English test and then devoted a lecture on Cubism right before the test. But these were somewhat minor compared to the corrective editing of tests by teachers and administrators.

There are also increased attempts to cheat on high-stakes college admission examinations. On October 29, 1996, *The New York Times* reported the arrest of George Kobayashi for helping students cheat on the Graduate Record Exam, the Graduate Management Admission Test, and the Test of English as a Foreign

Language. All of these tests are administered by the Educational Testing Service, which is the major gatekeeper to higher education and professional schools. In addition, the Educational Testing Service produces the Scholastic Aptitude Test, which makes it the major holder of high-stakes tests.

In Kobayashi's imaginative scheme, his company, the American Test Center, advertised a unique method costing $6,000 for preparing candidates for graduate school admission examinations. Relying on the difference in time zones, test takers flew to Los Angeles where they took the test three hours later than those taking it on the East Coast. Using anonymous names, Kobayashi's agents on the East Coast would first take the essay part of the examination and then during a recess telephone the questions to Kobayashi's office in Los Angeles. After the multiple-choice section of the examination, the agents would telephone the answers to the Los Angeles office. The answers were quickly inscribed in a special code on pencils that were given to Kobayashi's clients during their recess from the essay part of the examination.

"There's no way to tell how much cheating there actually is," claims Monty Neill, director of FairTest, a private education group opposed to the use of standardized tests, "but I get the sense nobody is looking too hard for abuses." Neill believes that because of high-stakes testing, "Schools are turning into test coaching centers, caught up in this frenzy of trying to look their best."

The future of high-stakes testing depends on the resolution of the problems associated with the cost, the effect on students from low-income families, the increasing residential segregation based on test scores, the increasing classroom time devoted to test preparation and test taking, the emphasis on lower-order thinking, the evaluation of teachers and school administrators, and cheating. These are not minor problems. In addition, there is now in place a testing industry that depends on schools using high-stakes testing for accountability. The testing industry is a major lobbyist for state and national testing. The final resolution of the issues raised by high-stakes testing will depend on the actions of politicians, school officials, and the testing industry.

## THE FEDERAL GOVERNMENT DECIDES THE READING WAR: NO CHILD LEFT BEHIND

Should the federal government mandate a particular method of instruction for American schools? You might be a fan of a particular method of teaching reading, but does this mean that you would favor federal laws requiring its use in the classroom? The No Child Left Behind Act supports one side of what is called the "reading wars." In a seemingly innocuous phrase, the "Reading First" part of the legislation alludes to "scientifically based reading research." This refers to the use of phonic methods in reading instruction. The actual wording of the legislation is:

> To provide assistance to State educational agencies and local educational agencies in establishing reading programs for students in kindergarten through grade 3 that are based on scientifically based reading research, to ensure that every student can read at grade level or above not later than the end of grade 3.

It is not within the scope of this text, nor is it appropriate within this limited space, to suggest the best methods of instruction. My purpose is to make you aware of the political nature of this debate. Teaching reading by using phonics methods is a staple of the conservative agenda for education, while liberals tend to support whole language methods. During the 2000 presidential campaign, candidate George W. Bush called for more federal money for reading programs. Attached to this proposal was the proviso that phonics would be the method used in federal reading programs. Bush's proposal reflected the conservative political push for phonics instruction in the schools. This was accomplished in the No Child Left Behind legislation. Prior to the 2000 presidential campaign, the California state legislature in 1997 passed a law requiring teacher trainers to sign an assurance clause, similar to a loyalty oath, that they would educate teachers to use phonics as the method for reading instruction.

Should presidential candidates and other national politicians be in the business of promoting a particular form of instruction? Should there be a public vote on methods of instruction, such as bilingual education? In fact, should there be state laws specifying instructional methodologies? Are state politicians qualified to make decisions about the best method of instruction?

What about assigning a special state committee to decide the best method for teaching mathematics? California did it in 1998, and the result was a heated political battle that caused Jack Price, the immediate past president of the National Council of Teachers of Mathematics, to conclude, "It isn't a question now of what is best for children, but who's going to win." The struggle can best be described as being between those advocating teaching math through conceptual understanding, mental computation and estimation, and cooperative work and those favoring traditional methods of memorization, paper-and-pencil computations, and drill and practice. On one side of the battle line was the California Mathematics Council, an organization of 12,000 teachers affiliated with the national math educators' council, which supported the newer conceptual approaches to teaching math. The president of the math council, Margaret DeArmond, defended the new methods because of "what kind of jobs students need in the future." On the other side, Martha Schwartz, one of the founders of the traditionalist group Mathematically Correct, argued, "We need to be much more specific and need to focus on skills."

## A CASE STUDY: STUDENT VIOLENCE AND FEDERAL ACTION

Of course, high-stakes testing and reading and math instruction are not the only worries confronting state and federal officials. The following stories of school violence caused federal officials to become involved in local school problems. In November 1998, five students in Burlington, Wisconsin, plotted to hold their high school principal hostage as they called 20 student victims from their classes for execution. Fortunately, the plan unraveled as the teenager with access to his father's rifles, shotguns, and handguns dropped out and another boy bragged about the scheme at a party. This gruesome plan included forcing the principal to announce over the school's intercom that all teachers were to keep their students in their classrooms while the juvenile terrorists searched through school files to find the classes of the victims. After calling their prey to the principal's office, the executioners envisioned a blood bath, including their own deaths along with those of the principal and students. A friend of the arrested conspirators described them as "the freaks" and "the Satan worshipers."

The Wisconsin conspiracy was reminiscent of shootings in the 1997–1998 school year that left 15 people dead and 42 wounded. Barry Loukatis, a 14-year-old honors student, contributed to that total when he walked into his algebra class at the Frontier Middle School in Moses Lake, Washington, dressed in black and armed with three family guns. After shooting his teacher in the back, Barry stood over a fellow student choking on his own blood and pronounced, "This sure beats algebra, doesn't it." In Jonesboro, Arkansas, two seventh grade students, Mitchell Johnson and Andrew Golden, successfully carried out a plan that included tripping the school fire alarm and killing five students and teachers leaving the school building. In West Paducah, Kentucky, 14-year-old Michael Carneal told his principal, "It was kind of like I was in a dream," after killing three girls and wounding five other students. In Springfield, Oregon, Kipland Kinkel was accused of killing 2 students and wounding 20 others with his father's semiautomatic rifle in a crowded school cafeteria. A Pearl, Mississippi, boy confessed to being enthralled with violent video games after randomly shooting students outside the town's high school.

In reaction to these and other scenes of school violence, U.S. Secretary of Education Richard Riley said, "We need to recognize that teaching young people coping and social skills that allow them to turn away from violence and drugs can take many forms." He recommended "character education, peer mediation, conflict resolution, and the establishment of student-run religious clubs." President Clinton chimed in, "When kids are more worried about guns and violence than math and science, we must all be committed to changing that."

The reaction to school violence provides a case study in federal influence. A central reason for federal involvement in the nineteenth century was the collection and distribution of education statistics. In keeping with this historical function, the U.S. Department of Education's National Center for Education Statistics in March 1998 issued the statistical report, "Violence and Discipline Problems in U.S. Public Schools: 1996–97." In 2000, the Federal Bureau of Investigation and the Department of Education teamed up to issue another report on school violence titled *Indicators of School Crime and Safety, 2000.* This report came to the happy conclusion for schools that "more victimizations happen away from school than at school." In other words, schools are safer than the home or streets. The report found that in 1998 students were twice as likely to be victims of serious violent crime away from school than at school. During 1998, students between the ages of 12 and 18 were victims of 2.7 million crimes. In school, students were victims of 253,000 serious violent crimes including rape, sexual assault, robbery, and aggravated assault. In addition, there were 60 school-associated violent deaths between July 1, 1997, and June 30, 1998—including 47 homicides.

Overall, the FBI report actually found a decline in school crimes during the 1990s. In fact, the study states, "As the rate of victimization in schools has declined or remained constant, students also seem to feel more secure at school now than just a few years ago. The percentage of students ages 12 through 18 who reported avoiding one or more places at school for their own safety decreased between 1995 and 1999—from 9 to 5 percent. Furthermore, the percentage of students who reported that street gangs were present at their schools decreased."

The executive of the FBI report concludes, "Therefore, the data shown in this report present a mixed picture of school safety. While overall school crime rates have declined, violence, gangs, and drugs are still evident in some schools, indicating that more work needs to be done."

In 2001, the Department of Justice teamed up with the Department of Education to issue a report, *Indicators of School Crime and Safety: 2001.* This document provided a summary of known facts about school violence. For instance, the report stated that in 1996–1997, 10 percent of all public schools reported at least one serious violent act such as murder, rape, sexual battery, suicide, use of a weapon, or robbery. Another 47 percent of public schools reported crimes such as a physical attack or fight without a weapon, theft/larceny, and vandalism.

Teachers were sometimes crime victims. Between 1995 and 1999, teachers were victims of approximately "1,708,000 nonfatal crimes at school, including 1,073,000 thefts and 635,000 violent crimes (rape or sexual assault, robbery, and aggravated and simple assault)." According to the report, there are "79 crimes per 1,000 teachers per year."

*Source:* Bob Englehart/*The Hartford Courant*

The logical next step after the collection of these statistics was for the federal government to become directly involved in funding violence prevention programs. This extended the federal government into another arena of education and added another step in the nationalization of the public school system. The No Child Left Behind Act of 2001 provided funds for violence reduction programs. The legislation declared that this section of the legislation would be called the Safe and Drug-Free Schools and Communities Act. The stated purpose of the legislation was "to support programs that prevent violence in and around schools; that prevent the illegal use of alcohol, tobacco, and drugs . . . through the provision of Federal assistance to . . . States for grants to local educational agencies."

The Safe and Drug-Free Schools and Communities Act highlights the structure of the current nationalization of schools. After identifying a problem—violence and drugs—the U.S. Congress passes a law that channels money through state governments to local school systems. The federal law specifies the type of programs that will be financially supported. To get these funds, state governments must act according to federal dictates. In turn, local schools seeking the funds must follow state guidelines. Consequently, administration of these funds requires three levels of administrators at the local, state, and federal levels.

## PRIVATE FOUNDATIONS: THE INVISIBLE POWER IN EDUCATION

Private foundations are an important means of nationalizing educational policies and practices. Often the activities of foundations result in government action. In *The Politics of Knowledge: The Carnegie Corporation, Philanthropy, and Public Policy,* Ellen Condliffe Lagemann writes, concerning a major foundation to affect educational policy, " . . . the Corporation's [Carnegie] policymakers sometimes helped government policymakers in realizing a program or plan . . . [In turn] the federal government often invited the Corporation to participate in policymaking or implemented the recommendations of Carnegie-supported groups."

In the United States, private foundations are established as philanthropic institutions by possessors of great wealth. Some of the largest foundations include the Ford Foundation, the Rockefeller Foundation, the Lilly Endowment, the W. K. Kellogg Foundation, and the Carnegie Corporation of New York. The names of the foundations suggest the sources of the fortunes that went into the establishment of these charitable organizations.

Because of their resources, private foundations can provide large sums of money to support studies, research, and organizations. These foundations have had a major impact on social policy in the United States. The broad scope and variety of activities sponsored by the foundations have led to their activities being attacked by both the political left and the political right in the United States. Right-wing groups attack foundations as instruments of large corporate wealth designed to promote a social policy that works against the interests of smaller industrial groups. Right-wing groups see foundations as restricting competition and supporting monopoly control of the marketplace through their funding of particular organizations and policies. In a similar fashion, left-wing political groups have been concerned about foundations exerting control over American social policy.

The real power of foundations lies in their ability to influence or control the areas in which they choose to spend money. Until the recent expansion of the federal government in the funding of research and social-action projects, foundations were the main source of funds for these activities in the United States. The decisions of foundations' boards of directors regarding funding of research, social projects, and organizations have determined the evolution and direction of scientific and social research and social policy in the United States.

Currently, the Carnegie Corporation of New York and the Rockefeller Foundation are playing leading roles in reshaping the profession of teaching. Money from both foundations supports the work of the National Commission on Teaching & America's Future. The Carnegie Corporation is the leading sponsor of the National Board for Professional Teaching Standards. If the plans of these two national groups are fulfilled, then the Carnegie and Rockefeller foundations will be responsible for national certification, national tests for state licensing, and national teacher-education standards.

Other foundations are responsible for many ideas associated with school choice and charter schools. In the 1970s, the head of the Olin Foundation, William Simon, called on business to donate money to foundations as part of a war against liberals. "I know of nothing more crucial," Simon wrote, "than to come to the aid of the intellectuals and writers who are fighting on my side. I strongly recommend that any businessmen with the slightest impulse for survival go and do likewise. The alliance between theorists and men of action in the capitalist world is long overdue."

Simon's call for business money to create a "counterintelligensia" against the liberal establishment resulted in large donations to existing conservative foundations and the creation of new ones. These conservative foundations include the Heritage Foundation, the American Enterprise Institute, the Hudson Institute, the Manhattan Institute, the Olin Foundation, and Empower America. These foundations supported leading conservative intellectuals interested in education, such as Diane Ravitch, William Bennett, Chester Finn, Jr., Denis Doyle, and Charles Murray. It is this group of conservative foundations and intellectuals that have campaigned for school choice, for-profit schools, charter schools, and privatization of schools.

In *Idea Brokers: Think Tanks and the Rise of the New Policy Elite,* James Allen Smith worries about the power of private money channeled through foundations to influence public policy and public opinion. Certainly, national certification, uniform teaching licenses, school choice, for-profit schools, charter schools, and privatization are major changes in public policy. Should private money be used to create major changes in public policies? Smith writes, "Ideas are indeed powerful political instruments. Masses can be moved, misled, or immobilized by them. Political leaders can seize upon ideas to uplift, to misinform, or to serve personal ambitions. Expert advisers, courtiers, and bureaucrats can use them to challenge authority, to curry favor, or to improve our understanding of politics and human affairs."

Therefore, foundations play an important role in shaping educational institutions. They act outside the arena of public influence. Often, the public is not even aware of their role in changing educational policy. The intellectuals who work for them, including college professors, are servants of power.

## SHOULD THE ROLE OF POLITICIANS IN EDUCATION BE LIMITED BY ELIMINATING COMPULSORY-EDUCATION LAWS?

Should some means be found to limit the role of politicians in education? One possibility is eliminating compulsory-education laws. The major authority states have for regulating public and private schools are compulsory-education laws. In most states parents can be arrested if they do not send their children to school. The state usually defines a school as an educational institution that conforms to state standards and regulation, including curriculum and teacher-certification requirements. This means that if an educational institution is not accredited by the state as complying with all state school requirements, its pupils are technically truant and their parents are liable for criminal prosecution. Without compulsory-school laws, parents would be free to send their children to educational institutions that do not conform to state regulations.

Compulsory-school-attendance laws vary from state to state in their actual form and interpretation by state courts. Robert P. Baker, a lawyer, reviewed judicial interpretations of the compulsory laws in an article titled "States Law and Judicial Interpretations" in *The Twelve Year Sentence,* edited by William F. Rickenbacker. Baker divides compulsory-schooling laws into what he calls the other-guy type and the cookie-cutter type. The argument given for the other-guy type of law is that although most people would educate their children without compulsory-schooling laws, there is somebody somewhere who would not educate his or her children. Compulsory-school laws then are designed to protect children from parents who are not willing to educate them. Where adopted, the other-guy type of interpretation results in a compulsory-schooling law requiring no more than what most parents would do anyway.

The cookie-cutter type of law is based on the idea that all children should have the same experiences within the same kind of institution. The most extreme example of a cookie-cutter type of law was a 1920 Oregon statute that required all children to attend public schools. One purpose of the law was to close Catholic schools. The U.S. Supreme Court ruled in 1925 that the law was not constitutional. The court stated, "The fundamental theory of liberty upon which all governments in this Union repose excludes any general power of the state to standardize its children by forcing them to accept instruction from public teachers only." Nevertheless, the ruling also upheld the right of the state to regulate private schools, which continued its right to enforce some form of standardization.

The differences between the other-guy and the cookie-cutter laws are best exemplified in judicial interpretations. For instance, in New Jersey in 1937 a Mr. and Mrs. Bongart were accused of being disorderly persons because they were educating their children in their home. The New Jersey compulsory-schooling law required attendance at school or equivalent instruction. Education in the home was not considered equivalent instruction by the trial judge because, in his words, "I cannot conceive how a child can receive instruction and experiences in group activity and in social outlook in any manner or form comparable to that provided in the public school." This is what Baker would call a cookie-cutter interpretation of the law. In a similar case, a young woman in Washington State was considered a delinquent and was made a ward of the court for not attending school. The trial court found that the instruction being given to the young woman in her home was at least the academic equivalent of that available in the public schools. Despite this finding, the Washington Supreme Court ruled against the child and her parents, with the argument that no school existed unless instruction was being given by a teacher certified by the state of Washington.

The other-guy type of judicial interpretation can result in a more flexible application of compulsory-schooling law. The most famous case was in Illinois in the 1950s in *People v. Levisen,* in which the parents, who were Seventh-Day Adventists, believed that educating their daughter in a public school would create an un-Christian character. The parents argued, "For the first eight or ten years of a child's life, the field or garden is the best schoolroom, the mother the best teacher, and nature the best lesson book." Education in the parents' home was considered adequate: The father was a college graduate and the mother had received training in pedagogy and educational psychology. Unlike the New Jersey and Washington courts, the Illinois courts formulated the other-guy philosophy in their ruling that "the law is not made to punish parents who provide their children with instruction equal or superior to that obtainable in the public schools. It is made for the parent who fails or refuses to properly educate his child."

The interpretation and application of state compulsory-schooling laws and education regulations will vary from state to state between the cookie-cutter and other-guy interpretations. In recent years all states have been limited in their application of the law as interpreted by the U.S. Supreme Court in the 1972 Amish case *State of Wisconsin, Petitioner v. Jonas Yoder et al.* In this case, Amish parents in Wisconsin were arrested in 1968 for refusing to comply with the state's compulsory-education law requiring the parents to enroll their children in high school. The Amish in Ohio, Pennsylvania, Iowa, and Wisconsin fought compulsory-schooling laws for years because they believed that high schools taught values that undermined their religious and communal lifestyle. The Amish eventually won their case against state-imposed compulsory education. The Court ruled that religious freedom was more important than state compulsory-schooling laws and that state law could not abridge the practice of religion (see Chapter 10 for a detailed analysis of their suit). This meant that if parents could prove in court that attending public school would interfere with the practice of their religion, they could not be forced to conform to state compulsory-schooling laws. Thus, the Supreme Court recognized that public schools were not always neutral as to religion. The social life, curriculum, and educational goals of the public schools could be in conflict with some religious customs and practices.

One of the most thorough criticisms of state regulation of education is made by one participant in the Amish case. Professor Donald Erickson provided expert educational testimony defending the right of the Amish to maintain their own educational practices. Erickson summarized some of his views in *Super-Parent: An Analysis of State Educational Controls,* written for the Illinois Advisory Committee on Nonpublic Schools. In his critique Erickson argues that two major reasons are given for state programmatic control of education. One reason is to ensure that all children have a reasonable chance to pursue happiness as free individuals. Education can give the individual some intellectual tools required for autonomous behavior. The second major reason given for state control of the schools is the protection of society from unemployment, indigence, crime, juvenile delinquency, mental illness, and political strife. This reason encompasses the social purposes of education discussed in the first chapter of this book.

In response to the first reason, that state-controlled education ensures autonomous individuals, Erickson points out that state-prescribed education is in direct conflict with the autonomy of all parents and does not give the child a model of a society of freely acting individuals. Erickson states, "In complex societies all over the world, however, state-controlled education arouses parental resistance. The reason is that child-rearing practices sponsored or required by the state in pluralistic societies are at odds with many parental views of the good life and how to prepare for it." Erickson argues that what is essential for the development of the autonomous individual in modern society is to learn reading, writing, arithmetic, and the fundamental workings of society's political, legal, and economic institutions. Still, even if we agree that knowledge of these subjects is essential for autonomous action, it does not, according to Erickson, justify the maintenance of the current system of compulsory school attendance and regulations. Parents and children could be given complete freedom to decide how the specified competencies were to be learned, and the child could be required to show through a national system of tests that progress is being made. This system would require compulsory education, but not compulsory school attendance.

The distinction between compulsory education and compulsory school attendance is very important for Erickson's argument. Compulsory education without compulsory school attendance would allow for the protection of those children suffering from parental neglect, without burdening all children with attendance at a state-regulated school. If during examinations the state found that a child was not learning the basics, it could prescribe some form of remedial action like required attendance at a state school.

As for education beyond elementary school, Erickson argues, there is no agreement among scholars about what knowledge is of most worth and what is essential for autonomous growth. This being the case, he feels that parents and children can decide what they should know and how they should learn it. Even if state officials can identify indispensable understandings and skills beyond the elementary ones already described, this does not require programmatic state regulation of schools. State intervention could be limited to those cases in which tests show that children are not making satisfactory progress toward the acquisition of required competencies.

Erickson rejects the second major reason given for state regulation of schools, which is protection of society from crime, unemployment, political strife, and other social problems. First, Erickson argues that no one knows what attitudes, understandings, and skills are truly necessary for the survival of a society. Second, no one knows how much a consensus about social and political beliefs is required before that same consensus actually becomes harmful to a society by limiting the freedom to find new ideas and adapt to new situations. You should remember from the first chapter that the argument for the achievement of the social and political purposes of schooling centers on the development of a consensus of political and social beliefs. Erickson rejects state involvement in this process with the argument that "state officials are probably the last group we should trust to decide how much commonality is essential to the general weal. It is in the interest of these officials to discourage the dissension and diversity that may jeopardize their positions, subject them to challenge, and make public institutions more difficult to govern smoothly."

In addition, it has never been proved that a relationship exists between the amount and quality of education available in a society and a decrease in crime, unemployment, and other social, economic, and political problems. In the twentieth century the education received by each person in society has steadily increased. At the same time crime has either remained the same or increased, unemployment has fluctuated with changes in the economy and labor market, indigence continues, and mental illness seems unaffected by the quantity of education. The nineteenth-century dream of schooling as a panacea for social problems does not seem to have been justified by the events of the twentieth century.

These facts might throw doubt on the reasons for compulsory-education laws, but there may be little chance of their demise. For instance, it would not be in the interest of teachers' unions to abandon compulsory-education laws because it would threaten student enrollments and teachers' jobs in public schools. In the past, teachers' unions strongly resisted vouchers and tuition tax credits for similar reasons.

Certainly, the combined interests of teachers' unions and the business community will continue to focus state efforts on issues of teacher compensation and the education of good workers. I will discuss the power of the federal government over educational policies in the next chapter.

## CONCLUSION

State and federal politicians are increasingly involved in issues of curriculum, methods of instruction, testing, and teacher certification. The trend is for more federal and state involvement in these areas. A pressing issue for the future is deciding whether there should be limits to political involvement in public schooling. Should federal and state politicians determine the content and methods of instruction?

## Suggested Readings and Works Cited in Chapter

ARCHER, JEFF. "R.I. Halts Exams in Wake of Wide-Scale Security Breaches." *Education Week on the Web* (17 March 2000). *This is a discussion of the Rhode Island scandal over cheating on standardized tests.*

BELLUCK, PAM. "Students Accused of Plotting Mass Slaying." *The New York Times* (17 November 1998). http://www.nytimes.com. *This is the story of the plot in Burlington, Wisconsin, to kill students and the principal.*

BIEBEL, CHARLES. "Private Foundations and Public Policy: The Case of Secondary Education during the Great Depression." *History of Education Quarterly* (Spring 1976). *Provides good examples of foundation influence over educational policy and organizations.*

BULLOCK, HENRY. *A History of Negro Education in the South.* New York: Praeger, 1970. *Chapter 5, "Deeds of Philanthropy," shows the influence of foundations on southern educational policy.*

CLINES, FRANCIS. "Cheating Report Renews Debate over Use of Tests to Evaluate Schools." *The New York Times on the Web* (12 June 2000). *This is a national report on the effect of cheating on the use of high-stakes tests.*

*Education Week. This weekly newspaper is one of the best sources of information on national educational politics.*

ERICKSON, DONALD. *Super-Parent: An Analysis of State Educational Controls. Written for the Illinois Advisory Committee on Nonpublic Schools, this is an important critique of the concept and practice of state regulation of schools.*

FUHRMAN, SUSAN. "State-Level Politics and School Financing." In *The Changing Politics of School Finance,* edited by Nelda Cambron-McCabe and Allan Odden. Cambridge, MA: Ballinger, 1982. *This is an analysis of the school finance reform movement on the structure of state politics of education.*

GOODNOUGH, ABBY. "If Test Scores of Students Swell, So May Superintendents' Wallets." *New York Times on the Web* (25 September 2002). *Describes bonus system for school superintendents based on student test scores.*

HANEY, WALT. "The Texas Miracle in Education." *Education Policy Analysis Archives: Center for Education, Research, Analysis, and Innovation* (21 August 2000). http://epaa.asu.edu/epaa/v8n41.

HARTOCOLLIS, ANEMONA. "9 Educators Accused of Encouraging Students to Cheat." *The New York Times on the Web* (3 May 2000). *This article reports on the New York City cheating scandal.*

HU, WINNIE. "9 Fired and 11 Others Face Dismissal in Cheating Scandal." *The New York Times on the Web* (12 December 1999). *This article reports on the New York City testing scandal.*

IANNACCONE, LAWRENCE. *Politics of Education.* West Nyack, NY: The Center for Applied Research in Education, 1967. *This book classifies the major types of state lobbying groups.*

*Indicators of School Crime and Safety, 2000.* Washington, DC: U.S. Printing Office, October 2000.

JOHNSTON, ROBERT. "Texas Presses Districts in Alleged Test-Tampering Cases." *Education Week on the Web* (15 March 2000). *Johnston discusses the testing scandal in Texas.*

KAUFMAN, PHILLIP, et al. *Indicators of School Crime and Safety: 2001.* U.S. Departments of Education and Justice. NCES 2002–113/NCJ–190075. Washington, DC: 2001. *Recent survey of school crime and violence.*

KEIM, ALBERT.   *Compulsory Education and the Amish.* Boston: Beacon Press, 1975. *This book provides background and discussions of* State of Wisconsin, Petitioner v. Jonas Yoder et al., *the important U.S. Supreme Court decision regarding compulsory education.*

KELLER, BESS.   "In State Campaigns, Schools Emerge as Topic." *Education Week on the Web* (20 September 2000). *Provides an analysis of the importance of education issues in the 2000 state elections.*

LAGEMANN, ELLEN CONDLIFFE.   *The Politics of Knowledge: The Carnegie Corporation, Philanthropy, and Public Policy.* Middletown, CT: Wesleyan University Press, 1989. *This is a history and analysis of the foundation that has had the greatest impact on educational policy in the United States.*

LAWTON, MILLICENT.   "Facing Deadline, Calif. Is Locked in Battle over How to Teach Math." *Education Week* (12 March 1997). http://www.edweek.org. *This article discusses California's political battle over the best method for teaching math.*

MANZO, KATHLEEN KENNEDY.   "Limitations on Approved Topics for Reading Sessions Rile Teacher Trainers." *Education Week* (5 November 1997). http://www.edweek.org. *This is a discussion of the California state law restricting the use of whole language methods to teach reading.*

MYRDAL, GUNNAR.   *An American Dilemma: The Negro Problem and Modern Democracy.* New York: Harper and Brothers, 1944. *Myrdal presents a Carnegie-sponsored study that has had a major influence on race relations in the United States.*

National Center for Education Statistics. *Violence and Discipline Problems in U.S. Public Schools: 1996–97.* Washington, DC: U.S. Department of Education, 1998. *This is a sweeping survey of violence in U.S. schools.*

NIELSEN, WALDEMAR.   *The Big Foundations.* New York: Columbia University Press, 1972. *This is a survey of the origins and activities of the major foundations in the United States.*

POPHAM, W. JAMES.   "Standardized Achievement Tests: Misnamed and Misleading." *Education Week* (19 September 2001). http://www.edweek.org. *A leading expert on test making, Popham criticizes the idea that standardized tests measure only achievement.*

PORTNER, JESSICA.   "Clinton Releases Findings of School Violence Survey." *Education Week* (25 March 1998). http://www.edweek.org. *President Clinton's comments on school violence are reported.*

Public Law 107–110, 107th Congress, Jan. 8, 2002 [H.R. 1]. "No Child Left Behind Act of 2001." Washington, DC: U.S. Printing Office, 2002. *Federal legislation dealing with high-stakes testing, reading, and school violence among other issues.*

"Resolution on Urging Reconsideration of High-Stakes Testing." Memorandum to NCTE from NCTE Committee on Resolutions, 2000 NCTE Resolutions, November 16, 2000. *This is the National Council of Teachers' resolution on the Test Takers Bill of Rights.*

RICHARDSON, LYNDA.   "Time-Zone Caper: Suspect Is Arrested in Testing Scheme." *The New York Times* (29 October 1996): 1, B17. *Reports on an example of one cheating scheme on high-stakes tests.*

RICKENBACKER, WILLIAM F., ed.   *The Twelve Year Sentence.* Chicago: Open Court, 1974. *Essays in this book discuss legal, historical, and philosophical arguments against compulsory education.*

SIMON, WILLIAM.   *A Time for Truth.* New York: McGraw-Hill, 1978. *Simon pleas for business to support conservative foundations to create a counterintelligentsia against liberals.*

SMITH, JAMES ALLEN.   *The Idea Brokers: Think Tanks and the Rise of the New Policy Elite.* New York: The Free Press, 1991. *Smith studies the influence of foundations on public policy.*

SPRING, JOEL.   *Conflict of Interests: The Politics of American Education.* New York: McGraw-Hill Companies, Inc. 2002. *This book provides an analysis of educational politics in the United States.*

_____. *Political Agendas for Education: From the Christian Coalition to the Green Party.* Mahwah, NJ: Lawrence Erlbaum, 1997. *This is a concise guide to the educational platforms of the major political organizations in the United States.*

U.S. Department of Education, National Center for Education Statistics. *Statistics of State School Systems; Revenues and Expenditures for Public Elementary and Secondary Education; and Common Core of Data Surveys* (May 2001). *Historical review of the proportion of revenues from local, state, and federal sources.*

WILGOEN, JODI. "National Study Examines Reasons Why Pupils Excel." *The New York Times on the Web* (26 July 2000). *This is a report on the Rand Corporation study on factors that contribute to high performance on high-stakes examinations.*

YARDLEY, JIM. "Critics Say a Focus on Test Scores Is Overshadowing Education in Texas." *The New York Times on the Web* (30 October 2000). *This is a summary of criticisms of the Texas government's emphasis on test scores as a method of improving education.*

## CHAPTER 8

# The Profession of Teaching

What is an American teacher? Guardian of morality and American character? Civilizer of western mining and ranching towns? Saint of freed slaves? Social worker in urban slums? Americanizer of immigrants? Protector against fascism and communism? Warrior against poverty? Champion of the global economy? As educational goals change so do the image and training of teachers. Now the profession is propelled by talk of the global economy. Protecting the U.S. role

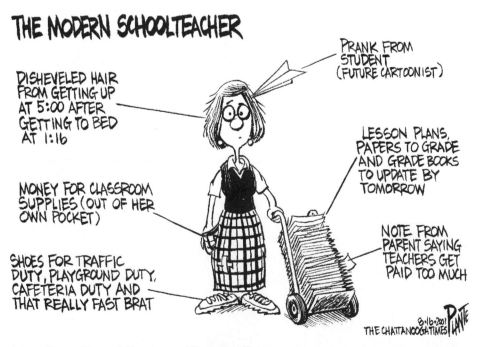

*Source:* Bruce Plante/*Chattanooga Times Free Press*

in the global economy continues the messianic vision of teachers as the saviors of society. In the nineteenth century, the development of professional teacher training paralleled the changing image of teachers from laughable weakling to the protector of American morality and character. In the 1830s, Horace Mann's declaration that common schools eliminate crime and morally reform society required the recruitment and training of moral teachers. The key was the feminization and professional training of the teaching force. Addressing the New York legislature in 1819, Emma Willard, founder of the Troy Female Seminary, whose main purpose was to educate teachers, declared the saving grace of female teachers: "Who knows how great and good a race of men may yet arise from the forming hands of mothers, enlightened by the bounty of that beloved country, to defend her liberties, to plan her future improvements and to raise her to unparalleled glory."

In 1839, Horace Mann supported establishment of a teacher-training institution in Lexington, Massachusetts. Called a normal school, this institution was designed primarily to train teachers for the elementary grades. In the twentieth century, many normal schools evolved into state colleges. Horace Mann quickly recognized the value of recruiting women into the teaching force. He wrote in 1846: "Reason and experience have long since demonstrated that children under 10 or 12 years of age can be more genially taught and more successfully governed by a female than by a male teacher." As protectors of morality, Mann emphasized the importance of teachers being "of pure tastes, of good manners, [and] exemplary morals." He charged local school committees with the responsibility of seeing that no teacher cross the school "threshold, who is not clothed, from the crown of his head to the sole of his foot, in garments of virtue."

Others echoed the sentiment that female teachers would be the guardians of American morality. The teacher was to save western mining and cow towns from lawlessness and immorality. Through the Board of National Popular Education, Catherine Beecher recruited teachers to civilize the West. Writing in the 1840s, Beecher envisioned "that in all parts of our country, in each neglected village, or new settlement, the Christian female teacher will quietly take her station . . . teaching . . . habits of neatness, order, and thrift; opening the book of knowledge, inspiring the principles of morality, and awakening the hope of immortality." After the Civil War, female teachers rushed into the South with a mission of creating social equality and political rights for freed slaves.

However, female teachers were often demeaned and exploited. Even into the twentieth century, most school districts did not allow female teachers to marry. In addition, teaching contracts warned female teachers not to be seen in public with men other than their fathers or brothers. Female teachers were to be moral models for their communities. In addition, female teachers were paid less than male teachers. The Boston Board of Education in 1841 urged the hiring of female teachers because "as a class, they [women] never look forward, as young men almost invariably do, to a period of legal emancipation from parental control, when they are to break away from the domestic circle and go abroad into the world, to build up a fortune for themselves; and hence, the sphere of hope and of effort is narrower, and the whole forces of the mind are more readily concentrated upon present duties."

Willard S. Elsbree, in *The American Teacher: Evolution of a Profession in a Democracy,* reports that from the 1830s up to the Civil War, increasing numbers of women entered teaching. The Civil War, with its demands for military manpower, completed the evolution of elementary school teaching from a male occupation to a primarily female occupation. For example, Elsbree states that in Indiana the number of male teachers in all grades dropped from 80 percent in 1859 to 58 percent in 1864; in Ohio the number of male teachers went from 52 percent in 1862 to 41 percent in 1864. The second-class citizenship of women in the nineteenth century made it possible to keep teachers' salaries low and contributed to the continuing low status of teaching as it became professionalized.

The growth of urban centers and immigration changed the image of teachers from protectors of morality to that of social welfare worker and vocational trainer. Teachers were enlisted to fight urban problems of crowding, epidemics, drugs, and crime. In addition, they were to prepare students for work in the modern factory. As the United States transformed from a rural to an industrialized nation in the late nineteenth and early twentieth centuries, teachers became workers in large educational bureaucracies. It was during this period, as I discuss later in the chapter, that teachers, following the lead of other workers, began to unionize.

Paralleling the new role of teachers as workers and defenders of industrial life, the professionalization of teaching moved from local control to the bureaucratic confines of state governments. Nineteenth-century teachers were usually certified by taking an examination administered by the employing school system or the county board of education. Licensing, or the granting of certificates to teach, was based primarily on examination and not on the number of education courses taken. Elsbree reports that in 1898 only four states had centralized certification or licensing at the state level. By 1933 forty-two states had centralized licensing at the state level; the primary requirement for gaining a teacher certificate was the completion of most courses in teacher education and other fields.

The centralization of certification and the dependence on teacher-education courses led to a rapid expansion of normal schools and colleges of education in the early twentieth century. State certification laws and expanded training in education completed the professionalization of teaching. Since 1933 this pattern of professionalization has continued with many normal schools becoming college and university departments of education. Course requirements in most states have generally increased and there has been a greater monitoring of teacher-education programs.

From the 1920s to the 1950s, teachers were asked to promote 100 percent Americanism against the threat of fascist and communist ideas. During this period, many states required teachers to take loyalty oaths. Organizations, such as the American Legion and Daughters of the American Revolution, helped purge schools of teachers with leftist ideas. When it appeared in the 1950s that the United States was slipping behind the Soviet Union in the military arms race and conquest of space, American teachers were called on to educate a generation of students to win the technological race. As worries shifted to poverty and race relations in the 1960s, teachers became warriors in War on Poverty programs. As unemployment and high inflation gripped the nation in the 1970s and 1980s, teachers were called on to guide students into the labor market.

Now, certification of teachers is being pushed to new levels of control and hierarchy. Teachers, as protectors of the U.S. role in the global economy, are being asked to obtain national certification and a professional education that will help students adapt to requirements of the international workforce.

The new training and role for teachers in the global economy raises a series of questions that are central to the evolution of the profession:

- Should teacher education change as the goals of schooling change?
- Should teacher education be focused on the imperatives of the global economy?
- Should teachers be trained to meet the special needs of children growing up in poverty, children from differing cultural backgrounds, children with special needs, and gay/lesbian students?
- Should teacher-education programs prepare teachers for training future citizens and inculcating moral and social values?

## TEACHER EDUCATION IN A GLOBAL ECONOMY

The teacher shortage is an important factor in reshaping the role of teachers for the global economy. The shortage sounds sweet to the ears of teacher educators because it provides the opportunity to tighten teacher examinations, require national certification, and control teacher education curricula. More new teachers mean a greater opportunity for departments and colleges of education to train a new generation of educators. As Linda Darling Hammond, director of the National Commission on Teaching and America's Future, excitedly told the press in August 1996, "We had huge hiring in the baby boom years of the '50s and '60s. By the time we restaff the schools in the next 10 to 15 years, it will be the biggest overhaul of the teaching force ever in our history."

It is estimated that half the teachers employed in the year 2005 will have been hired after 1996. Imagine replacing half the teaching force! One reason for the growing teacher shortage is a rapidly increasing student population. In 1996, 51.7 million students entered public and private elementary and secondary schools. This number surpassed the high during the baby boom of 51.3 million in 1971. Estimates project an increase of the student population to 55.9 million by the year 2005. Also, many teachers hired during the baby boom years are retiring. It is expected that the public school teaching force will grow from 2.8 million in 1991 to 3.3 million in the year 2002.

Another cause of the teacher shortage are the more favorable salaries in other white collar professions. Tables 8–1 and 8–2 provide a comparison of teacher salaries with that of other college graduates and professions for the 2000–2001 school year. As indicated in Table 8–1, college graduates entering

**TABLE 8–1. Average Starting Salaries for College Graduates 2000–2001**

| New College Graduates | Starting Salaries |
|---|---|
| Teaching | $28,986 |
| Accounting | 37,143 |
| Sales/Marketing | 40,033 |
| Math/Statistics | 49,548 |
| Computer Science | 49,749 |
| Engineering | 74,920 |

*Source:* "Good News/Bad News for Teacher Salaries, AFT Releases Latest State-by-State Teacher Salary Survey" (16 July 2002), http://www.aft.org/convention/salary_survey.html.

**TABLE 8–2. Average Salaries for White Collar Occupations 2000–2001**

| Occupation | Salary |
|---|---|
| Teacher | $43,250 |
| Mid-level Accountants | 52,664 |
| Computer System Analysts | 71,155 |
| Engineers | 74,920 |
| Attorneys | 82,712 |

*Source:* "Good News/Bad News for Teacher Salaries, AFT Releases Latest State-by-State Teacher Salary Survey" (16 July 2002), http://www.aft.org/convention/salary_survey.html.

teaching started at an average of $28,986 a year, while other graduates received higher starting salaries ranging from $37,143 for accounting majors to $74,920 for engineering majors. As indicated in Table 8–2, these differences were reflected in average white collar salaries with teachers earning on average $43,250 a year, while mid-level accountants earned $52,664 and attorneys $82,712. In examining these salary differences, it is important to remember that most experienced teachers are now required to have advanced professional training and degrees which in other white collar professions would result in much higher salaries.

Traditionally, teachers' salaries follow the laws of supply and demand. According to a 2002 report of the American Federation of Teachers, beginning teacher salaries are increasing at a steady rate; the average beginning teacher's salary in 2000–2001 was $28,986, up 4.4 percent from the previous year. However, the increases are primarily for beginning teacher salaries rather than for all teachers. School systems are interested in attracting new teachers rather than raising the salaries of experienced teachers. Sandra Feldman, President of the American Federation of Teachers commented, "The good news is that better starting salaries will attract more people to the teaching profession, but the bad news is that increases for experienced teachers are inadequate to keep them in the classroom. We need to retain quality teachers so that students and rookie teachers have the opportunity to learn from seasoned professionals."

# DISPARITIES IN TEACHER SALARIES
# AND EQUALITY OF EDUCATIONAL OPPORTUNITY

If we assume that high salaries attract the best teachers, then differences in teacher salaries between school districts might reflect differences in equality of educational opportunity for students. Students attending school districts with high teacher salaries might be receiving a better education than those attending school districts with low teacher salaries.

Two important questions are raised by the potential link between teacher salaries and equality of educational opportunity:

1. Should teacher salaries be equal between school districts within the same state?
2. Should teacher salaries be equal between states?

The first question deals with the existing disparity of teacher salaries between school districts in the same state as exemplified in Tables 8–3 and 8–4. The second question focuses on the disparities between states as exemplified in Table 8–5.

Table 8–3 provides an example of differences in teacher salaries as reported by Ohio's Legislative Office in 1999. Teachers with Master's degrees in the top

**TABLE 8–3. Differences in Salaries for Teachers with Master's Degrees for Selected Districts in Ohio, 1997–1998**

| School District | Average Salary |
| --- | --- |
| Perry (Lake) | $54,515 |
| Upper Arlington (Franklin) | 54,210 |
| Brecksville-Broadview Hts. (Cuyahoga) | 53,851 |
| Eastern (Meigs) | 29,918 |
| Austintown (Mahoning) | 25,221 |
| Buckeye (Ashatbula) | 22,162 |

*Source:* Legislative Budget Office, Ohio, *Policy Brief: Teacher Salaries* 1, no. 4 (21 January 1999), http://www.ohio.gov/.

**TABLE 8–4. Salary Differences Between Low-Need and High-Need School Districts in New York State**

| School District Need Status | Median Teacher Salary |
| --- | --- |
| Low need | $64,217 |
| Average need | 49,075 |
| High need, urban-suburban | 51,054 |
| High need, rural | 41,300 |

*Source:* New York State Department of Education, "Personal Attention and Access to Knowledge," http://www.emsc.nysed.gov/stateaidworkgroup/rsap-13.htm.

**TABLE 8–5. Average Teacher Salaries, 2000–2001, and Median Household Income, 2000, for Selected States**

| State | Average Teacher Salary | Median Household Income |
|---|---|---|
| Connecticut | $53,507 | $51,432 |
| California | 52,480 | 46,008 |
| New Jersey | 51,955 | 51,320 |
| New York | 51,020 | 41,504 |
| Michigan | 49,044 | 46,986 |
| Montana | 33,249 | 32,169 |
| Oklahoma | 32,545 | 33,235 |
| Mississippi | 31,954 | 32,581 |
| North Dakota | 30,891 | 34,665 |
| South Dakota | 30,265 | 36,681 |

*Source:* "Good News/Bad News for Teacher Salaries, AFT Releases Latest State-by-State Teacher Salary Survey" (16 July 2002), http://www.aft.org/convention/salary_survey.html; and U.S. Bureau of the Census, "Money Income in the United States: 2000" (Washington, DC: U.S. Government Printing Office, 2000).

three districts for salaries all earned over $50,000 a year, while those in the poorest-paying districts earned between $22,162 and 29,162 a year. In other words, those teachers in the highest-paying districts earned almost twice as much as those in the poorer-paying school districts.

In another example of salary disparities, New York State's Department of Education did a study of differences in teacher salaries between low-need and high-need school districts. Low-need school districts had few students who were at risk of academic failure. These districts were the most affluent school districts. High-need school districts were those with the most students who were at risk of failing and they tended to be the least affluent school districts. As indicated in Table 8–4, teachers with the highest salaries averaging $64,217 were concentrated in low-need school districts. High-need districts, which require the best teachers to help at-risk students, offered teacher salaries averaging $41,300 in rural areas and $51,054 in urban-suburban school districts.

There are also salary disparities between states as highlighted in Table 8–5. As indicated in the table, Connecticut, California, New Jersey, New York, and Michigan have the highest average teacher salaries in the United States, while Montana, Oklahoma, Mississippi, North Dakota, and South Dakota have the lowest. It is not surprising that the differences in teacher salaries also parallel the differences in household income. States with the highest teacher salaries have household incomes around $10,000 more than those states with the lowest teacher salaries. The differences are significant with Connecticut having the highest average teaching salaries at $53,507 a year and South Dakota the lowest at $30,265. This is a $23,242, or 56 percent, difference.

These examples of teacher salary differences can be found in most states. You might want to examine the differences in salaries in your own region and state.

# CURRENT ISSUES IN TEACHER EDUCATION

The scope of the National Commission on Teaching and America's Future's goals for teacher education evokes many questions. These questions involve some basic issues regarding teacher education. My intention is to use the following questions to highlight ongoing problems in educating teachers and organizing teaching as a profession:

- Should the goals and content of teacher education be determined by the needs of the global labor market?
- Should tests required for national licensing and certification determine the content of teacher-education programs and courses?
- Should career ladders for teachers be based on levels of certification?
- Should teachers be trained to "teach to the test"?

The first question repeats many issues related to the purposes of education. The major difference is the focus on training teachers to carry out the purposes of education. In this model, teachers do not act independent of the overall goals of schooling. The independence and creativity of the teacher are confined to discovering the best teaching strategies and educational materials to achieve the broader goal of preparing students to compete in a global labor market.

A convincing argument for relating teacher training to the general purposes of education is that the public pays for public schools and most teacher-training programs. Therefore, the public has a right to expect public benefits. Consequently, if the public wants schools to educate students for the global labor market, then teacher-education programs should prepare teachers to accomplish that goal. If a person wants to become a teacher, then he or she should expect to have his or her training geared to meet public needs.

## Control Through Testing: National Licensing and Certification

The second question is based on the National Commission on Teaching and America's Future's plan to use the power of assessment to change teacher education. The Commission prefers to use the word *assessment* because the word *test* evokes an image of simple paper-and-pencil examinations. Assessment encompasses paper-and-pencil tests, portfolios containing examples of work, videotapes, and observations. In reality, most licensing procedures will focus on the traditional examination form. On the other hand, national certification will be granted through a broad assessment of the candidate's qualifications.

The power of tests or assessments to control a system is quite simple. If you want to become a teacher, then you must learn the material that will be on the statewide teachers' examination. If departments or colleges of education want their students to be licensed, then they must prepare them to pass statewide examinations. To prepare for statewide examinations, the content of teacher-education courses must be organized around the content of the statewide examination.

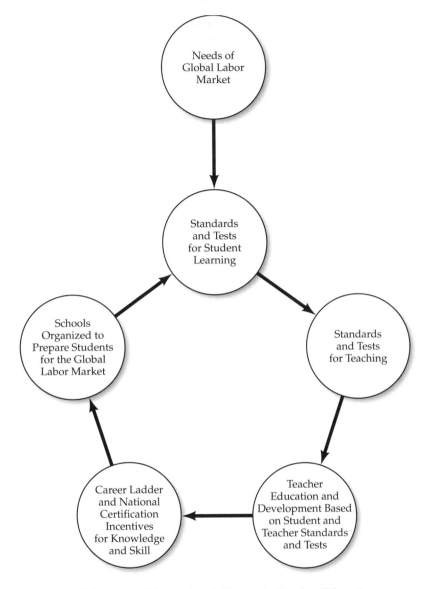

FIGURE 8–1. Elements of Control and Change in Teacher Education

The Commission proposes linking this model of control to national and state academic standards for students. As indicated in Figure 8–1, the standards for student learning determine the standards for teaching, which in turn determine teacher education and development. Eventually, the standards for students and teacher education determine the organization of schools. Some form of a test controls each stage of development.

In *What Matters Most: Teaching for America's Future,* the Commission provides an example of how the testing procedure can control teachers and school organizations. In this example, middle school mathematics teachers are concerned about the poor performance of their students on a statewide examination. Two teachers volunteer to organize material for study, including items from the test, scoring sheets, and student records. At the first meeting, the teachers decide to take the test. Afterward, "they analyze it closely for what it covers mathematically and what kind of things one needs to know and be able to do in order to do it." The teachers then spend a year studying the test, mathematics instruction, and learning theories so that they can organize their courses to prepare their students for the statewide test. For the Commission, this example exemplifies

> several elements of powerful professional education. . . . The teachers are bent on improving performance and they construct a way for themselves to investigate mathematics, assessment, learning, and teaching *using their need to look more closely at the test to understand it* [my emphasis]. . . . Their investigation of *what was causing students to do so poorly on the test* [my emphasis] gave them an opportunity to deepen their own understandings of mathematics, as well as of students' thinking and interpretation, and of the structure and worth of tasks.

The Commission envisions two major stages in using national examinations to control the content and programs in teacher education. The first stage is national licensing. Currently, licenses are granted by state governments. When teachers complete a teacher-preparation program and a statewide examination, they apply for a license from a state agency. This state-by-state procedure requires teachers to apply for a new license every time they move to a different state. In addition, according to the Commission, state-by-state licensing makes it difficult to create uniformity in teacher training.

## National Certification: The National Board for Professional Teaching Standards

The National Board for Professional Teaching Standards is issuing a national teaching certificate that it hopes will be recognized by all states. In addition, this national certification would supposedly identify master teachers. The Board was created in 1987 in the belief that the nation's schools were hindering America's ability to compete in the global economy. It was an outgrowth of the Task Force on Teaching's report *A Nation Prepared: Teachers for the 21st Century.* The report asserts that America can no longer compete in mass-production of goods in world markets. Consequently, the report argues, the nation must shift its economy to emphasize knowledge-based industries. In this context, the schools must stop teaching the repetitive skills needed in mass production and start teaching all students higher-order thinking skills. According to the report, the old educational requirements needed for a mass-production economy could be packaged in texts, and teachers could be trained to use those texts. A knowledge-based economy, on the other hand, requires students who are intellectually prepared to deal with a nonroutine world and unexpected events. The report argues that the training of students in higher-order skills requires abandoning traditional textbook teaching and developing new teaching strategies.

The National Board for Professional Teaching Standards' purpose is establishing standards for the profession of teaching and certifying that individuals meet these standards. Currently, the Board states its mission as:

1. Maintaining high and rigorous standards for what accomplished teachers should know and be able to do.
2. Providing a national voluntary system certifying teachers who meet these standards.
3. Advocating related education reforms to integrate National Board Certification in American education and to capitalize on the expertise of National Board Certified Teachers.

The National Board for Professional Teaching Standards identifies five teacher characteristics that they consider the hallmark of accomplished teaching. These five propositions guide the assessment process:

1. Teachers are committed to students and their learning. Accomplished teachers are dedicated to making knowledge accessible to all students. They act on the belief that all students can learn.
2. Teachers know the subjects they teach and how to teach those subjects to students. Accomplished teachers have a rich understanding of the subject(s) they teach and appreciate how knowledge in their subject is created, organized, linked to other disciplines, and applied to real-world settings.
3. Teachers are responsible for managing and monitoring student learning. Accomplished teachers create, enrich, maintain, and alter instructional settings to capture and sustain the interest of their students and to make the most effective use of time.
4. Teachers think systematically about their practice and learn from experience. Accomplished teachers are models of educated persons, exemplifying the virtues they seek to inspire in students—curiosity, tolerance, honesty, fairness, respect for diversity, and appreciation of cultural differences.
5. Teachers are members of learning communities. Accomplished teachers contribute to the effectiveness of the school by working collaboratively with other professionals on instructional policy, curriculum development, and staff development.

In 2000, the National Board for Professional Teaching Standards released a report that supports their claim that its test identifies effective teachers. The report compared a group of teachers who failed the test with a group who passed the test. The study found that teachers who passed the test had:

- A deeper understanding of why students succeeded and failed.
- Better ability to improvise skills when needed.
- More passion for teaching.
- Better ability to convey knowledge to students.
- Better ability to design lessons.
- Better ability to critique their instructional methods.

In 2002, the fee for National Board Certification was $2,300. This was expensive when you consider the average teacher salary was $43,250. Consequently, the Board has lobbied states to cover the testing fee. In 2002, thirty-one states along with many school districts provided financial aid to candidates to cover the high cost of the test fee. Also, many states and local districts guaranteed a salary supplement for those gaining National Board Certification.

## TEACHER EDUCATION

Teacher testing is one method for controlling the content of teacher education. Similar to other aspects of the high-stakes test model of equality of opportunity, there is an attempt to connect teacher education curricula to testing models such as that of the National Board for Professional Teaching Standards. Most of the current plans for teacher education originated from the concern to prepare U.S. students to compete in global markets. In 1992, a report of the American Association of State Colleges and Universities, *Teacher Education for the Twenty-First Century*, proposed organizing teacher education to meet the needs of a global economy. In addition, they recommended a requirement for "multicultural proficiency." The Association's report calls for the education of "teacher-scholars," who have a strong liberal arts education with an in-depth focus on subject matter and training in a professional school of education. The teacher-scholar, according to the report, should have a knowledge of methods of instruction, human development, learning theories, effective skills, and, of course, subject matter.

There continues to be an inherent logic to the educational requirements for teachers. It is logical that teachers know the

- Subject matter they are to teach.
- Psychological and physical natures of those they plan to teach.
- Political and social structures of the institutions in which they will be teaching.
- Methods by which people learn.
- Best methods for teaching a particular subject matter.

Most teacher-education programs include all of the preceding components. An introductory course on American education or educational foundations gives the future teacher an understanding of the political and social contexts in which he or she will be working. Courses in educational psychology, human development, and theories of learning give the prospective teacher an understanding of the individuals to be taught. In addition, courses in methods of instruction prepare a would-be teacher to teach in particular subject-matter areas. General education requirements are designed to ensure that a teacher knows his or her subject matter well.

Teaching not only requires knowing the subject matter, the learner, and the political and social context of learning, but it also involves skills that can be improved through actual practice. All teacher-education programs have some form of practice teaching that allows experienced teachers to aid prospective teachers in gaining teaching skills. Some teacher-education programs require observation periods before actual practice teaching. Other programs provide clinical experiences before or during practice teaching.

Most teacher educators agree that the preceding combination of knowledge and skill development should form the basic components of a teacher-education program yet there are disagreements about the actual content of each component, the proportion of time that should be devoted to each area, and the additional knowledge and skills necessary for teaching.

The Carnegie Foundation for the Advancement of Teaching's report, *High School*, provided specific recommendations for carrying out the general improvement of teacher education. The author of the report, Ernest Boyer, recommended that the first two years of college training be devoted to the study of a core of common learning. The responsibility for this core curriculum would be in the hands of the liberal arts faculty. Admission to a teacher-education program would occur in the junior year of college, and admission would require a "B" average or better plus strong recommendations from two professors. The teacher-education program would be three years long, with the first two years (the student's junior and senior years) devoted to completing a major in an academic discipline and to classroom observation.

After studying a core curriculum and completing an academic major, the prospective teacher would take teacher-education courses. Boyer is aware of the criticism directed at education courses. He writes, "While many speak disparagingly of teacher-education courses, we conclude there is important information uniquely relevant to teachers." Boyer believes that four areas of study should be part of the teacher-education curriculum. The first area is what the report calls "schooling in America." This course would be devoted to the history of education and current issues in education. The other three areas would deal with "learning theory and research," "teaching of writing," and "the use of technology." Boyer writes that "all teacher education students should study theories of learning, the ways teachers teach and students learn, and examine also the findings of current psychological and physiological research bearing on these themes." Boyer's emphasis on prospective teachers learning to teach writing reflects the general concern of the report with language instruction. The report argues that writing is not only an essential skill for self-expression but also an important means of teaching critical thinking. Boyer believes that all teachers should be prepared to teach students how to write better. Also, prospective teachers should study educational technology, including computers, for significantly improving classroom instruction. Besides the course work, Boyer recommends that the fifth year include classroom observation and practice teaching.

Reflecting the general trend to make teacher training a fifth-year program or graduate program, *A Nation Prepared: Teachers for the 21st Century* recommended restructuring teacher education by replacing undergraduate programs in education with graduate programs. Overall, *A Nation Prepared* advocates an undergraduate program devoted to a broad liberal arts education and a thorough study of the subject or subjects the student plans to teach. In keeping with the general trend toward a core curriculum, the report recommends an undergraduate curriculum that would provide rigorous study of history, government, science, literature, and the arts. The authors argue that elementary teachers need the same strong academic background as high school teachers because they have equal responsibility to impart our common culture and heritage. Professional courses in education would be provided at the graduate level in a master-in-teaching degree program to give teachers information about techniques of teaching, research on teaching, human development, and different learning styles. In addition, teachers seeking advanced certification would study philosophy of education, policies in education, and techniques of measurement.

## AMERICAN BOARD FOR CERTIFICATION OF TEACHER EXCELLENCE: ALTERNATIVE ROUTES TO TEACHING

In 2001, the U.S. Department of Education launched the American Board for Certification of Teacher Excellence to support alternative routes to certification for teachers from "nontraditional" backgrounds. These nontraditional backgrounds included professionals from other careers "who have the interest and ability to become teachers but who don't have the traditional teacher training and education." The program envisioned offering a "Passport" usable anywhere in the nation to qualified candidates. The Passport would supposedly attest to the mastery of subjects and professional skills needed for classroom effectiveness.

The federal government is also sponsoring the "Transition to Teaching Program" which provides grants for the recruitment, training, placement of people from other fields into teaching positions, and support for them during their first years in the classroom. The program targets mid-career professionals "who possess strong subject-matter skills and recent college graduates with outstanding academic records and a baccalaureate degree in a field other than teaching."

In addition, the Defense Department and the Education Department announced a joint program called "The Troops to Teachers Program." The stated goal of the program is "to help improve American education by providing mature, motivated, experienced, and dedicated ex-military personnel for the nation's classrooms. The current program provides referral assistance, placement services and stipends to military personnel interested in becoming teachers after their military service."

## THE REWARDS OF TEACHING

Why do people become teachers if the pay is low for a job that requires an extensive education and licensing? One answer is that teachers find their greatest reward in interacting with students. Also, in comparison with many corporate and factory jobs, teachers enjoy a great deal of autonomy in the classroom. It has been estimated that teachers make more than two hundred decisions an hour in their classrooms. These decisions range from curricular and teaching problems to behavioral problems. Compared with routine work, teachers can be involved in creative decision making. In a national survey, "Teachers' Working Conditions," Susan Choy found that "the vast majority of teachers thought that they had a good deal of control in their own classroom over practices such as evaluating and grading students, selecting teaching techniques, and determining the amount of homework to be assigned."

Other ancillary rewards of teaching are attractive to many individuals. A popular reward is the time for extended vacations and travel provided by the long summer vacation and other school holidays. Second to vacation time is the security of income and position. In most states teacher tenure laws provide a security not often found in other jobs.

In *A Place Called School* John Goodlad found a higher level of satisfaction among teachers than one would have suspected from the current criticism of the profession. In his sample, 74 percent felt their "career expectations had been fulfilled," and 69 percent said they would again "select education as a career."

Goodlad found that "personal frustration and dissatisfaction in the teaching situation" was the major reason teachers left teaching. Conflicts with fellow teachers, administrators, and students ranked low as reasons for leaving the profession. Goodlad argued that though interest in money was not a major reason given by teachers for entering the career of teaching, it was given as the second reason for leaving it. Goodlad writes:

> We might speculate that, anticipating rewards intrinsic to the work, teachers begin with a willingness to forego high salaries. However, when confronted with the frustration of these expectations, the fact that they sometimes are paid less than the bus drivers who bring their students to school may become a considerable source of dissatisfaction as well.

Another source of frustration for teachers is their relations to parents. In 1990 and 1991, Louis Harris and Associates conducted a survey of teachers' attitudes. Seventy percent of the teachers surveyed reported positive experiences with their students, and almost 60 percent reported positive relations with other teachers. On the other hand, only 50 percent reported that their working relationship with school principals was productive. The lowest percentage of teachers expressing satisfaction was with relations with parents. Only 25 percent reported finding their relations with parents to be cooperative and supporting.

Regarding the factors contributing to a person leaving teaching, the Harris survey found that the most often-cited reason was lack of parental support. The next most often-cited reason was low salary. In addition, the survey found that 20 percent of new teachers felt that they were very likely to leave the profession within their first five years of teaching.

Are teachers prepared to educate minority children and children from low-income families? Certainly the social background of many teachers does not prepare them for teaching the neediest children. In *Teachers for Our Nation's Schools* John Goodlad reports a survey of students enrolled in teacher-education programs, which includes 3,000 usable questionnaires and about 325 inter-

views with individual students. With regard to social and economic characteristics, 80 percent of students were female and 92 percent were white. In addition, 85 percent came from families earning more than a middle-class income.

On the other hand, the survey found that the top reasons given by students
for entering teaching are "having a satisfying job" and liking and wanting to
help children. Despite these altruistic reasons, most students faced critical comments from family members and friends. Some parents rejected the decision
and refused to support their child's schooling in teacher education. Despite
these reactions and recognition of the low status of teacher education and
teachers, students often clung to their belief in the importance of teaching.

The survey also found that students in teacher education primarily thought
of teaching basic subjects and not about the more general educational goals,
such as citizenship and morality. Even creativity was at the bottom of the educational purposes selected by students.

In addition, students in teacher education were more oriented toward practical issues, such as methods of teaching. Very few paid much attention to their
educational foundations courses, and many shrugged off their liberal arts requirements as courses they must endure. The result is that education students,
by undervaluing liberal arts and educational foundations courses, contribute to
the second-class academic status of education and, in part, the profession of
teaching.

The education faculty find themselves in the same status ranking as students. Viewed by the rest of the campus as teaching Mickey Mouse education
courses, the education college faculty are caught between the job requirements
and prestige scale of the college. Faculty in liberal arts might complain about
teacher-education programs being trivial. On the other hand, these same liberal
arts faculty will be quick to complain that teachers are not adequately trained.
Of course, in this context, improved training means improved methods of teaching courses that are branded by the same liberal arts faculty as Mickey Mouse.
This becomes a no-win discussion for both education faculty and students.

## WORKING CONDITIONS

Teachers average a 45-hour workweek. A national study of teachers' working
conditions found that full-time public school teachers at both the elementary
and secondary levels are required to be at school for an average of 33 hours a
week. In addition, teachers spend an average of 12 hours after and before
school and on weekends grading papers, preparing lessons, meeting with parents, and performing other school-related activities. Teachers at private schools
averaged about one more hour of required time at school and one more hour of
after-school work.

A major issue for teachers is class size. Besides affecting the quality of learning for students, class size has a direct bearing on the working conditions of
teachers. Large classes result in more papers to grade and more problems in class
discipline. Also, large classes affect the quality of interaction between students

...AND SO BEGINS ANOTHER DAY AT FIBBER McGEE ELEMENTARY...

*Source:* Jeff Parker/*Florida Today.* Reprinted with permission of Cagle Cartoons, Inc.

and teachers. If the major reason people enter teaching is the opportunity for interacting with students, then reward is enhanced through small classes.

In 1998, the federal government initiated a program to lower class sizes in the early grades to no more than 18 students. According to the U.S. Department of Education's report *The Class-Size Reduction Program* (September 2000), "Prior to the implementation of the federal Class-Size Program and similar initiatives in several states, more than 85 percent of our students were in classes with over 18 children, and about 33 percent were in classes of 25 or more students." The purpose of the program is to provide federal funds to school districts for the hiring of new teachers as a means of reducing class size. The average class size prior to the availability of government funds was 23 students. After the additional funds were received, average class size fell to 18 students. If the federal program is successful it will eliminate one of the major sources of teacher dissatisfaction.

Time pressures as a source of teacher dissatisfaction are vividly portrayed by Theodore Sizer in his description of a day in the life of high school English teacher Horace Smith. Sizer provides sympathetic insight into the life of a 28-year veteran of teaching who still cares about his work but is constantly forced to compromise his instructional ideals with the realities of public school teaching.

Sizer assures the reader that Horace's compromises are not the result of unusually poor working conditions. In fact, the reader is often reminded that Horace Smith teaches in a suburban school where conditions are far superior to those faced by teachers in central-city school systems. Sizer is also realistic. He recognizes that all jobs involve compromises between ideals and realities. But he feels the compromises required in teaching require more than ordinary adjustments to the realities of work. The compromises required in teaching not only shatter ideals but also cheat students of opportunities to learn.

Horace Smith is proud and committed to his job. His day begins at 5:45 A.M. with a brief breakfast and a 40-minute drive, bringing him to school by 7:00. He heads directly for the teachers' lounge, where he enjoys a cup of coffee and a cigarette before the beginning of his 7:30 class. The teachers' lounge is portrayed as a warm setting in which there are the smell of old cigarette smoke and a continual card game being played by groups of teachers during their off-hours. It is the one haven in the school where teachers can meet and share daily events and professional concerns.

Horace's three junior-level classes for the day are reading *Romeo and Juliet.* As a veteran teacher who has spent many years teaching *Romeo and Juliet,* he moves his classes quickly through the drama, anticipating their difficulties and avoiding distracting issues. His second-bell class is excused for an assembly, which allows him to return to his coffee cup in the teachers' lounge. His fourth-bell class is a senior advanced-placement class that is studying *Ulysses.* On this day, 13 of the 18 seniors are attending a United Nations week at a local college. Sizer describes Horace's annoyance at losing the teaching day but also his feeling of gratefulness at being able to avoid teaching, thus allowing his students time to read. Besides his five classes, Horace has a preparation period and a lunch hour.

The final bell ends the school day at 2:00 P.M. After conversations with students, Horace collects his papers, leaves his classroom at 2:30, and goes to the auditorium. Horace is a faculty adviser to the stage crew, for which he earns an extra $800 a year. For that small amount he puts in about four hours a week—and many more hours than that in the 10 days before a performance. After stopping in the auditorium, he drives to his brother-in-law's liquor store where he works behind the counter and in the stockroom from shortly after 4:00 P.M. until 6:30.

He eats dinner at 7:45 and then spends an hour grading papers. This is followed by several phone calls from sick students wanting assignments and students wanting to talk about the upcoming stage production. Finally, Horace ends his day by drifting off to sleep after the 11:00 news.

Horace's compromises are in the shortcuts he must take to deal with his busy day. He knows that he should be assigning his students a weekly essay of a page or two. But with a total of 120 students (central-city teachers often have more than 170 students) he is realistic and only assigns one or two paragraphs. Even with these short assignments, he estimates that grading and writing comments will take 15 to 20 minutes of his time per student. This still involves roughly 30 hours of grading. Again, Horace is realistic about his time and takes shortcuts in grading to reduce the time per student to five minutes. This means that even with reducing the assignment from a short theme to one or two paragraphs, and cutting corners while grading, Horace still must devote 10 hours a week to grading.

He must also take shortcuts in class preparations. He has taught some of his classes before, whereas others require more preparation. But even when classes are studying the same material, the differences among students require separate lesson plans. Horace recognizes that he should spend many more hours on preparation but again compromises and spends only about 10 minutes per class on preparation.

His shortcuts in grading and preparation, along with his teaching, administration, and extracurricular drama work, give him a 42-hour week. If he did not cut corners there would be another 20 hours of grading and possibly another 6 hours for preparation, which would mean a 68-hour week. On top of this is the time Horace spends working in his brother-in-law's liquor store to add to his inadequate salary. And, of course, there are the three full days he spends during Christmas vacation writing letters of reference for his students.

Lost in all these commitments is the time that should be used for reading professional journals and new literature and for doing those things that renew the life of the mind. As Sizer describes the situation, Horace hides his bitterness toward the critics who demand from teachers more scholarship and intellectual involvement. And, in the end, the students are as cheated as Horace's ideals.

In *High School*, Ernest Boyer provides similar descriptions of teachers who are overwhelmed by course loads and are forced to seek outside employment to add to their meager salaries. In many ways, Boyer paints an even grimmer picture of a high school teacher's life. His teachers have five to six classes a day with three different levels in a course. The different levels mean that more of the teachers' time is required to review subject matter and prepare for class. In addition, many teachers are assigned classes for which they have had no training. For instance, a social studies teacher might be assigned a science or mathematics course, which means endless hours of preparation. Added to this is the time spent on grading papers, preparing lesson plans, and counseling students.

Boyer found that a great deal of a teacher's time is spent on clerical and administrative chores. Many of these extra duties are nothing but baby-sitting and security tasks such as supervising hallways, lunchrooms, and student activities. Boyer found widespread complaints about clerical chores resulting from endless requests from both the school administration and the central administration of the school district. Also, teachers must keep elaborate student attendance records and send written reports to school counselors.

A great deal of a teacher's time is spent counseling students. Boyer gives the average pupil-to-counselor ratio in the United States as 319 to 1. This means there is little hope for the average student to find a counselor who has enough time to deal to any great extent with personal, academic, and career problems. This means students often turn to teachers for help. This creates a bind for many teachers because the better and more popular teachers often have the greatest demands on their time.

A feeling of isolation among teachers was also found in the high schools visited by Boyer. Teachers spend very little time in the company of other adults. Contact with other adults usually occurs only at lunchtime or during preparation periods in the faculty lounge. This situation gives teachers few opportunities to discuss common problems, professional issues, and intellectual topics with other teachers.

Teachers are also frequently without a permanent classroom, which means they are without their own desk: Most move from room to room carrying all their material. Many schools, particularly in central cities, are poorly maintained and have dirty windows and floors. In addition, there is often a shortage of school materials, and teachers dip into their own pockets to buy supplies.

For Boyer, a teacher's working conditions are made even more intolerable by a lack of public recognition and reward. There is a lack of respect from other adults outside teaching. Most teachers even avoid mentioning to other adults the nature of their occupation. One teacher, who works as a meat cutter during the summer, was told by a fellow butcher who discovered he was a teacher, "Man, that's a dead-end job. You must be a real dummy."

Although Sizer and Boyer analyze the lives of the high school teachers, many of their conclusions also apply to elementary school teachers. Elementary school teachers also feel time pressure in their class preparations and grading. They also feel the grim climate of isolation from adults, poor physical environment, and lack of community respect. They also must seek extracurricular school and summer employment to fill the gap left by inadequate salaries.

Many teachers find that contact with students, autonomy in the classroom, job security, and extended vacations compensate for poor working conditions and salaries. Personally, I enjoy teaching. I enjoy engaging students in dialogues over important questions. I enjoy students telling me that I made them think about the world in a different way. My philosophy of teaching is embodied in this book.

## TEACHERS' UNIONS AND TEACHER POLITICS

Calling her speech "Why Teachers Should Organize," Margaret Haley declared, as the first woman to ever speak from the floor of a national meeting of the National Education Association (NEA), "Two ideals are struggling for supremacy in American life today: one the industrial ideal, dominating thru [sic] supremacy of commercialism . . . the other, the ideal of democracy, the ideal of educators." Inviting teachers to organize to protect the interests of children, workers, and democracy, Haley exhorted, "It will be well indeed if the teachers have the courage of their convictions and face all that the labor unions have faced with the same courage and perseverance." Delivered in 1904, Haley's speech marked the rise of teacher unionism and the eventual founding of the American Federation of Teachers (AFT).

In 1998, echoing Haley's idealism, Mary Kimmel bemoaned the continued rivalry between the National Education Association (NEA) and AFT: "How can students learn if they don't have a full stomach and a safe environment? I don't know how we as educators can battle foes of public education if we're still fighting against ourselves." While struggling to overcome the differences between the two teachers' unions, organized teachers fulfilled Haley's dream of becoming an important force in American education and politics. Even national politicians paid attention to the power of the teachers' unions.

Both teachers' unions, the AFT and the NEA, actively participate in national elections. They work for both presidential and congressional candidates.

*Source:* www.Cartoonstock.com

Over the last two decades, they have given most of their support to candidates from the Democratic Party. This has created a split between the two national political parties over teachers' unions. Overall, Republicans oppose the work of teachers' unions, while Democrats are supportive. Of course, like other aspects of American politics, these alliances can vary from state to state.

Besides working in election campaigns, both unions have full-time Washington lobbyists who try to ensure that federal legislation does not jeopardize the welfare of teachers. Also, both unions maintain lobbyists at the state level and work for candidates to the state legislature. At the local level, teachers' unions have increasingly supported and campaigned for candidates in local school board elections. The involvement of teachers' unions in national, state, and local politics has made them a powerful political force.

## Differences between the Two Unions

The differences between the NEA and the AFT are a result of the historic split between professional and union organizations. As the following historical sketches show, the NEA traditionally limited its concerns to school organization and teachers. Consequently, the NEA restricts its membership to, in the words of their official description, "anyone who works for a public school district, a college or university, or any other public institution devoted primarily to education. . . . NEA also has special membership categories for . . . college students to become teachers."

On the other hand, the AFT traditionally embraced all educational workers, teachers, state and local government employees, and health workers. According to its official description, the AFT's membership includes "public and private school teachers, paraprofessional and school-related personnel, higher education faculty and professionals, employees of state and local governments, nurses and health professionals."

The AFT's commitment to a broad union movement is reflected by its membership along with 75 other unions in the 13.1-million-member AFL-CIO. The NEA remains unaffiliated with the general labor movement represented by the AFL-CIO. The following histories of the two organizations highlight the differences in labor affiliation and membership. These histories also illustrate the struggle of teachers to improve their working conditions. In reading these two brief histories, you should keep in mind the following questions:

- Should teachers organize into unions to protect and improve their working conditions, salaries, fringe benefits, and retirement funds?
- Should teachers' unions become actively involved in political campaigns and lobbying to support legislation favorable to the interests of teachers?
- Should the actions of teachers' unions reflect the interests of other unions, low- and middle-income families, children, or public schools?
- Should teachers' unions limit their activities to the welfare of teachers and other educational professionals?
- Should teachers' unions participate in general efforts to reform public schools?
- Should teachers' unions control and manage school budgets and curricula?
- Should teachers' unions attempt through collective bargaining to control class size, lengths of the school day and year, number of faculty meetings, and other school policies?
- What should be the purpose of a teachers' organization?

## A Brief History of the National Education Association (NEA)

Founded in 1857, the NEA adopted the goal of nationalizing the work of state education associations. This would be one of its major functions in the history of American education. The letter inviting representatives to the founding meeting states, "Believing that what state associations have accomplished for the states may be done for the whole country by a National Association, we, the undersigned, invite our fellow-teachers throughout the United States to assemble in Philadelphia."

The 1857 meeting in Philadelphia gave birth to an organization that in the nineteenth and early twentieth centuries had major influence over the shaping of American schools and contributed to the nationalizing of the American school system. From the platform of its conventions and the work of its committees came curriculum proposals and policy statements that were adopted from coast to coast. Until the 1960s the work of the NEA tended to be dominated by school superintendents, college professors, and administrators. These educational leaders would take the proposals of the NEA back to their local communities for discussion and possible adoption.

Examples of the work of the NEA include its major role in the shaping of the modern high school. In 1892 the NEA formed the Committee of Ten on Secondary School Studies, under the leadership of Charles Eliot, the president of Harvard University. The Committee of Ten appointed nine subcommittees with a total membership of 100 to decide the future of the American high school. The membership of these committees reflected the domination of the organization by school administrators and representatives of higher education: 53 were college presidents or professors, 23 were headmasters of private schools, and the rest were superintendents and representatives from teacher-training institutions. The work of the Committee of Ten set the stage for the creation in 1913 of the NEA Commission on the Reorganization of Secondary Education, which in 1918 issued its epoch-making report, *Cardinal Principles of Secondary Education.* This report urged the creation of comprehensive high schools offering a variety of curricula, as opposed to the establishment of separate high schools offering a single curriculum, such as college preparatory, vocational, and commercial. This report became the major formative document of the modern high school.

The NEA influenced the standardization of teacher training in the United States. The Normal Department of the NEA began surveying the status of institutions for teacher education in 1886, and debates began within the organization about the nature of teacher education. The official historian of the NEA, Edgar B. Wesley, stated in his *NEA: The First Hundred Years:* "By 1925 the training of teachers was rather systematically standardized." The work of the Normal Department of the NEA can claim a large share of the credit for this standardization.

NEA conventions and meetings also became a central arena for the discussion of curriculum changes in elementary and secondary schools. During the 1920s and 1930s many surveys, studies, yearbooks, and articles were published. In 1924 the Department of Superintendence began issuing what were to be successive yearbooks on various aspects of the curriculum at various grade levels. In 1943 the Society for Curriculum Study merged with the NEA Department of Supervisors and Directors of Instruction to form an enlarged department called the Association for Supervision and Curriculum Development (ASCD). The ASCD is still recognized as the major professional organization for the discussion of curriculum issues.

After the passage of the National Defense Education Act in 1958, the NEA's leadership role in the determination of national educational policy was greatly reduced as the federal government became the major springboard for national policy. The NEA became an organization whose central focus was teacher welfare and government lobbying. This shift was a result of several developments: the emergence of the leadership role of the federal government, demands within the NEA for more emphasis on teacher welfare, greater democratic control of the organization, and the success of the AFT in winning collective bargaining for its members (thus serving as a model for the NEA).

In 1962, the NEA's activities underwent a dramatic transformation when it launched a program for collective negotiations. This meant that local affiliates would attempt to achieve collective-bargaining agreements with local boards of education. This development completely changed the nature of local organizations and required a rewriting of local constitutions to include collective bargaining. Up to this point in time, local school administrators had controlled many local education associations, which used the local organizations to convey policies determined by the board and administration. Collective bargaining reversed this situation and turned the local affiliates into organizations that told boards and administrators which teachers they wanted.

Collective bargaining created a new relationship between locals of the NEA and local boards of education. Traditionally, local units of the NEA might plead for the interests of their members, but they most often simply helped to carry out policies of local school boards and administrators. Teachers bargained individually with the school board over salary and working conditions. With collective bargaining, teachers voted for an organization to represent their demands before the school board. Once selected as a representative of the local teachers, the organization would negotiate with the school board over working conditions and salaries. Many school boards were caught by surprise when their usually compliant local of the NEA suddenly demanded higher wages and better working conditions for all teachers.

The NEA's early approach to collective bargaining differed from that of the union-oriented AFT, which had pioneered collective bargaining in education. The NEA claimed it was involved in professional negotiating and not in union collective bargaining. Professional negotiation, according to the NEA, would remove negotiation procedures from labor precedents and laws and would resort to state educational associations, rather than those of labor, to mediate or resolve conflicts that could not be settled locally.

All pretense of the NEA not being a union ended in the 1970s, when the NEA joined the Coalition of American Public Employees (CAPE). CAPE is a nonprofit corporation comprising the National Education Association; American Federation of State, County, and Municipal Employees; National Treasury Employees Union; Physicians National Housestaff Association; and American Nurses Association. These organizations represent about 4 million public employees. The stated purpose of CAPE is "to provide a means of marshaling and coordinating the legislative, legal, financial, and public relations resources of the member organizations in matters of common concern." The most important of these matters "is supporting legislation to provide collective-bargaining rights to all public employees, including teachers."

By the 1980s, support of collective-bargaining legislation became one of many legislative goals of the NEA; the organization by this time was also directing a great deal of its energies to lobbying for legislation and support of political candidates. The turning point for the NEA was its endorsement of Jimmy Carter in the 1976 presidential election. This was the first time the NEA had supported a presidential candidate. After this initial involvement, the NEA expanded its activity to support candidates in primary elections. In 1980, the NEA worked actively in the primaries to ensure the victory of Jimmy Carter over Edward Kennedy for the Democratic nomination. Through the 1990s, the NEA committed itself to the support of Democratic candidates for the White House.

The major topic at the 1998 NEA convention was merger with its rival, the AFT. The consideration of a merger reflected the evolution of the organization from a professional organization to a politically active union. The evolution of the NEA is an important chapter in the political history of the United States. In recent years the NEA has emerged as the more socially concerned and militant of the two teachers' unions. By the 1990s, the NEA had become so politically active that its rival, the AFT, was accusing it of trying to be a political kingmaker. The historical irony of the AFT's claim is that it originated as an organization representing the broad political and social interests of the working class. By the 1990s, the AFT lost most of its early labor-union radicalism.

## A Brief History of the American Federation of Teachers (AFT)

Unlike the NEA's origins as a national policymaking organization, the AFT began in the struggle by female grade-school teachers for an adequate pension law in Illinois. The first union local, the Chicago Teachers Federation, was formed in 1897 under the leadership of Catherine Goggin and Margaret Haley. Its early fights centered on pensions and teacher salaries. Because of its success in winning salary increases, its membership increased to 2,500 by the end of its first year. In 1902, with the urging of famous settlement-house reformer Jane Addams, the Chicago Teachers Federation joined the Chicago Federation of Labor, which placed it under the broad umbrella of the American Federation of Labor (AFL).

From its beginnings, the AFT placed teacher-welfare issues and improving public education in the more general context of the labor movement in the United States. In an interview titled "The School-Teacher Unionized" in the November 1905 issue of the *Educational Review,* Margaret Haley declared: "We expect by affiliation with labor to arouse the workers and the whole people, through the workers, to the dangers confronting the public schools from the same interests and tendencies that are undermining the foundations of our democratic republic." Those "same interests" referred to in Haley's speech were big business organizations, against which Haley felt both labor and educators were struggling. The early union movement was based on the belief that there was unity between the educators' struggle to gain more financial support for the schools from big business and labor's struggle with the same interests to win collective-bargaining rights. Haley went on to state, "It is necessary to make labor a constructive force in society, or it will be a destructive force. If the educational question could be understood by the labor men, and the labor question by the educators, both soon would see they are working to the same end, and should work together."

Margaret Haley's comments highlighted the union's efforts to create mutually supportive roles between teachers and organized labor. On the one hand, teachers were to work for the interests of workers by fighting for better schools and working to remove antilabor material from the classroom. Teachers would fight to provide the best education for workers' children, while organized labor would provide the resources of its organization to support the teachers' struggle for improved working conditions and greater financial support for the schools. In addition, the type of education received by children in the schools would give children the economic and political knowledge needed to continue the work of the union movement, and teachers could share their knowledge with the adult members of the labor movement. Teachers would also increase their political and economic knowledge through their association with the labor movement.

In December 1912, the newly established magazine of the union movement, the *American Teacher,* issued a statement of the beliefs of the growing union movement in education. First, the statement argued that the improvement of American education depended on arousing teachers to realize that "their professional and social standing is far too low to enable them to produce effective results in teaching." Second, it was necessary for teachers to study the relation of education "to social progress, and to understand some important social and economic movements going on in the present-day world." Third, it was believed that teachers could use their experience in teaching to adjust education to the needs of modern living. Fourth, in one of the earliest declarations for the end of sexism in education, the statement called for high-quality teaching "without sex-antagonism."

In 1915, union locals from Chicago and Gary, Indiana, met and officially formed the AFT. In 1916 this group, along with locals from New York, Pennsylvania, Oklahoma, and Washington, DC, were accepted into the AFL. At the presentation ceremony, the head of the AFL, Samuel Gompers, welcomed the AFT to "the fold and the bond of unity and fraternity of the organized labor movement of our Republic. We earnestly hope . . . that it may . . . give and receive mutual sympathy and support which can be properly exerted for the betterment of all who toil and give service—aye, for all humanity."

It was not until 1944 that the AFT exercised any organizational control over a local school system. In 1944 the AFT local in Cicero, Illinois, signed the first collective-bargaining contract with a board of education. The form of the contract was that of a regular labor-union contract. It recognized the local as the sole bargaining agent of the teachers and listed pay schedules and grievance procedures. At the annual convention of the AFT in 1946 a committee was assigned to study collective bargaining and its application to school management. In addition, material was to be collected from trade unions on the education of shop stewards and union practices. With the introduction of collective bargaining, the AFT entered a new stage in its development.

The involvement of the AFT in collective bargaining led naturally to the question of teacher strikes. Since its founding the AFT had a no-strike policy. In 1946 the use of the strike for supporting teachers' demands became a major issue at the annual convention. Those supporting the use of the strike argued it was the only means available to arouse an apathetic citizenry to the problems in American education. It was also the only meaningful leverage teachers had against local school systems. AFT members who favored retention of the no-strike policy argued that teachers were in a public service profession and that work stoppage was a violation of public trust. In addition, it was argued that a strike deprived children of an education and was counter to the democratic ideal of a child's right to an education.

The AFT maintained its no-strike policy in the face of growing militancy among individual locals. In 1947 the Buffalo, New York, Teachers Federation declared a strike for higher salaries. The strike was considered at the time the worst teacher work stoppage in the history of the country. Other local unions supported the strikers, with local drivers delivering only enough fuel to the schools to keep the pipes from freezing. The Buffalo strike was important because it served as a model for action by other teachers around the country. School superintendents, school board associations, and state superintendents of education condemned these actions by local teachers. The national AFT maintained its no-strike policy and adopted a posture of aid and comfort but not official sanction. As William Edward Eaton states in his *The American Federation of Teachers, 1916–1961,* "Even with a no-strike policy, the AFT had emerged as the leader in teacher work stoppages."

The event that sparked the rapid growth of teacher militancy in the 1960s, and contributed to the NEA's rapid acceptance of collective bargaining, was the formation of the New York City local of the AFT, the United Federation of Teachers (UFT). In the late 1950s, the AFT decided to concentrate on organizing teachers in New York City and to provide special funds for that purpose. After the organization of the UFT in 1960, there was a vote for a strike over the issues of a dues checkoff plan, the conducting of a collective-bargaining election, sick pay for substitutes, 50-minute lunch periods for teachers, and changes in the salary schedules. On November 7, 1960, the UFT officially went on strike against the New York City school system. The union declared the strike effective when 15,000 of the city's 39,000 teachers did not report to school and 7,500 teachers joined picket lines around the schools. In the spring of 1961 the UFT won a collective-bargaining agreement with the school system and became one of the largest and most influential locals within the AFT.

During the 1960s, teachers increasingly accepted the idea of collective bargaining and the use of the strike. This was reflected in the rapid growth of membership in the AFT. In 1966 the membership of the AFT was 125,421. By 1981 the membership had more than quadrupled to 580,000. This increased membership plus the increased militancy of the NEA heralded a new era in the relationship between American teachers' organizations and the managers of American education. With the coming of age of the strike and collective bargaining, teachers in the NEA and AFT proved themselves willing to fight for their own welfare and the welfare of American public schools.

While the AFT did not support the Reagan and Bush administrations in the 1980s and early 1990s, it did adopt the view that one major purpose of education is to improve the ability of U.S. companies to compete in world markets. This goal is reflected in the AFT's policy statement "U.S. Education: The Task

Before Us" adopted at its 1992 annual convention. The policy statement opens with a call for the better education of "citizens of a democratic society" and "productive workers of a world-competitive economy." The AFT's adoption of this business agenda for educating productive workers reflects the conservative changes in the organization since the radical labor background of its early years.

## The NEA and the AFT Today

Reflecting the pressing educational problems of the day, the two unions are focusing on issues of standards, teacher training, charter schools, and teacher compensation. All of these directly effect the lives of the classroom teacher. At its 2002 meeting, NEA's President Reg Weaver urged delegates to bolster public confidence in education. "If we are to ensure success in our efforts," he said. "We cannot do it alone." Of particular concern to the NEA delegates was the effect of the federal government's No Child Left Behind Act of 2001. Delegates expressed particular interest in finding alternatives to high-stakes testing.

At the 2002 meeting of the AFT, President Sandra Feldman warned against the privatization of the educational system and the importance of close surveillance of charter schools. Reflecting the broader concerns of the AFT, her speech dealt with general labor issues including health care and right-to-work laws. She focused on union efforts to provide new designs for public schools. Called "Redesigning Schools to Raise Achievement," the program according to Feldman would "improve beginning reading instruction based on new research."

The two teachers unions play important roles in American education. I strongly recommend visiting the websites of the two unions (www.nea.org and www.aft.org) to examine their current reports and resources.

## A CASE STUDY: TOM MOONEY, AFT VICE PRESIDENT AND PRESIDENT OF THE OHIO FEDERATION OF TEACHERS

In the fall of 2002, Tom Mooney, President of the Ohio Federation of Teachers, was embroiled in efforts to defeat state legislation that would allow more opportunity for for-profit education companies to operate charter schools. In Mooney's words, "The bill gives private organizations the right to appropriate public funds." Tom Mooney had excelled as a classroom teacher and was now providing leadership to other teachers.

The purpose of this case study of Tom Mooney's role as union leader is to impart a knowledge of the inner workings of a teachers' union and the role of union leadership in effecting educational policy. My study of Tom Mooney's union career began in the 1980s when I had the opportunity to spend two months tagging along with him while he conducted union business. At the time, he was president of the Cincinnati Federation of Teachers, an AFT local.

Since that time, he advanced through the union ranks to become in 2000 the president of the Ohio Federation of Teachers and an AFT vice president. As a local president, he continuously held office from 1979 into the 1990s. My case study portrays the political world of a local union leader who must spend time convincing teachers that the union can provide better wages, benefits, and working conditions. The sketch gives a picture of the internal political life of a teachers' union and the ways in which unions become involved in a variety of political activities.

Tom Mooney describes his youth as being propelled by political activism and a compulsion to become self-supporting. He breezed through high school and college and in 1974, at the relatively young age of 20, earned his diploma from Antioch College. During the period of his attendance, Antioch College was known for its politically oriented student body support of social causes. While at Antioch, Mooney worked for the Farm Workers Union. As Mooney describes his entry into teaching at the age of 20, it was a classic case of being pointed toward a classroom and having to sink or swim. His college work did not prepare him for the realities of an inner-city junior high, nor did he receive much help from the school administration. He even had a difficult time understanding the language of the African American students, who made up the majority of the school's population.

With hindsight, it seems natural for a young teacher like Mooney to become interested in teacher union activities. He claims that his major motivation at the time was low teacher salaries and the fact that the school system had fouled up the operation of the schools. Mooney argues that school systems have traditionally expected teachers to dress and act like members of the middle class but they have never provided a high enough salary to allow a teacher to achieve a middle-class lifestyle. And from his perspective, the school system failed to provide decent working conditions and the services and supplies required to educate inner-city children.

His movement through the union organization was as swift as his high school and college career. During his first year of teaching, he had a chance to experience briefly a union position when he served as building representative for one week. The following year he transferred to another junior high school and joined the union's Educational Policy Committee. While on the committee he wrote a critique of the superintendent's 5-year plan for the school system. Mooney's report was adopted by the union as their official position. He became an area coordinator with the responsibility of coordinating union representatives from the various schools. When the Cincinnati Federation of Teachers conducted a major successful strike in 1977, he served on the union's bargaining team.

In 1979, when the union president decided not to run for re-election, Mooney launched a campaign for the position. The major parts of his platform were building a united bargaining council and influencing school board elections. A united bargaining council, which was later achieved, would bring together other workers in the system (like school office workers) with teachers so that a united front could be presented to the board of education. As I will discuss later, attempting to influence school board elections is part of Mooney's general concern with increasing teacher power.

Mooney won the election in 1979 and he is still president at the time of the publication of this book. After the election, Mooney moved into the union offices in a building occupied by other trade unions. Mooney's office reflects a dedication to trade unionism and progressive politics. On the wall directly in front of his desk hangs a picture of union leader Big Jim Larken giving a speech to a group of workers in Dublin in 1913. On the top of a bookcase sits a picture of Mooney with Senator Edward Kennedy. A picket sign from the successful 1977 strike hangs on the wall.

Mooney sees improving working conditions for teachers and increasing teacher power as his most important jobs. To understand his position on teacher power, one must also understand his general philosophy with regard to social action. He believes that the key to social action is convincing people that they have the power to make a change and a difference. This means overcoming the apathy and sense of powerlessness that pervade modern societies. One way to convince people that they can make a difference is to engage them in collective activity where they learn that working with others can bring about social and political change.

Mooney is concerned that teachers overcome a sense of powerlessness that has tended to dominate the profession. This can be accomplished by teachers learning through the collective work of the union that they can make a difference in the control and operation of a school system. This does not mean that the teachers' union can leap immediately into major attempts to exert control over the system. What must first take place is the gradual unfolding of awareness that greater influence is possible through collective action. One of the things Mooney claims he has learned since being in office is that things take time and that social and political goals require hard work and incremental steps. He feels that the union has accomplished major gains in salaries and working conditions but needs to exert more control over educational policy. This he believes is the next stage in the gradual unfolding of teacher power. Policy issues rather than wage issues are the items currently being stressed and negotiated by the union.

Regarding the ultimate goals for teachers' unions, Mooney would like to see teacher building committees sharing equal decision-making power with the principal. On a systemwide level, he would like to see the union sharing equal power with the board of education on issues involving educational policy.

Any discussion of teacher power leads to the issue of the potential conflict between the interests of teachers and the educational welfare of students. This issue is most often raised with regard to possible union protection of incompetent teachers, but it also includes union support of educational policies that might be detrimental to students.

The protection of incompetent teachers, Mooney argues, is a false issue usually raised by those who do not understand how school systems work. In the first place, most school systems put new teachers on an appraisal system for three or four years before giving them a permanent contract. Even after receiving a permanent contract, teachers can still be dismissed. According to Mooney, if incompetent teachers exist within a system, the guilt is on the shoulders of the administration and not the union. Clearly, continued employment of poor teachers has to be blamed on the inaction and failure of the school administrations to evaluate teachers adequately. The union's role in these situations is to ensure that the appraisal system is fair and to provide the teacher with help. Mooney describes the dismissal process as adversarial, with the administration presenting its case and the teacher organizing his or her case, but the decision rests with the administration. If the union feels that a teacher is unfairly dismissed, it can find some means of appeal through arbitration proceedings or through the courts.

The variety of issues and concerns related to the growth of teacher power and unionism is reflected in the types of activities Mooney engages in as union president. There is no such thing as a typical day for a union president because of the cyclical nature of some issues and the way other issues will suddenly burst onto the scene. The issues that generally follow a cycle involve negotiations with the local school board and meetings over the school budget. When these occur, they generally absorb a majority of Mooney's time. Some issues can appear suddenly, like a challenge from the local branch of the NEA that required a special election for teachers to determine their bargaining agent. When this occurred, Mooney found the majority of his time was devoted to campaigning.

On a typical day during the campaign, Mooney met with two groups of teachers at different elementary schools. The first meeting was scheduled during the first hour of school when teachers were free for their preparation period. It was held in the school library, with the head of the Teacher Building Committee acting as chairperson of the meeting. The other meeting was held informally in the teachers' lunchroom during their lunch break. In this situation, Mooney ran the meeting and answered questions from teachers.

Mooney's general strategy was to open meetings by emphasizing the benefits gained by the union. He was able to do this in an indirect manner by asking if the teachers had any questions about the new dental and medical benefits the union had negotiated with the school board. Mooney was guaranteed a stream of questions and an interest on the part of the teachers. After a lengthy discussion of these benefits, Mooney moved directly into a general campaign speech that emphasized the bargaining goals of the union and why a strong show of support by teachers in the coming election would strengthen the union's position at the bargaining table. Mooney was able to campaign by linking past negotiated gains with hope of future benefits.

Mooney's presence provided an opportunity for teachers to express their individual and collective problems. As a union leader and good politician, Mooney has a responsibility to respond and act on these concerns. At the school visited in the morning, teachers were upset by the conduct of their principal who, they complained, was often late to school and managed discipline poorly. In this situation, Mooney recommended that the Teacher Building Committee meet with the principal and express its concerns and pressure the principal into making formal rules to handle the discipline problems.

Following the morning meeting at the first school, Mooney was invited to the classrooms of two teachers to discuss their individual problems. The first had a complaint about the way the principal was handling her evaluation. He had not explained any of the procedures nor given her any written information about the appraisal process. Mooney assured her that the union would send her information and have a union representative stop by and check on the matter. The other teacher wanted to join the union but was hesitant about doing it in public. She was an older teacher who had never thought she would join a union. She wondered aloud why administrators made so much more money than teachers. After Mooney explained the payment of dues, she asked about the pension fund and the contribution made by the board of education. This led to a general discussion about retirement in which she voiced the opinion that teachers used to be able to teach 30, 40, and sometimes 50 years, but that this was no longer possible because they could no longer stand the stress of the job.

At another school, Mooney greeted teachers on their lunch hour with discussions about benefits and the future election. The teachers did not have any general complaints about the school, but one did request a private meeting over a personal problem. The teacher's husband had been fired from his job just prior to requiring hospitalization. When he was fired, he lost his hospitalization insurance. She called the board of education and asked that he be put under her insurance plan and was guaranteed immediate inclusion over the telephone. It had not occurred and now the couple had a $5,000 hospital bill with one member of the family still unemployed. Mooney copied down the details of the problem and promised to check with the board and insurance company to see if anything could be done about the bill.

This combination of concerns with union survival, teacher welfare, and educational policy was expressed at a meeting of the union Educational Policies Committee. The major issue of the meeting, as I observed, was the organization of middle schools to replace existing junior high schools. Mooney had expressed a concern to me before the meeting that middle schools might be one way the school administration had for attacking the union. The argument was that the administration was planning to require that middle school teachers have elementary certification. In the past, junior high schools were staffed by teachers with secondary certification, who usually were new teachers waiting for a position in a high school. It was from this pool of young junior high school teachers that the union received its strongest support and most active participation. Middle schools staffed by older elementary teachers would eliminate, according to Mooney, this most active union element in the city's teaching staff.

The meeting illustrated how teacher welfare issues, educational concerns, and union politics had to be balanced in dealing with the issue of the middle school. The major concern of the meeting was that most industrial arts and home economics teachers in the remaining junior high schools and middle schools would lose their jobs because there was no room in the planned schedule for those subjects. Of primary interest to the union was the protection of those teachers' jobs. In addition, the teachers on the committee argued that students of that age needed those types of educational experiences. The task the committee felt it had to perform was the creation of an alternative schedule that would allow for the inclusion of those courses. The plan was to take this alternative schedule to the administration and try to achieve some modification of their plans.

One plan that the teachers developed did seem to work, but it required all teachers to increase their workloads with the addition of one extra class. Mooney rejected this plan because it would not receive support from other middle and junior high school teachers. Or, in political terms, it would put Mooney in a difficult position to advocate a change of that nature. The safest plan politically required the hiring of extra staff so that the number of classes could be expanded without requiring teachers to work an extra class. Though politically a sound plan, it had its major drawback in the fact that the school system was short of cash and had stated several times that it would not be hiring new staff. Over issues of this type Mooney most often negotiates with members of the school administration rather than the board of education. From the perspective of his position, he has witnessed a real shift in power in recent years between the central administration and the board of education. Mooney argues that in recent years the board has given most of the power to the central administration. Consequently, the real power is in the hands of the middle managers who became stronger as the board became weaker. It is these middle managers, Mooney claims, who are now becoming the major adversaries of local union power.

The political picture that emerges from this case study is one where the union leader must attend to the welfare needs of teachers, protect teachers' jobs, and play politics with the school administration. In addition, the union leader must remain aware of any possible challenges to the union and to his or her position in the union. While this case study outlines the career route for Mooney from classroom teacher to president of the local teachers' union, it does not deal with career opportunities within the union. For instance, a president of a local teachers' union might want to climb up the union career ladder by gaining a position in the state or national union organization. This would add another dimension to the president's life as he or she does battle with the union's internal political forces.

Tom Mooney's concern about protecting teachers' jobs and improving wages, benefits, and working conditions reflects the general principles that have guided the activities of teachers' unions. Whether the issue is organizing middle schools or national certification of teachers, the first question teachers' unions ask is how will it affect jobs, salaries, and working conditions. As I discuss in the next section, this question defines the position of teachers' unions on most educational issues.

## *SHOULD TEACHERS STRIKE?*

The 2002 school year opened with its usual cycle of teacher strikes. *Education Week* reported at least a dozen strikes primarily over wages and health benefits. Reflecting on two strikes in Washington state school districts, Rich Wood, a spokesman for the NEA's Washington Education Association, commented, "Teacher pay and benefits are not competitive with the private sector or with schools in other states at a time when we have higher academic standards and expectations than ever before." On the other side of the strike issue, Janet Barry, school superintendent in Washington's Issaquah school district, claimed, "Their [the teachers' union] demand is still so far above the district's ability to pay that we're not truly bargaining. I see no signals that the union really intends to achieve a negotiated agreement that would settle this strike."

Across the country, teachers in New Jersey's Princeton Regional school district held a two-day strike on September 4 and 5 shortly after the opening of schools. They gained a new contract for salary increases of 4.5, 4.7, and 4.6 percent for the next three years, raising the average in the first year of the new contract to $58,376. Karen Joseph, a spokesperson for NEA's New Jersey Education Association, commented that with per capita yearly income in the district at $76,000, "The community clearly has the ability to pay [for the higher teachers' salaries]."

Striking is always a tough issue for teacher union members. Members know that they will encounter hostility from some parents and community members. Also, tensions are generated between those supporting the strike and those teachers who cross the picket line to work. Of course, Board of Education members and administrators often find themselves in conflict with teachers in a strike situation.

Strikes occur when a local teachers' union is unable to reach an agreement with the Board of Education regarding salary and working conditions. The steps leading up to striking begin with union representatives bargaining with a Board of Education over a new contract that will bind both sides to a particular wage scale and work rules. The wage scale includes salary and benefits such as health and dental insurance. Work rules involve length of school day, teaching load, class size, and a host of other work-related issues.

Conflict between the two sides is generated when the Board of Education wants to maintain existing salary scale and benefits and increase teachers' workload, while the union wants higher salaries and improved working conditions. Both sides will usually claim to be representing the interests of the students and community. When the bargaining process fails to reach a mutually acceptable contract, union members might authorize a strike. For instance, a recent strike in Yonkers, New York, occurred when the union rejected attempts by the administration to increase teachers' workloads by extending class time.

During a strike, the local teachers' union organizes picket lines around schools. Union members are assigned times and places for picketing. The purpose of the picket line is to keep members of other unions from entering the school. Theoretically, a union member is not supposed to cross the picket line of another union. For instance, truck drivers, usually members of the Teamster's Union, are not supposed to cross teachers' union picket lines to deliver goods to the school.

Picket lines also serve as a barrier to other teachers who refuse to strike. Teachers crossing picket lines are called "scabs." Conflict between teachers over a strike can result in years of hostile feelings. I have known situations where even 10 years after a strike union members still refuse to talk to "scabs" in faculty meeting rooms.

One of the questions frequently asked organizers for the NEA is, If we form a faculty union, will we have to go on strike? The NEA's answer is: "No. A strike can only be authorized by the faculty. State or national union officers or staff members cannot under any circumstances authorize or declare a strike. Faculty would have to vote on any strike action if they ever felt compelled to do so. In some states, a strike is an illegal activity."

While many states outlaw strikes by public employees, teachers' unions in those states still conduct strikes. I was involved in an illegal strike in Ohio where the final agreement between the two sides ruled out any criminal action against union members. On the other hand, there are cases where union leaders are arrested and jailed, and the local union heavily fined by the state.

Should teachers strike? On the one hand, some argue that teachers' strikes are sometimes necessary to improve the quality of education provided to students. Teacher welfare is directly related to student welfare. High pay and good working conditions attract and retain the best teachers. On the other hand, some argue that strikes only benefit teachers. Students lose valuable time at school while teachers are on strike. Communities are forced to raise taxes to pay for increased salaries that might result from a strike. Working parents' lives are disrupted when children are forced out of school by a strike. These conflicting concerns raise the following questions:

1. Do teacher strikes endanger the public welfare by denying an education to children and disrupting the employment of parents by requiring them to take charge of their own children during strike periods?
2. Should teachers only worry about fulfilling their instructional duties without concern for their wages or working conditions?
3. Do teachers' unions improve school instruction by improving teacher morale and creating conditions that foster good teaching?
4. Would you strike as a teacher?
5. Are there any salary or work-related issues that you might be willing to strike for?

## CONCLUSION

The profession of teaching has changed greatly since the nineteenth century model of teachers as paragons of morality. The changes in the profession parallel changes in the goals of U.S. schools. Essentially, the changes were from a moral to a global model. Teacher issues and concerns range from teacher education and licensing to high-stakes tests and classroom conditions.

Teachers are not passively manipulated by policymakers. Teachers' unions are a powerful force in American politics and in the formulation of educational policies. Unions protect the wages and working conditions and allow for the voice of teachers in national and local educational policy decisions.

## Suggested Readings and Works Cited in Chapter

The best sources of current information about the teachers' unions can be found on their websites. The information used in this chapter on recent NEA and AFT policies was taken from their official websites. The NEA site is www.nea.org. The AFT site is www.aft.org.

AHMAD, NASHIAH. "Strikes Hit Two Washington State Districts." *Education Week* (18 September 2002). www.edweek.org. *Review of teacher strikes at the opening of the 2002–2003 school year.*

American Federation of Teachers. "Good News/Bad News for Teacher Salaries, AFT Releases Latest State-by-State Teacher Salary Survey." (16 July 2002). http://www.aft.org/convention/salary_survey.html.

BERUBE, MAURICE. *Teacher Politics: The Influence of Unions.* Westport, CT: Greenwood Press, 1988. *This is a very good introduction to the contemporary politics of teachers' unions.*

BORROWMAN, MERLE. *The Liberal and Technical in Teacher Education: A Historical Survey of American Thought.* New York: Teachers College Press, 1956. *This is the classic study of the debates that have surrounded the development of teacher education in the United States. The book provides the best introduction to the history and issues regarding teacher education.*

BOYER, ERNEST L. *High School.* New York: Harper and Row, 1983. *This study, conducted for the Carnegie Foundation for the Advancement of Teaching, contains important descriptions of the work life of teachers and recommendations for the reform of teaching.*

BRADLEY, ANN. "Revamp Teacher Recruitment, Training, Continuing Education, Colleges Urged." *Education Week* (2 December 1992): 8. *This article summarizes the report of the American Association of State Colleges and Universities, Teacher Education for the Twenty-First Century.*

EATON, WILLIAM E. *The American Federation of Teachers, 1916–1961.* Carbondale: Southern Illinois University Press, 1975. *This is a good history of the development of the AFT.*

ELSBREE, WILLARD S. *The American Teacher: Evolution of a Profession in a Democracy.* New York: American Book, 1939. *This is still the best history of the profession of teaching in the United States. Unfortunately it traces the professionalization of teaching only to the 1930s.*

GOODLAD, JOHN. *A Place Called School.* New York: McGraw-Hill, 1984. *This detailed study of American schools contains surveys and recommendations about the profession of teaching.*

————. *Teachers for Our Nation's Schools.* San Francisco: Jossey-Bass Publishers, 1990. *This study of teacher education in the United States contains surveys and recommendations for the teaching profession.*

HERBST, JURGEN. *And Sadly Teach: Teacher Education and Professionalization in American Culture.* Madison: University of Wisconsin, 1989. *This is a good source on the professionalization of teaching.*

HOFFMAN, NANCY. *Woman's "True" Profession: Voices from the History of Teaching.* New York: Feminist Press, 1981. *This is an important collection of essays on the history of women in teaching.*

Legislative Budget Office, Ohio. *Policy Brief: Teacher Salaries* 1, no. 4 (21 January 1999). http://www.ohio.gov/. *A study of teacher salary disparities in Ohio.*

LORTIE, DAN. *Schoolteacher: A Sociological Study.* Chicago: University of Chicago Press, 1975. *This is the most complete study of the social interactions and world of the American teacher.*

MILLER, JANET. *Creating Spaces and Finding Voices: Teachers Collaborating for Empowerment.* White Plains, NY: Longman, Inc., 1990. *This book explores the role of teachers as researchers.*

MURPHY, MARJORIE. *Blackboard Unions: The AFT & NEA.* Ithaca: Cornell University Press, 1992. *This is a good introduction to teacher unionism.*

National Education Association. "Frequently Asked Questions." http://www.nea.org/he/bargain/faq.html. *This NEA Web page answers questions dealing with collective bargaining and strikes.*

New York State Department of Education. "Personal Attention and Access to Knowledge." http://www.emsc.nysed.gov/stateaidworkgroup/rsap2000/rsap-13.htm. *Study of equality of educational opportunity in New York school districts, including teacher salary differences between low-need and high-need school systems.*

Report of the National Commission on Teaching and America's Future. *What Matters Most: Teaching for America's Future.* New York: National Commission on Teaching and America's Future, 1996.

SCHUBERT, WILLIAM H., and WILLIAM C. AYERS, eds. *Teacher Lore: Learning from Our Own Experience.* White Plains, NY: Longman, 1992. *This is a collection of analyses by teachers of their own teaching.*

SIZER, THEODORE. *Horace's Compromise: The Dilemma of the American High School.* Boston: Houghton Mifflin, 1984. *This study of the American high school contains important insights into the problems encountered by teachers.*

Task Force on Teaching as a Profession. *A Nation Prepared: Teachers for the 21st Century.* New York: Carnegie Corporation of New York, 1986. *This important report calls for the restructuring of the teaching profession and the establishment of a national certification board.*

U.S. Department of Education. "Teacher Quality: Ensuring Excellence in Every Classroom." http://www.ed.gov/offices/OIIA/stmresources/march/teacherquality.html. *Provides a Web guide to alternative certification and Troops to Teachers programs.*

———. *The Class-Size Reduction Program: Boosting Student Achievement in Schools across the Nation.* Washington, DC: Editorial Publications, U.S. Department of Education, 2000.

URBAN, WAYNE. *Why Teachers Organized.* Detroit, MI: Wayne State University, 1982. *This excellent history of teachers' unions argues that the primary reason for the formation of these unions was protection of wages and seniority.*

WESLEY, EDGAR. *NEA: The First Hundred Years.* New York: Harper and Brothers, 1957. *This is the main source of information, in addition to original sources, about the early years of the NEA.*

## CHAPTER 9

# Textbooks, Curriculum, Internet E-Learning, and Instruction

Should biology courses teach evolutionary and biblical theories on the origin of life? Should public groups be allowed to censor school textbooks? Should state agencies censor material quoted in high-stakes tests? Who should determine the content of state academic standards? Should student access to the Internet be censored? Is Bible history an appropriate course in the public school curriculum?

## CENSORSHIP ISSUES

Disputes over the content of the school curriculum and textbooks, Internet access, and methods of instruction are a constant in public education. The People for the American Way, a self-appointed watchdog over school censorship, reports the following causes of demands for censorship of textbooks:

- Sexual content 44 percent of the time.
- Offensive language or profanity 24 percent of the time.
- Anti-Christian or endorsement of another religion 18 percent of the time.
- Objections to historical interpretations, environmentalism, feminism, discussions of government, and other issues 14 percent of the time.

In 2002, it was revealed that officials in the New York State Department of Education had altered literary quotes in the English Regents examination. Passing this examination is required for high school graduation in New York State. Consequently, all New York seniors were required to read the same altered passages. The modification of literary passages in the exam was uncovered by Jeanne Heifetz, the mother of a Brooklyn, New York, high school student. She found that state officials "sanitized" passages from the works of noted authors such as Issac Bashevis Singer, Anton Chekhov, and William Maxwell. The so-called sanitization of literary passages removed practically any reference to race, religion, ethnicity, sex, nudity, and alcohol. For instance, Bashevis Singer's works focus on the Jewish experience. Quotes from his texts on the exam eliminated all mentions of Judaism. "Most Jewish women" was changed to "most women." The entire line "Jews are Jews and Gentiles are Gentiles" was removed from an excerpt. Removed from a passage taken from Annie Dillard's memoir *An American Childhood* were all racial references from a description of her childhood trip to a library in a black neighborhood that had few white visitors. The purpose of Dillard's description was to highlight racial issues. The following changes were made in other passages used on New York State's English Regents exam:

- In a speech by U.N. Secretary Kolfi Annan "fine California wine and seafood" changed to "fine seafood."
- In Anton Chekov's "The Upheaval" portion deleted about wealthy woman strip-searching household staff to find a missing brooch.
- In Carol Saline's "Mothers and Daughters" "went out to bar" changed to "went out."
- In Ernesto Galarza's "Barrio Boy" "skinny" changed to "thin" and "fat" to "heavy" in describing boys.
- In Frank Conroy's "Stop-Time" deleted sentence where boys declare intent to kill a snake because of potential violence.

The changes were defended by Roseanne De Fabio, the New York Education Department's assistant commissioner for curriculum, instruction, and assessment. She admitted, "We do shorten the passages and alter the passages to make them suitable for testing situations." The passages were changed using the department's "sensitivity review guidelines." The purpose, she said, was to ensure that no students were "uncomfortable in a testing situation. Even the most wonderful writers don't write literature for children to take on a test."

In response to the revelations about the New York Regents exam, Cathy Popkin, Lionel Trilling professor in the humanities at Columbia University, wrote, "I implore you to put a stop to the scandalous practice of censoring literary texts, ostensibly in the interest of our students. It is dishonest. It is dangerous. It is an embarrassment. It is the practice of fools." Author Frank Conroy wondered, "Who are these people who think they have a right to 'tidy up' my prose? The New York State Political Police? The Correct Theme Authority?"

There are many other examples of censorship over the last decade. Maya Angelou's *I Know Why the Caged Bird Sings* was banned from a tenth grade college preparatory class by school board members in West Chester, Ohio. Board members complained that *I Know Why the Caged Bird Sings* contained a description of rape that was "too graphic" and "inappropriate." In Hudson, Ohio, school board members denounced the use of a history textbook titled *The American People* because it contained too many details about women, African Americans, Native Americans, indentured servants, immigrants, farmers, and industrial workers. The following are other examples of complaints against books used in schools.

- J. K. Rowling's *Harry Potter* series of children's literature was criticized for promoting witchcraft and the occult. Some people complained the books are the work of the Devil himself.

- Madeleine L'Engle's *A Wrinkle in Time* was criticized for allegedly teaching demon worship and mysticism.
- Ernest Hemingway's short story "The Killers" was found objectionable because it contains the word "nigger."
- Mark Twain's *The Adventures of Huckleberry Finn* was criticized for racial stereotypes and offensive language.

Censorship of school books can't simply be dismissed as the work of extremists or concerned bureaucrats. There are reasonable objections that can be raised about the content of instruction in public schools. After all, parents must send their children to a public school if they can't afford a private school. What should parents do if they are offended by the books their children are required to read?

Parental objections also include methods of instruction. Some parents want their children to be taught by methods that emphasize independent thinking, critical thinking, and self-motivated learning. Other parents want an emphasis on rote learning and authoritarian instructional methods. Usually, fundamentalist Christian parents stress obedience to the authority of God and the Bible.

Religious objections to textbooks and instructional methods open the constitutional question of separation of religion and government. Some religious groups argue that public schools do not teach students to rely on the authority of God. Consequently, these religious groups maintain public schools are violating religious beliefs protected by the Constitution. In addition, some groups claim teaching evolutionary theory in science classes is a violation of religious rights. Court cases and legal decisions touching on these issues will be discussed in detail in Chapter 10 in the sections "School Prayer, Bible Reading, and Meditation," "Secular Humanism," "Evolution and Creationism," and "Parents' Rights."

Efforts at censorship of books and methods of instruction raise important issues regarding the role of public schools in a democratic society. Democracy depends on the free exchange of ideas and the diversity of ideas. On the other hand, education is compulsory. In the following sections I discuss the politics of textbooks, national standards, the history of the public school curriculum, and methods of instruction. These topics raise the following set of questions. There is no correct answer to any of these questions, but they do highlight the dilemmas facing a government-operated school system in a society based on freedom of thought. In thinking about these questions remember that attendance at public schools is compulsory unless parents can afford a private school. In addition, the majority of voters elect school boards. This raises the issue of whether minority opinions should be overruled by the majority.

- Should children in public schools be forced to read books approved by the school board that are objectionable to the children's parents?
- Should children in public schools be taught by methods of instruction approved by the school board but found objectionable by students' parents?
- Who should decide what knowledge is most worth teaching in public schools?

- Who should decide the content of textbooks and tests?
- What type of curriculum should be used in public schools?
- What methods of instruction should be used in public schools?
- Would you approve of your children reading any book?
- What curriculum and methods of instruction would you want for your children?

## WEB SCRUB: A NEW FORM OF CENSORSHIP?

In George Orwell's classic novel *1984,* political leaders controlled the future writing of historical events by tossing documents down the memory hole to their destruction. Today, a similar phenomenon is occurring with the removal of files from websites. This process is called "Web scrub" in reference to the cleaning out of unwanted files from websites. What happens when decisions regarding removal of items from a website are determined by political beliefs?

*Education Week*'s Michelle Davis reported on September 18, 2002, that the U.S. Department of Education was engaged in a massive Web scrub that would "ensure that material on the site meshes with the Bush administration's political philosophy." The Department of Education's website was originally created in March 1994 during President Bill Clinton's administration. As of 2002, the site provided access to 50,000 files and received 84,000 visits a day. The large number of daily visits to the site indicates its importance for providing public information.

Reporter Michelle Davis claims that "some researchers and government watchdogs say the department's decision to scrap some information based on whether it comports with Bush administration initiatives could set an unsettling precedent." Would it mean that every time a new president is elected government websites would be purged of files containing opposing political viewpoints? If a Democrat is elected after a Republican leaves office would it mean another purge of Web files?

Web scrubs raise unforeseen issues regarding government websites. In the past, paper documents would have simply been stored and, therefore, they would have remained available to researchers. Electronic files are simply erased and lost to future generations. Reporter Davis raises the issue: "Just what responsibility do political officials have to preserve the products of those who came before, particularly if their predecessors saw the issues in a different light?"

## TEXTBOOKS

During the hot summer of 2002, the Texas State School Board began public hearings to select textbooks in history and social studies for its 4 million students. These were subject areas that were bound to attract comments from all sides of the political spectrum. Texas's textbook hearings were notorious for their strident demands by opposing interest groups to add and delete material from textbooks. At the opening of the hearings, there already seemed to be agreement among board members not to select for advanced placement classes Pearson Prentice Hall's history text *Out of Many: A History of the American People* despite it being among the best sellers. The problem was two paragraphs dealing with prostitution in late nineteenth century cattle towns. "It makes it sound that every woman west of the Mississippi was a prostitute," said Grace Shore, the Republican chairwoman of the Texas State Board of Education. "The book says that there were 50,000 prostitutes west of the Mississippi. I doubt it, but even if there were, is that something that should be emphasized? Is that an important historical fact?"

Texas and California's textbook hearings are extremely important for publishers. They are 2 of 22 states in which government committees select textbooks for public schools. Texas represents 8 percent of the $2.2 billion dollar national market in textbooks, while California represents 12 percent. Consequently, these two states exert enormous influence over the content of textbooks used throughout the United States. As Carol Jones, the field director of the Texas chapter of Citizens for a Sound Economy, commented, "The bottom line is that Texas and California are the biggest buyers of textbooks in the country, and what we adopt in Texas is what the rest of the country gets." Her organization examines textbooks to ensure accuracy and any information that lends a liberal political slant.

During the hearings, *Out of Many: A History of the American People* was criticized not only for its section "Cowgirls and Prostitutes" but also for its mention of Margaret Sanger and the development of contraception, and the gay rights movement. Complaining about the books' content, Peggy Venable, director of the Texas chapter of Citizens for a Sound Economy, said, "I don't mean that we should sweep things under the rug. But the children should see the hope and the good things about America."

Texas textbook selection is governed by state laws which require the promotion of democracy, patriotism, and free enterprise. These innocent-sounding terms are open to dispute. Is a discussion of the possible value of federal government farm subsidies a violation of the requirement to promote "free enterprise?" Is any criticism of the actions of the federal government a violation of the requirement to promote "patriotism?"

Also at stake in 2002 was approval of science textbooks. Contrary to expectations that science texts would not be as controversial as history books, the issue of global warming caused a major uproar. Science textbooks were condemned for saying that there was a scientific consensus that the earth's climate was changing because of global warming. This claim was labeled as "anti-technology," "anti-Christian," and "anti-American. The Board rejected Jane L. Person's *Environmental Science: How the World Works and Your Place in It* because of statements such as "Destruction of the tropical rain forest could affect weather over the entire planet" and "Most experts on global warming feel that immediate action should be taken to curb global warming." To gain acceptance by the Texas Board, the statements were changed to: "Tropical rain forest ecosystems impact weather over the entire planet" and "In the past, the earth has been much warmer than it is now, and fossils of sea creatures show us that the sea level was much higher than it is today. So does it really matter if the world gets warmer?"

In 2001, the Texas Board singled out for censorship Daniel Chiras' *Environmental Science: Creating a Sustainable Future*. The book opened with phrases such as "Things can't go on as they have been," "We must change our ways," "throwaway mentality," and "obsession with growth." The Board attacked the text for using the "oft-used falsehood that over 100 million Americans are breathing unhealthy air."

One text that did win approval was financed by a consortium of mining companies. Titled *Global Science: Energy, Resources, Environment*, the book was praised before the Texas Board by Duggan Flanakin, formerly of the U.S. Bureau of Mines and currently a member of the Texas Policy Foundation. The book was also commended by Ms. Shore, chair of the Texas Board and co-owner of TEC Well Service. TEC is a producer of gas and oil and repairs and deepens oil wells. From Ms. Shore's perspective, the oil and gas industries "always get a raw deal" in environmental science textbooks.

While environmental science courses threatened rampant consumerism, home economics courses embraced consumerism under the new name Family and Consumer Sciences.

Texas has also been the scene of important arguments about the content of health books. Regarding a high school health text published by Holt, Rinehart & Winston, Inc., Monte Hasie, a member of the Texas Board of Education, said, "They were promoting homosexuality as an acceptable alternative lifestyle and promoting sex as being O.K. if you use a condom. We were going to put *Playboy* and *Penthouse* out of business." After months of hearing testimony from family planning, antiabortion, gay advocacy, fundamentalist Christians, and other groups, the Board mandated that the health book and four others under consideration delete toll-free numbers for gay, lesbian, and teenage suicide-prevention groups, illustrations for examinations for testicular cancer, and sections on homosexuality. They also asked for inclusion of descriptions of Texas laws against sodomy. In an unusual decision in March 1994, the publisher decided not to sell its book in Texas rather than make changes demanded by the Texas Board of Education. Concerning the Texas controversies, Gilbert T. Sewall, director of the American Textbook Council, commented, "This underlines how hard it is getting to produce a textbook that appeals to a general audience and to satisfy all the pressure groups."

California has been the scene of struggles over another seemingly innocuous subject area, namely, mathematics. In 2000, Brian Hoey, publisher of the College Preparatory Mathematics Program, announced that his company would be withdrawing its textbooks from consideration by the California school system. Hoey complained, "Why would I want to submit my books when [decision makers] are on record as opposing them? The deck is stacked against any math program that isn't in a traditional format." This shocked the textbook publishing world because in 1999 a federal panel had stated that the companies' books were "exemplary." At issue was a new California law that requires that math instruction emphasize basic skills and repeated drills as opposed to concepts and problem-solving using real-life situations.

In contrast to California, some schools around the country are adopting math textbooks from Singapore because they don't emphasize basic skills and drill. Singapore's books are without the eye-catching graphics used in U.S. texts. These plain books, according to Yoram Sagher, a mathematics professor at the University of Illinois at Chicago, insist "on full understanding, and an avoidance of mindless rituals that lead to a solution." Felicity Messner Ross, a middle school math teacher in Baltimore, said, "I think these books really empower students as problem-solvers."

Besides state governments, many national organizations try to influence textbook publishers. A group specifically organized for this purpose is People for the American Way. Contrary to the impression conveyed by its name, this is a politically liberal group claiming a membership of 277,000, which was created to combat the influence of the religious right on textbooks. An example of its tactics was a national mailing in 1989 asking recipients to send three enclosed postcards to leading publishers showing support for including evolutionary theory in science textbooks. The letter warned, "The Far Right's objective is to force publishers to censor the theory of evolution and replace it with the biblical story of creation as scientific fact." The postscript to the letter pleaded, "Help me stop the far right from controlling what children in our public schools are taught."

As veterans of many textbook wars, leaders of People for the American Way know where to apply political pressure. In fact, as their letter stated, they see themselves competing with the religious right for influence on two key states' selection processes—California's and Texas's. "The censors [religious right] know," the letter advised, "that if they change textbooks in Texas and California—the two largest textbook buyers that account for more than 20 percent of the total national market—publishers will print those texts as national editions." The letter warned that officials in California were preparing to tell publishers what to include in textbooks and that the Texas State Textbook Committee would be meeting to select biology and science textbooks.

Members of People for the American Way know that textbook publishers try to avoid any controversy that might hurt sales. The reality is that very few administrators are willing to select for their schools textbooks that could cause controversy in the community. Often a local school superintendent walks a thin political line. Certainly, the desire to protect their jobs would cause administrators to avoid controversial situations. Recognizing this situation, publishers know that they will have a difficult time selling controversial books to local schools. In the words of the president of People for the American Way, Arthur Kropp, "To avoid controversy, publishers may downplay or eliminate ideas criticized by the censorship groups. They've caved into Far Right pressure in the past."

As a result of the activities of these differing pressure groups and state laws textbook content is highly politicized. Of course, textbooks do not have that appearance. Usually, textbooks seem bland and boring compendiums of facts containing no political messages. In part, this appearance is caused by the wish of textbook publishers to avoid controversy. On the other hand, imbedded in the blandness are facts and ideas that are the product of a whole host of political debates and decisions.

The question of who should control knowledge in a democratic society can be asked specifically about curriculum, instruction, and textbooks. The battles that happen, particularly over the curriculum and the content of textbooks, are often unnoticed by the public. In fact, I encounter very few public school students who are aware that political decisions determine the contents of their textbooks.

## CURRICULUM STANDARDS AND THE POLITICAL NATURE OF KNOWLEDGE

Like many other areas of education, the No Child Left Behind Act of 2001 directedly impacted national discussions of academic standards. My concern is the role of academic standards in the control of knowledge. As discussed in Chapter 7, academic or curriculum standards prescribe what a student should know about a particular subject for each grade level. Advocates of academic standards argue that standards are necessary to ensure that teachers instruct students in what the state education agency considers the important parts of each subject. In addition, high-stakes state tests linked to state standards ensure that students have learned the subject-matter prescribed by the state. It is also argued that academic standards can be used to force teachers to teach more material. In turn, this will require the student to learn more.

The No Child Left Behind Act requires that states create academic standards. The opening section of the legislation declares as its first purpose: "(1) ensuring that high-quality academic assessments, accountability systems, teacher preparation and training, curriculum, and instructional materials are aligned with challenging State academic standards so that students, teachers, parents, and administrators can measure progress against common expectations for student academic achievement."

Who should determine the content of academic standards now that all states are required to have them? Consider the ongoing issue of the place of evolutionary theory in the academic standards for science. The No Child Left Behind Act mandates that states measure students' scientific knowledge by 2008. In a report accompanying the legislation, it is suggested that the intent of the law was for state science curriculums to "help students to understand the full range of scientific views that exist." The report specifically mentions evolutionary theory as a controversial scientific theory. Those wanting evolutionary theory to be presented to science students as controversial also want students to learn about biblical statements on the origin of life and theories associated with intelligent design.

The debate over science standards and evolutionary theory began in 1999 when a majority of members of the Kansas State Board of Education removed the teaching of evolutionary theory and discussion of the origin of the Universe from the state's science standards. This gave school districts the option to exclude or include evolutionary theory in the local curriculum. The catch was that state standards determined the content of state high-stakes tests, so questions about evolutionary theory would not appear on state science examinations. This meant that science teachers would not be motivated by the threat of testing to teach evolutionary theory. A political furor resulted from the Kansas State Board's decision. Five seats on the 10-member school board came up for election in November 2000. The major focus of election rhetoric was on the evolutionary theory issue.

The decision of the Kansas State Board of Education received the widespread support by many members of the religious right. On the other hand, scientists complained that evolutionary theory was an important part of biological science. According to the National Academy of Science, evolutionary theory has become the "central unifying concept of biology."

In 2001, a newly elected Kansas Board of Education voted 7 to 3 to restore evolutionary theory to the state's science standards. In the same year, the Alabama State Board of Education unanimously decided to include in its state's science standards a disclaimer clause declaring evolutionary theory as "controversial." The disclaimer states:

> It is controversial because it states that natural selection provides the basis for the modern scientific explanation for the diversity of living things. Since natural selection has been observed to play a role in influencing small changes in the population, it is assumed, based on the study of artifacts, that it produces large changes, even though this has not been directly observed.

In 2002, Ohio became a battleground over evolutionary theory in the state's science standards. In the end, supporters of evolutionary theory declared a victory when it was included in the state's standards. An opponent, Robert Lattimer, complained, "The current draft standards have an evolution-only approach. It does not address any of the points about teaching the controversy. He argued that the standards should allow teachers to present alternative theories.

In Cobb County, Georgia's second largest school district, the school board in 2002 adopted a policy requiring teachers to provide students with a "balanced education" by giving equal weight to biblical and evolutionary theories on the origin of life. Insurance salesman and minister, Russell Brock, told the school board, "To deny there is a God is to stand on a building and deny there is a building."

The debate over science standards and evolutionary theory raises a number of questions:

- Should curriculums standards be determined by state governments?
- Should politicians determine the content of the curriculum or should that be done by academic experts. (For example, should a scientist, as opposed to an elected member of the state board of education, determine the appropriate content of biology instruction?)

Do state curriculum standards effect the actions of teachers in the classroom? A 2000 study of fourth grade teachers in New Jersey found that teachers were adding material to their courses as a result of the state standards. Kathleen Manzo, a reporter for *Education Week,* summarized the study's findings: "In mathematics, the traditional classroom diet of whole-number facts is being balanced with such topics as probability and the use of data. In science, lessons in chemistry, physics, and investigative skills, as well as the use of math in science, are supplementing long-standing course work in areas such as weather and ecosystems." These changes highlight the important effect of state standards on what children learn. On the other hand, the study found little effect of the standards on teaching methods.

Attempts to create curriculum standards have been plagued by controversies over what should be included. In *The New York Times,* the headline to an article on proposed national standards for teaching history declared, "Plan to Teach U.S. History Is Said to Slight White Males." "They make it sound as if everything in America is wrong and grim," Lynne Cheney, conservative chair of the National Endowment for the Humanities during the Reagan and Bush administrations, told a *Times* reporter. Presenting what she called a warped history of the United States, she claimed that proposed standards made 17 references to the Ku Klux Klan and 19 references to McCarthyism without mentioning Paul Revere and Thomas Edison. While it is important to study women and minorities, Cheney argued, "politically incorrect white males" should not be pushed aside.

The problem in creating national standards is determining what knowledge is of most worth to teach. And basic to answering this question is the other question of who should determine what knowledge is of most worth. In addition, knowledge is not politically neutral or agreed upon by all scholars. In any discipline there is wide disagreement over what is truth. Walk down the halls of any university and you will encounter many different theories competing for dominance in a particular discipline. For instance, in psychology there are a variety of competing theories of human behavior and research methods. In areas such as history and political science, what is considered truth is often relative to the political beliefs of a particular professor. Since it is impossible to teach all things to all elementary and secondary students, some selection of content must be made. Among all the competing theories in a discipline, some decision must be made about what knowledge is of most worth to teach.

Even in a supposedly politically neutral field such as science, important decisions must be made about what knowledge is most worth teaching to elementary and secondary students. For instance, consider the list of issues developed by the National Academy of Sciences in 1992 in its preparation for development of national standards:

1. Should science standards be differentiated by the ability of the students?
2. What should be the boundary of school science? Should science instruction include topics in engineering, technology, and the social sciences?
3. Should science instruction reflect the tradition and culture of mainstream science?

The first of these questions reflects the debate about tracking. The danger of a differentiated approach is that it might support inequality of educational opportunity and inequality of opportunity. Since an understanding of science is important for access to many high-paying jobs as symbolic-analysts, those students taught a science program for low-ability groups would be at a disadvantage compared with those learning a science program designed for high achievers. On the other hand, it could be argued that low achievers cannot understand science as well as high achievers. Whatever position a person takes on this issue has important implications for issues involving equality of opportunity.

Question 2 reflects the lack of a standardized body of scientific thought. The fact that science spills over into many areas of human living and many other intellectual fields makes it difficult to establish boundaries. Again, a trip down the hall of a science department at a university would probably elicit as many answers to this question as there are professors. Therefore, an equally important question in answer to this question is, Who should decide the boundaries of school science?

The third question is the most politically explosive. At a 1992 meeting of the American Association for the Advancement of Science, one member objected to the routine exclusion of Afrocentric approaches to science teaching. Of course, Native Americans could object to national standards in science based on a European approach to the teaching of science. From the perspective of Native Americans, European science has resulted in death and destruction by the weapons developed for modern warfare, and the destruction of the environment. Native Americans might argue that science should be focused on living with nature and not on trying to exploit nature.

Returning to the issue of history standards, I would raise questions similar to those asked by the National Academy of Sciences.

1. What should be the boundary of school history? Should history taught in schools include political history, economic history, social history, and intellectual history?
2. Should U.S. history be taught from the perspective of European Americans?

Defining the boundaries of history often reflects political values. Conservatives believe that school history should focus on political history to help the student understand the operation of the U.S. government and to build patriotism. On the other hand, liberals believe that social history is important so that students understand the sources of social inequality and learn how to be political activists. Again, I want to remind you that neither the conservative nor liberal position represents truth. What is important to understand is that the determination of the boundaries of school history does involve political values.

This is also true with respect to the perspective to be used in the teaching of history. Teaching history from the viewpoint of Native Americans and African Americans does not cast U.S. institutions in a very positive light. For instance, it would be very difficult to use history for building patriotism if students were required to read Dee Brown's *Bury My Heart at Wounded Knee: An Indian History of the American West.* Told from the perspective of Native

Americans, this history presents the U.S. government as a treacherous institution not to be trusted and the U.S. military as a band of savages involved in massacres and mutilations.

Again, the issue is not which view of history is correct, but the fact that there are different perspectives. With national standards, decisions about the boundaries and interpretations of history would be decided by political forces. These issues came to the forefront in discussions about standards for world history. How should the role of Western nations be portrayed in world history? John J. Patrick, the director of the Social Studies Development Center at Indiana University, argues, "We're not interested in a history that is Eurocentric. We're interested in global history." In contrast, Mary Bicouvaris, 1989 National Teacher of the Year, implored the National Council for History Standards not to discard all emphasis on Western nations. "Why are we turning away from the rise of the West?" she asked. "Is there a contempt for the rise of the West?"

While the goal in establishing academic standards is improving student achievement, the process opens the door to ideological control of the curriculum by politicians and special interest groups. Knowledge is not politically neutral.

## CURRICULUM

As exemplified by the political issues surrounding state standards, the public school curriculum has been a battleground in American education. Business groups, radical reformers, religious organizations, welfare associations, left-wing and right-wing politicians, and many other groups want the public schools to teach subjects that will serve their interests. During the twentieth century, the curriculum has varied with changes in the political, economic, and social climates.

In *The Struggle for the American Curriculum, 1893–1958,* Herbert M. Kliebard identifies four types of curricula that have vied for dominance in American public schools. Each of these curricula receives support from issues generated by particular social, economic, and political factors. The curricular struggle Kliebard portrays continues into the 1990s. Kliebard's four curriculum categories are

1. Social efficiency
2. Humanism
3. Social meliorism
4. Developmentalism

The *social-efficiency* curriculum has the greatest influence in American schools. Backed by those who want the schools primarily to serve the needs of the economy, it is designed to prepare students for the workforce. Often, social-efficiency curricula emphasize vocational subjects and are associated with the educational goals of human capital.

In sharp contrast to the advocate of social efficiency, the *humanist* wants the curriculum to introduce students to the cultural traditions of society. A humanist spurns the idea of a vocational curriculum and favors the development of general intellectual skills. Often the humanist wants the curriculum to be organized around standard academic subjects like literature, history, foreign languages, the arts, and science.

The *social meliorist* wants the curriculum to cause social improvement and change. Social meliorism reflects the reform element in American education. At the most extreme, the social meliorist will ask for courses to solve each new social problem. Sometimes this means educating students to bring about general political and economic changes. But more often it means the advocacy of courses to solve problems such as alcoholism, drug abuse, AIDS, and traffic accidents.

In many ways, *developmentalism* is the most radical of the four curriculum types. The developmentalist wants the curriculum organized around the psychological development of the child. This means a curriculum focused on the needs of the individual child as opposed to the focus of social-efficiency educators, humanists, and social meliorists, respectively, on economic needs, the passing on of culture, and social reform. Of the four curriculum types, developmentalism has had the least influence on the public school curriculum. The child-centered curriculum of the developmentalist is often rejected by supporters of the other types of curricula for being anti-intellectual and failing to give the student the necessary skills to function in society and the world of work.

In the twenty-first century, preparation for the global economy has become a combination of social-efficiency and humanist curriculum goals. Based on a human capitalist model, the social efficiency model strives to educate workers for new jobs in a rapidly changing technological society. In this rapidly changing global economy, workers must be prepared to continually update their skills with each technological advancement. Humanism receives support because of its contribution to teaching students how to learn and general intellectual skills. Humanists advocate that all students be required to take a core curriculum emphasizing traditional academic subjects.

The current blend of social-efficiency and humanistic curricula marks a sharp contrast to the traditional divisions between these two points-of-view. In the early part of the twentieth century, humanists resisted the growing vocationalization of U.S. schools by trying to preserve the teaching of Greek and Latin in the schools. They argued, in the tradition of the liberal arts, that the purpose of education should be the training of the mind and, because of that training, the development of character. For humanists, the study of classical languages, literature, and history would give students the mental tools and character to be moral and successful.

Social-efficiency educators in the early twentieth century, however, argued that the school should provide individualized training based on a person's future destination in the labor force. The worth of all public school courses, they argued, should be judged by their contribution to a person's social worth in the world of work. Therefore, social-efficiency educators called for abandoning the long-standing tradition of teaching Latin and Greek for more vocational courses.

In their enthusiasm for the practical, social-efficiency educators went so far as to advocate that particular courses be geared to a student's future work. For example, they asked why a prospective mechanic or bricklayer should be taught Shakespeare, when the intended occupation required only minimal language skills. Instead, they proposed that occupations should be analyzed to decide their specific academic requirements, and courses could then be organized around those requirements. Future bricklayers, then, would be taught only the English, arithmetic, and science actually needed for that occupation.

By the 1920s, the battle lines were clearly drawn between the humanists and social-efficiency advocates. Neither side could claim victory, but the social-efficiency philosophy did replace many traditional humanist components of the curriculum. In the 1930s, a new group of humanists working under the label of *essentialist* reacted against the too-specialized curriculum of the social-efficiency advocates and declared the need for a common core curriculum. While essentialist did not base their proposals for a core curriculum on a traditional classical education, they emphasized the importance of teaching a common cultural tradition. Unlike earlier humanists who looked to the past, essentialists examined the cultural requirements of the present.

While the humanist argument for a core curriculum was being modified by the practical outlook of the essentialist of the 1930s, social meliorists were calling for major transformations in the public school curriculum. Since the early days of the common-school movement of the 1830s and 1840s, public schools had been viewed as a source of social change and improvement. The depression of the 1930s sparked widespread concern with social and economic conditions. Many Americans began to believe that the only hope lay in basic changes in the economic organization of the society.

Influenced by these arguments, a group of educators calling themselves *social reconstructionists* argued for the teaching of subjects that would prepare the individual to be an active participant in the economic transformation of society. Often this meant a stress on social studies courses designed to give students the skills to analyze political and economic conditions. In contrast to the social meliorist who accepted the basic structure of society and wanted to reform the individual, the social reconstructionist envisioned social improvement as a product of individual empowerment. For political radicals, social reconstructionism offered the hope that public schools could be used to make fundamental changes in society.

The *postwar* period of the late 1940s shifted the concern of American educators from the economic problems of the depression to the international problems of the cold war between the United States and the Soviet Union. The rhetoric of the cold war dominated curriculum discussions from the 1940s into the 1960s. The result was a strange amalgam of humanist and social-efficiency ideas. Social-efficiency ideas were present in the call for more courses in mathematics and science to train students to be engineers, scientists, and mathematicians to win the military race with the Soviet Union. In addition, there was a call for the teaching of more and a greater variety of foreign languages so that the United States could compete with the Soviet Union for influence in other countries. The common rhetoric of the period was that American schools needed to meet human power needs or the United States would succumb to the power of the communist threat.

Humanists joined the chorus of those arguing that the schools needed to meet the human power needs of the cold war by stressing the importance of academic rigor and the teaching of intellectual skills. Within the concerns of the cold war, the humanist stress on intellectual skills was complemented by the social-efficiency demand to produce highly trained workers for the war machine. Humanists declared American public schools anti-intellectual and called on academic scholars to gain control of the public school curriculum.

By the 1960s, the cold war concerns of educators gave way to the pressures of the civil rights movement and fears of increasing poverty. Again, social meliorists were prominent in calls for changes in the curriculum that would prepare minorities and poor people for more equal participation in the economy. For social meliorists of the 1960s, a major goal of education became the elimination of poverty and racism. Discussions of new science and math courses gave way to proposals for compensatory education and Head Start courses. These changes in the curriculum were designed to provide the children of the poor with equal access to education by improving their basic skills. Combined with desegregation, these curriculum changes were to end poverty and racism.

In the late 1960s, the social unrest sparked by the Vietnam War dimmed the hopes of social meliorists. Campus protests and disruptions alarmed conservatives and created demands for the restoration of law and order. Republicans attacked the curriculum changes of the social meliorists as unproven social experimentation. War protesters, however, linked antiwar activities with greater demands for cultural freedom. Included in these demands was greater educational freedom for students to pursue their own interests. In addition, the financial cost of the war and energy problems in the 1970s caused unemployment and economic stagnation.

Thus, in the late 1960s and early 1970s, a confused period of curriculum change occurred with conservatives demanding more discipline in the schools, cultural and antiwar protesters demanding more freedom in the schools, and social-efficiency advocates demanding changes in the curriculum to solve the problems of unemployment and economic stagnation. The result in the 1970s was that conservatives and social-efficiency advocates joined forces to emphasize, as a solution to both discipline and economic problems, career-education courses, expanded vocational offerings, and closer linkages between the curriculum and the needs of the labor market. Mostly, those seeking greater educational freedom established private alternative schools outside the organization of the public schools. Although many reasons might be given for the short life of these schools, certainly financial problems made it difficult for them to compete with public schools.

It is important to understand that the private alternative schools established in the 1960s and 1970s were part of a long tradition of efforts to organize a curriculum based on student choice and interest. Usually this tradition flourished in private schools. A major difficulty in organizing a student-centered curriculum in a public school is that the public school exists to serve the interests of society overall. This means, as we have discussed, that the public school curriculum is primarily determined by constantly shifting social, economic, and political goals.

The attempt to create a child-centered curriculum is part of the developmentalist tradition of adjusting the curriculum to the child's nature. The assumption is that the source of motivation, interest, and learning is within the nature of the child. Education, therefore, involves providing the opportunity for children to learn as their interests and desires unfold. Some educators in this tradition argue that a child passes through different stages of development and that the curriculum should be adjusted for each developmental stage.

The private alternative schools of the late 1960s and early 1970s were often called *free schools* because children were given freedom to learn according to their own needs and interests. They were identified with the English school Summerhill, established in the 1920s by A. S. Neill. Neill believed that aggression was primarily a product of the repression of a child's free development. Authority and discipline, according to Neill, rather than making a child socially responsible, often created a personality that was destructive and aggressive. At Summerhill children were given complete freedom to decide what they studied and how they lived. The only restriction was that they not interfere with the freedom of others. Neill believed that a free school educated individuals who would strive for a free and peaceful world.

Summerhill was one of many alternative schools in the 1920s. In the United States a variety of schools appeared in the early part of the twentieth century devoted to freedom of learning and natural development. The Modern School opened in New Jersey before World War I and lasted into the 1950s. It was dedicated to a nonauthoritarian education where the children determined their own learning. The Walden School was opened in the 1920s by Margaret Naumberg, who believed that the individuality of the child developed through the study and practice of art. The politically radical Manumit School opened during the same period based on the idea that children should manage their education in the same manner as workers organized in unions. Labor-management contracts defined the relationship between students and teachers.

## JOHN DEWEY AND PROGRESSIVE EDUCATION

The educational philosopher most often associated with the development of curricula based on student self-interests is John Dewey. It is difficult to measure the impact of Dewey on American education. Certainly his ideas on learning and curriculum have been widely discussed since the beginning of the twentieth century. However, there is little evidence that his ideas caused significant changes in the public schools.

Dewey evaluated the impact of the child-centered education movement on the public schools in a *Time* magazine article in 1952. On the positive side, he said the movement made teachers more aware of the growing human being and personal relations and that the "older gross manifestations . . . of education by fear and repression . . . have, generally speaking, been eliminated. . . ." On the negative side, while these grosser forms disappeared, Dewey argued, the "fundamental authoritarianism of the old education persists in various modified forms." Indeed, he found little cooperative and democratic learning in American schools.

A problem in discussing Dewey's impact is the complexity of his thinking and the varying interpretations that can be made of his writings. Consequently, Dewey's ideas have been attacked as anti-intellectual and catering too much to the whims of children, as politically radical, and as promoting group conformity.

Probably the two most controversial aspects of Dewey's thinking, and the source of his ideas on curriculum organization, are the beliefs that all knowledge has a social origin and that the interests of the child are the primary sources of learning. Of course, the conviction that all knowledge has a social origin is rejected by religious groups who believe that God is the source of knowledge. This is one reason many religious groups have attacked Dewey's ideas. Dewey argues that all knowledge and ideas, including ideas about social organizations and morality, are relative to the social situations that produced them. Principles of morality and the organization of society, according to Dewey, must constantly change to adapt to new problems and social situations. Therefore, the curriculum should be organized, Dewey argues, so that the child learns that knowledge has a social origin and is socially useful. Rather than the teacher acting as if knowledge fell out of the sky, the teacher is to guide the student to an understanding of the historical and social conditions that produced particular knowledge. For instance, arithmetic can be taught as an abstract set of rules or it can be taught in situations where students learn its social usefulness such as counting other children or objects for a particular purpose.

In keeping with the belief that standards of social conduct and of institutions must constantly adapt to changing situations, Dewey believes schools must adapt to the needs of today. A primary problem in the modern industrial and urban world, he states, is the need for a sense of cooperation. He argues that today the stress on individual economic competition needs to be replaced with economic cooperation. Since modern industry and urban life are not fostering cooperation, Dewey maintains, the school needs to change and become the center for teaching cooperation. For instance, Dewey replaced individual classroom desks with group tables on the belief those individual desks promoted individual economic competition while working at tables promoted cooperation.

Dewey rejects the idea that children are primarily motivated to learn by rewards and punishments. He argues that the source of individual action is not stimulation from an outside reward or punishment, but originates in individual interests and desires.

Dewey's beliefs resulted in a curriculum based on student interests and designed to teach the social origins of knowledge and cooperation. In this curriculum, teachers guide student interests to sources of knowledge. In addition, knowledge is taught as a whole and not isolated fragments. Cooperative group activity is the method of learning. Thus, a student or students might express an interest in milk. The teacher would guide the students to sources of the production, chemistry, and distribution of milk. Groups of students might visit the local dairy and develop a group project on milk for the classroom. During this group study of milk, students might learn chemistry, economics, arithmetic, social history, and cooperation. Even though Dewey did not agree with many experiments in child-centered curricula, his name is most often associated with the movement.

## HUMANISTIC SOCIAL EFFICIENCY FOR THE TWENTY-FIRST CENTURY

From the middle of the 1970s through the 1980s, conservatives blamed progressive education and social-efficiency curricula for the supposed decline in the academic quality of schools which was linked to the weakening of the U.S. economy. In what seemed like a replay of the 1950s, critics argued that the curriculum did not develop the intellectual skills needed to compete in the development of new technology. Humanists, such as Mortimer Adler and Secretary of Education William Bennett, advocated a core curriculum where all students developed intellectual skills through the study of important historical documents and literature. Overall, critics argued that the vocational orientation of schools needed to be replaced with an academic orientation.

The result is the curriculum of the early twenty-first century, which combines an emphasis on academic skills with the needs of the global economy. Science and math are now the basis for vocational training. The problem is the neglect of the humanistic emphasis on the arts. Humanism has been compromised by the social-efficiency goals of the twenty-first century. Traditional hu-

*Source:* Bruce Beattie/Copley News Service

manists would argue for a major role for the arts in education—including visual and performing arts. However, those concerned with global economy place more emphasis on science and math instruction to the detriment of visual and performing arts. Consequently, the twenty-first century curriculum could be called "humanistic social efficiency" in which the meaning and content of a humanistic curriculum is determined by economic needs.

The constant changes in the American public school curriculum are primarily the result of constantly changing political and economic needs. Since the public school serves public purposes, its curriculum will constantly change. The shifting patterns of the public school curriculum primarily involve humanistic concerns with cultural traditions and intellectual skills; social-efficiency advocates wanting the schools to serve the economic needs of society; and social meliorists wanting the curriculum organized to promote social reform. Often, the public school curriculum is a blend of all three curricular patterns with one or more dominating because of the particular political and economic conditions of the time.

## THE INTERNET AND E-LEARNING

The wiring of American schools raises questions about student access to the world's knowledge. Here is a wonderful means of learning that is as significant as the earlier development of printed books. However, should students be allowed access to *all* the world's knowledge? Should public schools allow students to access pornography, bomb-building plans, prescriptions for terrorism, or the proclamations of racial hate groups?

These questions plague educators and noneducators as the Internet is being toted as the new revolution in learning. Called e-learning, school activities using the Internet are designed to teach both the use of computer technology and provide a new mode for learning other subjects. Through e-learning, a student becomes literate in the new means of communication including the use of search engines and electronic libraries. In addition, e-learning involves distance learning and Web-enabled classrooms.

E-learning is supposed to transform classroom learning. Rather than just learning from textbooks, the student can now access online resources. E-learning opens up the opportunity for students to extend discussions beyond the walls of the classroom through continued discussions with the teacher and other students. In addition, e-learning can involve Web-based tutoring in school or at home. Course assignments and grades can be posted on a website which allows students access to this information from home.

Naturally, the idea of e-learning is tied to the educational requirements of the global economy. Writing in *Education Week,* Peter J. Stokes, author of the government-sponsored essay, "How E-Learning Will Transform Education," hopes that e-learning "can help us more effectively develop the 'knowledge workers' required to sustain the growth of the new economy— workers, after all, who must possess a fluent understanding of both the ideas and communications systems of the modern workplace."

E-learning has also contributed to the growth of for-profit education. The University of Phoenix, the largest private university in the world, relies on e-learning through distance learning. For many adult workers, it is easier and more convenient to sit at home and join class discussions through chat rooms, answer questions by e-mail, download assignments including reading materials, and take Internet examinations than to go to a classroom at a prescribed time. Flexibility, resources, and interaction are the key ingredients to good distance learning.

Teachers and cost represent an ongoing problem for e-learning. Most teachers are not adequately trained to handle e-learning. In addition, e-learning represents a potential threat to teachers' jobs, particularly in higher education. I have taught in colleges where faculty members are openly resistant to distance learning. For teacher training, this means the existence in college departments of education of faculty members who refuse to teach about e-learning and who refuse to participate in distance learning.

Cost is another important factor. The wiring of schools for the Internet, the use of online services, the purchase and installation of computers, and the maintenance of computers adds a heavy burden to local school budgets. To help local schools join the Internet age, the federal government provides support for Internet access, including the costs of cables, communications hubs, and switches to carry information between school buildings. This support is called E-rate and is provided by the 1996 Telecommunications Act which mandated that the Federal Communications Commission make Internet services affordable for all schools and libraries. As a result, the federal program made it possible by 2000 for two-thirds of the nation's classrooms to gain Internet access.

Is the cost of e-learning worth the results? The international organization Alliance for Childhood calls for a moratorium on investment in classroom computers until their worth in classroom instruction has been proven. Joan Almon, head of the organization, argues, "We've gone down this highway of bringing computers into elementary schools with so little debate, and spending such huge sums. If we were spending so much money on other aspects of education with so little evidence of gain, we'd be ashamed of ourselves." The organization argues that there is little direct evidence that shows computer use results in higher school achievement.

On the other hand, *Education Week*'s 2002 report, "Technology Counts 2002," found that the Florida Virtual School is successfully educating high school students. The school is a state-sponsored online school. Sixty-eight percent of the virtual school students say their online courses are as difficult or more difficult than regular high school courses. A major issue with virtual high schools is aligning the online courses with state academic standards.

## THE CHILD ONLINE PROTECTION ACT OF 1999

The Child Online Protection Act of 1999 makes it a crime for commercial websites to make pornography available to students. In addition, it requires libraries and schools receiving federal technology funding to equip their computers with

Internet filters. Specifically, the law requires the use of technological measures that block or filter Internet access to "visual depictions" that are "harmful to minors." It also requires schools to have a plan for monitoring students' online activities. The law does contain a provision that allows the disabling of filters for adults conducting "bona fide research or other lawful purposes."

The problem is that filters often block access to nonpornographic sites. Consequently, a federal district court in Philadelphia ruled against the requirement of Internet filters in libraries because "plaintiffs demonstrated that thousands of Web pages containing protected speech are wrongly blocked by the four leading filtering programs." However, filters remain on school computers. A supporter of the law, Heather Cirio, a spokeswoman for the conservative Family Research Council, contends, "We should make sure the computers purchased with tax dollars contain filters that would protect children from obscene and pornographic materials."

Internet filters also have opponents. Peacefire, an opponent of filtering, tested five filters on a randomly selected list of 1,000 websites and reported that 20 to 80 percent of the blocked sites were blocked in error. In other words, filters often block sites that were not intended to be blocked and thereby reduce the promise of the Internet to provide access to the world's knowledge. "Candidly," said Mark Uncapher of the Information Technology Association of America, "there's no silver bullet for filtering."

There are also problems involving student use of websites. Jean O'Brien, a student at Westlake High School near Cleveland, Ohio, created a home-based website containing a photo of his high school band instructor. The student's website described that band teacher as "an overweight middle-age man who doesn't like to get haircuts . . . [and who] likes to involve himself in everything you do." As a result, O'Brien was suspended from school for 10 days. A student in McKinney, Texas was suspended for setting up on the school computer a website called C.H.O.W. or Chihuahua Haters of the World. A student in Statesboro, Georgia, was arrested for posting on his personal website terrorist threats against his school principal.

According to Ann Besson of the American Civil Liberties Union, the Internet is creating a whole new generation of educational censorship issues. "These Web cases," she said, "have become somewhat analogous to the student newspaper cases of the past, where the school tries to say, 'You can't talk about condoms in the school newspaper.' Except that with Web sites, people tend to become more alarmed because people outside the school find out about them."

Some school districts allow students an appeal process when their access to an Internet site is blocked. For instance, Clark County, Nevada, students can ask a teacher for access to a blocked site. The teacher then notifies the school's network authority. If the school administration and the network authority composed of nine members consider the website appropriate, then it is unblocked. "We realized that no filtering software is perfect," commented Karlene Lee, the district's director of technology services.

Other school districts are adopting tough policies regarding Web usage. Utah's Salt Lake City school district will suspend students for "improper" use of the Internet. Students are not allowed access to any website that mentions birth control, condoms, or abortion.

In summary, the e-learning revolution has created the promise of new methods of learning and greater access to knowledge along with a whole host of problems associated with teacher training, costs, and censorship. E-learning also creates another arena for the development of for-profit education corporations. But researchers using data from the California and U.S. departments of education reported in 2002 that the use of the Internet has no measurable impact on student achievement. University of Chicago researcher Austan Goolsbee concluded, "We haven't found any evidence that it [Internet access] is [providing academic benefits]."Despite these difficulties, e-learning will probably become an essential part of public schooling.

## *INSTRUCTION*

Although the curriculum of the public schools shifts with changing political and economic goals, the actual methods of instruction, despite attempts at reform, remain relatively constant. One reason is that to achieve social and economic goals, the schools must manage student behavior and learning. Certainly, allowing students freedom in learning would not ensure the achievement of the goals of most public school curricula. Even social reconstructionists want to manage students to achieve politically radical ends.

In *How Teachers Taught: Constancy and Change in American Classrooms, 1890–1980,* Larry Cuban details the factors that made public school instruction primarily *teacher-centered* as opposed to *student-centered*. Cuban, for the purposes of his history of instruction, defines teacher-centered instruction as occurring when "teacher talk" dominates the classroom, instruction is primarily given to the whole class as opposed to small groups or individuals, the teacher determines the use of classroom time, and the classroom is arranged in rows of desks facing the front of the room. On the other hand, Cuban describes the opposing student-centered tradition as occurring when student discussion of learning tasks is equal to or greater than teacher talk, instruction is individual or in small groups, students participate in determining the rules of the classroom, and instructional materials are available for students to use individually or in groups.

Cuban portrays the history of instruction as attempts by advocates of student-centered instruction to change, with modest success, the entrenched patterns of teacher-centered instruction. At the beginning of the century, the physical conditions of schools influenced patterns of instruction. Urban classrooms were constructed for 40 and 60 students with bolted-down desks in rows facing the front of the room. The classroom organization was standardized between the 1890s and the 1920s by the architect for the New York Board of Education, C. B. J. Snyder. In addition, teachers were poorly trained and often had to cover 10 different subjects daily by using textbooks and curricula prescribed by the central administration. The effect on teachers of large classes, arranged classrooms, prescribed textbooks and curricula, and many preparations for teaching, Cuban argues, was the continued reliance on teacher-centered instruction and textbooks as sources of knowledge.

Besides the physical and working conditions of teaching, social-efficiency ideas reinforced patterns of teacher-centered instruction. During the early part of the twentieth century, school administrators developed a mania for bureaucratic efficiency. Viewing the schools as factories, they stressed standardization and uniformity of instruction. Efficiency administrators compared themselves with factory managers, where power flowed from the top of the organization to the bottom. This meant that just as they believed administrators should control and dominate teachers, teachers should dominate and control students.

While working conditions and ideas of social efficiency reinforced patterns of teacher-centered instruction in the early twentieth century, advocates of student-centered instruction, led by John Dewey, began to press their reforms on the public schools. But most of these instructional reforms were unable to penetrate the organizational structure of the public schools and received their greatest acceptance in private schools.

Cuban describes many attempts before 1940 to introduce student-centered instruction in public schools with the results being only minor and affecting only a few teachers. For instance, the New York City school system began in 1934 to experiment with what was called an *activity program,* which stressed teachers and students working together to select subject matter and learning activities, and a focus on the needs and interests of the students. In addition, classroom schedules were to be flexible, with the standard teacher-dominated recitation being replaced by excursions, research, dramatization, and sharing. Controlled discipline was to be replaced by self-control. In 1942, after eight years of attempted instructional reform, it was estimated that only 25 percent of all city elementary schools incorporated activity methods in some classrooms. In a survey of New York teachers in the same year, 93 percent said they preferred conventional forms of instruction.

Between 1920 and 1940, Denver public schools were widely hailed as leaders of student-centered instructional reform. Under the leadership of four superintendents dedicated to the implementation of student-centered instruction, the school district emphasized teacher-constructed curricula, an activity program like that of the New York schools, and the *project method.* The project method involved students learning through the development of individual or group projects. In evaluating the effects of these reforms on high school teaching, Cuban found that only 20 percent of the classrooms during this period had extensive student-centered instruction.

Overall, Cuban concludes, reforms based on student-centered instruction between 1920 and 1940 did not significantly change the instructional methods of American teachers because of the structure and organization of the schools. The primary method of instruction remained that of the teacher standing in front of the room, talking to the whole class, and questioning students who mainly listened to the teacher talk. Teachers retained control of the subject matter and manner of instruction.

Although these standard practices remained, student-centered reforms, according to Cuban, did loosen up the atmosphere of the classroom. More student movement in the classroom was permitted, desks became movable, and there was less formal recitation, characterized by students rising and speaking by their desks.

Following World War II, student-centered instruction came under attack as causing a deterioration of the academic standards considered necessary for winning the cold war with the Soviet Union. Advocates of student-centered instruction, including John Dewey, were accused by the extreme political right of being communists trying to undermine the country by destroying discipline and academic standards in the classroom. Even more-moderate observers claimed that the schools were made anti-intellectual by student-centered instructional methods. Consequently, advocates of student-centered instructional reforms made a hasty retreat and did not appear on the scene again until the late 1960s.

As described in the previous section on curriculum, the late 1960s witnessed the growth of alternative schools based on differing forms of student-centered instruction. In the public schools, the major attempt to introduce student-centered instruction came as the *open classroom.* Originally developed in England, the open classroom captured the imagination of many American educators in the 1960s and early 1970s. A flood of newspaper and journal articles and experiments in public school systems seemed to show that this instructional method would become standard. Indeed, many schools built during this period incorporated the principles of the open classroom into their design.

Like other forms of student-centered instruction, the open classroom emphasized active as opposed to passive learning, and student-directed learning as opposed to teacher-determined instruction. Classrooms were to be large open spaces divided into interest areas or learning centers. Each learning center was to contain a variety of learning materials. Students were to plan their own learning and move from interest station to interest station. The open classroom movement quickly ended by the middle of the 1970s with demands for student discipline and an emphasis on basic subjects.

*Competency-based instruction* replaced the open classroom movement. In the framework of competency-based instruction, teachers develop specific instructional objectives, develop methods to achieve those objectives, and measure the achievement of those objectives. Students learn discrete skills in incremental steps by using preplanned instructional packages. The emphasis on measurement contributed to the rise in the importance of standardized testing. Often, this meant the standardized test had a controlling influence over the actions of the teacher and students.

Larry Cuban cites several examples of the organizational difficulties encountered in the introduction of student-centered learning in the 1960s and 1970s. For instance, consider the 1968 staff bulletin from the central administration of the New York public school system, which told teachers that students must raise their hands during recitation, they must ask permission to go to the bathroom, and they must regularly clean their desks under the supervision of a teacher. According to Cuban, one New York teacher during this period stated that students were whipped into shape by sitting at their desks for long hours and by using textbooks and notebooks to study formally organized lessons. Silence and good behavior were the standards of classroom conduct.

Cuban identifies three major reasons for the lack of significant change in instructional methods in American public school classrooms in the twentieth century. The first is that public schools exist to serve larger social purposes, to "instill behaviors required by the prevailing economic system. This produces teaching practices that emphasize uniformity, authority, and other traits required by bureaucratic organizations. Student-centered instruction, on the other hand, develops traits of individual choice and expression that run counter to the demands of society on the public schools."

The second reason for the persistence of teacher-centered practices, according to Cuban, is the organizational structure of the public school. In most situations, teachers are expected to maintain control, use a textbook, and teach from a prescribed curriculum. Class size and structure inhibit the use of student-centered activities. Teachers find it convenient under these circumstances to have students seated according to a seating chart, to have students raise their hands and wait their turn before speaking, and to allow student movement only with the permission of the teacher. It is also most convenient for the teacher to instruct with lectures, seatwork, and homework by using textbooks. Student-centered instruction, on the other hand, does not fit the organizational and structural requirements of the public school, is inconvenient for the teacher, and creates more work.

The third reason for the lack of change in instructional practices is the culture of teaching. According to Cuban, teachers are socialized to be conservative and resistant to change. Often their teaching is modeled on that of the teachers they had in school and on the teachers who supervised their student teaching. This modeling perpetuates standard methods of instruction.

In addition, Cuban argues that teacher beliefs and administrative ineptness contribute to a failure to change. Those teachers who believed in student-centered instruction did change their classroom practices, but large groups of teachers continued to believe in traditional methods. When attempts to start student-centered instruction did occur, school administrators, Cuban argues, failed adequately to carry through their plans.

For all these reasons, classroom instruction has changed little in the twentieth century. Classroom practices did soften with the introduction of movable chairs, the decline of the requirement that students stand by their desks when speaking, and the growth of informality between teachers and students. But teachers continue to instruct from textbooks by using planned lessons, and students remain passive learners.

## CRITICAL PEDAGOGY

During the 1970s new instructional methods developed based on the work of Brazilian educational philosopher Paulo Freire. Compared in importance to John Dewey and hailed as the leading educational philosopher of his time, Freire's book *Pedagogy of the Oppressed* provided a methodology for educating the world's oppressed peoples. In the framework of Kliebard's curriculum categories, Freire would be classified as a social reconstructionist interested in reforming the world. Freire's concerns go beyond the usual educational issues involved in providing equality of opportunity and equality of educational opportunity. He argues that most educational systems attempt to integrate oppressed people into the very social system that caused their oppression. Obviously, from Freire's perspective, this approach does not provide a permanent solution. His goal is to provide an educational methodology that will teach people to understand the economic and political forces determining the structure of society and that will prepare them to work for social change.

The central focus of Freire's methods is to help people understand the world in which they live. For instance, one might display to a group of learners a picture of a common scene from their daily lives. Through a process of discussion, people take apart the elements of the scene. Out of this discussion, a critical awareness of the social and political forces in society is developed. In addition, words used by the participants to describe the scene become the basis for the development of reading material. Freire believes that the learning of language can result in enslavement or freedom. When learning to read for freedom, reading is a means for understanding one's world.

An important role for the teacher is that of *problem-posing*. Problem-posing is directly related to the lives of students. Teachers pose problems about aspects of their students' lives. Students and teachers then engage in a dialogue about these problems—and from this dialogue emerge words that are frequently used by the students to describe their lives. These words become the basis for the teaching of reading. In this manner, there is a direct connection between learning how to read and learning how to think about one's world.

To begin this educational process, teachers must investigate the lives of their students. During Freire's early work in adult literacy, teachers would first explain their purpose and then spend time observing their students' lives. The purpose of this observation is to discover themes in students' lives that can be used in a problem-posing dialogue. For instance, teachers in a small village or urban barrio, Freire states, should take notes on the way people talk, their behavior at church and work, and the general social life of the community. In the initial stages of this process, the teachers frequently gather to compare their observations. It is assumed that their initial observations are distorted by their own beliefs and knowledge.

The dialogue between the teachers helps to raise their consciousness about the social conditions being investigated and about the way in which they perceive the world. As in all Freirian-type dialogues, learning takes place at several levels. At one level, the teachers learn about their surrounding world. At another level, they learn how they think about the world. Finally, they learn why they think about the world the way they do. Freire calls this last process *reflection*.

Reflection involves thinking about the consequences of one's actions and the causes for one's thinking. For instance, a person can make a choice to act in a certain manner. That action will affect the world. In turn, the person can reflect on the impact of that choice and why he or she made the choice in the first place. This process then affects future choices that, in turn, become objects of reflection.

As teachers go through this process of reflection on their observations, they identify contradictions in the lives of their students that can be used in dialogues. These contradictions are then developed into what Freire calls *codifications,* such as sketches, photographs, dramatizations, and tape recordings. These codifications must reflect the real lives of the participants so that they can recognize the situations depicted within them. Also, they should not be overly explicit or be too obscure. Ideally, the codification will spark a dialogue that will lead to other themes in the lives of the students.

Codification presents students with a representation of their lives for *dialogue.* For instance, a codification presented to tenement residents living in Santiago depicted a drunk staggering down the street and men conversing on the corner. In this situation, many tenement dwellers live in a culture of silence but by living in a culture of silence, people do not make their lives an object of reflection—they just act. In Freire's language, they are dehumanized. They are objects of history as opposed to being subjects of history. They do not make history; history makes them.

Many people living in a culture of silence, according to Freire, have never considered their lives as an object to be discussed. In presenting these codifications, Freire warns, teachers must not assume that they know reality. For instance, in the codification depicting the drunk, an educator might assume that the person is drunk because of unemployment or lack of virtue. In the actual dialogue, the investigator, who had selected the codification because he had identified alcoholism as a problem in the community, learned that the drunk was considered by the tenement dwellers to be a productive worker who turned to drink because of worries about low wages and supporting his family.

Freire argues that presentation of codifications causes participants to make explicit their consciousness of the world. The participants see how they act while analyzing a situation that they have experienced. For instance, the tenement dwellers in Santiago see how they act when they are drunk and they analyze the reasons for getting drunk. The process of analysis forces the participants to change their perception of their actions while drinking. This creates new perceptions and the development of new knowledge in the participants.

For example, originally, the participants might have gotten drunk without any thought given to the reasons and consequences. After the process of engaging in a dialogue about the codification of their behavior, the participants might now perceive their actions to be a result of their economic conditions. This perception would fundamentally alter their consciousness about their own actions and the causes of alcoholism. The participants might then engage in reflection on their past perceptions and knowledge. Freire describes this process as "perception of the previous perception" and "knowledge of the previous knowledge." In other words, the participants reflect on why they originally gave little thought to the causes of their own drinking.

Out of the process of codification and dialogue emerge *generative words* to be used in teaching reading. These generative words must have pragmatic value in helping participants to break with their culture of silence. The generative words are words that participants use in describing their own reality. Of course, some consideration must be given to phonetic difficulty in selection of the initial generative words. Ideally, each new word added to the vocabulary would be of increasing phonetic difficulty and would reflect an increasing level of consciousness. In the dialogue about the drunk walking up the street, the teachers might choose for reading instruction words such as *drunk, street, walk, work, wages,* and *family.* As the dialogue progresses, the participants might be introduced to words such as *alcoholism, exploitation, economics, tenement, employment,* and *unemployment.*

The process of learning these words also aids in heightening the consciousness of the students. These words stand as objects of a person's actions. To read or write about one's actions is a process of objectification. In this process of objectification, a person reflects on the action embodied in the word. This process of reflection can transform a person's future actions. For instance, if a person learns the words *drunk, low wages,* and *family* and the person is engaged in a dialogue about the reasons for drinking, then in the future he or she might consciously think of his or her desire for alcohol as resulting from low wages and poor living conditions. With these thoughts affecting their future actions, people might—at least Freire hopes—decide to engage in political actions that will eliminate the social causes of alcoholism. In other words, they will consciously engage in the reconstruction of the world.

One goal of reflection is expulsion of the oppressor from the consciousness of the participants. This reflective process begins with the question, Why did I think the way I did? For the tenement dwellers the question might be, Why did I just accept a life of low wages and seek escape from my misery through alcohol? In reflecting on this question, participants would have to seek the reasons for their previous lack of awareness of how economic and social conditions caused drinking and why they never acted to change their conditions.

In summary, Freire identifies five stages in a dialogue about a codification. In the first stage, the participants simply describe what they see in the theme. In stage two, the teacher poses problems regarding the codified presentation. In the preceding example, the teacher might ask why the person is drunk and why other men linger on street corners. The problem-posing stage helps participants see their way of life as an object that can be discussed and as something that can be changed. In the third stage, the participants reflect on their previous state of silence regarding their culture. For instance, the participants might wonder why they had never questioned the heavy drinking by so many in their community, and why they never linked low wages and family problems as a cause of drinking. In the fourth stage, participants go through increasing levels of critical awareness as they come to understand how their lives and thinking were shaped by political and economic circumstances. And in the fifth stage, they eject the controlling influence of the oppressor from their minds.

## CONCLUSION

While actual classroom procedures have varied little since the beginning of the twentieth century, there continues to be a struggle over the content of textbooks, state standards, the goals of the curriculum, and access to the Internet.

These struggles are an inevitable part of a system of education designed to reach all members of the public. Self-interest along with religious and political convictions are the driving forces in these disputes. Different types of businesses ranging from the dairy industry to advertising want to be treated in a positive light by textbooks and in the school curriculum. Religious groups are concerned that their fundamental beliefs are not disparaged in textbooks and the school curriculum. Those supporting or attacking differing political causes, such as environmental regulations and national health plans, are concerned about how these issues are treated.

I could argue that the democratic processes of a civil society are reflected in the continual challenges to textbooks, curriculum, and Internet usage. (By "civil society" I mean nongovernment organizations.) In the case of education, civil society is constantly attempting to influence in different ways the knowledge taught by schools. On the other hand, it could be argued that action by a civil society means the influence of those organizations that are most active or have the most money. The most active, such as religious groups, organize and devote time to campaign to change what is taught in schools. Without this type of organization, the average citizen has little voice in a civil society. Money can also buy influence of the type that is not available to most people.

The questions raised by the influence of a civil society lead directly to the larger questions: Who should control knowledge in a democratic society? Should control be given to the most active and those with money? Should voters decide directly on what is taught in public schools? Should the decisions be made by politicians acting as representatives of the voters?

## Suggested Readings and Works Cited in Chapter

The Associated Press. "Group: Re-Evaluate School Computers." *The New York Times on the Web* (12 September 2000). *This article discusses the demand by the Alliance for Children for research to assess the educational value of classroom computer use. The organization believes too much money has been spent on school computers without a knowledge of their benefits.*

BEALE, HOWARD. *Are American Teachers Free?* New York: Scribner, 1936. *This is a study of the political pressures placed on teachers and textbook publishers in the 1920s and 1930s.*

BLAIR, JULIE. "Kansas Primary Seen as Signaling Shift in Evolution Stance." *Education Week on the Web* (6 September 2000). *This article discusses the continuing political struggle in Kansas over the issue of evolutionary theory in the state science standards.*

BLAIR, JULIE, and DAVID HOFF. "Evolution Restored to Kansas Standards, but Called 'Controversial' in Alabama." *Education Week on the Web* (21 February 2001). *Covers the continuing controversy over the place of evolution in state standards.*

BORJA, RHEA R. "Internet Filtering Is Balancing Act for Many Schools." *Education Week on the Web* (16 January 2002). *A discussion of the techniques used by various school districts to filter the Internet.*

BROWN, DEE. *Bury My Heart at Wounded Knee: An Indian History of the American West.* New York: Henry Holt and Company, 1970. *This is an excellent example of a U.S. history book written from the perspective of a non-European-American.*

CUBAN, LARRY. *How Teachers Taught: Constancy and Change in American Classrooms, 1890–1980.* White Plains, NY: Longman, 1984. *A study of how teachers actually taught in classrooms in American public schools.*

DAVIS, MICHELLE.   "No URL Left Behind? Web Scrub Raises Concerns." *Education Week on the Web* (18 September 2002). *This article discusses the removal of files from the U.S. Department of Education website that are not compatible with the educational philosophy of the Bush Administration.*

DELEFATTORE, JOAN.   *What Johnny Shouldn't Read: Textbook Censorship in America.* New Haven, CT: Yale University Press, 1992. *A study of textbook censorship in the United States.*

DIEGMULLER, KAREN.   "Removal of Literary Works from Calif. Test Stirs Flap." *Education Week* (9 March 1994): 11. *This article describes the controversy over the removal of stories by Alice Walker and Annie Dillard from the California Learning Assessment System.*

_____. "Model Exam in Calif. Is Target of New Attacks." *Education Week* (4 May 1994): 1, 12. *A discussion of the political controversy over the California Learning Assessment System.*

_____. "Standards for World History a Tough Task." *Education Week* (1 June 1994): 1, 10. *This article reports the problems in establishing standards for the teaching of world history.*

DILLON, SAM. "Publisher Pulls a Textbook in Furor on Sexual Content." *The New York Times* (17 March 1994): B10. *This article reports on the 1994 furor over health textbooks in Texas.*

DWORKIN, MARTIN, ed.   *Dewey on Education.* New York: Teachers College University Press, 1959. *A collection of Dewey's writings including Dewey's 1952 statement on the effect of progressive education on the public schools as quoted in this chapter.*

*Education Week.* "Technology Counts 2002." http:www.edweek.org. *This report discusses the latest advances in e-learning. It can be easily downloaded from the* Education Week *website.*

FITZGERALD, FRANCES.   *America Revised: History Schoolbooks in the Twentieth Century.* Boston: Little, Brown, 1979. *This is a history of history textbooks that depicts the major debates and changes in content in these public school texts.*

FREIRE, PAULO.   *Pedagogy of the Oppressed.* New York: Continuum, 1970. *This is the basic text in critical pedagogy.*

HOFF, DAVID.   "And Congress Said, 'Let There Be Other Views', Or Did It?" *Education Week on the Web* (12 June 2002). *Discussion of whether or not the No Child Left Behind legislation intended to include evolutionary theory in state science standards as a controversial theory.*

_____. "Exemplary Texts Withdrawn from California Adoption Process." *Education Week on the Web* (18 October 2000). *Discussion of the effect of California skill and drill math legislation on math textbooks.*

_____. "Kansas To Revise Standards Without Citing Evolution." *Education Week on the Web* (20 October 1999). *Discussion of removal of evolutionary theory and the origin of the Universe from the Kansas State science standards.*

_____. "New Ohio Draft Ignores Alternative to Evolution." *Education Week on the Web* (18 September 2002). *Discusses controversy in Ohio on the place of evolutionary theory in the state's science standards.*

GLUCK, CAROL.   "Let the Debate Continue." *The New York Times* (19 November 1994): 23. *The debate over history standards.*

KLEINFIELD, N. R.   "The Elderly Man and the Sea? Test Sanitizes Literary Texts." *The New York Times on the Web* (2 June 2002). *This article deals with the censorship of literary excerpts included in the New York Regents exam.*

KLIEBARD, HERBERT M.   *The Struggle for the American Curriculum, 1893–1958.* Boston: Routledge and Kegan Paul, 1986. *Kliebard's history of curriculum in the twentieth cen-*

tury stresses the conflict among social-efficiency advocates, humanists, social meliorists, and developmentalists.

MANZO, KATHLEEN KENNEDY. "N.J. Standards Beginning to Alter What Is Taught, But Not How." *Education Week on the Web* (3 May 2000). *A discussion of the effect of state standards on classroom instruction.*

MCMANUS, TERRY. "Home Web Sites Thrust Students into Censorship Disputes." *The New York Times on the Web* (13 August 1998). *This article surveys the increasing cases of school censorship of student websites.*

"Plan to Teach U.S. History Is Said to Slight White Males." *The New York Times* (26 October 1994): B12. *This article discusses Lynne Cheney's reactions to the proposed history standards.*

"Rejected Textbook." *Compuserve Executive News Service Associated Press* (26 June 1996). *A report on the objections of Hudson, Ohio, parents to the history text,* The American People.

RIECHMANN, DEB. "School Censorship." *Compuserve Executive News Service Associated Press* (4 September 1996). *A report on the number of censorship cases during the 1995–1996 school year.*

SACK, KEVIN. "Regents Vote to Revise Teaching of History." *The New York Times* (17 February 1990): 129. *This article discusses New York State's Education Commissioner's plan to revise American history curriculum and textbooks.*

"School Bans Angelou Autobiography." *Compuserve Executive News Service United Press International* (27 September 1996). *Report on the banning by the West Chester, Ohio, school board of Maya Angelou's* I Know Why the Caged Bird Sings.

SPRING, JOEL. *Conflict of Interests: The Politics of American Education.* White Plains, NY: Longman, 1988. Chapter 6, *"The Knowledge Industry," discusses the politics of publishing and testing. Quotes from the 1986 Texas Textbook Committee are taken from this chapter.*

STILLE, ALEXANDRA. "Textbook Publishers Learn to Avoid Messing with Texas." *The New York Times on the Web* (June 29, 2002). *This article discusses the struggle over the content of history and science textbooks before the Texas State Board of Education.*

STOKES, PETER. "How E-Learning Will Transform Education." *Education Week on the Web* (13 September 2000). *This article describes the range of possibilities for e-learning to enhance education.*

TROTTER, ANDREW. "FCC Issues Rules for Filtering Access to Internet Sites." *Education Week on the Web* (18 April 2001). *This article discusses rules governing the filtering of the Internet in schools and libraries.*

_____. "Internet Access Has No Impact On Test Scores, Study Says." *Education Week on the Web* (4 September 2002). *Using data from California and U.S. departments of education, researchers conclude that Internet access has no measurable impact on student achievement.*

_____. "Rating the E-Rate." *Education Week on the Web* (20 September 2000). *Report on the effect of federal financing on the wiring of schools for the Internet.*

VIADERO, DEBRA. "U.S. Schools Importing Singaporean Texts." *Education Week on the Web* (27 September 2000). *Discussion of the use of math texts from Singapore because they are oriented toward problem solving.*

WEST, PETER. "Academy Unveils 'Principles' for Science Standards." *Education Week* (4 November 1992): 10. *This article outlines the important questions regarding national standards, including differential standards, boundaries of a discipline, and cultural perspective.*

WILLARD, NANCY. "Filtering the Internet." *Education Week on the Web* (27 March 2002). *This is a discussion of the continuing problems associated with Internet filters.*

ZERNIKE, KATE.   "Georgia School Board Requires Balance of Evolution and Bible." *The New York Times on the Web* (23 August 2002). *The second-largest school district in Georgia requires teachers to present biblical interpretations on the origins of life along with evolutionary thought.*

# CHAPTER 10

# *The Courts and the Schools*

Can public schools require urine samples from middle and high school students enrolled in extracurricular activities such as band, choir, and Future Homemakers of America? Can publically funded school vouchers be used to purchase an education at a religious school?

The answer to both questions is yes! These are just two examples of court decisions that affect every aspect of schooling. Constitutional issues are involved in school activities ranging from student publications to the selection of books for the school library. One result is the involvement of the courts in the control and regulation of public schools. Only a limited number of constitutional issues involving the school are discussed here. Each day court decisions are made and legal issues become more complex. Anyone planning a career in teaching should investigate the rights and responsibilities of both teachers and students. Education law is now a whole field of study, and many lawyers are becoming specialists in education issues as school systems spend increasing amounts of time in the courts.

Many court cases involve the First and Fourteenth Amendments to the U.S. Constitution. The Fourteenth Amendment guarantees that states cannot take away any rights granted to an individual as a citizen of the United States; this means that although states have the right to provide schools, they cannot in their provision of schools violate citizen rights granted by the Constitution. The wording of Section 1 of the Fourteenth Amendment is extremely important in a variety of constitutional issues related to education:

> All persons born or naturalized in the United States, and subject to the jurisdiction thereof, are citizens of the United States and of the State wherein they reside. No State shall make or enforce any law which shall abridge the privileges or immunities of citizens of the United States; nor shall any State deprive any person of life, liberty, or property without due process of law [Due Process Clause]; nor deny to any person within its jurisdiction the equal protection of the laws [Equal Protection Clause].

These few lines are important for state-provided and state-regulated schools. For instance, "no state shall make or enforce any law which shall abridge the privileges or immunities of citizens of the United States" means that the courts can protect the constitutional rights of students and teachers particularly with regard to freedom of speech and issues related to religion. The Due Process Clause is invoked in cases that involve student suspensions and teacher firings. Since states provide schools to all citizens, they cannot dismiss a student or teacher without due process. As we shall see later in this chapter, the courts established guidelines for student dismissals.

All the protections of the Fourteenth Amendment depend on the states making some provision for education. Once a state government provides a system for education, it must provide it equally to all people in the state. The Equal Protection Clause is invoked in cases that involve equal educational opportunity and is central to cases that involve school segregation, non-English-speaking children, school finance, and children with special needs. You will recall from an earlier chapter that the famous *Brown v. Board of Education of Topeka* decision in 1954 centered on whether segregated schools provided equal educational opportunity for all students. Before that decision, the Supreme Court had ruled that segregated schools were constitutional; the importance of the 1954 case was the decision that the educational opportunity provided in segregated schools was inherently unequal.

As you can see from the preceding discussion, the Fourteenth Amendment allows for constitutional protection in the schools. What is important, and generates controversy, is the protection of the rights granted in the First Amendment:

> Congress shall make no law respecting an establishment of religion [Establishment Clause], or prohibiting the free exercise [Free Exercise Clause] thereof; or abridging the freedom of speech [Free Speech Clause], or of the press; or the right of the people peaceably to assemble, and to petition the Government for a redress of grievances.

The Establishment Clause of the First Amendment is important for decisions involving school prayer and religious exercises in the schools. The section dealing with laws prohibiting the free exercise of religion, the Free Exercise Clause, is important when religious groups claim that public schools interfere with their religious practices or that public schools are teaching something that is offensive to their religious beliefs.

There is a thin line between not allowing the establishment of religion and interfering with the free exercise of religion. For instance, as we will see later in this chapter, the U.S. Supreme Court prohibits school prayer because it involves the government in the establishment of religion. On the other hand, groups defending school prayer claim that the Court's decision interferes with their free exercise of religion.

The same problem plagues the issue of freedom of speech. On the one hand, the courts recognize the importance of protecting the free speech of students and teachers; on the other hand, the courts recognize the necessity for maintaining order in schools and for school boards to exercise control over teachers. This dilemma also exists in the interpretation of the Eighth Amendment, which reads: "Excessive bail shall not be required, nor excessive fines imposed, nor cruel and unusual punishments inflicted." But when does punishment of a student become cruel and unusual punishment? This, as we will see later in the chapter, is a major issue in court cases dealing with corporal punishment. The first issue I discuss is student rights.

## DRUG TESTING OF STUDENTS

Let's begin considering student rights in the framework of the 2002 U.S. Supreme Court ruling on drug testing. The case, *Board of Education of Independent School District No. 92 of Pottawatomie County et al. v. Earls et al.*, involved a 1998 Student Activities Drug Testing Policy of the Tecumseh, Oklahoma, school district which required students to submit to a urinalysis for illegal drugs (e.g., amphetamines, marijuana, cocaine, opiates, and barbiturates) prior to participating in competitive extracurricular activities. The extracurricular activities included in the school district policy were the Academic Team, Future Farmers of America, Future Homemakers of America, band, choir, pom pom, cheerleading, and athletics.

Two students at the Tecumseh High School, Lindsay Earls and Daniel James, and their parents, claimed that students' Fourth Amendment rights to protection from "unreasonable searches" and the requirement of "probable cause" were being violated. In other words, was the urinalysis an "unreasonable search?" Was there a "probable cause" of drug usage by students engaged in competitive extracurricular activities?

The Fourth Amendment states that:

> The right of the people to be secure in their persons, houses, papers, and effects, against unreasonable searches and seizures, shall not be violated, and no warrants shall issue, but upon probable cause, supported by oath or affirmation, and particularly describing the place to be searched, and the persons or things to be seized.

Regarding "unreasonable search," the U.S. Supreme Court identifies the right to privacy as a key issue. Is the invasion of personal privacy by the urinalysis an "unreasonable search?" The Court's decision states that students in school are in "temporary custody of the state" and a "student privacy interest is limited in a public school environment." The Court also argues that students participating in extracurricular activities, such as athletics or those requiring travel, involve "communal undress." In addition, the manner in which the school district collects the urine samples is not invasion of privacy. The U.S. Supreme Court decision provides the following description of the Tecumseh school district's collection of urine samples:

> A faculty monitor waits outside the closed restroom stall for the student to produce a sample and must listen for the normal sounds of urination in order to guard against tampered specimens and to insure an accurate chain of custody. The monitor then pours the sample into two bottles that are sealed and placed into a mailing pouch along with a consent form signed by the student. This

procedure . . . additionally protects privacy by allowing male students to produce their samples behind a closed stall.

Based on the school's custodial care of the student, "communal undressing," and
"given the minimally intrusive nature of the sample collection," the U.S. Supreme
Court concludes "that the invasion of students privacy is not significant."

Is there a "probable cause" requiring drug testing? Are students using
drugs while engaging in extracurricular activities? First, the U.S. Supreme
Court decision declares, based on previous cases, "that a warrant and finding
of probable cause are unnecessary in the public school context because such requirements would unduly interfere with the maintenance of the swift and informal disciplinary procedures [that are] needed." In other words, school authorities do not have to prove "probable cause" before searching a student's
possessions as along as the search is conducted in a reasonable manner. Also,
school authorities can test for drugs even though there is no suspicion that the
student has actually used drugs.

In addition, the Court felt that the Tecumseh school district had identified
a drug problem in the school district. The following evidence of drug usage is
given in the Court's decision:

> Teachers testified that they had seen students who appeared to be under the in-
> fluence of drugs and that they had heard students speaking openly about using
> drugs. A drug dog found marijuana cigarettes near the school parking lot. Po-
> lice officers once found drugs or drug paraphernalia in a car driven by a Future
> Farmers of America member. And the school board president reported that
> people in the community were calling the board to discuss the drug situation.

Based on the above reasoning, the U.S. Supreme Court ruled that the
Tecumseh school district's Student Activities Drug Testing Policy is not a violation of the Fourth Amendment's prohibition of "unreasonable searches" and
the requirement of "probable cause." The result of this decision means that any
public school district can legally adopt a drug policy modeled on that of the
Tecumseh school district.

Following the Supreme Court decision, John P. Walters, the director of the
White House Office of National Drug Control Policy, sent a booklet to local
school districts urging the use of drug testing. He writes that drug testing had
"enormous potential benefits' and that concerns about privacy were "largely
unfounded." "Already," he contends, "testing has been shown to be extremely
effective at reducing drug use in schools and businesses all over the country. As
a deterrent, few methods work better or deliver clearer results."

The Supreme Court decision was not supported by many groups including
the National Education Association and the American Academy of Pediatrics.
These groups were concerned about privacy issues involved in requiring all
students participating in extracurricular activities to be drug tested. Some communities have divided over the issue. For instance in New Buffalo, Michigan,
there were weekly meetings in August 2002 to hammer out a drug policy. The
superintendent, Michael Lindley, stated, "It cuts deep down to how one sees
the world, and people have different views. Some say it's invasive and you're

assuming my child is guilty until proved otherwise. Others say if kids have nothing to hide, it's not invasive."

Many school districts adopted the Tecumseh school district's stated policies to avoid any future legal problems. "I tell districts," said Paul Lyle, a lawyer representing 50 Texas school districts, "that if they adopt the same verbatim policy as Tecumseh, that would be safe. But I tell them, if you change a comma, it could open the door to something." Raymond Lusk, superintendent of the Lockney, Texas, school district, commented, "We'll probably get 85 percent of the kids in extracurriculars. I think it would be fairer to test everybody, because why are some kids more important than others?"

## STUDENTS' FREE SPEECH RIGHTS

In addition to the Fourth Amendment, students' rights are affected by the Free Speech Clause of the First Amendment which, as previously stated, provides that "Congress shall make no law . . . abridging the freedom of speech." *Tinker v. Des Moines Independent School District* (1969) is the landmark case involving free speech rights for students.

The *Tinker* case originated when a group of students decided to express their objections to the war in Vietnam by wearing black armbands. School authorities in Des Moines adopted a policy that any student wearing an armband would be suspended. When the case was decided by the U.S. Supreme Court, clear recognition was given to the constitutional rights of students. The Court stated that a student "may express his opinion, even on controversial subjects like the conflict in Vietnam. . . . Under our Constitution, free speech is not a right that is given only to be so circumscribed that it exists in principle but not in fact."

One extremely important condition is placed on the right of free speech of students and that is the possibility of disruption of the educational process. The Court does not provide any specific guidelines for interpreting this condition and limitation. What it means is that school authorities have an obligation to protect the constitutional rights of students and, at the same time, an obligation to ensure that there is no interference with the normal activities of the school.

In recent years, student rights were limited by claims of interference with the educational purposes and activities of schools. A federal appellate court ruled that a school administration can disqualify a student campaigning for student body president because of remarks about the vice principal and school administration. The appellate court reasoned that the administration's educational concerns allowed it to censor comments that might hurt the feelings of others. This form of censorship taught students to respect others.

In *Hazelwood School District v. Kuhlemier* (1988), the U.S. Supreme Court ruled that school administrators have the right to control the content of school-sponsored publications because they are part of the curriculum. The case involved a newspaper published by the journalism class at Missouri's Hazelwood High School. The newspaper contained articles about student pregnancies and students from divorced families. False names were used to protect the students interviewed for the articles. The school's principal objected to the articles because the interviewed students might be identifiable to other students, and he considered the sexual discussions inappropriate for high school students. The authors of the articles responded that both divorce and pregnancy were appropriate topics for modern youth and that they were widely discussed among students.

The right of school administrators to censor student publications was expanded to include all school activities. School administrators have the right to refuse to produce student plays, to prohibit student publication of articles that are poorly written and vulgar, and to ban student expression that advocates drugs, alcohol, and permissive sex. In censorship cases of this type, the legal test is whether the school administration's actions are based on legitimate educational concerns.

School authorities are also allowed to punish student speech that they consider to be lewd and indecent. In *Bethel v. Fraser* (1986), the U.S. Supreme Court ruled that school administrators in the Bethel, Washington, school system could punish a high school senior, Matthew Fraser, for giving a nominating speech at a school assembly that used an "elaborate, graphic, and explicit sexual metaphor." The Court said that school officials had the right to determine what is vulgar and offensive in the classroom and at school activities and to prohibit vulgar and offensive speech. This decision did not apply to speech about political, religious, educational, and public policy issues; it was limited to the issue of indecent speech.

## GAYS, BOY SCOUTS, AND NO CHILD LEFT BEHIND ACT OF 2001

In the 1990s, the decision by the Boy Scouts to deny membership to homosexuals was extremely contentious. In 2000, the U.S. Supreme Court ruled in *Boy Scouts of America v. Dale* that it was a private association with the right to set its own standards for membership and leadership. As a result, school districts across the country banned the Boy Scouts from using school facilities. For instance, when the Minneapolis school district denied the Boy Scouts access to school buildings, Carol Johnson, the superintendent, contended, "We are an inclusive organization. It would be very difficult to continue to partner with them [Boy Scouts] and be consistent with our nondiscrimination policy." Evan Wolfson, a senior staff lawyer with the Lambda Legal Defense and Education Fund, a gay-rights group, asserted, "Schools, as public entities, cannot be accomplices to discrimination, especially discrimination that hurts our kids."

The issue of Boy Scout access to schools was resolved in the No Child Left Behind Act. In a special section titled "Boy Scouts of America Equal Access Act," the legislation states:

> Notwithstanding any other provision of law, no public elementary school, public secondary school, local educational agency, or State educational agency that

has a designated open forum or a limited public forum and that receives funds made available through the Department shall deny equal access or a fair opportunity to meet to, or discriminate against, any group officially affiliated with the Boy Scouts of America.

## SEXUAL HARASSMENT AND DISCRIMINATION

In *Franklin v. Gwinnett* (1992), the U.S. Supreme Court ruled that students who were victimized by sexual harassment and other forms of sexual discrimination by school officials could sue for monetary damages. The case involved a Georgia high school student who was sexually harassed and abused by a teacher. This decision was made in the context of Title IX, which bars discrimination based on gender. The school district was required to conform to Title IX. In making its decision, the U.S. Supreme Court relied on a previous decision barring supervisors from sexually harassing a subordinate. The Court extended this ruling to include teachers and students.

In contrast, the U.S. Supreme Court in 1996 let stand the decision by the U.S. Court of Appeals for the Fifth District that school systems were not liable for sexual harassment of students by other students. The case involved two eighth grade girls in Bryan, Texas, who were sexually harassed on a school bus.

The decision by the U.S. Supreme Court not to review the Texas case left school officials in a state of confusion. In a California decision, a state court jury awarded $500,000 to a family of a sixth grade student who was tormented by other students calling her "slut" and "bitch." Alarmed at the possibility of other suits, school officials in North Carolina and New York City punished first and second grade boys for kissing female classmates. These punishments caused a great deal of public criticism. Until the U.S. Supreme Court clarifies the issue, school officials will continue to worry about potential suits over sexual harassment between students.

## STUDENTS' ACCESS TO BOOKS

A First Amendment case involved balancing the right of students to have access to books in the school library with the right of the school board to decide which books should be in the school library. The case *Board of Island Union Free School District v. Steven A. Pico* (1982) concerned the removal of books from the school library by the board of education because the content of the books was considered unsuitable for high school students. The issue originated when several members of the board of education attended a conference of a politically conservative organization of parents concerned with educational legislation in the state of New York. While they were at the conference the board members received a list of books considered morally and politically inappropriate for high school students. Upon returning from the conference, the board members investigated the contents of their high school library and discovered nine books that had been on the list. Subsequently, the board ordered the removal of the books from the library shelves. The books included *Best Short Stories of Negro Writers* edited by Langston Hughes, *Down These Mean Streets* by Piri Thomas, *The Fixer* by Bernard Malamud, *Go Ask Alice* of anonymous authorship, *A Hero Ain't Nothin but a Sandwich* by Alice Childress, *Naked Ape* by Desmond Morris, *A Reader for Writers* by Jerome Archer, *Slaughterhouse Five* by Kurt Vonnegut, Jr., and *Soul on Ice* by Eldridge Cleaver.

In its decision the U.S. Supreme Court gave full recognition to the power of school boards to select books for the school library and to the importance of avoiding judicial interference in the operation of local school systems. On the other hand, the Court recognized its obligation to ensure that public institutions do not suppress ideas. Here, there was a clear intention to suppress ideas by making decisions about book removal based on a list from a political organization.

The Supreme Court's method of handling the preceding dilemma was to recognize the right of the school board to determine the content of the library, if its decisions on content were not based on partisan or political motives. In the words of the Court, "If a Democratic school board, motivated by party affiliation, ordered the removal of all books written by or in favor of Republicans, few would doubt that the order violated the constitutional rights of the students denied access to those books." In another illustration, the Court argued, "The same conclusion would surely apply if an all-white school board, motivated by racial animus, decided to remove all books authored by blacks or advocating racial equality and integration." Or, as the Court more simply stated, "Our Constitution does not permit the official suppression of ideas."

On the other hand, the Court argued that books could be removed if the decision were based solely on their educational suitability. The Court also limited its decision to apply only to books removed from school library shelves, not to decisions about books added to the shelves. In summary, the Court stated:

> We hold that local school boards may not remove books from school library shelves simply because they dislike the ideas contained in those books and seek by their removal to prescribe what shall be orthodox in politics, nationalism, religion, or other matters of opinion.

## STUDENT SUSPENSIONS

A student's "property interest" in education is the result of a state statutory entitlement to a public education. The right to attend public schools is usually conferred on children by state law. This law, of course, can vary from state to state.

Property interest and the right to an education were major considerations of the U.S. Supreme Court in dealing with due process and suspensions from school in *Goss v. Lopez* (1975). This case dealt with suspensions from school of junior and senior high school students. The Court ruled that due process "requires, in connection with a suspension of 10 days or less, that the student be given oral or written notice of the charges against him and, if he denies them, an explanation of the evidence the authorities have and an opportunity to present his side of the story." The Court based its decision on "legitimate claims of entitlement to public education" as given in state law. What this meant was that a student's right to an education could not be taken away in an arbitrary manner.

The *Goss* decision established a precedent that due process is required before a school-dismissal decision. R. Lawrence Dessem, in a 1976 article in the *Journal of Law and Education,* "Student Due Process Rights in Academic Dismissals from the Public Schools," argues that in the future the due-process requirement might be applied to cases involving dismissal from school for academic reasons. The *Goss* decision dealt only with suspension for disciplinary reasons. In either case there may be a clear obligation upon school authorities to guarantee due process for all students.

Dessem outlines in his article the basic procedures that must take place to ensure due process for students. First, there must be an attempt to decide the basis of fact. Second, there must be some provision to guarantee future review of any decisions. And third, just procedures must be followed in reaching any decisions.

In practice, these three procedures mean very specific things. A student must be provided with a notice detailing the charges, and the notice must be received in sufficient time for the student to prepare answers to the charges. A student must be given the chance to present answers to the charges in a hearing before an unbiased group. Dessem argues that schools cannot be required to have groups outside the school conduct the hearings because of the expense. Dessem states: "A hearing before a panel of disinterested teachers and school administrators would seem to strike an acceptable balance between the right of the student to an impartial arbitrator and the school's interest in keeping the expense and inconvenience of such hearings to a minimum." Students do have a right to have the decision based only on the evidence presented.

In *Goss,* the U.S. Supreme Court did place a limit on the procedural elements of due process by refusing to require that students be given the right to call witnesses and have legal counsel. "The Supreme Court's rationale," states Dessem, "for refusing to mandate this and several other procedures was that since 'brief disciplinary suspensions are almost countless, to impose in each such case even truncated trial type procedures might well overwhelm administrative facilities in many places.'"

The *Tinker* decision has provided some protection for the freedom of speech of students in public schools, and the *Goss* decision has provided protection from arbitrary dismissal of students from public schools. Both decisions represent the continuing expansion of civil liberties granted under the Constitution of the United States. Teachers and other school authorities have a duty and an obligation to ensure that these rights are protected. Teachers also have an obligation to protect their constitutional rights, thereby serving as models for students and setting an example for interpreting the meaning of civil liberties in the United States.

# DO SCHOOL AUTHORITIES HAVE THE RIGHT
# TO PADDLE CHILDREN?

Consider the following situations and compare your opinions with the decisions of the courts. Assume the following set of circumstances: The family of a child cannot afford private schooling. Due to compulsory-education laws, the family is forced to send the child to a local public school where the primary means of discipline is corporal punishment. The parents do not believe in the use of physical punishment, have never used physical punishment at home, and do not want the public school to use physical punishment on their child. In this situation, can school authorities spank the child? Can the child be forced to attend an institution that gives its personnel the right to use physical punishment, contrary to practices in the child's home?

Part of the answer to these questions was given in the U.S. Supreme Court decision *Ingraham v. Wright* (1977). A junior high school student, James Ingraham, in Dade County, Florida, refused to let the principal of his school, Willie Wright, paddle him for not leaving the stage of the school auditorium promptly. (Ingraham claimed that he had left the stage when requested by the principal.) When Ingraham refused to be paddled, Principal Wright called in his two assistant principals, who held Ingraham's legs and arms. The student was hit 20 times on the buttocks with a two-foot-long wooden paddle. His mother examined him when he arrived home and immediately took him to a local hospital, where the doctor prescribed pain pills, ice packs, and a laxative and recommended that Ingraham stay home for a week.

At a Florida trial court hearing, many other students complained about beatings at the school. Children described being pushed up against urinals in the boys' bathroom and being beaten on the legs, back, and across the neck. One boy described how he refused to take a whipping because he felt he was innocent and was beaten with a board across the head. Within a few days of the beating, the student underwent an operation to have a lump removed from his head; he claimed a subsequent loss of memory.

After a weeklong trial, the Florida court granted the defense a motion for dismissal, arguing that there was no showing of severe punishment and that corporal punishment was not unacceptable according to the standards of contemporary society. This ruling was overturned by the Fifth Circuit Court of Appeals because the punishment at the junior high school violated the Eighth Amendment's prohibition against cruel and unusual punishment. A further appeal reversed this ruling and set the stage for a decision by the U.S. Supreme Court.

On April 19, 1977, the U.S. Supreme Court ruled that the Cruel and Unusual Punishment Clause of the Eighth Amendment does not apply to corporal punishment, nor does the Due Process Clause of the Fourteenth Amendment require that notice be given to students before they are subjected to corporal punishment. The Court argued that corporal punishment is the traditional means of maintaining discipline in the public schools and that although public opinion is divided on the issue, there is not any trend to eliminate its use.

The Court found no reason for extending the Eighth Amendment to the schools.

The Court felt that community pressure and common-law safeguards should be used to ensure that corporal punishment be used in a reasonable manner. This argument paralleled the lower court's argument that here criminal charges could be brought against the junior high school principal and assistant principal. In other words, public school authorities can beat children, but the extent of the punishment must be reasonable.

Determining what is reasonable creates a difficult problem for courts and the community. A teacher or administrator who inflicts one or two spankings a year without causing any lasting physical damage would be considered reasonable. But what about the teacher or principal who paddles so violently that students are left with black-and-blue marks? A principal of a Kentucky high school, in a recent lecture at my university, argued that administrators and teachers who use corporal punishment excessively exhibit behavior usually associated with child abusers.

But what if parents object to the use of corporal punishment? A decision regarding this issue was made by the Fourth Circuit Court of Appeals on May 9, 1980, in *Hall v. Tauney*. Thomas Flygare describes this case in the September 1980 issue of the *Phi Delta Kappan*. A West Virginia grade school student was, in Flygare's words, "repeatedly and violently struck on the hip and thigh by a teacher using a homemade hard rubber paddle about five inches in width. She alleged that because of this paddling she was hospitalized for ten days and has received the treatment of specialists for possible permanent injuries to the lower spine."

Since argument about the Eighth Amendment's Cruel and Unusual Punishment Clause had failed in the Ingraham case, Hall's lawyers decided to use a different tactic. The lawyers argued that the paddling, as Flygare states, "violated the right of her parents to determine the means by which she could be disciplined."

The Fourth Circuit Court ruled that parents had no constitutional right to exempt their children from corporal punishment in the schools. The statement of the court raised a whole host of issues regarding the power of parents versus the power of the school. Reflect on the statement by the court that "the state interest in maintaining order in the schools limits the rights of particular parents unilaterally to except their children from the regime to which other children are subject."

## COMPULSION AND RELIGION

Since their founding public schools have been in conflict with religious groups. The Establishment Clause of the First Amendment to the U.S. Constitution states that "Congress shall make no law respecting an establishment of religion, or prohibiting the free exercise thereof." The problem is that many religions believe education cannot be separated from religion. Both education and religion are concerned with the moral and social development of the individual. Religion, education, and the First Amendment conflict when certain religious groups are forced to send their children to public school and conform to the practices of the school, and when religious groups demand that the public schools engage in certain religious practices, such as school prayer. In the first case, forced attendance and compliance with school regulations can be an infringement on an individual's right to practice religion, if school practices conflict with religious beliefs. In the second case, religious activities in public schools can mean that the government is giving support to particular religious practices.

## VOUCHERS AND RELIGIOUS SCHOOLS

In 2002, the U.S. Supreme Court issued a landmark decision on school vouchers and religious schools. In *Zelman v. Simmons-Harris,* the primary issue was the use of government-funded vouchers by students to attend schools with religious affiliations. Was the use of these government vouchers a violation of the Establishment Clause ("Congress shall make no law respecting an establishment of religion") of the First Amendment?

As I discussed in Chapter 6, the state of Ohio's Pilot Project Scholarship Program provides tuition aid vouchers to families residing in the Cleveland City school district. These vouchers can be used to attend any accredited private school or public schools in other school districts adjacent to the Cleveland City school district. The Establishment Clause became an issue because, as stated in the U.S. Supreme Court decision, "82% of the participating private schools had a religious affiliation, none of the adjacent public schools [in other school districts] participated, and 96% of the students participating in the scholarship program were enrolled in religiously affiliated schools." Clearly, religious schools were receiving the bulk of the voucher money provided under the Pilot Project Scholarship Program.

In the decision regarding Ohio's Pilot Project Scholarship Program, the U.S. Supreme Court relied on a previous decision, *Mueller v. Allen* (1983) which dealt with a Minnesota law that allowed state taxpayers to take deductions from gross income for expenses incurred for "tuition, textbooks, and transportation" for dependents attending elementary and secondary schools. The majority of beneficiaries (96 percent) of the Minnesota law were parents of children attending religious schools. In *Mueller,* the U.S. Supreme Court argued that the law did not violate the Constitution because "the deduction is available for educational expenses incurred by all parents, including those whose children attend public schools and those whose children attend nonsectarian private schools or sectarian private schools." The Court reasoned that the intent of the law was primarily secular, it did not advance religion, and it did not cause an excessive entanglement between the government and religion.

What about the fact that under both the Minnesota and Ohio laws the majority of the government benefits went to parents sending their children to religious schools? Wasn't this a violation of the Establishment Clause? No, the U.S. Supreme Court answered, because the intent of the law was secular. The fact that the majority of benefits went to religious institutions was the result of the choices made by parents. In the words of the U.S. Supreme Court's decision regarding Ohio's Pilot Project Scholarship Program, "The amount of government aid channeled to religious institutions by individual aid recipients was not relevant to the constitutional inquiry."

Based on the above reasoning, the Court concluded that Ohio's Pilot Project Scholarship Program was not a violation of the Establishment Clause. However, the decision left many questions unanswered. In reality, Cleveland parents were limited in choice to private schools because none of the surrounding school districts were willing to participate in the program. This fact highlights the efforts by suburban school districts to protect their educational advantages.

## CHILD-BENEFIT THEORY

The now-famous voucher decision in *Zelman v. Simmons-Harris* followed previous attempts to distinguish between religious and secular intents of laws. One approach is referred to as the *child-benefit theory*. The child-benefit theory was articulated by the U.S. Supreme Court in *Cochran v. Louisiana State Board of Education* (1930). At issue was a Louisiana law permitting the purchase and distribution of textbooks to all schoolchildren. Under this law textbooks were provided to children attending private religious schools. The U.S. Supreme Court affirmed the Louisiana Supreme Court ruling that the law did not sanction the support of religious schools. Taxpayers' money was spent to purchase books that went directly to schoolchildren. The law existed for the benefit of children, not for the support of religious institutions.

The same reasoning was involved in the 1947 U.S. Supreme Court decision *Everson v. Board of Education*, which allowed public support of school transportation for parochial students. Here the support again went directly to the child and not to a religious institution. The Court stated, "We cannot say that the First Amendment prohibits . . . spending tax-raised funds to pay the bus fares of parochial school pupils as a part of a general program under which it pays fares of pupils attending public and other schools."

One difficult issue is the participation by religious schools in federally funded programs, such as Title I programs for remedial education. In 1978, a group called Public Education and Religious Liberty (PEARL) argued that the presence of publically funded teachers, such as Title I teachers, in religious schools was a violation of the Establishment Clause of the First Amendment. In 1985 the U.S. Supreme Court in *Aguilar v. Felton* agreed with PEARL; as a result, Title I teachers at religious schools were housed in off-campus mobile classrooms or other facilities. In 1997 the U.S. Supreme Court in *Agostini v. Felton* reversed the 1985 decision arguing that there was no reason to think that Title I teachers would give religious lessons in their classrooms. For many teachers, such as Maxine Bender, a New York public school teacher, it was a pleasure to be able to teach remedial reading inside the Sacred Heart Catholic school. "It makes a tremendous difference," she said, "to be back inside the building." In 2000 the U.S. Supreme Court ruled in favor of a federal program that provided computers and library books to religious schools. This decision reversed an earlier decision barring the federal government from giving maps, charts, overhead projectors, and other instructional materials to religious schools.

A 1971 U.S. Supreme Court case, *Lemon v. Kurzman,* established a three-part test for determining the constitutionality of government programs that benefit religion. The case involved laws in Rhode Island and Pennsylvania that provided salary supplements to teachers in private religious schools. Under the *Lemon* test, government aid to religious schools

- Must have a secular purpose.
- Must not inhibit or advance religion.
- Must not cause excessive entanglement of government in religion.

## CAN STATES REGULATE PRIVATE SCHOOLS?

The issue of state regulation of private schools appeared in the U.S. Supreme Court case dealing with the conflict between compulsory schooling and religious freedom. In *Pierce v. Society of Sisters* (1925), the Court ruled on Oregon's Compulsory Education Act (1922), which required every parent, guardian, or other person having control or charge or custody of a child between 8 and 16 years of age to send the child to a public school. The act was clearly an attempt to close parochial schools by forcing all children to attend public schools. Two private schools in Oregon immediately obtained injunctions against Governor Pierce and Oregon state officials.

The First Amendment was not directly involved in the case because the law affected both religious and nonreligious private schools. The Supreme Court did indirectly support the guarantee of religious liberty, however, by maintaining the right to choose a religious school instead of a public school. The Court stated that the "fundamental theory of liberty upon which all governments in this Union repose excludes any general power of the State to standardize its children by forcing them to accept instruction from public teachers only."

The Supreme Court ruling in *Pierce v. Society of Sisters* was based on an earlier ruling involving a Nebraska law that required all subjects in private and public schools be taught in the English language. The purpose of the law was to curb German nationalism during World War I by limiting the use of foreign languages. In *Meyer v. Nebraska,* they declared the law unconstitutional. Nevertheless, the Court did recognize the right of the teacher "to teach and the right of parents to engage him so to instruct their children." The importance of the Meyer decision was the recognition of the parental right to direct the upbringing of their children within the reasonable limitations of the law.

In *Pierce v. Society of Sisters* these rights were again confirmed in declaring the 1922 Oregon law unconstitutional. The Court stated, "Under the doctrine of

*Meyer v. Nebraska* . . . we think it entirely plain that the Act of 1922 unreasonably interferes with the liberty of parents and guardians to direct the upbringing and education of children under their control." But the Court did not recognize the complete control of the parents and guardians over the education of their children; it very clearly defined the power of the states regarding education.

Probably the most important part of the *Pierce* decision, besides declaring that children could not be forced to attend public schools, was the recognition of the power of the state to regulate education and compel students to attend school. The Court stated, "No question is raised concerning the power of the State reasonably to regulate all schools, to inspect, supervise and examine them, their teachers and pupils; to require that all children of proper age attend some school." Besides recognizing the right of regulation and requirements to attend, the Court also recognized the right of the state to certify teachers and regulate the curriculum regarding citizenship studies. The Court ruled that the state had the right to require "that teachers shall be of good moral character and patriotic disposition, that certain studies plainly essential to good citizenship must be taught, and that nothing be taught which is manifestly inimical to the public welfare."

These qualifications to the *Pierce* decision placed important limitations on the right of parents and guardians to direct the education of their children. The state had the right to force attendance at an educational institution that met state requirements concerning teachers, curriculum, and other reasonable standards. The only right recognized for parents was the choice between public and private schools, and this right was limited by the ability to pay for private schooling. The unresolved issue was what would happen if the state standards used to regulate public and private schools differed from religious practices and the state required attendance at a state-accredited school. This is the problem that the Amish encountered.

## RELIGION AND STATE SCHOOL REQUIREMENTS

The Amish are a subgroup of the Anabaptist-Mennonite tradition that has refused to be assimilated into the mainstream of American society and the modern urban and industrial world. They first came to America in the eighteenth century and settled in eastern Pennsylvania in compact communities. They retained in America their original European dress-style of men wearing black clothes and wide-brimmed hats and women wearing capes and aprons. In areas of Pennsylvania, Ohio, Indiana, Iowa, and Wisconsin, communities of Amish continue to exist with traditional religious practices, clothes, and community living. The Amish continue to use horse-and-buggy transportation and avoid the use of electricity and telephones.

One major threat to the Amish way of life is the public school and compulsory education. The public school threatens the destruction of the Amish community by the teaching of values contrary to its traditions and by the introduction of the children to modern lifestyles. For the Amish, this threat can occur in areas that might seem unimportant to other people. For instance, one objection of Amish parents to compulsory high school attendance is the requirement that young women wear shorts for physical education, which is in serious violation of Amish beliefs. In the nineteenth century the Amish began to object to the rise of public schools. In an article entitled "From Erlanback to New Glarus" in a book he edited titled *Compulsory Education and the Amish,* Albert N. Keim quotes a nineteenth-century Amish leader: "The righteousness that counts before God is neither sought nor found in the public or free schools; they are interested only to impart worldly knowledge, to ensure earthly success and to make good citizens of the state."

The Amish particularly object to public high school because of its broader curriculum and preparation for a vocation or college. The Amish do their own vocational training within their communities. Amish education stresses following instructions, respecting authority, and mastering basic information. Amish disapprove of modern education that stresses critical thinking and asking questions. They see obedience to authority and tradition as essential for the survival of the community.

New Glarus, Wisconsin, was the scene of the final confrontation between the Amish and compulsory-education laws. In 1968, public school authorities insisted that the Amish community comply with a Wisconsin law requiring school attendance until 16 years of age. The county court upheld the school authorities. The Amish appealed the case to the Wisconsin Supreme Court, which rejected the lower court's decision and ruled that compulsory schooling of Amish children beyond the eighth grade was a violation of the free exercise of religious rights. In 1972 the U.S. Supreme Court in *State of Wisconsin, Petitioner v. Jonas Yoder et al.* upheld the Wisconsin Supreme Court decision.

In the *Yoder* decision the U.S. Supreme Court placed some limitations on the right of a state to compel school attendance, as recognized in *Pierce v. Society of Sisters.* The Court stated in the Pierce decision that there was recognition given that the "values of parental direction of the religious upbringing and education of their children in their early and formative years have a high place in our society." In addition, the Court argued that a state's interest in universal education should not be at the sacrifice of other rights, specifically those of the First Amendment. In the words of the Court, "We can accept it as settled, therefore, that however strong the State's interest in universal compulsory education, it is by no means absolute to the exclusion or subordination of all other interests."

The *Yoder* decision also placed limitations on state educational requirements. The Court stated that there were two primary arguments for maintaining a system of compulsory education. One argument was the necessity for citizens to be prepared to participate intelligently in an open political system. The other argument was that education was necessary to prepare people to be self-reliant and self-sufficient in society. The Court clearly stated concerning these two arguments: "We accept these propositions." The Court then went on to argue that the requirement that the Amish attend school beyond the eighth grade did not aid in the achievement of these educational goals. The Court stated that the Amish community was a highly successful social unit and its members were productive and law-abiding. Education within the community therefore appeared to fulfill the state interests in education.

The importance of the 1972 *Yoder* decision is in the placing of First Amendment religious freedoms above those of the state's interest in education. This would mean that in the future the courts would decide any conflict between religious practices and compulsory schooling in favor of individual religious freedom. The decision also requires that, in any future cases dealing with compulsory schooling, the state must show some relationship between its educational requirements and standards and its interest in educating self-sufficient and intelligent citizens. State standards cannot be arbitrary and unrelated to these objectives.

The U.S. Supreme Court also protects First Amendment rights when required practices in the schools conflict with religious beliefs. This decision involved objections of Jehovah's Witnesses to saluting and pledging allegiance to the flag. The case began in the early 1940s when the West Virginia Board of Education ordered that the flag salute become a regular part of the school program and that all teachers and pupils be required to salute the flag and say the Pledge of Allegiance. Refusal to participate was to be viewed as an act of insubordination, and pupils who failed to conform were to be expelled from school. Pupils expelled from school were considered delinquent and could possibly be sent to juvenile reformatories.

Jehovah's Witnesses object to the flag ceremony because they believe that the obligations imposed by the law of God are superior to the laws of government. One law of God taken literally by Jehovah's Witnesses is: "Thou shall not make unto thee any graven image, or any likeness of anything that is in heaven above, or that is in the earth beneath, or that is in the water under the earth; thou shalt not bow down thyself to them nor serve them." Jehovah's Witnesses believe that the flag is an image and refuse, for religious reasons, to salute it.

The U.S. Supreme Court ruling in *West Virginia State Board of Education v. Barnette* declared the West Virginia School Board ruling unconstitutional because of its abridgment of First Amendment freedoms. In its decision the Court went beyond the issue of protection of religious practices to the issue of protection within public schools of all constitutional privileges. The Court argued: "That they are educating the young for citizenship is reason for scrupulous protection of Constitutional freedoms of the individual, if we are not to strangle the free mind at its source and teach youth to discount important principles of our government as mere platitudes." Within the same framework, the Court emphasized that patriotic exercises should not be made compulsory. In the words of the Court, "To believe that patriotism will not flourish if patriotic ceremonies are voluntary and spontaneous instead of a compulsory routine is to make an unflattering estimate of the appeal of our institutions to free minds."

Another controversial issue is religious practices in schools. There is a great deal of pressure to introduce religious practice into schools as Bible reading, prayer, and meditation. All three practices conflict with the Establishment Clause of the First Amendment.

## SCHOOL PRAYER, BIBLE READING, AND MEDITATION

Many religious groups were outraged by the 1962 school-prayer decision in *Engel v. Vitale.* The decision denied the right of a public school system to conduct prayer services within school buildings during regular school hours. Those groups of people whom the decision angers argue that it made education godless, and they seek an amendment to the Constitution that would allow for prayer ceremonies in the school. The Court decision against school prayer was primarily based on the argument that school prayer involved the state in the establishment of religion. This is considered a violation of the Establishment Clause of the First Amendment.

The school-prayer case began when the New York Board of Regents granted a local school system the right to have a brief prayer said in each class at the beginning of the school day. The prayer, considered denominationally neutral, read, "Almighty God, we acknowledge our dependence upon Thee, and we beg Thy blessings upon us, our parents, our teachers and our country." The New York courts granted the right of local school systems to use this prayer. The one requirement was that they could not compel students to say the prayer if they or their parents objected.

It was the decision of the New York courts against which the U.S. Supreme Court ruled in *Engel v. Vitale.* One major objection of the Court was the fact that government officials wrote the prayer. This seemed to put the government directly in the business of establishing religion. The Court stated that "in this country it is not part of the business of government to compose official prayers for any group of the American people to recite as a part of the religious program carried on by government." The Court reviewed the early history of the United States, and the struggle for religious freedom and the ending of government support of churches. The Court argued: "By the time of the adoption of the Constitution, our history shows that there was a widespread awareness among many Americans of the dangers of a union of Church and State." The writing of a prayer by government officials ran counter to this long-standing struggle in the United States.

The Court rejected the argument that the school-prayer law did not violate any rights because it did not require students to recite the prayer and the prayer was nondenominational. The Court argued that this confused the right of free exercise of religion with the prohibition against the state establishing and supporting religion. Excusing students from reciting the prayer might protect their free exercise of religion, but the very existence of the prayer involved the establishment of religion. In the words of the Court, "The Establishment Clause, unlike the Free Exercise Clause, does not depend upon any showing of direct governmental compulsion and is violated by the enactment of laws which establish an official religion whether those laws operate directly to coerce nonobserving individuals or not."

In 1963, the Court applied the same reasoning to the issue of Bible reading in the public schools. In *Abington School District v. Schempp* the issue was a

Pennsylvania law that permitted the reading of 10 verses from the Bible at the opening of each public school day. The verses were to be read without comment, and any child could be excused from reading the verses or attending the Bible reading, upon the written request of the parents or guardians. Like the school-prayer issue, the Court felt that a Bible-reading service of this type involved the state in the establishment of religion. The Court made it clear that it did not reject the idea of Bible reading as a part of a study of comparative religion or the history of religion. Nor did the Court exclude the possibility of studying the Bible as a piece of literature. What the Court objected to was the reading of the Bible as part of a religious exercise.

The courts are somewhat ambivalent on the issue of meditation in schools. Massachusetts passed a law requiring a moment of silence "for meditation or prayer" in public schools. Here, the Court said that meditation could refer to any subject because the law used the word *or*, which inferred a secular intent for meditation. Therefore, a student might be expected to meditate on anything, including schoolwork or family life. In this situation, the law was not violating the Establishment Clause.

A Louisiana law allowing meditation was struck down as a violation of the Establishment Clause. Here, the law included the permission for teachers to ask students if they were interested in praying. An Alabama law allowing for meditation or voluntary prayer and for teachers to lead classes in prayer was also ruled as violating the Establishment Clause. The argument then was that the law lacked a secular purpose and that it was intended to support school prayers.

In 2000 the U.S. District Court in Alexander, Virginia, ruled that the state's law requiring students to observe a "minute of silence" did not violate the ban on government-established religion. During the minute of silence students are allowed to "meditate, pray, or engage in any other silent activity."

The test in all these cases is whether the intent is secular or religious. If the intention is religious, then it is a violation of the Establishment Clause.

## STUDENT PRAYERS

In 1992, the U.S. Supreme Court, in a dispute originating over prayers given by a Rabbi at a middle school graduation in Providence, Rhode Island, ruled that prayers conducted at a public school graduation were unconstitutional. Writing for the majority of the court in *Lee v. Weisman*, Supreme Court Justice Anthony Kennedy declared:

> The Constitution forbids the state to exact religious conformity from a student as the price of attending her own high school graduation. No holding by this Court suggests that a school can persuade or compel a student to participate in a religious exercise. That is being done here, and it is forbidden by the Establishment Clause of the First Amendment.

Student-led graduation prayers were declared unconstitutional in 1996 by the U.S. Court of Appeals. The case involved a 1993 graduation exercise at New

Jersey's Highland Regional High School. Before the graduation ceremony a majority of seniors voted to have a graduation prayer. A student sued and won an injunction against the prayer. The Appeals Court argued that the religious rights of students who did not want a prayer could not be compromised by a majority vote.

On the other hand, an Appeals Court ruling in 1998 approved the Madison school district of Rexburg, Idaho, policy of allowing the top four graduating seniors to speak on any topic including the reciting of prayers and singing of religious songs. In *Doe v. Madison,* the U.S. Court of Appeals for the Ninth Circuit Court argued that in this case the control of religious content was in the hands of the individual student as opposed to the school. The Appeals Court cited the following factors:

- Students and not clergy delivered the prayers.
- Student speakers were selected on academic standing.
- School officials allowed the students to choose the content of their speeches.

In 1996, the U.S. Supreme Court let stand a ruling barring voluntary student prayers during schools events. At issue was a 1994 Mississippi law allowing "nonsectarian, nonproselytizing student-initiated voluntary prayer" during student events. The Mississippi state legislature passed the law in protest of the firing of a Jackson, Mississippi, high school principal. The principal, Bishop Knox, allowed students to pray over the school's intercom. "A state policy of prayer at school," states the Fifth Circuit Court ruling upheld by the Supreme Court, "tells students that the state wants them to pray. The school-prayer statute is an unconstitutional endorsement of religion." This decision was upheld in 1998, when the U.S. Supreme Court rejected an appeal by Governor Fob James, Jr., of Alabama, who sought to restore the right to student-led prayers in Alabama schools.

Do religious groups have the right to use public school facilities for religious services? New York City allows the rental of schools for community activities including religious discussion. It does not allow their use for religious services. A coalition of Christian and Jewish religious groups sued demanding equal access to public schools for conducting religious ceremonies. In 1998 the U.S. Supreme Court, by rejecting an appeal of a decision by the U.S. Court of Appeals for the Second Circuit, let stand a decision that public schools are limited forums rather than public forums. It is difficult to limit free speech in public forums, such as on sidewalks or in parks. However, they argued, public schools are limited forums and, therefore, school officials can limit free speech for the purpose of not being identified with a particular religious service.

In 2000 the U.S. Supreme Court ruled that student-led prayers at football games violated the Establishment Clause. In this situation, the Santa Fe, Texas, school district authorized a student vote on whether to have a prayer before football games. The U.S. Supreme Court ruled that this amounted to district sponsorship of a religious activity.

# SCHOOL PRAYER AND THE NO CHILD LEFT BEHIND ACT OF 2001

A special section of the No Child Left Behind Act of 2001 titled "School Prayer" gives the U.S. Department of Education an active role in ensuring that school districts allow for school prayer within the boundaries of the law. The legislation orders the U.S. Secretary of Education to provide guidance in writing and on the Internet to local schools "on constitutionally protected prayer in public elementary schools and secondary schools."

More importantly, under this legislation, local school districts must certify in writing "no policy of the local educational agency prevents, or otherwise denies participation in, constitutionally protected prayer in public elementary schools and secondary schools." Consequently, this legislation directly involves the federal government in monitoring prayer issues in local school districts.

# SECULAR HUMANISM AND THE RELIGION OF PUBLIC SCHOOLS

An interesting set of court cases in the 1970s and 1980s involved claims that the public schools taught a religion, secular humanism, which could be a violation of the rights of those not subscribing to secular-humanist values. The issue arose over state regulation of private schools. During the latter part of the 1970s and into the 1980s, the fastest-growing private schools were those identified as Christian. These were usually associated with a fundamentalist Christian organization. At first, people outside the movement assumed the growth of Christian schools was a result of white flight from desegregated school systems. But when Christian schools began to multiply in rural areas of Wisconsin and Alaska, where segregation was not an issue, it became evident that the movement was a result of strongly held religious values.

Problems began in the Christian school movement when state authorities demanded that the schools conform to state minimum educational standards. Most state minimum standards are not a small list of requirements but a vast set of statutes and regulations covering everything from the design of the water fountain to the curriculum. Christian schools did not have any problems with regulations related to the safety of school buildings, but they did object to curriculum requirements that interfered with the Christian objectives of their schools.

Of primary concern were state regulations that required the schools to teach ethical values that the Christian schools called *secular humanism*. The simplest definition of secular humanism is that it comprises a set of ethical standards that places primary emphasis on a person's ability to interpret and guide his or her own moral actions. This is against the Christian fundamentalist viewpoint, which holds that the sources of ethical and moral values should be the Bible and God. Secular humanism relies on the authority of human beings, while Christian fundamentalism relies on the authority of the Scriptures.

One of the earliest and most famous cases dealing with the issue was decided by the Ohio Supreme Court in 1976 in *State v. Whisner*. The case originated when Levi Whisner opened the doors of the Tabernacle Christian School in Bradford, Ohio, in 1973. The issue for Pastor Whisner was not whether the school met minimum state standards, but whether he should even apply for a charter from the state. Keep in mind the fact that compulsory-education laws in most states require attendance at a school approved by the state. If the student does not attend an approved school, the student can be considered truant and the parents and student can be held liable for the truancy.

James Carper of Tulane University reported in a paper delivered at the 1980 meeting of the American Educational Studies Association that after reading the 149-paged *Minimum Standards for Ohio Elementary Schools, Revised 1970*, "Whisner and the governing board of the school concluded that as a matter of religious principle they could not conform to all of the standards and, therefore, decided not to initiate the prescribed procedures for obtaining a charter." The consequence of that action was immediately felt by the parents and their children when, within a month of the school's opening, the local probation officer sent out letters informing the parents that if their children did not attend a school that met minimum standards, a complaint against the parents would be filed in the local juvenile court. In November, two months after the opening of the school, 15 parents were indicted by the county prosecutor's office for not sending their children to school. After some negotiation, the trial date was set for May 7, 1974. Professor Carper wrote: "The trial court proceedings revealed again that to the state the primary issue was the noncompliance with state law while the defendants believed that free exercise of religion was at the heart of the matter." One point revealed in the first trial was that the Ohio Department of Education required total compliance with state minimum standards and that one of those standards was a written statement of philosophy of education. The interesting question raised by this standard was how conflicts between a school's statement of philosophy and other department standards would be resolved. It was revealed during the trial that "if the statement of a school's philosophy of education, a mandated standard, ran counter to other minimum standards and made it impossible fully to embrace them, the department would not approve the school."

In August 1974 the trial court found the 15 parents guilty; after an appeal, the Supreme Court of Ohio agreed to hear the case in October 1975. On July 28, 1976, the Supreme Court of Ohio reversed the lower court's decision and argued that Pastor Whisner and the appellants had "sustained their burden of establishing that the 'minimum standards' infringe upon the right guaranteed them by the First Amendment to the Constitution of the United States, and by Section 7 of the Ohio Constitution, to the free exercise of religion."

This decision gave legal recognition to the argument that the state minimum standards did require the teaching of a philosophy, secular humanism, which differed from the religious values of the appellants. To understand this conflict it is best to review some specific points in the state's minimum standards objected to by Pastor Whisner.

Alan Grover, in his book *Ohio's Trojan Horse: A Warning to Christian Schools Everywhere*, provides a detailed summary of Whisner's objections to the minimum standards. For our purposes, I will deal with only a few of these objections, for highlighting the issue of secular humanism. In Grover's words, "The 'Minimum Standards' philosophy points to the wisdom and self-sufficiency of man in finding solutions to all of society's problems." This, of course, is contrary to the belief that humans need the Scriptures and God to deal with social problems. As examples of the Ohio minimum standards' emphasis on the wisdom and self-sufficiency of humans, Grover cited the following statements from the standards:

> Problems are solved by group discussion and decisions. Man's comprehension of the present and his wisdom in planning for the future depend upon his understanding of the events of the past and of the various forces and agencies in society that influence the present. Through all time and in all regions of the world, man has worked to meet common basic human needs and to satisfy common human desires and aspirations. The health of the child is perhaps the greatest single factor in the development of a well-rounded personality. (The objection to this is the belief that the spiritual condition of the individual is more important.)

The preceding quotation was taken from the curriculum section of the state standards. What should be remembered is that the state required compliance with all standards and, consequently, Pastor Whisner considered compliance a violation of his religious beliefs. This case has opened the door to similar cases in other states and has made it possible to argue that compulsory attendance at a public school might be a violation of religious freedom. And it was certainly clear in the mind of Pastor Whisner that the public schools taught the religion of secular humanism.

A 1987 ruling by the Eleventh Circuit Court of Appeals brushed aside parental claims that 45 books approved for Alabama schools taught secular humanism. Alabama's Governor George Wallace supported the parents in declaring, "I don't want to teach ungodly humanism in the schools where I'm governor." The case required the plaintiffs to prove that secular humanism was a religion and that secular humanism was being imposed on children in public schools. Testimony was presented in the trial that teaching independent thinking regarding moral issues was a religious position and, therefore, violated the Establishment Clause. Initially, Judge Brevard Hand ruled that secular humanism was indeed a religion and books based on secular humanism should be removed from the schools but Judge Hand's decision was reversed by the Eleventh Circuit Court of Appeals. The Appeals Court ruled that the books did not violate the Establishment Clause. The court stated:

> Rather the message [in the books] is one of a governmental attempt to instill in Alabama public school children such values as independent thought, tolerance of diverse views, self-respect, maturity, self-reliance, and logical decision-making. This is an entirely appropriate secular effect.

## EVOLUTION AND CREATIONISM

Evolution theory challenges a basic premise of many religions about the creation of life. Some Christians believe evolutionary arguments deny the divine authority of the Bible. In March 1996, presidential candidate Pat Buchanan told ABC, "I think [parents] have a right to insist that Godless evolution not be taught to their children or their children not be indoctrinated in it." Antievolutionists are pressing for public school science courses to expose students to creationism along with evolutionary theory. Creationism maintains that humans did not evolve but were created as part of an intelligent design of the Universe. Creationist ideas are also called abrupt appearance theory or intelligent design theory.

In 1982 the Louisiana legislature passed a law requiring that any public school teaching evolution must give equal time to explaining creationism. The Creationism Act did not require the teaching of either theory unless the other was taught. The legislation defined theories as "the scientific evidences for [creation or evolution] and inferences from those scientific evidences."

In 1987, the U.S. Supreme Court in *Edwards v. Aguillard* declared the legislation unconstitutional. In the majority opinion, Justice William Brennan, Jr., wrote, "The Act impermissibly endorses religion by advancing the religious belief that a supernatural being created humankind. The legislative history proves that the term 'creation science,' as contemplated by the state legislature, embraces this religious teaching." Based on this reasoning, the Court found the legislation violating the Establishment Clause.

Applying the *Lemon* test to the legislation, the U.S. Supreme Court found that the Creationism Act did have a religious intent. Justice Brennan argued, "Teaching a variety of scientific theories about the origins of humankind to schoolchildren might be validly done with the clear secular intent of enhancing the effectiveness of science instruction. But because the primary purpose of the Creationism Act is to endorse a particular religious doctrine, the Act furthers religion, violating the Establishment Clause."

## PARENTS' RIGHTS

Debates over censorship, secular humanism, and evolution highlight the issue of parents' rights. Do parents have the right to protect their children from exposure to school services and educational materials that the parents consider objectionable? In 1989, Jason Newkirk's father refused permission for his son to receive school counseling. Authorities in an East Lansing, Michigan, school district found Jason had difficulty interacting with other children and sent him to see a school counselor. The parents claimed the psychological tests administered during counseling caused Jason to have panic attacks and separation-anxiety disorder. The Newkirks sued, contending their parental rights were violated because the school acted without their permission. A federal district court rejected their arguments. In 1995, the U.S. Supreme Court, by declining to review the case, let the lower-court decision stand.

In 1991, the Falmouth, Massachusetts, school district adopted a policy of making condoms available to junior and senior high school students. The school nurse distributed the condoms along with AIDS-prevention pamphlets. Condom vending machines were placed in high school restrooms. Some parents protested the policy contending that their constitutional rights to direct their children's upbringing were violated; they also argued that the policy was a violation of the Free Exercise clause.

Ruling against the parents, the Supreme Judicial Court of Massachusetts maintained, "Parents have no right to tailor public school programs to meet their individual religious and moral preferences." The court argued that students were not compelled to accept a condom and that the parents could instruct their children not to accept condoms. In 1996, the U.S. Supreme Court rejected the parents' appeal.

The Chelmsford, Massachusetts, High School required students to attend an AIDS-prevention assembly featuring comic Suzanne Landolphi of the Hot, Sexy and Safer Productions. Two parents sued claiming they were not given an opportunity to remove their children from the assembly. They lost the case in

*"Please remind your mom and dad that it's a parent–teacher conference, not a parent–teacher–attorney conference."*

the federal district court and in the U.S. Court of Appeals for the First Circuit. The U.S. Supreme Court rejected the parents' appeal on March 4, 1996.

The U.S. Court of Appeals' written decision in the Chelmsford High School case reflects the general policy of courts to deny parental control of the public school curriculum. The Appeals Court stated:

> If all parents had a fundamental constitutional right to dictate individually what the schools teach their children, the schools would be forced to cater a curriculum for each student whose parents had genuine moral disagreements with the school's choice of subject matter.

## TEACHERS' RIGHTS

During the nineteenth and early twentieth centuries, schoolteachers were expected to be models of purity. Pressure was placed on teachers to be circumspect outside the school regarding dress, speech, religion, and types of friends. Within the school, a teacher's freedom of speech was abridged at the whim of the school administrator. Some school administrators allowed teachers to discuss controversial topics freely within the classrooms; others fired teachers who spoke of things within the classroom that were not approved by the administration. Very often, teachers were fired for their political beliefs and activities.

During the last several decades, court actions, the activities of teachers' associations, and state laws granting teachers tenure expanded academic freedom in the public schools and protected the free speech of teachers. The expansion of academic freedom in the United States first took place at the college level and later in elementary and secondary schools. The concept of academic freedom was brought to the United States in the latter part of the nineteenth century by scholars who received their training in Germany. The basic argument for academic freedom was that if scientific research were to advance civilization, scholars had to be free to do research and to lecture on anything they felt was important. The advancement of science depended on free inquiry. In Germany this was accomplished by appointing individuals to professorships for life.

The concept of academic freedom was not immediately accepted in institutions of higher education in the United States. Many professors were fired in the late nineteenth and early twentieth centuries for investigating certain economic problems and for backing reforms such as child labor laws. College professors found it necessary to organize the American Association of University Professors (AAUP) to fight for academic freedom. The major protection of academic freedom in American universities is provided by tenure. The idea behind tenure is that after individuals prove they are competent as teachers and scholars, they are guaranteed a position until retirement, if they do not commit some major act of misconduct.

Tenure and academic freedom are supported by the NEA and AFT as ways of protecting the free speech of public school teachers. Many states adopted tenure laws for the express purpose of protecting the rights of teachers. Court decisions also played an important role in extending academic freedom. But there are major differences between the way academic freedom functions at the university level and how it functions at the secondary and elementary levels. The organizational nature of public schools and the age of children in them places some important limitations on the extent of teachers' academic freedom.

Before they teach in the public schools, teachers must understand their rights and the limitations of their rights. There are three major types of rights about which teachers must be concerned. The first deals with the rights and limitations of speech and conduct of teachers in relationship to administrators and school boards. The second deals with rights and limitations of the speech of teachers in the classroom. And the third deals with the rights of teachers outside the school.

The most important U.S. Supreme Court decision dealing with the rights of teachers in relationship to school boards and administrators is *Pickering v. Board of Education of Township High School* (1967). The case involved an Illinois schoolteacher who was dismissed for writing a letter to the local school board criticizing the district superintendent and school board for the methods being used to raise money for the schools. The letter specifically attacked the way money was being allocated among academic and athletic programs and stated that the superintendent was attempting to keep teachers from criticizing the proposed bond issue. In court it was proved that there were factually incorrect statements in the letter.

The U.S. Supreme Court ruled that teachers could not be dismissed for public criticism of their school system. In fact, the Court argued in *Pickering:* "Teachers are, as a class, the members of a community most likely to have informed and definite opinions how funds allotted to the operation of the schools should be spent. Accordingly, it is essential that they can speak out freely on such questions without fear of retaliatory dismissal." Here, the participation of teachers in free and open debate on questions put to popular vote was considered "vital to informed decision making by the electorate."

The Court did not consider the factual errors in the public criticism grounds for dismissal; it did not find that erroneous public statements in any way interfered with the teacher's performance of daily classroom activities or hindered the regular operation of the school. "In these circumstances," the Court stated, "we conclude that the interest of the school administration in limiting teachers' opportunities to contribute to public debate is not significantly greater than its interest in limiting a similar contribution by any member of the general public."

The *Pickering* decision did place some important limitations on the rights of teachers to criticize their school system. The major limitation was on the right to criticize publicly immediate superiors in the school system. In the words of the Court, immediate superiors were those whom the teacher "would normally be in contact with in the course of his daily work." The Court, however, did not consider the teacher's employment relationship to the board of education or superintendent to be a close working relationship. One could imply from the decision that teachers could be dismissed for public criticism of their immediate supervisor or building principal. But what was meant by close working relationship was not clearly defined in the decision. The Court stated in a footnote: "Positions in public employment in which the relationship between superior and subordinate is of such a personal and intimate nature that certain forms of public criticism of the superior by the subordinate would seriously undermine the effectiveness of the working relationship between them can also be imagined."

There is a possible procedural limitation on a teacher's right to criticize a school system if the school system has a grievance procedure. This issue is dealt with in a very important book on teachers' rights published under the sponsorship of the American Civil Liberties Union (ACLU). The question is asked in David Rubin's *The Rights of Teachers:* "Does a teacher have the right to complain publicly about the operation of his school system even if a grievance procedure exists for processing such complaints?" The answer given by this ACLU handbook is "probably not." The handbook states that this issue has not been clarified by the courts, but there have been suggestions in court decisions that if a formal grievance procedure exists within the school system, a teacher must exhaust these procedures before making any public statements.

*The Rights of Teachers* also argues that a teacher is protected by the Constitution against dismissal for bringing problems in the school system to the attention of superiors. But, again, the teacher must first exhaust all grievance procedures. The example in the ACLU handbook was of a superintendent who dismissed a teacher because her second grade class wrote a letter to the cafeteria supervisor asking that raw carrots be served rather than cooked carrots, because of the higher nutritional value of the raw vegetable. In addition, when the drinking fountain went unrepaired in her classroom, her students drew pictures of wilted flowers and of children begging for water, and presented them to the principal. The ACLU handbook states that the Court decision found "the school policy was arbitrary and unreasonable and in violation of . . . First and Fourteenth Amendment rights of free speech and freedom peaceably to petition for redress of grievances."

Concerning freedom of speech in the classroom, one of the most important things for public elementary and secondary teachers to know is that the courts seem to recognize certain limitations. The three things that the courts consider are whether the material used in the classroom and the statements made by the teacher are appropriate for the age of the students, related to the curriculum for the course, and approved by other members of the profession.

An example of the courts considering the age of students, given by the ACLU in *The Rights of Teachers,* is a case in Alabama where a high school teacher had been dismissed for assigning Kurt Vonnegut's "Welcome to the Monkey House" to her eleventh grade English class. The principal and associate superintendent of the school called the story "literary garbage," and several disgruntled parents complained to the school. School officials told the teacher not to use the story in class. The teacher responded that she thought the story was a good literary work and felt she had a professional obligation to use the story in class. The school system dismissed her for insubordination. The first question asked by the Court was whether the story was appropriate reading material for eleventh grade students. In its final decision, the Court found that the teacher's dismissal was a denial of First Amendment rights, since it had not been proved that the material was inappropriate for the grade level or that the story disrupted the educational processes of the school.

Another important issue is whether the classroom statements of a teacher are related to the subject matter being taught. One example given in *The Rights of Teachers* is of a teacher of a basic English class making statements about the Vietnam War and anti-Semitism, although the lessons dealt with language instruction. The Court found that his remarks had minimum relevance to the material being taught but might have been appropriate in courses such as current events and political science. What is important for teachers to know is that their freedom of speech in the classroom is limited by the curriculum and subject being taught.

Whether the method used by the teacher is considered appropriate by other members of the teaching profession might be another consideration of the courts. In a case in Massachusetts, an eleventh grade English teacher wrote an example of a taboo word on the board and asked the class for a socially acceptable definition. The teacher was dismissed for conduct unbecoming a teacher. The teacher went to court and argued that taboo words are an important topic in the curriculum and that eleventh grade boys and girls are old enough to deal with the material. The ACLU handbook states that the Court ruled that a teacher could be dismissed for using in good faith a teaching method "if he does not prove that it has the support of the preponderant opinion of the teaching profession or of the part of which he belongs."

On the other hand, officially stated school policies can limit the free speech of teachers in a classroom. A 1998 Colorado Supreme Court decision involved school regulations requiring teachers to get the principal's approval before using controversial materials in the classroom. A Jefferson County, Colorado, schoolteacher failed to get approval before showing the Bernardo Bertolucci film *1900* to his high school logic and debate class. The Colorado court upheld the firing of the teacher because the film depicted "full frontal nudity, oral sex, masturbation, profanity, cocaine abuse, and graphic violence." These scenes, according to the court, clearly fell under the school district's controversial-materials policy.

In another case, Cecil Lacks, a Missouri high school teacher, was fired for not complying with the school district's policy prohibiting profane language. She allowed students to use street language in writing plays and poetry dealing with sex, teenage pregnancy, gangs, and drugs. Other teachers defended her methods as being student-centered. The Eighth District Circuit Court supported the school district's firing of Lacks because she had willfully violated school board policies against the use of profane language in school.

Besides the question of academic freedom regarding curriculum and instruction, there is the issue of teachers' freedom of conscience. For instance, a New York high school teacher was dismissed from her job for refusing to participate in a daily flag ceremony. The teacher stood silently while a fellow teacher conducted the ceremony. In *Russo v. Central School District No. 1* (1972), a federal circuit court ruled in favor of the teacher. The U.S. Supreme Court refused to review the case and, therefore, the circuit court decision was allowed to stand. The circuit court ruled that the teacher's actions were a matter of conscience and not disloyalty.

Although teachers do not have to participate in flag ceremonies or say the Pledge of Allegiance if it is a violation of their conscience, they cannot refuse to follow the curriculum of a school because of religious and personal beliefs. In *Palmer v. Board of Education* (1979), the U.S. Court of Appeals decided, and the decision was later upheld by the U.S. Supreme Court, that the Chicago public schools had the right to fire a teacher for refusing to follow the curriculum because of religious reasons. The teacher was a Jehovah's Witness and she informed her principal that because of her religious beliefs she refused "to teach any subjects having to do with love of country, the flag or other patriotic matters in the prescribed curriculum." The court declared, "The First Amendment was not a teacher license for uncontrolled expression at variance with established curricular content."

Can school districts require urine testing of teachers? In 1998, the U.S. Court of Appeals for the Fifth District struck down two Louisiana school districts' drug policies on testing teachers. The court argued that there has to be some identified problem of drug abuse before requiring tests. The ruling stated, "Despite hints of the school boards, the testing here does not respond to any identified problem of drug use by teachers or their teachers' aides or clerical workers."

In summary, teachers do not lose their constitutional rights when they enter the classroom, but their employment does put certain limitations on those rights. Important is the requirement that teachers follow the prescribed curriculum of the school. In addition, they must comply with any school policies regarding controversial materials and profane speech. Teachers have freedom of speech in the classroom if their comments are related to the curriculum but when exercising the right to freedom of speech, teachers must consider whether their comments are appropriate for the age of the students and would be considered appropriate by other educational professionals. While teachers are required to follow a prescribed curriculum, they do not have to participate in flag ceremonies and other political ceremonies if it is a violation of their personal beliefs.

## THE LIABILITY OF TEACHERS

Is a teacher liable for monetary damages if a student is seriously injured by rocks thrown by another student? The answer in some situations is yes! In this example, Margaret Sheehan, an eighth grade student, was taken along with other female students by her teacher to an athletic field. The teacher told the students to sit on a log while she returned to school. During her absence, a group of boys began throwing rocks at the girls, resulting in serious injury to Margaret's eye. In *Sheehan v. St. Peter's Catholic School* (1971), the Minnesota Supreme Court declared: "It is the duty of a school to use ordinary care and to protect its students from injury resulting from the conduct of other students under circumstances where such conduct would reasonably have been foreseen and could have been prevented by the use of ordinary care."

The issue of teacher liability for student injuries is extremely important because of the potential for the teacher being sued for monetary damages. To protect themselves in these types of situations, teachers should carry some form of professional liability insurance. Often, this insurance coverage is provided by teachers' unions. In some cases, teachers might want to contact their insurance agents about coverage.

In *Teachers and the Law,* Louis Fischer, David Schimmel, and Cynthia Kelly state that teachers can be held liable for student injuries under the following conditions:

1. Teachers injure the student or do not protect the student from injury.
2. Teachers do not use due care.
3. Teachers' carelessness results in student injury.
4. Students sustained provable injuries.

Are school districts liable for a teacher's sexual harassment of a student? In a small Texas school district, a high school teacher was fired after district officials discovered he was having an affair with one of his students. The student, Alida Gebser, testified that the teacher, Frank Walrop, began giving her special attention in 1991 when, as a 14-year-old, she attended an after-school Great Books discussion group. She stated that the 52-year-old teacher acted as a mentor; however, she became "terrified" when he made sexual advances. The following year, the teacher and student began having sexual relations until the police discovered them having sex in a wooded area. The teacher was barred from school and lost his state teaching certificate. The student and her mother sued the school district. The plaintiffs argued before the U.S. Supreme Court that the school district was responsible for the conduct of the teacher and that they should be rewarded monetary damages under Title IX, which prohibits discrimination based on sex in any school receiving federal funds. Ruling that the school district was not liable in *Gebser v. Lago Vista Independent School District* (1998), Justice Sandra Day O'Connor stated in the majority opinion that school officials are only liable if they have "actual knowledge of discrimination . . . and fail adequately to respond."

Can gay or lesbian teachers inform students of their sexual orientation? In 1998, U.S. District Judge Bruce Jenkins ruled that Wendy Weaver could not be fired from coaching high school volleyball because she answered yes when asked by a student, "Are you gay?" The judge said her free speech and equal protection rights were violated. "Although the Constitution cannot control prejudices, neither this court nor any other court should, directly or indirectly, legitimize them," Judge Jenkins stated.

## TEACHERS' PRIVATE LIVES

Another concern is teachers' activity outside the school. A controversial issue is whether a teacher's membership in a radical political organization is grounds for dismissal or denial of employment. The two most important U.S. Supreme Court decisions on this issue both originated in cases resulting from New York's Feinberg Law. The Feinberg Law was adopted in New York in 1949, during a period of hysteria about possible communist infiltration of public schools. The law ordered the New York Board of Regents to compile a list of organizations that taught or advocated the overthrow of the U.S. government by force or violence. The law authorized the board of regents to give notice that membership in any organization on the list would disqualify any person from membership or retention in any office or position in the school system.

The first decision concerning the Feinberg Law was given by the U.S. Supreme Court in *Adler v. Board of Education of New York* (1952). This ruling upheld the right of the state of New York to use membership in particular organizations as a basis for not hiring and for dismissal. The Court argued that New York had the right to establish reasonable terms for employment in its school system. The Court also recognized the right of a school system to screen its employees carefully because, as stated by the Court, "A teacher works in a sensitive area in a schoolroom. There he shapes the attitude of young minds toward the society in which they live. In this, the state has a vital concern." The Court went on to state that not only did schools have the right to screen employees concerning professional qualifications, but also "the state may very properly inquire into the company they keep, and we know of no rule, constitutional or otherwise, that prevents the state, when determining the fitness and loyalty . . . from considering the organizations and persons with whom they associate."

The *Adler* decision underwent major modification when the Feinberg Law again came before the U.S. Supreme Court 15 years later in *Keyishian v. Board of Regents of New York* (1967). Here a teacher at the State University of New York at Buffalo refused to state in writing that he was not a communist. This time the Court decision declared the Feinberg Law unconstitutional. The reasoning of the Court was that membership in an organization did not mean that an individual subscribed to all the goals of the organization. The Court stated: "A law that applies to membership, without the specific intent to further the illegal aims of the organization, infringes unnecessarily on protected freedoms. It rests on the doctrine of guilt by association which has no place here."

The *Keyishian* decision did not deny the right of school systems to screen employees or to dismiss them if they personally advocated the overthrow of the U.S. government. What the *Keyishian* decision meant was that mere membership in an organization could not be the basis for denial of employment or for dismissal.

Whether a teacher's private life can be a basis for dismissal from a school system has not been clearly defined by the U.S. Supreme Court. The ACLU argues in *The Rights of Teachers* that courts are increasingly reluctant to uphold the right of school authorities to dismiss teachers because they disapprove of a teacher's private life. Examples given by the ACLU include an Ohio court ruling that a teacher could not be dismissed for using offensive language in a confidential letter to a former student. The Ohio court ruled that a teacher's private actions are not the concern of school authorities unless they interfere with the ability to teach. The California Supreme Court ruled that a teacher could not be dismissed because of a homosexual relationship with another teacher. The court could not find that the relationship hindered the ability to teach.

It would appear that the major concern of the courts is whether teachers' private lives interfere with their professional conduct as teachers. But the difficulty of establishing precise relationships between private actions and ability to teach allows for broad interpretation by different courts and school authorities. Teachers should be aware that there are no precise guidelines in this area. The best protection for teachers is to develop some form of agreement between their teachers' organization and their school district regarding the use of private actions as a basis for dismissal and evaluation.

One limiting condition applied by the U.S. Supreme Court is that teachers' and students' actions cannot interfere with normal school activities. For instance, in *Board of Education v. James* (1972), the U.S. Supreme Court upheld a lower-court ruling that a teacher could not be dismissed for wearing an armband in class as a protest against the Vietnam War. The lower court reasoned that the wearing of the armband did not disrupt classroom activities and, therefore, there was no reason for school authorities to limit a teacher's freedom of expression.

## THE LANGUAGE OF THE SCHOOLS

Court rulings are quite clear that the primary task of the schools is to teach standard English and that other languages and black English are to be used as a means to achieve that goal. On the other hand, schools must provide special help to students who have limited use of English. The landmark case is the 1974 U.S. Supreme Court decision in *Lau et al. v. Nichols et al.* The case was a class-action suit brought for non-English-speaking Chinese students in the San Francisco school district. The complaint was that no special instruction for learning standard English was provided to these students. The complaint did not ask for any specific instructional methods to remedy this situation. In the words of the Court decision: "Teaching English to the students of Chinese ancestry who do not speak the language is one choice. Giving instructions to this group in Chinese is another. There may be others." This point created a good deal of controversy in 1980, when the federal government issued regulations for a specific remedy to *Lau*. It was argued that specific remedies were not defined under the *Lau* decision. Those regulations were withdrawn in 1981.

The claim in *Lau* was that the lack of special instruction to help non-English-speaking students learn standard English provided unequal educational opportunity and therefore violated the Fourteenth Amendment to the Constitution. The Court did not use the Fourteenth Amendment in its ruling, but relied on Title VI of the 1964 Civil Rights Act. This law bans discrimination based on "race, color, or national origin" in "any program or activity receiving Federal financial assistance." The Supreme Court ruled: "It seems obvious that the Chinese-speaking minority receives fewer benefits than the English-speaking majority from the respondents' school system that denies them a meaningful opportunity to participate in the educational program—all earmarks of the discrimination banned by the regulations." Although the Court did not give a specific remedy to the situation, its ruling meant that all public school systems receiving any form of federal aid must ensure that children from non-English-speaking backgrounds be given some form of special help in learning standard English so that they may have equal educational opportunity.

The problem that was not addressed in *Lau* was that of specific remedies for the situation of children from non-standard-English backgrounds. A decision regarding this issue was made by the U.S. District Court in 1979 in *Martin Luther King Junior Elementary School Children et al. v. Ann Arbor School District.* The court was quite clear that the case was "not an effort on the part of the plaintiffs to require that they be taught 'black English' or that a dual language program be provided." As the court defined the problem, it was the ability to teach standard English to "children who, it is alleged, speak 'black English' as a matter of course at home and in their home community." The plaintiffs introduced into the case the testimony of expert witnesses who argued that attempts to teach standard English without appreciating the dialect used by the children at home and in the community could cause the children to be ashamed of their language and hinder their ability to learn standard English.

The court gave recognition to the existence of a bilingual culture within the African American community, in which individuals would speak African American English with peers and standard English with the larger community. In the words of the court, the African American children "retain fluency in 'black English' to maintain status in the community and they become fluent in standard English to succeed in the general society."

After reviewing the evidence and the expert testimony, the court argued that there was a possible relationship between poor reading ability and the school's not taking into account the home language of the children. This prevented children from taking full advantage of their schooling and was a denial of equal educational opportunity. This argument was based on the reasonable premise that knowing how to read was one of the most important factors in achievement in school.

The court gave a very specific remedy to the situation, a remedy that might be used as a guide in future cases. The court directed the school system to develop within 30 days a plan that would "identify children speaking 'black English' and the language spoken as a home or community language." Second, the school system was directed to "use that knowledge in teaching such students how to read standard English." The language of the school is one aspect of providing equal educational opportunity. Another aspect is equality of funding of schools.

## SCHOOL FINANCES

Equalizing school finances is an important step in providing equal educational opportunity. The problem is that how much money spent per public school student varies between school districts because of differences in local property taxes. There are differences between school districts in the value of the property to be taxed and the amount a community is willing to tax its property. For instance, some communities have several large industries and expensive residential and commercial areas that can be taxed for support of schools. Other communities are composed of modest residential areas and do not have any large industries. Both communities might levy equal taxes. This would not result in equal revenue, due to the unequal value of property in the two communities. This could mean, for instance, that a homeowner in one community could pay the same amount of taxes on a house as a homeowner with a house of the same value in another community, but very different sums might be spent on the education of their children because of the disparity in total value of property between the two communities.

The disparities that exist between school systems in the same state is illustrated in a report in the March 5, 1990, issue of *The New York Times*, which compared the schools of East Orange and Millburn, New Jersey. Millburn spends $6,247 on each schoolchild while East Orange spends $4,867. The difference in per-pupil expenditures is almost $1,400. The difference in expenditures reflects differences in property values. Millburn is a community of spacious homes and quaint country lanes. In 1988, the median sales price of a home in Millburn was $370,000. On the other hand, East Orange is an urban school district with a median sales price for a home in 1988 being $80,000.

The differences in school expenditures are evident in both systems. When Scott High School in East Orange needed a new library, a gymnasium was converted. Millburn built a new high school library in a large courtyard. East Orange's teachers average 14 years' experience and earn $35,000 a year. Millburn's teachers average 20 years' experience and earn $41,520 a year. The pupil-teacher ratio in East Orange averages 27 to 1, while in Millburn it is 18 to 1. Millburn offers 14 advanced-placement courses; East Orange offers none. *The New York Times* explained that Millburn High has plenty of classroom space, but

> Scott High [East Orange], built here 52 years ago for 800 students, is bulging now with 1,200. The other day, Deborah Mayes's American history class was squeezed into the music room, next to the piano. Ester Lundy was teaching a first-year business course in the typing room as her students tried to balance their open texts atop typewriters.

The first major judicial decision dealing with school finances was made by the California Supreme Court in *Serrano v. Priest* (1971). This case involved the two sons of John Serrano, who lived in a poor, mainly Mexican American, community in Los Angeles. The local school in the area had rapidly increasing class sizes and a consequent shortage of textbooks and supplies. Local school authorities told John Serrano that the financial situation in the schools would not improve. According to Charles Tesconi and Emanuel Hurwitz in their book, *Education for Whom?*, the family was forced to mortgage their property and move to another community to provide a better education for the two sons.

The case presented before the California Supreme Court put the situation of the Serrano family in the following terms: "Plaintiffs contend that the school financing system classifies on the basis of wealth. We find this proposition irrefutable. . . ." The court went on to assert that this was a direct result of the method of financing the schools. The example given by the court was of "Baldwin Park citizens, who paid a school tax of $5.48 per $100 of assessed valuation, were able to spend less than half as much on education as Beverly Hills residents, who were taxed only $2.38 per $100."

The California Supreme Court ruled in the Serrano case that the California school financing system, with its dependence upon local property taxes, violated the Equal Protection Clause of the Fourteenth Amendment. The court stated: "We have determined that this funding scheme invidiously discriminates against the poor because it makes the quality of a child's education a function of the wealth of his parents and his neighbors."

*Serrano* was a landmark decision for action within state court systems. When the issue finally reached the U.S. Supreme Court, a major setback in the legal struggles occurred. In 1973 the Supreme Court ruled in one school financing case, *Rodriguez v. San Antonio Independent School District,* that the right to an education was not implicitly protected by the Fourteenth Amendment and was not entitled to constitutional protection. The Court declared: "The consideration and initiation of fundamental reforms with respect to state taxation and education are matters reserved for the legislative processes of the various states."

The *Rodriguez* decision meant that school financing cases would have to be argued within the courts of each state under state constitutions. This would mean a long struggle within each state to achieve a method of providing equal financial support to the schools. One cannot predict whether this will occur in all states in the country, but it is one important part of the attempt to achieve equality of educational opportunity in the United States.

## CONCLUSION

The courts continue to play an essential role in protecting individual rights within the public schools. Because public schools attempt to educate a large population having a variety of backgrounds and beliefs, there is always the danger that minority rights will be lost or forgotten within the school. In addition, public schooling is a property right and in most states is compulsory. These conditions mean that some institutions must exercise vigilance in the protection of rights in education. This is the important role that the courts have assumed and will continue to assume in American education.

### Suggested Readings and Works Cited in Chapter

COONS, JOHN E., WILLIAM H. CLUNE, and STEPHEN SUGARMAN. *Private Wealth and Public Education.* Cambridge, MA: Harvard University Press, 1970. *This is the book that provided the basic arguments for the school finance cases.*

DELEFATTORE, JOAN. *What Johnny Shouldn't Read: Textbook Censorship in America.* New Haven, CT: Yale University Press, 1992. *This book contains discussions of court cases involving claims of secular humanism in textbooks.*

DESSEM, LAWRENCE. "Student Due Process Rights in Academic Dismissals from the Public Schools." *Journal of Law and Education 5,* no. 3 (July 1976).

FISCHER, LOUIS, et al. *Teachers and the Law,* 5th ed. New York: Addison-Wesley, 1998. *Written in a question-and-answer format, this is a very useful and up-to-date guide to laws that affect the teaching profession.*

"Gay Teacher Faced Discrimination." *The New York Times* (26 November 1998). http://www.nytimes.com. *This article describes how the court supported a schoolteacher who told a student that she was a lesbian.*

GROVER, ALAN. *Ohio's Trojan Horse: A Warning to Christian Schools Everywhere.* Greenville, SC: Bob Jones University Press, 1977. *The book contains a description of the Whisner case and the arguments regarding secular humanism.*

HANLEY, ROBERT. "New Jersey Schools: Rich, Poor, Unequal." *The New York Times* (5 March 1990): B1, B4. *This article describes the disparities between the school systems of Millburn and East Orange, New Jersey.*

HILL, DAVID. "Counter Evolutionary." *Education Week* (20 November 1996). http://www.edweek.org. *Hill reviews cases that involve the teaching of evolution.*

KEIM, ALBERT N., ed. *Compulsory Education and the Amish.* Boston: Beacon, 1972. *This book contains articles about the Amish and their struggle against compulsory education.*

LAPATI, AMERICO. *Education and the Federal Government.* New York: Mason/Chapter, 1975. *The last section of this book reviews all the major U.S. Supreme Court cases regarding education.*

LEHNE, RICHARD. *The Quest for Justice: The Politics of School Finance Reform.* New York and London: Longman, 1978. *This is an excellent analysis of the movement for equitably sharing the cost of school finances.*

LEWIN, TAMAR. "With Court Nod, Parents Debate School Drug Tests." *The New York Times on the Web* (29 September 2002). *A survey of the reaction of local school districts to the U.S. Supreme Court decision to allow drug testing of students involved in extracurricular activities.*

PORTNER, JESSICA. "Federal Court Upholds Va. Minute of Silence." *Education Week on the Web* (8 November 2000). *Portner reports on the Federal District Court decision that the Virginia law requiring a minute of silence in public schools is not a violation of the Establishment Clause.*

RUBIN, DAVID. *The Rights of Teachers.* New York: Avon, 1972. *This is the American Civil Liberties Union handbook of teachers' rights.*

"Supreme Court on Aid to Religious Schools." *Education Week* (6 September 1995). http://www.edweek.org. *Provides a review of cases that involve government aid to religious schools.*

TESCONI, CHARLES, and EMANUEL HURWITZ. *Education for Whom?* New York: Dodd, Mead, 1974. *This book contains essays about the school finance cases.*

WALSH, MARK. "Appeals Court Allows Student-Led Graduation Prayers." *Education Week* (3 June 1998). *Walsh reports on the U.S. Court of Appeals decision that allows student-led graduation prayers when students are allowed the choice of speaking on any topic at graduation.*

_____. "Appeals Court Rejects Employee-Drug-Test Policies." *Education Week* (10 June 1998). *Walsh reports that a federal appeals court struck down two Louisiana school districts' policies for drug testing of teachers.*

_____. "Bills in Six States Address Student-Led Prayers." *Education Week* (23 February 1994): 10. *This article describes the continuing effort to get prayers back into the schools.*

_____. "Court Allows Vouchers in Milwaukee." *Education Week* (17 June 1998). *Walsh reports on the Wisconsin Supreme Court decision that declares the Milwaukee voucher system, which allows students to attend private religious schools, constitutional.*

_____. "Court Clears Cleveland's Voucher Pilot." *Education Week* (7 August 1996). *This is a discussion of the lower-court decision stating that the Ohio voucher law is not unconstitutional.*

_____. with Laura Miller. "Court Upholds Drug Tests for Student Athletes." *Education Week on the Web* (12 July 1995). *The recent ruling on drug tests for school athletics is reported.*

_____. "Education and the Supreme Court: The 1999–2000." *Education Week on the Web* (12 July 2000). *Provides recent educational rulings of the U.S. Supreme Court.*

_____. "High Court Lets Stand Ruling on Religious Uses of Public Schools." *Education Week on the Web* (29 April 1998). *Walsh reports on how the U.S. Supreme Court upholds the right of school districts to bar the use of school facilities for religious services.*

_____. "High Court Limits District Liability on Harassment." *Education Week on the Web* (24 June 1998). *This article describes how the U.S. Supreme Court denies parents the right to sue the school district for monetary rewards in a case involving sexual relations between a teacher and student.*

_____. "High Court Rejects Two Appeals on Religion in Schools." *Education Week on the Web* (8 July 1998). *This article deals with the U.S. Supreme Court's refusal to overturn a federal district judge's rulings that struck down a state law allowing student-led prayers in public schools.*

_____. "High Court's Ban on Graduation Prayers Disappoints Districts." *Education Week* (5 August 1992): 1, 41–43. *This article discusses the U.S. Supreme Court case* Lee v. Weisman *(1992), which banned prayers from public school graduation services. The article contains lengthy excerpts from the decision.*

_____. "Religious Schools Welcome Back On-Site Title I Services." *Education Week* (8 July 1998). *This article discusses the U.S. Supreme Court decision to allow federally funded programs to be conducted on the site of religious schools.*

_____. "Scouts' Ban on Gays Is Prompting Schools to Reconsider Ties." *Education Week on the Web* (25 October 2000). *A report on school districts' reactions to the Boy Scout ban on gay leaders and members.*

_____. "Students Claiming Sex Harassment Win Right to Sue." *Education Week* (4 March 1992): 1, 24. *This article discusses the U.S. Supreme Court ruling in* Franklin v. Gwinnett County Public Schools *(1992), which provides students with protection from sexual harassment by teachers.*

_____. "Supreme Court Declines to Accept Student Sexual-Harassment Case." *Education Week on the Web* (16 October 1996). *This article tells how the Supreme Court avoids clarifying the legal issues involving a public school student sexually harassing another student.*

_____. "Supreme Court Lets Stand Rulings on Drug Tests, Teaching Materials." *Education Week on the Web* (14 September 1998). *Walsh reports on the U.S. Supreme Court decision to uphold the right of school districts to perform random drug tests on students participating in extracurricular activities.*

_____. "Teachers Fired over Classroom Practices Lose Appeals." *Education Week on the Web* (7 August 1998). *Walsh reports on how the courts upheld the firing of teachers for using a film and class methodologies that violated school policies on controversial materials and the use of profane language.*

_____. "White House Backs Wider Drug Testing in Schools." *Education Week on the Web* (11 September 2002). *Discussion of booklet issued by the White House Office of National Drug Control Policy urging drug testing of students involved in extracurricular activities.*

WEEKS, J. DEVEREUX. *Student Rights under the Constitution: Selected Federal Decisions Affecting the Public School Community.* Athens: University of Georgia Press, 1992. *This is a guide to student rights under the U.S. Constitution.*

# Index